ANCIENT JAPAN

ANCIENT JAPAN

Richard Pearson

with contributions by

Doi Takashi

Harada Masayuki

Inokuma Kanekatsu

Kawagoe Shun'ichi

Kawahara Sumiyuki

Kobayashi Tatsuo

Morimitsu Toshihiko

Okamura Michio

Sahara Makoto

Shiraishi Taichirō

Tanabe Ikuo

Tanaka Migaku

Tateno Kazumi

Tsude Hiroshi

George Braziller, Inc., New York

Arthur M. Sackler Gallery
Smithsonian Institution, Washington, D.C.

This book is published on the occasion of the exhibition *Ancient Japan*, organized by the Arthur M. Sackler Gallery, Smithsonian Institution, Washington, D.C., in cooperation with the Agency for Cultural Affairs of the Government of Japan. The exhibition, publications, and related programs are made possible in part by grants from the Smithsonian Institution Special Exhibition Fund and the Japan Foundation and by an indemnity from the Federal Council on the Arts and the Humanities. Additional support has been provided by All Nippon Airways Co., Ltd., Japan Airlines Co., Ltd., Matsushita Electric Corporation of America, and NHK Japan Broadcasting Corporation.

Exhibition dates:
Arthur M. Sackler Gallery
August 9–November 1, 1992

Library of Congress Cataloging-in-Publication Data
Pearson, Richard J.
    Ancient Japan / Richard Pearson.
        p.   cm.
    Published on the occasion of an exhibition at the Sackler Gallery, 8/9–11/1/92.   ISBN 0-8076-1282-0 (Braziller: cloth)
    1. Japan—Civilization—to 794—Exhibitions. 2. Japan—Antiquities—Exhibitions. I. Arthur M. Sackler Gallery (Smithsonian Institution) II. Title.
    DS822.P44   1992
    952'.01–dc20   92-15138
                                CIP

The site essays and catalogue entries were translated from the Japanese by Kazue Pearson. The text was proofread by Kathryn Stafford and indexed by Andrew Christenson. Maps and line drawings were adapted by Patricia Condit.

Edited by Jane McAllister and Kathleen Preciado
Designed by Susan Rabin
Typeset in Gill Sans Bold and Garamond 3
by Graphic Composition, Inc., Athens, Georgia
Printed by Schneidereith & Sons, Baltimore, Maryland

Front cover: Ring pommel [169]
Back cover: Ear ornaments [70–72]
Frontispiece: Mirror with design of houses [153]

CONTENTS

LENDERS TO
THE EXHIBITION

Agency for Cultural Affairs, Government of Japan
Aichi Prefectural Kiyosu Kaigarayama Shell Mound Museum,
    Kiyosu Township
Akita Prefectural Museum, Akita City
Amagi City Museum, Fukuoka Prefecture
Aomori Prefectural Education Commission, Aomori City
Aomori Prefectural Museum, Aomori City
Asuka National Museum, Nara Prefecture
Asuka Village Education Commission, Nara Prefecture
Chino City Education Commission, Nagano Prefecture
Chitose City Education Commission, Hokkaidō
Fujiidera City Education Commission, Osaka Prefecture
Fukuoka Municipal Museum
Fukuoka Prefectural Amagi Historical Museum, Amagi City
Gumma Prefectural Archaeological Research Center,
    Kitatachibana Village
Gumma Prefectural History Museum, Maebashi
Habikino City Education Commission, Osaka Prefecture
Hachinohe City Education Commission, Aomori Prefecture
Hayashi Shigeki
Higashi Osaka Municipal Museum, Osaka Prefecture
Hōhoku Township Education Commission, Yamaguchi Prefecture
Hokkaidō Education Commission, Sapporo
Hokkaidō Historical Museum, Sapporo
Ibaraki City Education Commission, Osaka Prefecture
Ibaraki Prefectural History Museum, Mito
Imagane Township Education Commission, Hokkaidō
Imperial Household Agency, Tokyo
Isonokami Shrine, Tenri City, Nara Prefecture
Iwate Prefectural Archaeological Research Center, Tonan Village
Iwate Prefectural Museum, Morioka City
Izunagaoka Township Education Commission, Shizuoka Prefecture
Kamiina Education Institution, Inc., Ina City, Nagano Prefecture
Kiryū City Education Commission, Gumma Prefecture

Kobe City Museum, Hyōgo Prefecture
Kondō Atsuho
Kyoto University
Maebaru Township Education Commission, Fukuoka Prefecture
Meiji University Museum of Archaeology, Tokyo
Minami Kayabe Township Education Commission, Hokkaidō
Mitsui Library Foundation, Tokyo
Morioka City Education Commission, Iwate Prefecture
Nagaoka Municipal Museum of Science, Niigata Prefecture
Nagatoro Museum, Saitama Prefecture
Namegawa Hiroshi
Nara National Cultural Properties Research Institute
Nara National Museum
Nara Prefectural Kashihara Archaeological Research Institute
National Museum of Japanese History, Sakura City, Chiba Prefecture
Nojiriko Museum, Shinano Township, Nagano Prefecture
Okaya City Education Commission, Nagano Prefecture
Okayama Prefectural Museum, Okayama City
Okazaki City Education Commission, Aichi Prefecture
Prefectural Amagi Museum, Fukuoka Prefecture
Saga Prefectural Museum, Saga City
Sapporo Medical University, Hokkaidō
Senpoku Archaeological Museum, Sakai City, Osaka Prefecture
Tatsuuma Archaeological Museum, Nishinomiya City, Hyōgo Prefecture
Tawaramoto Township Education Commission, Nara Prefecture
Tōhoku Historical Museum, Tagajō City, Miyagi Prefecture
Tōhoku University Archaeological Research Laboratory, Sendai City,
    Miyagi Prefecture
Tōkamachi Municipal Museum, Niigata Prefecture
Tokyo National Museum
Tokyo University Museum
Utsunomiya City Education Commission, Tochigi Prefecture
Yamagata Prefectural Museum, Yamagata City
Yasu Township Education Commission, Fukuoka Prefecture

CONTRIBUTING AUTHORS

Doi Takashi, Agency for Cultural Affairs, Government of Japan, Tokyo

Harada Masayuki, Agency for Cultural Affairs, Government of Japan, Tokyo

Inokuma Kanekatsu, Nara National Cultural Properties Research Institute

Kawagoe Shun'ichi, Nara National Cultural Properties Research Institute

Kawahara Sumiyuki, Agency for Cultural Affairs, Government of Japan, Tokyo

Kobayashi Tatsuo, Kokugakuin University, Tokyo

Morimitsu Toshihiko, Nara National Cultural Properties Research Institute

Okamura Michio, Agency for Cultural Affairs, Government of Japan, Tokyo

Richard Pearson, University of British Columbia, Vancouver, Canada

Sahara Makoto, Nara National Cultural Properties Research Institute

Shiraishi Taichirō, National Museum of Japanese History, Sakura City, Chiba Prefecture

Tanabe Ikuo, Agency for Cultural Affairs, Government of Japan, Tokyo

Tanaka Migaku, Agency for Cultural Affairs, Government of Japan, Tokyo

Tateno Kazumi, Nara National Cultural Properties Research Institute

Tsude Hiroshi, Osaka University

STATEMENT

With its long history and rich heritage, Japan is blessed with an abundance of cultural properties. When most people think of ancient Japan, they undoubtedly recall the Buddhist temples and sculptures from the Asuka and Nara periods. But preceding those eras was a long formative age considered to be the wellspring of Japanese civilization. During this prolonged epoch—now divided into four periods termed Paleolithic, Jōmon, Yayoi, and Kofun—a culture that would bear a uniquely Japanese character came into being.

The material remains from such early periods are, of course, not found aboveground. Beneath contemporary Japan is a deep repository of treasures spanning the nation's history of more than two hundred thousand years. Today, excavators in search of such relics are locating, one after another, priceless remains. From these they can reconstruct not only the pre-Buddhist culture of Japan but also the transitions from each prehistoric era to the next.

Supported by such research, this book and exhibition contribute to a comprehensive understanding of ancient Japan. The objects discussed represent a broad selection of the finest examples, beginning with Paleolithic stone tools—among the oldest in Japan, dating to about two hundred thousand years ago—and including *haniwa* funerary figures, bronze weapons, and other artifacts. Also presented are the impressive horse trappings from the Fujinoki Kofun. These have recently undergone conservation treatment to reveal their original gilding. The exhibition marks the first time these precious archaeological relics have been shown outside Japan.

The Agency for Cultural Affairs sincerely hopes that the book and exhibition will contribute to a wider appreciation and understanding of ancient Japanese culture and will enhance cultural exchange between the United States and Japan. *Ancient Japan* has been realized as a collaborative project between our two nations through the efforts of Milo Cleveland Beach, Director, and the staff of the Arthur M. Sackler Gallery.

I would like to express my sincere appreciation to the many people who have cooperated on this project as well as my gratitude for the goodwill of the owners of the cultural properties, who have supported the goals of the exhibition and graciously allowed their priceless artifacts to be displayed.

Kawamura Tsuneaki
Commissioner-General
Agency for Cultural Affairs

FOREWORD

As a national museum of Asian art, the Arthur M. Sackler Gallery of the Smithsonian Institution seeks to stimulate interest in and expand knowledge of the artistic and cultural traditions of Asia. To achieve that goal, the Gallery actively pursues a wide variety of programs.

Publication of the book *Ancient Japan* marks the occasion of the first loan exhibition from Japan to be held at the Sackler Gallery. The book and exhibition promise to number among many cooperative projects undertaken by the Gallery and the Agency for Cultural Affairs (Bunka-chō) of the Government of Japan.

The member research institutes of the Agency for Cultural Affairs have maintained a long-standing collaborative relationship with scientists and historians at the Smithsonian. Within recent years, specific investigations, formally organized to involve several Smithsonian bureaus, including the Department of Conservation and Scientific Research of the Arthur M. Sackler Gallery and the Freer Gallery of Art, have been pursued.

Plans for a major loan exhibition of Japanese art at the Sackler Gallery were initiated with the Agency for Cultural Affairs even before the Gallery opened to the public in 1987. Eventually, it became clear that an exploration of Japanese prehistory could make an especially important and original contribution to a wider understanding of Japanese art and culture. Such an exploration would also allow the presentation of visually exciting works that might be unfamiliar to many individuals.

The proposal for the project was presented to Yamamoto Nobuyoshi, former director of the Fine Arts and Crafts Division of the Agency for Cultural Affairs and now director of the Nara National Museum, during his visit to Washington, D.C., in 1985. His enthusiastic endorsement was immediately augmented by the involvement of Miwa Karoku, director of the Department of Restoration Techniques, Tokyo National Research Institute for Cultural Properties. Without their knowledgeable assistance, the book and exhibition would not have been possible.

The Sackler Gallery is also grateful to Ueki Hiroshi, former commissioner-general of the Agency for Cultural Affairs, for his initial approval, and to his successor, Kawamura Tsuneaki. These colleagues provided unwavering support and allowed and encouraged the substantial involvement of Agency staff members. Watanabe Akiyoshi, director of the Fine Arts and Crafts Division, has been particularly generous with help and guidance at every stage of discussion and planning.

The intellectual underpinning of *Ancient Japan* was conceived by Professor Richard Pearson, chairman of the Department of Anthropology and Sociology at the University of British Columbia, Vancouver, to whom the Gallery is much indebted. The success of the book and exhibition for an audience outside Japan is in large measure attributable to his broad expertise and sound judgment.

Ann Yonemura, associate curator of Japanese art, ably guided and coordinated the multifaceted project. Patrick Sears, assistant director for exhibitions and facilities, and Sarah Newmeyer, assistant director for administration, bore major responsibility for the achievement of this complex undertaking. Any enterprise as ambitious as this involves every person on the Gallery staff, and I would like to acknowledge with thanks the thoughtful and diligent efforts of all.

The success and importance of such an endeavor are dependent ultimately on the quality and significance of the featured works of art. Institutional and private collectors in Japan have been unusually cooperative in allowing their greatest treasures to be shown in the United States. The Arthur M. Sackler Gallery is immensely grateful for their generosity.

Milo Cleveland Beach
Director
Arthur M. Sackler Gallery and Freer Gallery of Art

INTRODUCTION AND ACKNOWLEDGMENTS

Throughout the Japanese islands more than twenty thousand sites are excavated each year. The investigations yield artifacts and reveal contextual features created by cultures that existed as recently as a few hundred or possibly as long as tens of thousands of years ago. Practiced on a remarkable scale, which has been expanding since the 1960s, archaeological excavation and reporting in Japan are the focus of intense scholarly and public interest. The current rapid pace of excavation has been driven in large part by the threatened destruction of historic and prehistoric sites by new construction and the extension of utilities and transportation systems from densely populated cities such as Tokyo into outlying rural areas. The scarcity of flatland owing to Japan's steep, mountainous topography ensures that most urban and agricultural areas overlie earlier historic or prehistoric sites.

This volume and the accompanying exhibition of more than 250 objects, most recovered in excavations conducted over the past two decades, survey the archaeology of ancient Japan from the first evidence of human activity during the Paleolithic period through the establishment of a central state in the seventh and eighth centuries A.D. The archaeology of ancient Japan has never before been explored in an exhibition of this scope outside Japan.

Historical Japan, with its roots in the seventh century, is relatively well known to us through documents, monuments, and works of art. The seventh century spans the critical transition between the beginnings of Japanese history and the buried and substantially effaced cultures that are the subject of *Ancient Japan*.

Whereas objects are essential to the art historian, the features of a site, whether or not objects are found there, may be as informative as artifacts for the archaeologist. Many recently unearthed sites expand our insight into aspects of daily life in ancient Japan that have proved difficult to confirm. For example, a wide cross section dug down through several feet of earth at the Tama New Town excavation site in Tokyo has revealed for the first time the location of a clay mine, which was used as a source of raw material for Jōmon pottery approximately four thousand years ago. Traces of compacted earth and the impressions of footprints of humans and domesticated animals have led archaeologists to uncover rice paddies more than fourteen hundred years old (see p. 224).

For archaeologists, objects in the aggregate and their disposition within sites possess an informative value independent of their aesthetic qualities. In that respect, the central focus of curators in art museums in selecting and exhibiting objects differs fundamentally from the inclusive approach of archaeologists, who seek to identify patterns rather than to highlight the unusually beautiful and technically refined object. Although there are exceptions, such as the utilitarian implements presented here to illustrate major changes in modes of subsistence and technology, many objects in this exhibition reflect the partiality of the art museum curator toward the outstanding object. This selection, however, does not concentrate only on masterpieces without reference to chronology or geography. Wherever possible, groups of objects from one site assume precedence over a sampling from many localities.

Following a chronological sequence of chapters, the authors of this volume discuss ancient Japan as revealed by recent archaeology. Each chapter begins with an essay written by Richard Pearson of the University of British Columbia. By employing anthropological methods of analysis, Dr. Pearson examines various sites and artifacts. He provides a broad interpretive context for the archaeological record of each period, in terms of function, social organization, and interaction through trade and political alliances. Dr. Pearson also discusses divergencies of scholarly opinion concerning interpretation of archaeological data and comparative material from cultures outside Japan.

Seven eminent archaeologists—Inokuma Kanekatsu, Kobayashi Tatsuo, Okamura Michio, Sahara Makoto, Shiraishi Taichirō, Tanaka Migaku, and Tsude Hiroshi—have contributed essays outlining important recent excavations and their significance for the evolving understanding of ancient Japan. These authors describe many characteristics of the practice of archaeology in Japan. Some sites are noteworthy for the type, quantity, or disposition of artifacts preserved; others for features disclosing previously unknown evidence of urban or rural life. The catalogue entries for individual or groups of objects were written by seven scholars of the Agency for Cultural Affairs and the Nara National Cultural Properties Research Institute: Doi Takashi, Harada Masayuki, Kawagoe Shun'ichi, Kawahara Sumiyuki, Morimitsu Toshihiko, Tanabe Ikuo, and Tateno Kazumi.

Insofar as possible the individual opinions expressed by each author have been maintained. Contrasting approaches to interpretation will be apparent. The chapter essays disclose an anthropological concern with describing societies and comparative data; the site essays and catalogue entries emphasize a detailed description of objects, locations, and chronological and interregional relationships.

No endeavor of the scope of *Ancient Japan* is accomplished without the support and cooperation of many dedicated individuals and institutions. Planning for the exhibition has been encouraged and supported by Kawamura Tsuneaki, commissioner-general of the Agency for Cultural Affairs, and his predecessor, Ueki Hiroshi. Members of the Agency's Fine Arts and Crafts Division, particularly Tanabe Ikuo, chief inspector of cultural properties, and Doi Takashi, inspector of cultural properties, merit special acknowledgment for their tireless dedication in performing the many tasks involved in shaping and coordinating the exhibition, in negotiating loans, supervising photography, and arranging for transport of the objects. Harada Masayuki, Okamura Michio, and Yoshinaga Shōji, also of the Fine Arts and Crafts Division, have contributed substantially to this project.

The Japanese scholars who wrote essays and catalogue entries warrant recognition for their willingness to take time from their extremely busy schedules to participate in this project and share their knowledge with an English-speaking audience. Sahara Makoto of the Nara National Cultural Properties Research Institute helped coordinate the site essays and accompanying illustrations.

Several Japanese museums and research institutes have been most gracious in advising the Sackler Gallery staff. To the Nara National Cultural Properties Research Institute, the National Museum of Japanese History, the Gumma Prefectural Archaeological Research Center, the Gumma Prefectural Museum of History, and the Tokyo Metropolitan Archaeological Center, we extend our unreserved thanks.

The lenders to the exhibition have been extraordinarily generous in entrusting highly important and fragile works—the treasures of their collections—to travel to Washington, D.C. Some objects are shown for the first time outside Japan.

Support for the exhibition at the Sackler Gallery has been provided by two grants from the Special Exhibition Fund of the Smithsonian Institution. The Federal Council on the Arts and the Humanities granted an indemnity for the exhibition. Publication of this book was assisted by a grant from the Japan Foundation, which also made possible the presentation of an international symposium. Generous support was provided by All Nippon Airways, Co., Ltd., Japan Airlines Co., Ltd., Matsushita Electric Corporation of America, and NHK Japan Broadcasting Corporation.

Each of my colleagues at the Arthur M. Sackler Gallery has contributed in some way to the publication, exhibition, and public programs for *Ancient Japan,* and I am grateful for their willingness to apply their expertise and talent to this project. Milo Cleveland Beach, director of the Arthur M. Sackler Gallery and the Freer Gallery of Art, has fully and energetically supported this endeavor. Discussions of the project were begun by Thomas Lawton, former director of the galleries and now senior research scholar. Patrick Sears, assistant director for exhibitions and facilities, and Sarah Newmeyer, assistant director for administration, have provided invaluable administrative guidance.

The publication benefited from the skills of editors Jane McAllister and Kathleen Preciado, who had the daunting task of shaping a unified text from the work of fifteen authors. Portions of the manuscript written originally in Japanese were translated by Kazue Pearson, whose knowledge of archaeological terminology proved invaluable. The handsome design of the book reflects the skill of Susan Rabin. The maps and line illustrations were ably drawn by Patricia Condit. Rebecca Kingery typed many complex manuscript revisions. Carol Beehler, head graphic designer, offered insightful guidance during preparatory stages of the production of the book. Thanks also go to Karen Sagstetter, editor in chief.

For the exhibition, Jane Norman, exhibits conservator, and Bruce Young, registrar, worked closely with the Agency for Cultural Affairs in arranging for the safe transport and handling of the objects. A highly effective installation for the exhibition was designed by John Zelenik. Yael Gen, Richard Skinner, Jeff Baxter, Cornell Evans, and the staff of the Exhibitions Department devoted their talents to meeting the particular challenges of the exhibition. Sarah Ridley and Lucia Pierce of the Education Department worked with customary enthusiasm coordinating public programs and interpretive materials. Reiko Yoshimura developed library holdings in the field of Japanese archaeology, and Head Librarian Lily Kecskes verified romanization of Chinese terms. Laurel Muro tirelessly pursued funding sources. Susan Bliss and Mary Patton prepared material for the press and organized an extensive publicity campaign. Patricia Bragdon managed all special events related to the exhibition.

Lee Bruschke-Johnson, curatorial assistant for Japanese art, Barbara Brooks, secretary, and Marie Deemer, volunteer, are to be credited for their efficient handling of diverse responsibilities—from responding to countless requests for information to proofreading and verifying bibliographic references and technical terms. Tomoko Hirata and Sanae Iida Reeves, volunteers, and Maribeth Garnier, University of Maryland museum fellow, provided valuable assistance in the final months of preparation for the exhibition.

The outstanding efforts of all these individuals and many more, including lenders, sponsors, and other staff members and volunteers of the Arthur M. Sackler Gallery, the Agency for Cultural Affairs, and museums and universities in Japan, have contributed immeasurably to the realization of this book and exhibition. The results of the collaboration will provide for the first time in an exhibition in the United States a comprehensive view of ancient Japan, an image that continues to evolve as new excavations yield long-buried treasures.

Ann Yonemura
Associate Curator of Japanese Art
Arthur M. Sackler Gallery and Freer Gallery of Art

CHRONOLOGY

No standard chronology is accepted by all archaeologists for the periods of Japanese prehistory discussed in this book. Specifically, the dating of the earliest Paleolithic sites, for which this chronology reflects the earliest proposed dates, prompts considerable scholarly debate. For later periods, especially the Yayoi and Kofun, the beginning and ending dates vary and may overlap, depending on the criteria adopted for defining those periods. The continuation of earlier cultural patterns in outlying areas, after the occurrence of significant shifts in the politically powerful centers, makes a clear line of demarcation between major periods problematic. A specific example is the Late Kofun period and early Asuka period, during which the construction of *kofun* continued through the seventh century in regions such as Gumma Prefecture. Variations also exist in the definition of subdivisions within major periods.

Japan

Paleolithic,
200,000 (?)–10,500 B.C.
Early, 200,000 (?)–30,000 B.C.
Late, 30,000–10,500 B.C.

Jōmon, 10,500–400 B.C.
Incipient, 10,500–8000 B.C.
Initial, 8000–5000 B.C.
Early, 5000–2500 B.C.
Middle, 2500–1500 B.C.
Late, 1500–1000 B.C.
Final, 1000–400 B.C.

Yayoi, 400 B.C.–A.D. 250
Initial, 400–300 B.C.
Early, 300–100 B.C.
Middle, 100 B.C.–A.D. 100
Late, A.D. 100–250

Kofun, A.D. 250–600
Early, A.D. 250–400
Middle, A.D. 400–500
Late, A.D. 500–600

Asuka, A.D. 600–710

Nara, A.D. 710–794

Heian, A.D. 794–1185

Kamakura, A.D. 1185–1333

Muromachi, A.D. 1333–1573

Momoyama, A.D. 1573–1615

Edo, A.D. 1615–1868

Meiji, A.D. 1868–1912

Taishō, A.D. 1912–1926

Shōwa, A.D. 1926–1989

Heisei, since A.D. 1989

Korea

Paleolithic,
50,000 (?)–10,000 (?) B.C.

Mesolithic, 10,000–5000 B.C.

Neolithic, 5000–1000 B.C.

Bronze Age, 1000–300 B.C.

Proto-Three Kingdoms,
300 B.C.–A.D. 100

Lelang Garrison under
Chinese rule,
108 B.C.–A.D. 343

Three Kingdoms,
57 B.C.–A.D. 668
Silla, 57 B.C.–A.D. 668
Paekche, 18 B.C.–A.D. 660
Koguryŏ, 18 B.C.–A.D. 668

Unified Silla, A.D. 668–918

China

Paleolithic,
1,000,000 (?)–10,000 B.C.

Mesolithic,
ca. 10,000–7,000 B.C.

Neolithic, ca. 7000–1700 B.C.

Shang dynasty, 1700–1050 B.C.

Zhou dynasty, 1050–221 B.C.
Western Zhou, 1050–771 B.C.
Eastern Zhou, 770–221 B.C.
    Spring and Autumn,
    770–481 B.C.
    Warring States, 480–221 B.C.

Qin dynasty, 221–206 B.C.

Han dynasty, 206 B.C.–A.D. 220
Western Han, 206 B.C.–A.D. 8
Xin (Wang Mang), A.D. 8–25
Eastern Han, A.D. 25–220

Six Dynasties, A.D. 220–589
Three Kingdoms, A.D. 220–280
Western Jin, A.D. 265–317
Southern Dynasties,
A.D. 317–589
Northern Dynasties,
A.D. 304–581

Sui dynasty, A.D. 581–618

Tang dynasty, A.D. 618–907

NOTE TO THE READER

Dimensions are given in inches, followed in parentheses by centimeters. The metric measurement is more precise. Measurements in inches have been rounded down to the nearest 1/16 inch. Unless otherwise noted, height (or length) precedes width and depth.

Numbers in brackets [ ] refer to catalogue entries. References are abbreviated. A complete list of sources begins on page 312.

Japanese and Chinese personal names appear in traditional style, with family names preceding given names. Macrons are used over the long vowel in all Japanese words except well-known place-names (Kyoto, Osaka, Tokyo). Words that have entered the English language (Shinto) are not italicized and do not appear with diacritical markings.

Map 1
Japan and surrounding region.

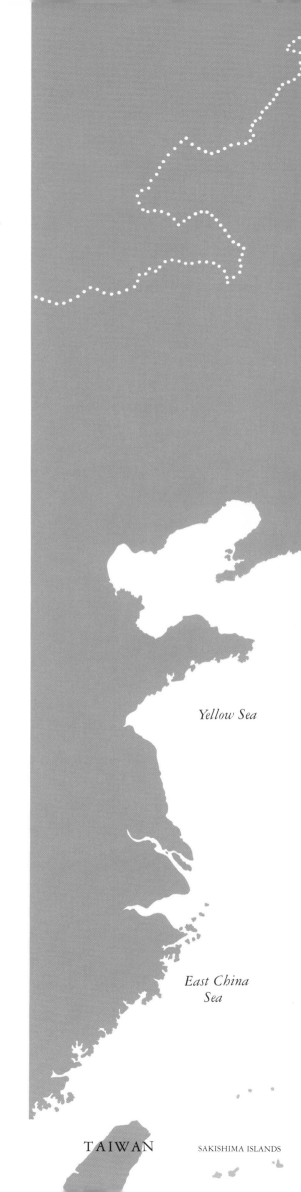

Yellow Sea

East China Sea

TAIWAN   SAKISHIMA ISLANDS

CHINA

Sōya Strait

KURIL ISLANDS

HOKKAIDŌ

Tsugaru Strait

Shimokita
Peninsula

Sea of Japan

Mizuki River

HONSHŪ

Echigo
Range

Japanese
Alps

Kantō
Plain

Hida
Range

Mount
Yatsugatake

Kantō Range

KOREA

Kiso
Range

Mount Fuji

Lake
Biwa

Korea Strait

Mount
Daisen

Mount
Hakone

Tokyo
Bay

TSUSHIMA

Nara
Basin

Osaka
Bay

Ise
Bay

Izu
Peninsula

Oyashio (Kuril Current)

N

Tsushima Strait

Kii
Peninsula

IZU
ISLANDS

SHIKOKU

Kawachi
Plain

Inland Sea

KYUSHU

A

TANEGASHIMA

Kuroshio (Black Current)

P

Pacific Ocean

SATSUNAN
ISLANDS

A

J

OKINAWA

RYŪKYŪ ISLANDS

N

0   50   100   150   miles

100   200   300   kilometers

I

ANCIENT JAPANESE
CULTURE AND SOCIETY

The roots of Japanese civilization are found in the vigorous hunting and gathering cultures of the Asian temperate forests. Today, as each modern highway or factory is planned, archaeologists labor to recover the buried evidence of early peoples. Whole villages are exposed, their houses and cemeteries intact under the soil of rice paddies or ash flows spewed from now-dormant volcanoes. Razor-sharp blades shaped of volcanic glass, fragments of the world's oldest pottery, villages of contending chiefs who cherished their swords and daggers, and palaces of the first ruling clans are meticulously examined by teams of archaeologists employed by national, regional, and local governments. The complex record of ancient Japan has been pieced together over the past several decades through extensive excavations. The care and energy devoted by the Japanese to the recovery of artifacts and to the preservation of their ancient culture are remarkable.

In addition to scientifically precious fragments of charred food, manufacturing by-products, soil samples, and traces of settlement, Japanese archaeological sites have yielded vast quantities of artifacts. Among the recovered material are tools for hunting, gathering, and cultivation; vessels for the storage, preparation, and display of food; and objects of personal adornment. Some are artifacts of religious veneration, from local cult to state religion, and symbols of prestige and authority. Others identify group membership. Artifacts from later periods include weapons and trappings as well as inscribed objects, the products of a literate elite. They reflect different social means of production, from village hunter to specialized foreign artisan working under state control. While most objects were locally manufactured, those of foreign origin represent the ties between ancient Japan and other Asian societies.

Five Periods of Ancient Japan

The archaeology of ancient Japan presents a panorama of development and change. The forested, insular environment of Japan played a prominent role in the development of its ancient societies. Rich plant life and fish resources, rarely found together in such abundance, fostered a stable foraging existence that lasted for an unusually long time after it was set in place during the Early Jōmon period. An extended era of forest adaptation gave way to rapid agricultural expansion and political change, stimulated and affected by contacts with continental Asia. The reasons for the abandonment of that pattern in favor of rice-paddy cultivation around 400 B.C. have complex historical and social dimensions, and the consequences of the shift were dramatic. In a span of eight centuries

Detail of a *haniwa* figure [158]

Map 2
Prefectures of Japan.

1 Hokkaidō

Tōhoku Region
2 Aomori
3 Iwate
4 Miyagi
5 Akita
6 Yamagata
7 Fukushima

Kantō Region
8 Ibaraki
9 Tochigi
10 Gumma
11 Saitama
12 Tokyo
13 Kanagawa
14 Chiba

Chūbu Region
15 Niigata
16 Toyama
17 Ishikawa
18 Fukui
19 Yamanashi
20 Nagano
21 Gifu
22 Shizuoka
23 Aichi

Kinki Area
24 Mie
25 Shiga
26 Kyoto
27 Osaka
28 Hyōgo
29 Nara
30 Wakayama

Chūgoku Region
31 Okayama
32 Yamaguchi
33 Tottori
34 Shimane
35 Hiroshima

Shikoku Island
36 Kagawa
37 Ehime
38 Tokushima
39 Kōchi

Kyūshū Island
40 Fukuoka
41 Saga
42 Nagasaki
43 Kumamoto
44 Miyazaki
45 Ōita
46 Kagoshima

47 Okinawa

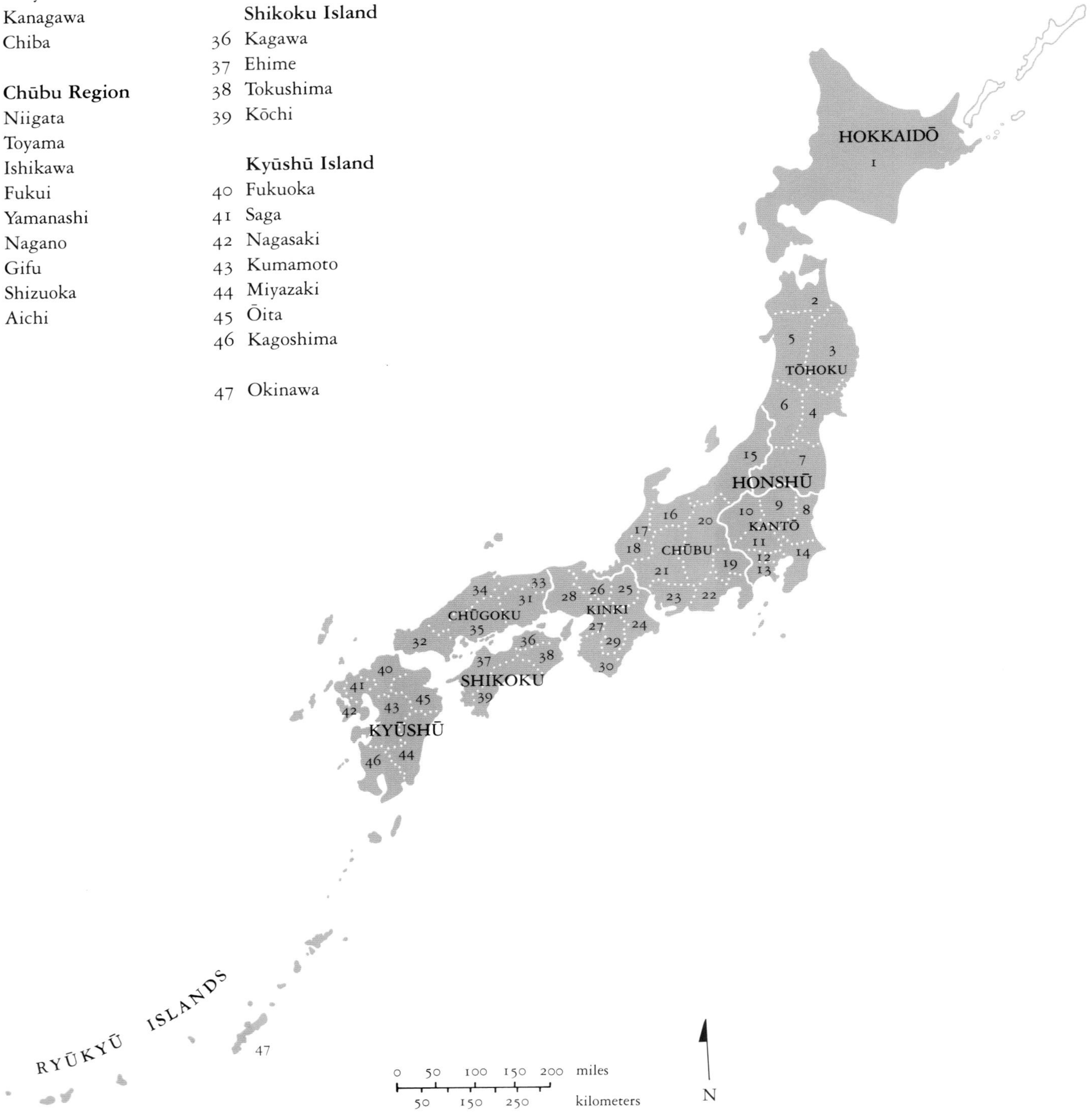

HOKKAIDŌ
1

TŌHOKU
HONSHŪ
KANTŌ
CHŪBU
CHŪGOKU
KINKI
SHIKOKU
KYŪSHŪ

RYŪKYŪ ISLANDS
47

0 50 100 150 200 miles

50 150 250 kilometers

N

Japan's subsistence pattern passed from incipient cultivation to intensified agricultural and state-level organization.

The first humans to inhabit the Japanese islands appeared as early as 200,000 B.C., during the last stages of the Pleistocene period (ca. 1.6 million–ca. 8500 B.C.). Although the dating of the earliest finds is debated, it is agreed that by thirty thousand years ago a vigorous Paleolithic pattern of hunting and gathering was well established.

Hunters and gatherers, adapting to the abundant resources of the Japanese forests and coastlines and experimenting with plant cultivation, were also present in Japan during the Jōmon period. During that time a stable pattern of settlement developed and crafts of all kinds, particularly pottery making, flourished. That way of life persisted until 400 to 300 B.C., when intensive rice cultivation appeared, together with migrating people from the Asian continent who brought with them various kinds of technology such as metalworking and glassmaking.

The Yayoi period marked the establishment of an agrarian society in Japan. Increasing productivity, especially of cultivated food, led to a larger population and greater social competition. The Yayoi chiefly communities presaged a relatively long period of ranked (hierarchical) society of differing complexity. Shifting alliances and centers of power gave way to a group of contending paramount chiefdoms around the late fourth century A.D. in the Kinai region (centered in the Nara Basin and adjacent regions of the Kawachi Plain and southern Kyoto Prefecture).

New ideology and burial rituals, which altered radically in the third century A.D., and changes in styles of artifacts marked the beginning of the Kofun period, named for its impressive burial mounds. By the fifth century the scale of public works as exemplified in these tumuli rivaled that of any world civilization. The period was also notable for agricultural innovations and the organization of political confederacies. Combining under a central authority resources from several productive alluvial plains may have provided the stable food supplies that made possible the grand burial displays.[1] By the Late Kofun social and political organization had reached the level of a state.

Yamato, the first state to evolve in Japan, was consolidated by the introduction and adaption of Chinese systems of land allotment and regional administration, binding together outlying chiefdoms and internal factions.[2] A bureaucracy based on a Chinese model was only partially achieved in Japan, however, and in later centuries a Japanese system prevailed. The Nara Basin, a small, well-watered plain with maritime links to the Asian continent, assumed a central role, connecting an inner circle of polities and an outer ring of politically independent regions.

The organization of the Yamato state evolved substantially during the Asuka period. Buddhism was adopted from neighboring kingdoms in Korea and China, and expansion and consolidation of the bureaucracy and the legal system took place. The study of the social role of Buddhism as the legitimizing and organizing principle for elite competition may provide important ways of examining the archaeological record. The role of foreign ideas and foreign specialists in the building of the Yamato state during the Asuka period underlines a theme in the development of every world civilization: interethnic diversity and cooperation. Both were important in the formation of ancient Japan.

The vast archaeological record of artistic and technological accomplishments of Japan's indigenous, pre-Buddhist roots is becoming ever more clear. Small-population groups contributed to the development of Japanese culture throughout the period. While Japan was not a continental crossroads, communication with other early Asian civilizations was significant. We know, however, that Japan was not inundated by waves of migrants who destroyed earlier cultural traces. Rather, each prehistoric culture built on its predecessor and regional and temporal diversity was significant throughout prehistory. The pace of social change throughout the Japanese archipelago was neither constant nor uniform. The evolution of Japanese society followed a broad path toward complexity and was marked by dramatic changes of pace that have only recently become apparent.

Anthropological Interpretations of Change in Ancient Japanese Society

Each chapter of this book begins with an introduction and brief discussion of the chronology of the period. Archaeological materials are introduced and aspects of culture and society are reconstructed from an examination of artifacts and sites. For the Asuka period, for which historical documents are essential, the historical record is introduced before the archaeological record. The aim of this anthropological perspective is to interpret from the excavated evidence how people's lives changed throughout the millennia of Japanese prehistory and protohistory and also to illuminate the social and cultural context of recovered objects. The main subjects are the size and organization of household, village, or community groups; the methods of securing and distributing vital resources; technology and the social groups who control it; and the "glue" of society: rituals, festivals, trade, and exchange. In each essay the archaeological record from excavations is linked to the social reconstruction. The five archaeological periods of ancient Japan—Paleolithic, Jōmon, Yayoi, Kofun, Asuka—are based on pottery wares and burial methods rather than on social or economic changes. Levels of social complexity, such as band, tribe, chiefdom, and state, do not fit neatly, therefore, into the archaeological periods.

Social Organization

From the study of living societies and archaeological sequences from around the world, anthropologists have classified societies according to the size and structure of social and political groups. Such categories provide points of comparison between Japan and other areas. Also, when ancient cultures known only through archaeological remains share certain types of sites or artifacts with present-day societies, loose analogies can be drawn from living examples to flesh out impressions of ancient patterns.

The types of societies described by anthropological models are abstractions. They do not account for particular solutions to unique problems nor do they preclude alternative forms of development. In any one period, particularly in Japan, it is likely that many different types of society existed side by side. Their coexistence was often a necessary prerequisite for their being; their symbiotic relationships provided a variety of sources for goods and services to which one type of society alone did not have access.

The purpose of introducing well-established theoretical models of social organization is not to force Japan into an evolutionary framework derived from Western anthropological models but to establish reference points for exploring prehistoric social relations based on archaeological data. A comparative perspective is useful in drawing significant conclusions from the plethora of Japanese archaeological materials.

Bands

The simplest societies in ancient Japan existed during the late Pleistocene. The earliest finds are of uncertain date but could be as old as two hundred thousand years. Small groups of one or two multigenerational families lived by hunting wild animals, gathering plant foods, and probably fishing. Those small groups of people, which archaeologists call "bands," were generally egalitarian, with their social distinctions based on sex and age (Fried 1967, 35). Elders guided the group by their experience in locating game and plant foods and their knowledge of the collective traditions of the group.

Bands lived in seasonal settlements, moving through a large territory in search of food. Tools with similar uses are found over wide areas of the world, although some bands adopted distinct styles of tools or decorated them in specific ways to mark ethnic boundaries. Burials of band members were often made at points along the seasonal migration and usually differed little in the display of social status except for those of prominent hunters or shamans. Owing to the impermanence of the shifting settlements, cemeteries are rare. Although bands were generally self-sufficient, even the simplest were linked socially in exchange networks by which scarce commodities, such as exotic stones for ornaments and fine materials for toolmaking, were secured. Bands differed in size of territory, permanence of dwellings, and stability of settlement. Small bands may have comprised about twenty individuals, while large bands in the post-Pleistocene may have ranged up to 150. A great shift came at the end of the Pleistocene, around 11,000 B.C., when Jōmon people developed the use of pottery and new hunting, gathering, and food-processing techniques. Judging from the increasing distinctiveness of pottery styles, local band territories seem to have been reduced in size over time.

Tribes

Band societies, the prevalent form of organization in Japan during the Paleolithic period, continued into the Jōmon period, especially in remote regions. In parts of southwestern Honshū and Okinawa and in the deep mountains, small groups of people persisted at the band level of organization.

Tribal societies emerged in Jōmon cultural centers. These societies are characterized by larger and more permanent settlements, greater population densities, and increasingly complex social relations (Service 1971, 132). Some tribal groups, referred to as segmentary tribes, are aggregates of small local groups with little integration or cohesion (Sahlins 1968, 20). Others develop into chiefdoms, which maintain an elaborate political superstructure and organized ideology, economy, and ritual customs. Not all anthropologists believe that tribal societies represent a separate stage in the evolution of political organization (Fried 1967, 173). Many, however, consider tribal societies to be a necessary step between egalitarian and ranked societies. Judging from the distribution of similar Jōmon pottery styles, the boundaries of large tribal groups seem to have coincided with natural boundaries such as river systems. Such regions probably marked linguistic divisions as well.

Most archaeologists believe that Jōmon society was not hierarchical, that no groups held higher status over others through inherited wealth or power. The family was the basic unit of production. Archaeological remains show uniformity among domiciles and an absence of specialized workshops, except where they were shared informally by several families. The archaeological record of houses and burials seems to indicate that Jōmon ceramic vessels and figures—despite their complexity and artistic quality—were for general use and not concentrated in the hands of elites. The topic has not been adequately investigated however. The study of the social implications of Jōmon pottery—the relationship of pottery styles to settlements, parts of settlements, houses, and burials— is in its infancy.

Jōmon settlements yield exceptionally large structures for ceremonial gatherings and other forms of communal architecture, such as stone circles. Fine crafts made by local, part-time specialists also are found. Such goods may have passed between communities as marriage payments or blood compensations. Evidence has been established of kinship networks between villages engaged in cooperative labor and exchange. The presence of ritual centers in some areas of Jōmon culture suggests that groups may have assembled for great ceremonies conducted by religious practitioners, an aspect of Jōmon life reflecting pantribal institutions.

Political relations between tribal groups within a valley or river-drainage system were coordinated by a council of elders of equal authority. Comparisons may be made between Jōmon social groups and the hunting, fishing, and gathering tribes of North America. Tribes of the Pacific Northwest depended on the exceptionally rich resources of salmon and nuts (Sahlins 1968, 39). Comparably rich food resources were the mainstay of Jōmon subsistence (Aikens & Dumond 1986).

Chiefdoms

Chiefdoms are societies having two or three levels of social hierarchy. Such societies are also called "rank societies" (Fried 1967). Within kin groups are elite members who hold family titles and prerogatives; other members do not enjoy those privileges. The chief, selected by a council, arbitrates disputes and is in charge of political relations and occasionally warfare with other chiefdoms. He or she controls the use of prestige items—nonutilitarian goods that cannot be bartered in the manner of staples but are exchanged among people of high rank to establish or consolidate political relationships. Chiefs also coordinate long-distance exchange. Some anthropologists believe that competition among chiefs motivates efforts to expand into new territories, engage in warfare, and create impressive residential and burial facilities. Others, who disagree with that elite-dominated view of social evolution, hold that the primary incentive lies in increased agricultural productivity and technology and that warfare and competition result from pressure over land.

Burial goods help identify chiefs and their families for archaeologists. Elaborate burials, often spatially segregated from those of other people, may be of distinctive types, with ornaments, weapons, and replicas of utilitarian items. Residences of chiefs may be larger or set off in some way, such as on a mound, from those of lower-ranking families. Chiefs rule by persuasion, without a written legal code, constitution, army, or taxation. Goods may, however, be brought to them as tribute, and chiefs consequently act as agents for the redistribution of specialized goods and services.

Ancient Japan was particularly rich in different kinds of chiefdoms. Some burial facilities from the Early Yayoi period contain more artifacts and are larger than the burials of commoners. By the Early Kofun period several ranks of chiefs joined in alliances. As early as the third century A.D. paramount chiefs dominated a court in the Kinai region.

During the fifth century A.D. state government emerged in the Kinai region while chiefdoms continued to exist. In outlying regions, such as Hokkaidō and Okinawa, however, tribal societies persisted for many centuries. Ancient Japan can thus be seen as a mosaic of varying levels of social complexity.

States

State-level societies are characterized by hereditary rulers at the top of at least three levels of hierarchy. They legitimize power through a militia, criminal code, and legal constitution. The ruler governs with the aid of written law and institutionalized force. Most theorists stress the importance of defining states in terms of social stratification and differentiation of categories of population according to their access to basic resources (Fried 1967, 230). The fluid system of social ranking in chiefdoms gives way in states to more rigid social classes. The appropriation of local goods and services by the state center, without intervention by surrounding chiefs, is an important threshold of state evolution.

Religion and ritual became important forces for the organization of the state and in the shaping of ancient Japan. Evidence of state control through tribute systems or religious networks can be seen in seventh- and eighth-century Japan in the form of inscribed wooden tablets (*mokkan*) documenting the flow of goods from the hinterland to the capital and in the uniform roof tiles of Buddhist temples belonging to the state religious system. According to later fragmentary written accounts, however, centralized control had emanated directly from a series of successive Yamato capitals in the Nara Basin to outlying areas by about A.D. 500, before the tribute system and state religion affected the reorganization of the Japanese state. Surprisingly, although taxation is a universal, definitive characteristic of early states, currency does not appear until state organization has become sufficiently complex to require a common medium of exchange for goods transported from disparate outlying areas. Currency did not come into use in Japan until the early eighth century A.D.

Integral to state organization is the central place, the ceremonial and administrative capital. In Japan, capitals shifted each generation until the end of the seventh century A.D. The area through which they were moved, however, is not large, less than 37 miles (60 km) at most. In early times administrative functions were carried out in the residential buildings of a palace complex; later, separate buildings were erected to house state offices.

Most but not all states adopt a writing system for ceremonial or commercial purposes. When states later write their histories, illustrious ancestry is recorded, edited, and enhanced to legitimize the claim of the rulers to their position. In Japan, where writing had not developed independently, Chinese characters were in limited use by the fourth century A.D. In the earliest Japanese documents, history was compiled and reworked.

The Yamato state that developed by the late fifth century A.D. was secondary rather than primary; that is, it grew in interaction with already established states. All states, secondary or primary, evolve from a local base of agricultural production, requisite population levels, and sufficient technological expertise. It is often remarked that state organization was adopted or "spread to Japan." But foreign ideas alone were not sufficient to build the Japanese state. State organization cannot be achieved without local food surpluses to feed the bureaucrats, large numbers of people to contribute labor for goods and services, and local technology to process raw material into buildings and objects. Japan was nevertheless in complex interaction with states in Korea and China, from which came expert technicians, administrators, and religious practitioners. Specialists from abroad were assimilated into all levels of society and contributed substantially to Japanese culture.

Environment

Despite their small landmass, the islands of Japan extend latitudinally over a long span, roughly one-quarter of the distance from the equator to the North Pole (maps 1, 2). The configuration of the islands in relation to climate, ocean currents, and access to the Asian continent greatly affected the evolution of Japanese culture.

The Japanese island arc, part of the volcanic Rim of Fire surrounding the Pacific Ocean, encompasses a chain of islands flanking the Pacific coast of Asia. Extending from about twenty-five to forty-five degrees north latitude, it consists of four large islands—Hokkaidō, Honshū, Shikoku, and Kyūshū. At each end of the large island group, small islands run further north (Kuril Islands) and south (Ryūkyū Islands). The total landmass is 145,833 square miles (377,708 sq m), about the size of Montana. Placed along the east coast of the United States, the islands would run from Maine to the Florida Keys; along the Pacific Coast they would extend from northern Washington State to the tip of Baja California. Thus, considerably diverse natural resources and growing conditions for cultivated crops are found in Japan.

The closest points to the Asian mainland occur between Hokkaidō and Siberia in the north and between Kyūshū and Korea in the south. These locations became accessible destinations for the migration of ancient populations as well as contact points between the islands and the mainland. Ideas also flowed along these routes. In addition, the southernmost Ryūkyū Islands lie only 62 miles (100 km) from Taiwan. Straits between the islands are of differing depths; thus, at times in the past when sea levels were lower, land bridges were created.[3]

The Japanese islands are mountainous, with indented coastlines, short, swift rivers, and scarce flatland, which comprises only some 15 percent of the total area, or about 20,000 square miles (51,800 sq km). The flatland is partitioned by mountains into small pockets, which gave rise to distinctive local cultures. Steep mountain barriers often restricted communication and thus stimulated the use of sea routes. The largest flat area in the country is the 5,000-square-mile (12,950 sq km) Kantō Plain around Tokyo. The center of the Yamato state, the Nara Basin in northern Nara Prefecture, is 116 square miles (300 sq km). On the island of Kyūshū the Fukuoka Plain, the location of Early Yayoi chiefdoms, is 164 square miles (425 sq km).[4]

The Japanese climate varies dramatically with latitude and altitude. In Hokkaidō, with only 90 to 150 frost-free days annually, traditional Japanese crops such as tea and edible bamboo will not grow. Varieties of rice have been cultivated in southern Hokkaidō only in the last century. The Kantō Plain has about 220 frost-free days annually, while Kyūshū has about 250, and the Ryūkyū Islands are entirely frost free. The traditional image in the West of Japanese food, including rice, tea, and tangerines, comes from the heartland of Japanese civilization; the outlying areas produce quite different foods. The monsoon, which brings about 20 days of rain in late spring and early summer, affects the entire archipelago. Late summer rain is often caused by typhoon storms, and winters tend to be dry in most locations. The typical East Asian climate of dry winters and wet summers provides a set of conditions to which East Asian food plants are highly adapted.

Ocean currents affect the climate of Japan and bring an abundance of marine resources. The warm Black Current (Kuroshio) flows north from the Philippines along the Pacific shores of the Ryūkyūs and into the Sea of Japan. The main current moves north as far as the general latitude of Tokyo Bay and then turns east into the Pacific. The cold Kuril Current (Oyashio) flows southward along the Pacific coast of Japan from Siberia until it meets the Black Current and is deflected east into the Pacific. Where the currents come together the surrounding ocean is rich in sea life. The plentiful food resources in the northern current fostered a vigorous maritime tradition in Japan as early as the Jōmon period.

Two basic forest types cover the central Japanese islands. In central and northern Honshū, broadleaf deciduous forests, which resemble those of the eastern United States, predominate. In winter and early spring many wild plants, often tuberous, grow rampant on the forest floor before their light is cut off by the summer foliage of trees. Many of these seasonal plants provide important native foods. Broadleaf evergreen forests grow in Kyūshū and western Honshū. Dense, multitiered, and dominated by evergreen oaks, this forest type is also found in the Himalayas and central China.

Nuts are abundant in the deciduous and evergreen forests, but wild game is more plentiful in the former. The deciduous forests of eastern Japan yielded a rich subsistence base for the Jōmon people. Tea, rice, and citrus were not indigenous to Japan but came from the broadleaf evergreen forest zone of China and were adapted to Japanese conditions in later periods.

Unlike the heartland of Japan, the outlying regions support variants of the deciduous and evergreen vegetation types. In the north, Hokkaidō forests are a mix of broadleaf deciduous and coniferous. Sharing some tool types with Siberia, the hunting and gathering cultures of Hokkaidō flourished. In the south, the Ryūkyūs are covered with broadleaf evergreen forests in the interior and Indo-Pacific subtropical forests along the coast. The islands have shallow lagoons and extensive coral reefs rich in fish and shellfish, which provided abundant seafood for ancient populations.

Notes

1. Alluvial plains are flat areas composed of deposits made by rivers or steams.

2. Comparative studies suggest that secondary states pass through a process of consolidation and codification through emulation of more advanced polities.

3. The Tsushima Strait between Korea and Japan ranges from 328 to 426 feet (100–130 m) deep, except for a north-south channel that is about 656 feet (200 m) deep. The Tsugaru Strait between Honshū and Hokkaidō is 426 feet (130 m) deep, while the greatest depth of the channel between Hokkaidō and the Asian continent is only 164 feet (50 m).

4. Trewartha 1965. In Hokkaidō the central plain is about 800 square miles (2,072 sq km). On the east coast of the Tōhoku region (northeastern Honshū) the Sendai Plain is 580 square miles (1,502 sq km), while on the west coast the Niigata Plain is 700 square miles (1,813 sq km). Nōbi Plain near Nagoya, Aichi Prefecture, is about 695 square miles (1,800 sq km); Osaka Plain is 293 square miles (760 sq km).

2

PALEOLITHIC PERIOD

200,000 (?)–10,500 B.C.

The Paleolithic period has been recognized in Japan since the discovery in 1948 of hand-made stone artifacts at Iwajuku in Gumma Prefecture, west of Tokyo (fig. 1). Since that discovery, which first confirmed human settlement in Japan during the Pleistocene, thousands of Paleolithic sites have been recorded, with as much as 90 percent of all information on the Japanese Paleolithic collected over the past twenty years (Keally 1990). Most Japanese Paleolithic sites have been dated between 12.5 and 30 thousand years ago. They are categorized in Japan as Late Paleolithic.[1]

The term "Paleolithic" has been used since the nineteenth century to describe the prehistoric Stone Age cultures of Europe. Also called "Preceramic," in Japan, it refers to a way of life relying on chipped or flaked stone tools, before the invention of grinding or polishing stone, pottery making, or metalworking. Since Paleolithic cultures were first found in Europe many ideas about their growth and characteristics are based on European examples.

During the period of intense nationalism before World War II, Japanese archaeologists were forbidden to contradict the "Imperial Myth of Origin," which stated that the ancestors of the Japanese people descended from heaven to Kyūshū in 660 B.C. Working before the advent of radiocarbon dating in 1949, postwar archaeologists believed that Japan was first inhabited during the Jōmon period, perhaps around 3000 B.C. In the late 1940s chipped stone tools were found in the Tachikawa Loam at Iwajuku. Although undated at the time, Tachikawa Loam was known to be older than any layer bearing specimens of Jōmon pottery because it was below those levels.

Not all archaeologists initially accepted the new discovery, but in the past forty years Paleolithic research in Japan has far surpassed that conducted in the rest of Asia. We now have a rough idea of the range of human occupation, kinds of tools and techniques of manufacture, and environments in which people lived. We still know little about the Paleolithic cultural adaptations and diet or the internal structure of the settlements. We know most about the stone tools of the last thirty thousand years of human occupation, since they are well preserved and most sites fall within that time span.

While heavy choppers, chopping tools, and large scrapers have been found in Japanese Paleolithic sites, the distinguishing tools of the assemblages are stone blades having a wide variety of shapes and fashioned into knives and graving tools.[2] Obsidian, or volcanic glass, one of the most desirable kinds of stone for toolmaking, is abundant in Japan owing to the primarily volcanic origin of the Japanese islands. The prevalence of

Stone points [13, 14]

obsidian, which can be precisely and quickly worked, contributed to the elaboration of manufacturing techniques and increase in types of stone tools. For a short period in Japan, near the end of the Pleistocene, sophisticated methods were developed for making stone microblades.

Chronology

The question of the existence of Paleolithic cultures in Japan thirty thousand years ago has generated continual debate, with archaeologists proposing dates ranging from thirty-five to two hundred thousand years ago for the same site. Although the human fossils that have been found in Japan date no earlier than thirty thousand years ago, many archaeolo-

Figure 1
Paleolithic sites mentioned
in the text.

 1 Pirika 1
 2 Zasaragi
 3 Babadan A
 4 Nakamine C
 5 Shibiki
 6 Kitamae
 7 Yamada Uenodaira
 8 Sugikubo
 9 Iwajuku
10 Hoshino
11 Kirihara
12 Mikoshiba
13 Musashidai
14 Sunagawa
15 Kōzushima
16 Kou
17 Hasamiyama
18 Nyū
19 Sōzudai
20 Minatogawa

gists have proposed the existence of an earlier Paleolithic culture. They argue that the Japanese islands were joined to the Asian mainland for most of the Pleistocene, except for a narrow channel between Tsushima and Korea. The landmass did not become fully separated until eighteen thousand years ago. Since animal populations migrated from both northern and southern Asia across those bridges, it is thought that humans must have also moved into the Japanese islands. Not all researchers, however, have accepted the dating of the sites considered to be Early Paleolithic.

Unfortunately, few food remains have been found in the acidic soils of Japan. Most studies, therefore, have focused on stone-tool typology and fabrication methods. Many questions concerning the manner in which stone tools were used and their relationship to tasks in the daily life of people living in various sites and environments have yet to be answered. Despite the poor conditions of preservation of archaeological finds, remains of houses and burials have recently come to light to provide more information on ancient societies.

Several methods have been used to establish the chronology of the Japanese Paleolithic. Stratigraphic analysis of terraces and layers of gravel, volcanic ash, or loam provides relative dates by superposition.[3] Volcanic eruptions produced pumice layers that can be identified by tephrachronology.[4] Pumice layers blanketed significant parts of Japan and thus enable cross dating of widely separated sites.[5] Volcanic ash layers, however, are difficult to detect in the Kansai region (Kyoto-Osaka region), and the dating of Kansai sites is thus problematic.[6] In addition to dating on the basis of stratigraphy, radiocarbon and fission track dating have been utilized for Paleolithic sites.[7]

In the Kantō Plain three geological formations created by the sea and volcanic eruptions formed the environment in which ancient people lived. The reliability of artifacts in these ancient layers and their identification as actual products of human manufacture are debated. The earliest of the formations is Shimosueyoshi Formation, a marine deposit laid down when the sea covered the Kantō Plain, around two hundred thousand years ago, during the interglacial stage before the Würm Glaciation.[8] The marine deposit was cut by wave action to form a terrace when the sea receded, an event dated around two hundred thousand years ago. Over the Shimosueyoshi Terrace lies the Shimosueyoshi Loam, formed by airborne volcanic deposits up to 23 feet (7 m) thick, dating around 66 to 130 thousand years ago.[9] Above this, the Musashino Loam, a volcanic-ash layer, contains the Tokyo pumice layer.[10] The Tachikawa Loam, the third layer, dates roughly from thirteen to thirty-three thousand years ago (Aikens & Higuchi 1982, 27–35).[11]

The classic stratigraphy of the Kantō geological sequence remains a kind of baseline for archaeological dating in Japan. Pumice layers, typological comparisons of artifacts, and absolute dating methods established by the Kantō Sequence have been extrapolated to other regions where the geological stratigraphy is less clear.[12] Many archaeological sites have been found in the Tachikawa Loam and its stratigraphic equivalents elsewhere in Japan.

Whether Paleolithic sites exist in geological formations dating earlier than the Tachikawa Loam is a topic of much controversy. Resolving the continuing scholarly debates concerning Paleolithic chronology in Japan will require the study of each site found in layers below the Tachikawa Loam. Artifacts must be evaluated on the reliability of the context and by demonstration that they are actually human-made tools rather than objects shaped by natural forces.

Cultural Phases

Serizawa Chōsuke, the pioneer of Japanese Paleolithic archaeology, proposed that artifacts from sites such as Nyū and Sōzudai in Ōita Prefecture and Hoshino in Tochigi Prefecture predate those recovered from the Tachikawa Loam, which, he suggested, may date to two hundred thousand years ago. The objects are often crude, heavy flakes made of materials that are difficult to work. They are thought to indicate the Early Paleolithic period, which predates the advent of backed blades and other refined tools of the Late Paleolithic. Many archaeologists deny the existence of such a typological separation. Others insist that no Japanese sites can be reliably dated to more than thirty-five thousand years ago (Oda & Keally 1986). Ikawa-Smith has discussed at length the debate on the Early Paleolithic.[13] She believes that Serizawa was led, in some instances, to disregard geological opinion and to rely heavily on typological comparisons with Lower Paleolithic assemblages from abroad, mainly China.[14]

A series of sites located at Babadan A and Zasaragi in Miyagi Prefecture has recently been dated, on the basis of geological context and typological similarity, to 150 to 200 hundred thousand years ago. The associated tools are said to resemble those from the upper layers of the Zhoukoudian cave deposit of northern China.[15] Although no human fossil evidence has been recovered from these early sites, the excavators postulate that a migration of *Homo erectus* to Japan could have occurred.

Around sixty-five thousand years ago another migration, from the region of Mongolia and Lake Baikal in southern Siberia, is said to have introduced varied tool types, such as sawtooth knives, points, and knives made of flakes. The excavator Okamura Michio has theorized that around thirty-three thousand years ago the migration of a new group of people brought about an abrupt change. According to Okamura (1988, 152), the sudden appearance of knife technology and edge grinding demarcates the beginning of the Late Paleolithic, which bears little connection to the Early Paleolithic.

Two Tokyo archaeologists, Oda Shizuo and Charles T. Keally, have rejected Okamura's dating for the Early Paleolithic. They contend that the artifacts recovered at the Miyagi sites were vertically displaced from their original layers, as shown by reversals in sequences of thermoluminescence dates and absence of flaking debris or flakes that can be refitted onto cores.[16] Moreover, they argue that the artifact sample is too small and that the dates assigned by some archaeologists to particular geological strata do not agree with the actual measurements provided by absolute methods. Oda and Keally (1986, 349) have concluded that artifacts from layers 12 and 13 at Zasaragi, layer 10 at Babadan A, layers 7 and 8 at Shibiki, and some materials from layers 15 and 17 at Kitamae should be dated 18,000 to 33,000 B.C., a difference of 70 to 165 thousand years from the earliest dates proposed.[17] Despite the divergent opinions, many archaeologists at present support Okamura's views.

Environment

Around forty thousand years ago the warmer climate between the last two cold periods of the final Ice Age ended with the onset of cooler, drier weather. The peak of the last glaciation occurred around eighteen to twenty-one thousand years ago; around fifteen thousand years ago the Japanese climate began a gradual warming trend.[18]

Around twenty thousand years ago large coastal plains in most regions of Japan were exposed as the sea level became lower and the islands of Kyūshū, Shikoku, and Honshū were formed into one large landmass. Hokkaidō, separated from that landmass by the Tsugaru Strait, was joined to Siberia; the Sōya Strait between Siberia and Hokkaidō was particularly shallow. Many large Pleistocene herbivores, such as deer, elk, and mammoth, lived throughout the islands. In the tundra and boreal forests of northeastern Japan, remains of moose, brown bear, steppe bison, aurochs, Japanese horse, and Asian wild ass were found.[19] The Tsushima Strait between Japan and Korea also remained open, although much diminished, during the Pleistocene (Keally 1990, 3). Some researchers, however, favor the idea of a continuous land bridge between Japan and Korea throughout the period.

The main vegetation zones of Japan were transformed during the episode of cold climate. The warm, temperate broadleaf evergreen zone was reduced to the southern tip of Kyūshū. A temperate coniferous forest covered the Kantō Plain and most of western Japan except the Setouchi Basin near the Inland Sea, which was primarily treeless.[20] Boreal coniferous forests covered western Hokkaidō, northern Honshū, the central mountains, and the higher regions of western Japan, while the eastern half of Hokkaidō was tundra or park tundra.[21]

Plant foods were very limited in both the boreal and temperate coniferous forests at the height of the glacial maximum; since the forests were also extremely dense, the number of animals, especially grazing herbivores, was reduced. After 13,000 B.C., with the warming climate, the Pleistocene animals of the north became extinct, while animals that had lived only in the warm, temperate forests of southern Kyūshū, such as wild boar, Japanese serow, and Himalayan black bear, expanded into areas of eastern Japan and the environments they occupy today (Keally 1990, 4–6).

Human Fossils in Japan

Although human fossils were found in Japan in the 1960s in Shizuoka and Ōita prefectures, they were extremely fragmentary and did not yield cranial fragments, which are particularly useful for paleoanthropological studies. The most important finds have been made in the limestone regions of Okinawa, southwest of the central Japanese islands. Dating between ten to thirty thousand years ago, these fossils belong to *Homo sapiens*. No fossils of earlier hominids similar to the finds in China of *Homo erectus* (Beijing Man), for instance, have been recovered in Japan.[22]

The best-documented Pleistocene hominid fossils in Japan come from the Minatogawa limestone fissure in Okinawa. They were discovered by amateur archaeologists, the Ōyama family, who found fossils in limestone formations in the front wall of their residence and traced the stone to the original quarry. The bones were of three women and one man.[23] The upper bodies were relatively slender, but the legs were heavy, typical of hunter-gatherers.[24] In general, the fossils are morphologically close to the Liujiang fossil from southern China.[25] Radiocarbon dating for the Minatogawa specimens ranges from 16,000 to 14,000 B.C. (Kokuritsu Kagaku Hakubutsukan 1988, 40–46). While fossils have been found on Kume and Miyako islands, elsewhere in the Ryūkyūs, their Pleistocene dating is not universally accepted.

Technology

For the following discussion of the Late Paleolithic period, the dating scheme based on stone-tool typology devised by Charles T. Keally is adopted but simplified (1990). The general sequence of cultural phases is similar to that presented for the Kantō Plain in a bilingual English-Japanese publication by three innovative archaeologists, Akazawa Takeru, Oda Shizuo, and Yamanaka Ichirō (1980). The scheme used here may convey the impression that the chronology of the Paleolithic is completely known in great detail. That is not the case. Different methods of dating, particularly for the earlier part of the sequence, yield substantial discrepancies.

A small number of accepted sites is known from the Tokyo area, together with a few localities in the Chūbu region of central Japan and eastern Tōhoku in northern Honshū. Tools that have been recovered are small, undifferentiated flake tools, a few larger amorphous flake tools, and some larger pebble tools. Layer Xb of Musashidai site in Tokyo Prefecture contained several edge-ground axlike stone tools, the oldest of their kind. The early sites appear to have been situated in a cool, temperate-forest microenvironment.

Fumiko Ikawa-Smith (1986, 202) has proposed that a flexible and opportunistic production strategy would have been the most efficient adaptation when population density was low and each band had access to a large territory. Amorphous flakes with minimum retouching would have been useful for making tools from wood and bone.

Toolmaking

Pebble tools, large flake tools, and large blade flakes were found in a few sites in the Musashino Upland of the southern Kantō Plain. Dating from 25,000 to 21,000 B.C., the sites are distributed from northern Tōhoku to Kyūshū and, although it is difficult to determine, appear to be culturally uniform.[26] The people who occupied these sites lived in the maximum cold of the last glacial period. It is thought that they resided in both the boreal and temperate-forest zones.

Distinctive tools include axlike artifacts with edge grinding. Unusual in Paleolithic technology, this technique was used to produce a durable edge that could be repaired without reworking the entire tool (Ikawa-

Smith 1986, 204). Mikoshiba in Nagano Prefecture has yielded many such edge-ground tools [16–25]. Some lightly retouched blade flakes were formed as knifelike tools. Some of these tools, made of obsidian, are the oldest examples of the use of this type of stone in Japan. The raw material came from the Chūbu region and from Kōzushima, an island off the Izu Peninsula.

Backed blades, which date from 21,000 to 17,000 B.C., were produced by blunting one of the edges of a stone blade by direct blows. The tool thus resembles the blade of a penknife. Sites of this period also yield flakes and flake tools, blade flakes and true blades, and some pebble tools. Sites in which backed blades are found are roughly contemporaneous with the Aira Tanzawa pumice or slightly later.

The sites, which appear to have been small, impermanent encampments, were inhabited during the glacial maximum in three different kinds of environments.[27] Those in the Kantō and Kyūshū regions were located in temperate coniferous forest. Sites in the Tōhoku region were situated in dense boreal forest; those on Hokkaidō are thought to have been located in sparse boreal forest or park tundra (fig. 2).

Between thirteen and nineteen thousand years ago blades were produced by what is called the Setouchi or side-blow technique, from the side of a small core and then blunted. Sites with this type of tool are abundant in the Setouchi Basin, an open, temperate coniferous forest. Other sites are found from Osaka to Kyūshū and in a wide variety of environments. Sites also exist in the thick boreal forest and tundra regions of Hokkaidō, where large boreal herbivores were present.

Producing regularly shaped blades was a means to economize on the amount of required raw material that had to be carried while people moved through their territory. Efficient, durable stone tools could thus be adapted to specific functions (Ikawa-Smith 1986, 206).

After 14,000 B.C. knife-shaped tools made from blades proliferated. In the Kantō Plain the tools are associated with thumbnail scrapers and partially bifoliate points. The refinement of blade technology and production of knife-shaped tools occurred during a warming trend after the first glacial maximum and in the period of extinction of the Pleistocene megafauna.[28] Keally has noted that the distribution of knife blades coincides with the temperate-forest zone. Very different tools based on microblade production predominated in Hokkaidō.

"Microblade technology" refers to a method of producing small blades by applying pressure to a carefully produced stone core, which was sometimes shaped as a bifacial tool.[29] The resulting tiny blades are thought to have been used for carving and engraving, when hafted or set in slotted pieces of bone. A fine series of microblades from Pirika 1 in Hokkaidō displays this technology [8–10].

Distinct shapes of microcores and methods of removing the blades are evident in different regions of Japan. Microblades were used in all three major environmental zones dating from nine to eleven thousand years ago: boreal forest and tundra in Hokkaidō, temperate forest in the Kantō Plain, and broadleaf forest in Kyūshū. Keally (1990, 10) notes that the dating of the microlithic period is unclear, radiocarbon giving dates that are almost two thousand years too old.

Figure 2
Important artifact types
of the Late Paleolithic
(30,000–10,500 B.C.).

1 Sempukuji
2 Nodake
3 Hyakkadai
4, 6 Tanukidani
5, 7 Komagatakoya
8, 9 Uwaba
10 Magano
11 Kamikuroiwa
12 Higashi
13, 15 Onbara
14 Itaiteragaya
16 Kobayashigawara
17, 18 Itaiteragaya
19 Nakazuchi
20 Uenohira
21 Nozawa A
22 Shiroiwa Yabunoue
23 Tsukimino Kamino
24 Shimbashi
25 Higashibayashiato
26–28 Suzuki
29, 31 Shimofureushibuse
30 Suwanishi
32 Isoyama
33 Kakuniyama
34 Ōdairayamamoto (the
    scale of this artifact
    is reduced to half that
    of other artifacts)
35 Higashiyama
36, 38 Konokakesawa
37 Kazanashidai II
39 Shirataki Hattoridai
40 Hokushin
41 Shukubai Sankakuyama
42 Shimaki

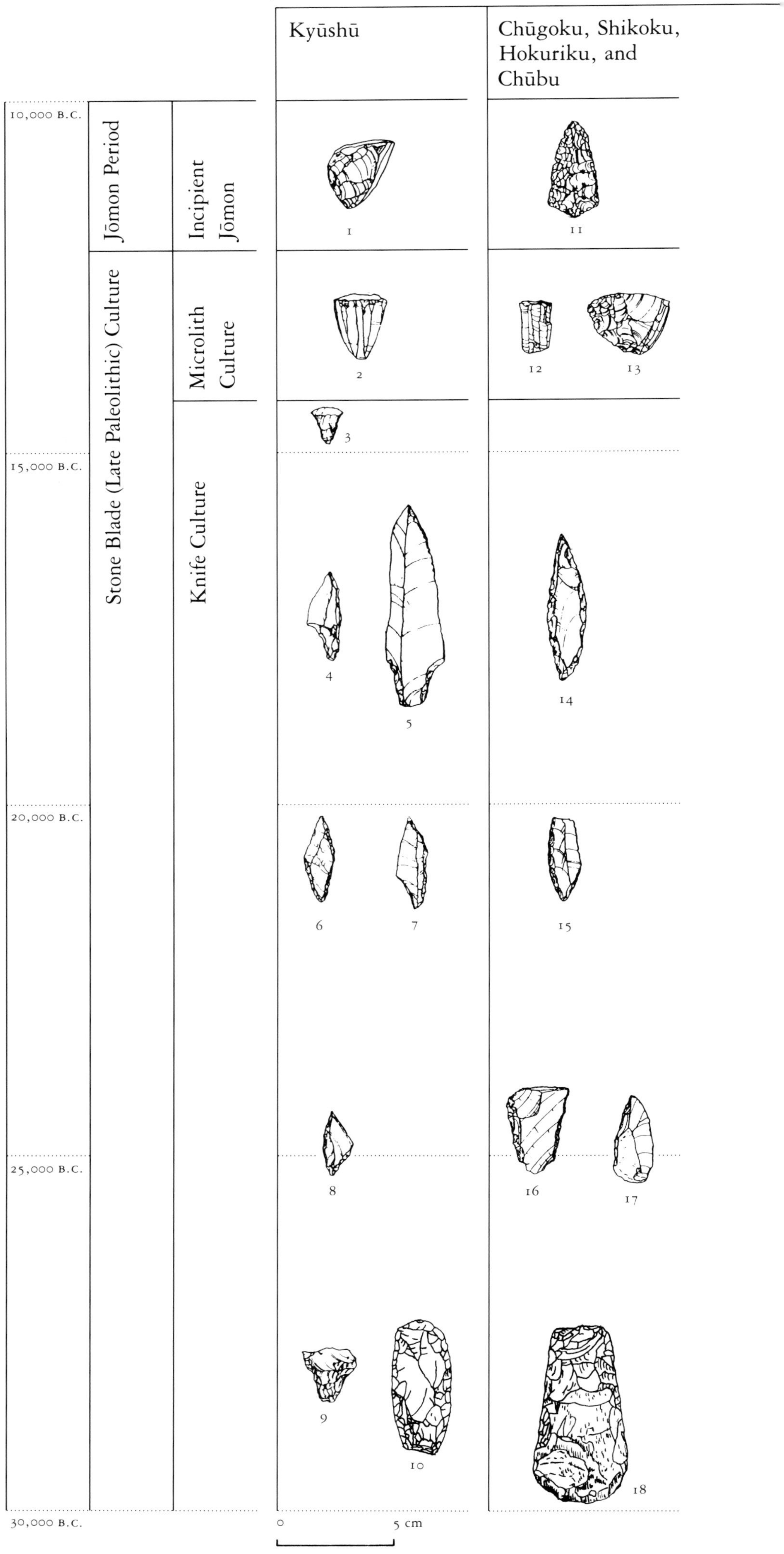

			Kyūshū	Chūgoku, Shikoku, Hokuriku, and Chūbu
10,000 B.C.	Jōmon Period	Incipient Jōmon	1	11
	Stone Blade (Late Paleolithic) Culture	Microlith Culture	2	12 13
			3	
15,000 B.C.		Knife Culture	4 5	14
20,000 B.C.			6 7	15
25,000 B.C.			8	16 17
30,000 B.C.			9 10	18

0 _____ 5 cm

Chūgoku, Shikoku, Hokuriku, and Chūbu	Southern Kantō	Northern Kantō	Tōhoku	Hokkaidō

Figure 3
From such concentrations ("lithic scatters") of stone tools and raw materials left from toolmaking, archaeologists are able to identify sites occupied by prehistoric peoples. The Pirika site in Hokkaidō yielded more than one hundred thousand stone artifacts, unfinished tools, and raw stone materials.

Living Patterns

In the absence of well-preserved animal bones and other organic remains, it has been difficult to reconstruct the living patterns of Japan's earliest inhabitants. The distribution of artifacts and stone debris, however, provides some clues. Paleolithic sites, which are often located on natural terraces near small tributary rivers, average 21,530 to 32,290 square feet (2,000–3,000 sq m), with a few large ones of 53,820 square feet (5,000 sq m). They consist of localized artifact concentrations called "blocks" in Japanese. Since "blocks" can be confused with the English-language names for excavation units, a better term for this discussion might be "lithic scatters" (fig. 3).[30]

A site generally consists of a number of scatters within one cultural layer. When a scatter is composed of one type of raw stone material, it is assumed that it was left by a single social group. A site with two types of scatters is considered to have been occupied by two social groups. In addition to lithic scatters, gravel concentrations appear to represent temporary campfires. These are difficult to recognize, however, because little evidence remains of changes in soil color caused by burning (Inada 1988b, 105–24).

In some sites storage pits up to 39⅜ inches (1 m) deep have been recognized from earth discoloration. A single family would leave three to five scatters, containing up to more than ten stone cores. They may have stayed in one place for several days to several weeks, then moved to a new site when 30 to 60 percent of the stone cores used as material for blade tools were depleted (Inada 1988b, 122). Groups kept to a single river-drainage system for foraging and did not move their camp-sites far but may have traveled great distances to pursue large game.

Some sites have yielded irregular circular patterns of small stones, thought to be weights placed around temporary, hide-covered shelters, which contain remains of hearths and sometimes postholes. The dwellings were not pit houses but lay close to the surface. The postholes for these dwellings vary widely in size and do not deeply penetrate the soil. Dwellings lie close to the ground surface, making them difficult to recognize and in many cases distinguish from later cultural layers superimposed directly on them. At the Hasamiyama site in Fujiidera City, Osaka Prefecture, there is evidence for a circular dwelling on one side of a small depression or moist area, with graves on the other.[31]

The exchange network of obsidian for making artifacts covered large distances, from the mountains of Nagano Prefecture, northwest of Tokyo, to Kōzushima, some 31 miles (50 km) offshore Izu Peninsula. Other kinds of stone were available locally. Even in the Kantō Plain—where layers of volcanic ash blanketed the entire landscape—chert, andesite, rhyolite, basalt, and slate have been recovered from deep gravel layers, where they were exposed by stream erosion. The relative volume of exotic stone that was exchanged varied over time; later sites have more obsidian. Sites near Nogawa, a river close to Tokyo, reveal the predominance of local stone from twenty-two to thirty thousand years ago, whereas obsidian tools increased in that area to 60 percent from eleven to twenty thousand years ago (Inada 1988b, 127). Variables other than simple chronology may account for shifts in the relative use of exotic material.

The emergence of different techniques for making and finishing knives from fifteen to twenty thousand years ago may reflect cultural differences within Japan. Knives are grouped into three major categories: the Higashiyama knife of the Tōhoku region, the Kou knife of the Osaka region, and the Moro knife of the Kantō Plain (fig. 4). Knives of the Higashiyama type are found as far away as Hiroshima to the southwest, and the Kou knife as far north as Yamagata. Typical blades of the Kou, Moro, and Sugikubo types were used in the same manner as the backed blades of nineteen to twenty-three thousand years ago but demonstrate different stylistic characteristics in the finishing of the tools. Their distribution suggests that finished artifacts were exchanged interregionally on a small scale (Inada 1988b, 131–36).

Summary

At the close of the Paleolithic, large leaf-shaped spearheads, found with partially ground adzlike stone tools in Tōhoku, appeared during the transition to a variety of smaller-stemmed points throughout the main islands of Japan. The earliest pottery, dating between 11,000 and 10,000 B.C., is found in the same layers as various types of stone tools, including bifacial foliate points in Honshū and the last survivals of microblades on Kyūshū.

Although knowledge of the social organization of Paleolithic bands in Japan is hampered by a lack of well-preserved organic material, including human bones, and the fact that most sites are open rather than sealed-cave deposits, the finding of storage areas and burials suggests that by the end of the period small groups of people stayed in relatively permanent base camps within a hunting territory. Thus the settling-down process, which later took place among Jōmon foragers, must have started during the Paleolithic. Social networks can be seen in the exchange of obsidian. Moreover, the stylistic similarities of backed blades suggest that the population of Japan may have been composed of several

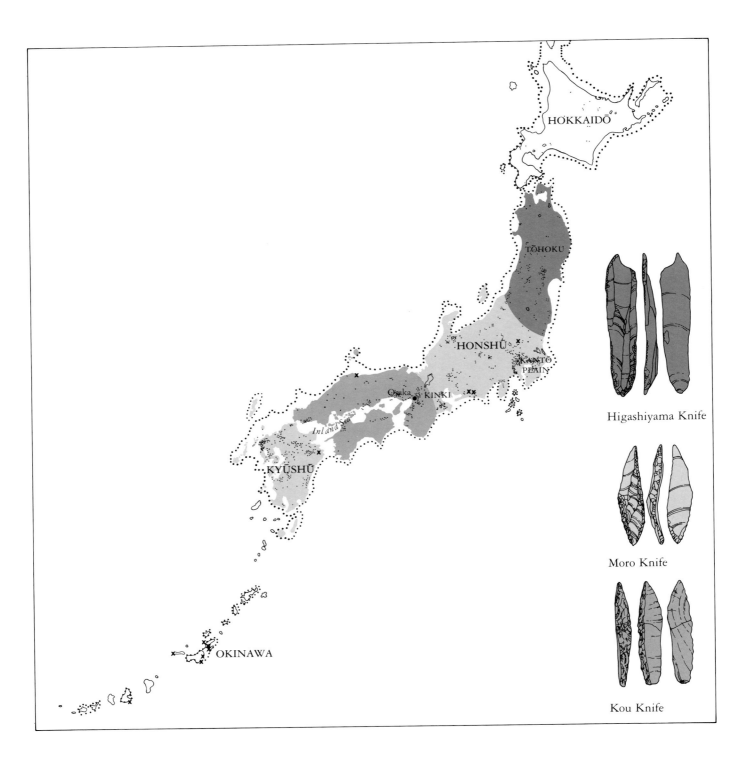

HOKKAIDŌ

TŌHOKU

HONSHŪ
KANTŌ
PLAIN

Osaka KINKI

Inland Sea

KYŪSHŪ

OKINAWA

Higashiyama Knife

Moro Knife

Kou Knife

Figure 4
Late Paleolithic backed-blade stone knives, sites, and finds of human fossils. The Higashiyama-type knife is found in the Tōhoku region and in Hokkaidō; the Moro knife, in the Kantō region of central Honshū and in Kyūshū; and the Kou knife, along the Inland Sea in the Osaka region.

The coastline of Japan about twenty thousand years ago is defined by a dotted line; black dots indicate sites yielding Paleolithic backed-blade stone knives; Xs indicate sites yielding human fossils.

broad cultural groups. The inclusion of large cores in the Hasamiyama burial site may indicate respect for a master hunter or accomplished toolmaker. Is it symbolically important that the grave offerings were cores rather than functioning tools?

Edge grinding suggests that access to sources of the best kinds of tool materials was regulated. The raw material must have been passed from one group to another and, since it was scarce, new methods of conserving tools were invented. The preparation of microblades in which many tools were produced efficiently from a small amount of stone also indicates increasing population densities and complex social networks.

Despite the meager archaeological remains found on each site, there is sufficient evidence to suggest that band organization was complex and population density relatively high during the Late Paleolithic. The conditions of the Late Paleolithic are similar to those of the succeeding Jōmon period.

Notes

1. The Late Paleolithic in Japan corresponds to the Upper Paleolithic elsewhere, a stage in stone toolmaking in which long, uniform stone blades were made from carefully prepared stone cores.

2. The edge of a chopper is made by flaking from one side; the edge of a chopping tool is made by flaking from both sides.

3. Superposition is the formation of one layer on top of another of soil or tools and other artifacts.

4. Tephrachronology is the analysis of undisturbed beds of volcanic ash with the aim of constructing a time sequence. Different kinds of ash are traced to their sources, which are dated by certain kinds of archaeological dating such as fission track or obsidian hydration (see below, n. 7).

5. The so-called Tokyo pumice layer is dated to 47,000 B.C., the Daisen Kuniyoshi pumice from Mount Daisen to 43,000 B.C., and the Aira Tanzawa pumice to 20,000 B.C. The eruption of Aira Caldera Volcano spread ash throughout Kyūshū, Shikoku, and Honshū, making it possible to cross date the Tachikawa Loam with other regions of Japan. Aira Caldera, 12½ miles (20 km) in diameter, now forms Kagoshima Bay on Kyūshū; a smaller volcano, Sakurajima, on the rim of the old caldera, is still active.

6. The eruption of a volcano near the tiny Korean island of Ullŭng-do in the Sea of Japan has been dated to 7300 B.C.; the eruption of Suwanose, south of Kagoshima, to 4300 B.C.; and the eruption at Mount Paektu in northern Korea to about A.D. 1000 (Inada 1988a).

7. Fission track dating is the dating of volcanic glass such as obsidian by counting the density of microscopic tracks created by spontaneous fission of uranium 235 in the obsidian. The density of the tracks depends on the amount of time lapsed since the cooling of the rock and the amount of uranium in the sample.

8. The Shimosueyoshi Formation lies 33 to 43 feet (10–13 m) deep and about 130 feet (40 m) above the present sea level. The interglacial stage is a warm period intervening between glacial periods, usually lasting for ten thousand years or more, and as warm as or warmer than the present.

   The Würm Glaciation is the last great glacial episode of the Pleistocene in Europe, which began around one hundred thousand years ago and is thought to have ended in different regions between six and eleven thousand years ago.

9. The Shimosueyoshi Loam was formed by weathered deposits of volcanic ash, dating from 60 to 130 thousand years ago. The Shimosueyoshi Terrace, a wave-cut terrace, was formed when the receding ocean cut into the Shimosueyoshi Formation, between 130 and 200 hundred thousand years ago.

10. Dating around forty-nine thousand years ago, the Musashino Loam, one layer of the formation of the Kantō Sequence, is composed of weathered volcanic ash 10 to 13 feet (3–4 m) thick.

11. Whereas the Musashino Loam is thought to have been deposited by the central volcanoes of Hakone, north of Tokyo, the Tachikawa Loam layers, which vary between 6½ and 13 feet (2–4 m) in thickness, are thought to have come from Mount Fuji to the southwest.

12. Absolute dating methods result in dating by calendar years as contrasted to relative dating by layers or stylistic changes, for example.

13. According to Fumiko Ikawa-Smith (1978, 273), the debate has centered on the validity of the stratigraphic context for the specimens, interpretation of stratigraphy and geology, establishment of human fabrication of the specimens, and appropriateness of the comparative reference material.

14. The Lower Paleolithic is a period marked by the manufacture of crude flake tools, before the production of blades. It is the earliest stage of human culture and took place at different times in different parts of the world.

15. Zhoukoudian, the cave site of Beijing Man, is dated from 230 to 460 thousand years ago. Located some 12⅜ miles (20 km) southwest of Beijing, it is the most important site of the Chinese Lower Paleolithic. If the typological similarities between Babadan A and Zasaragi and the upper portion of the main deposit of Zhoukoudian can be supported, this would be of great significance in the confirmation of the Early Paleolithic in Japan.

16. Sites with such artifacts include not only those of Miyagi Prefecture, such as Babadan A and Zasaragi, but also Yamada Uenodaira and Kirihara in Gumma Prefecture.

    Thermoluminescence dating is a technique used to measure the amount of low-level energy absorbed by materials such as pottery or its grit tempering, which are known to be metastable. When pottery or baked clay objects are fired for the first time, energy is driven off as the heat accelerates electrons in the materials. Later when such objects are heated in a laboratory, the amount of low-level energy given off as light is dependent on the time elapsed between the two firings.

17. Note that in his essay in this publication (pp. 49, 50) Okamura Michio dates layer 10 to about sixty thousand years ago.

18. The final glaciation is the period of the last ice sheets of the Pleistocene, which began around one hundred thousand years ago and reached a peak between twenty and twenty-five thousand years ago.

19. Charles T. Keally (1990, 5) has proposed that the animals crossed to Honshū before 18,000 B.C., probably over a winter ice-bridge spanning Tsugaru Strait.

20. Briefly, the warm, temperate forest is characterized by evergreen oak species (*Cyclobalanopsis* and *Castanopsis*). The temperate forest contained species of spruce, larch, and fir (*Picea, Larix,* and *Abies*) as well as deciduous oaks (*Castanea* and *Quercus*).

21. The northern boreal forest, adapted to a colder climate than the temperate coniferous forest, contained birch and hemlock (*Betula* and *Tsuga*) as well as spruce, larch, and fir. The lowlands supported willow (*Salix*) and alder (*Alnus*). The tundra or park tundra was largely treeless, except for shrubs such as willow and birch (*Betula*) in protected areas (Keally 1990, 4).

22. Hominids are modern humans (*Homo sapiens sapiens*) and their immediate relatives, such as *Australopithecus, Homo erectus,* and *Homo sapiens neanderthalensis.*
   Homo erectus are human beings who lived from around one hundred thousand to one million years ago. They possessed larger brains than their predecessors, made more elaborate tools, and settled in environments found in western Europe, Asia, and tropical Africa. *Homo sapiens* are modern humans who probably evolved in Africa more than one hundred thousand years ago. Archaic *Homo sapiens* are thought to represent a transition between *Homo erectus* and *Homo sapiens* and to have shared some physical features of both.

23. The height of the females is estimated to have been about 4½ feet (1.4 m) and of the males about 5 feet (1.5 m). It is possible that one of the women, with the lower median incisors absent and the gum resorbed, exhibits tooth extraction, a custom practiced by the Jōmon people as well as the Neolithic people of the China coast.

24. The arm and leg bones differ slightly from those of later Jōmon skeletons, which have longer forearms and lower-legs.

25. The Liujiang skull, found in 1958 in Guangxi Province, southern China, is one of the earliest skulls of a modern *Homo sapiens.* It is dated around forty thousand years ago. Thus the Minatogawa people are considered *Homo sapiens* of an old type, sometimes referred to as archaic Mongoloids.

26. Keally believes that sites with such assemblages represent pioneer settlements, at least in the Tōhoku region.

27. The glacial maximum is a period of maximum cold temperature during the Pleistocene, achieved at the time of the maximum area of the ice sheets. These periods were marked by low sea levels and depressed temperatures. Glaciation was limited in Japan, but the effects of the continental ice sheets on local climate were pronounced.

28. Pleistocene megafauna are giant animals that lived during the Pleistocene. Many of them became extinct at its end.

29. These small blades are ⅜ to ¾ inches (1–2 cm) long and less than ⅜ inch (1 cm) wide.

30. Lithic scatter refers to the distribution of tools and debris created by toolmaking and daily living.

31. The dwelling, which had seven posts 3¼ to 5⅝ feet (1–1.7 m) apart, yielded an assortment of Kou-type knives and side-blow flakes. In a feature thought to be a burial, no skeletal material was found, but two extremely large cores, 8¼ and 10¼ inches (21–26 cm), of sanukite (a dense volcanic rock similar to andesite), a material not found near the site, were thought to be grave offerings (Inada 1988b, 115, 116).

BABADAN A

OKAMURA MICHIO

Archaeologists have since 1965 discussed the probability of cultures older than those of the Late Paleolithic. One central issue has been that naturally produced eoliths (irregularly shaped stone) can be confused with stone artifacts, a circumstance that has made it difficult for archaeologists to be convinced of the existence of older tools. Nevertheless, in 1980 the Sekki Bunka Danwakai, an organization of amateur archaeologists, found true stone artifacts from a layer dated around forty thousand years ago at Zasaragi, Miyagi Prefecture. The discovery confirmed that archaic *Homo sapiens* in the Japanese islands had left cultural remains older than the Late Paleolithic. One after another, sites predating the Late Paleolithic have been found in Miyagi, and the search for the oldest site has intensified. Groups of stone artifacts about two hundred thousand years old have been found in Babadan A and Nakamine C, Miyagi Prefecture, in the Tōhoku region.

The excavations at Babadan A were carried out from 1984 to 1987, primarily by the Tōhoku Historical Museum. At Babadan A, thirty-three layers of volcanic ash had accumulated to a depth of more than 19⅝ feet (6 m). Stone artifacts were recovered from layers 33, 32, 30, 20, 19, 10, 7, 6, and 3, counting from the oldest (about two hundred thousand years ago) to the most recent (about ten thousand years ago). Finds from the superimposed layers elucidated the changes in morphology of the stone artifacts. From the surface of layer 20 (fig. 5), datable to around 130 thousand years ago, excavators uncovered small artifacts of

Figure 5
Excavations at the Babadan A site, Miyagi Prefecture. In layer 20, datable to around 130 thousand years ago, excavators found scrapers, awls, knife-shaped tools, and gravers.

agate or chalcedony, including circular scrapers, awls, knife-shaped tools, and gravers. Large stone artifacts, such as chopping tools made of roughly chipped, rough-grain andesite, have been found at other sites of the same period and seem to be contemporaneous with the stone tools discovered at Babadan A. Future excavations will likely reveal that stone artifacts existed in Japan nearly one million years ago.

Large, well-made tools of shale or quartzite, such as axes, scrapers, and ovoid objects, were unearthed from layer 19 at Babadan A, datable to around one hundred thousand years ago. The sample of stone artifacts is not large enough, however, to ascertain the total range of tools from that level.

On the surface of layer 10, datable to around sixty thousand years ago, the stone material was more silicified and the toolmaking techniques more sophisticated: well-trimmed discoidal cores were left by the process of making triangular or trapezoidal flakes; the edges of the flakes were carefully thinned to produce various kinds of scrapers. The same technique is evident in tools from layer 7, which contained, in addition, bifacially shaped points and sawtooth-edged tools. At present, artifacts from that level of stone-tool development have been found widely distributed among sites near Tokyo and northern Honshū. Their characteristics and variety resemble those of northeastern China up to above fifty degrees north latitude, from the Altai Mountains to Lake Baikal. Changes in artifacts occurring in Japan around fifty to sixty thousand years ago may indicate cultural influence or human migration from northeastern Asia.

In excavations of Babadan A, tephra dates were measured by using various methods from above and below the artifact-bearing layers of volcanic ash. The pumice layer, dated by tephrachronology to around 130 thousand years ago, was peeled away carefully at a level about 11½ feet (3.5 m) below the present earth surface. It overlay the original ground surface, layer 20. On its gently undulating surface were twenty to forty stone artifacts in seven scatters surrounding a shallow swamp accessible from the south. An extremely small amount of fatty acid left from animal remains was detected there. Archaeomagnetic studies revealed that an open fire had been located within a vacant space in the center of each concentration of stone artifacts.[1] From the remnants of horn, bone, leather, and meat found on the stone tools, one can surmise that seven small groups of people had arranged their shelters in a circular pattern and spent a short time there, processing animals and cooking meat around open fires. Babadan A offers clues to a culture predating the Late Paleolithic and to changes in stone artifacts and human living patterns, which have only recently come to light in Japan.

Note

1. Archaeomagnetic studies use magnetic alignments from burned features, such as pottery kilns or hearths, for dating by comparison with known fluctuations in the earth's magnetic field.

Early Paleolithic period,
ca. 200,000 B.C.
Excavated at Babadan A,
Miyagi Prefecture
Stone
Tōhoku Historical Museum,
Tagajō City, Miyagi Prefecture

Left to right, top to bottom:

1
Scraper (?)
1½ × 1 1/16 × ⅜ in.
(3.9 × 2.7 × 1.0 cm)

2
Burin (?)
1½ × 1⅜ × ⅜ in.
(3.9 × 3.6 × 1.0 cm)

3
Scraper (?)
1 × ⅞ × ⅜ in.
(2.6 × 2.3 × 0.9 cm)

4
Awl (?)
1⅜ × 1⅛ × ½ in.
(3.5 × 2.9 × 1.2 cm)

5
Core (?)
1¾ × 1 3/16 × ½ in.
(4.4 × 3.0 × 1.4 cm)

These stone artifacts were unearthed from one of the oldest sites in Japan, located in northwestern Miyagi Prefecture, in the Tōhoku region. Babadan A can be traced to the Early Paleolithic period, or around two hundred thousand years ago; the time span of the site can be roughly divided into two stages. The specimens here were unearthed from a layer dating to more than 150 thousand years ago. Both small and large stone implements were recovered, with end scrapers and stone awls the most conspicuous. Bifacial techniques were used for some tools.

The techniques of sharpening, retouching, and abrading are evident in the stone artifacts. Such tools cannot, however, be classified according to fixed types such as "awl," "burin," or "scraper." It may be misleading, therefore, to identify them individually by such specific terms. Nevertheless, these stone artifacts constitute important evidence for the antiquity of human habitation in the Japanese islands.

DOI TAKASHI

Late Paleolithic period,
13,000–11,000 B.C.
Excavated at Pirika 1, Hokkaidō
Stone
Imagane Township Education
Commission, Hokkaidō
Important Cultural Property

Left to right, top to bottom:

6
Burin
2⅜ × ¾ × ⅜ in.
(6.0 × 1.9 × 0.9 cm)

7
Burin
2⅝ × ½ × 3/16 in.
(6.8 × 1.4 × 0.5 cm)

8
Microblade
1⅛ × 3/16 × 1/16 in.
(2.8 × 0.5 × 0.1 cm)

9
Microblade
1⅛ × 3/16 × 1/16 in.
(2.9 × 0.5 × 0.2 cm)

10
Microblade
1 3/16 × ⅛ × 1/16 in.
(3.0 × 0.5 × 0.2 cm)

11
Microlithic core
2¾ × 1½ × 1¼ in.
(6.9 × 4.0 × 3.3 cm)

12
Microlithic core
1¼ × 1½ × ¾ in.
(3.3 × 3.8 × 1.9 cm)

13
Point
10 × 3 × ⅞ in.
(25.3 × 7.7 × 2.4 cm)

14
Point
13 × 3 × ¾ in.
(33.1 × 7.5 × 1.8 cm)

15
Unfinished artifacts (refitted)
Each approx. 2¾ × 7 × 1¼ in.
(6.9 × 17.8 × 3.3 cm)

These specimens represent the Late Paleolithic period in Hokkaidō. The most important tools at that time were microblades [8–10], which were inserted into grooved or slotted wood or bone handles, and the burins used to make such grooves [6, 7]. The burin's cutting edge was created by striking an oblique, irregular flake from the tip of a stone blade.

The exhausted microlithic cores [11, 12] left after the removal of the microblades resemble those from northern China, Siberia, and Alaska, suggesting that Hokkaidō belonged to the North Pacific Paleolithic cultural area. Excavations have gradually revealed a wide exchange network. Stone material for making pendantlike ornaments was transported to Hokkaidō from the Lake Baikal area in Siberia. Conversely, obsidian for making stone implements was taken from Hokkaidō to Siberia.

Pirika 1 is remarkable for the huge amount of stone artifacts it has yielded—as many as 110 thousand. Also recovered are unfinished tools and pieces of raw stone material, which reveal the process of tool manufacture [15]. The abundance of stone implements at Pirika 1 may be related to the site's proximity to the original source of the stone.

The stone point [14] is one of the largest found in Japan, and the method of its production is extremely sophisticated. It is dated to the same period as certain tools from Mikoshiba, Nagano Prefecture [see 16–25].

DOI TAKASHI

Late Paleolithic period,
ca. 11,000 B.C.
Excavated at Mikoshiba,
Nagano Prefecture
Stone
Collection of Hayashi Shigeki; on
deposit at Kamiina Education Insti-
tution, Inc., Ina City, Nagano
Prefecture
Important Cultural Property

16
Point
6 × 1¾ × ⅝ in.
(15.4 × 4.5 × 1.5 cm)

17
Point
6¾ × 1¾ × ½ in.
(17.1 × 4.5 × 1.4 cm)

18
Adz
8⅝ × 2⅞ × 1⅝ in.
(22.0 × 7.4 × 3.9 cm)

19
Adz
8 × 2¾ × 1⅝ in.
(20.3 × 6.9 × 4.1 cm)

20
Adz
8⅜ × 3⅛ × 1⅝ in.
(21.2 × 8.0 × 4.2 cm)

21
Adz
9 × 3¼ × 1¾ in.
(23.0 × 8.2 × 4.5 cm)

Illustrated next page:

22
Scraper
4 × 1¹⁄₁₆ × ¼ in.
(10.3 × 2.7 × 0.6 cm)

23
Scraper
5⅝ × 1½ × ⅝ in.
(14.2 × 3.8 × 1.6 cm)

24
Core
4⅜ × 3⅞ × 1¾ in.
(11.0 × 9.9 × 4.5 cm)

25
Core
4¾ × 4⅝ × 1¾ in.
(12.0 × 11.8 × 4.4 cm)

These stone artifacts represent the period contemporaneous with the emergence of earthenware pottery. The most typical stone tools of the period were elegant points and partially polished adzes.

More than eighty stone artifacts were unearthed at Mikoshiba in Nagano Prefecture, in an area 13⅛ feet (4.0 m) wide. The stone points [16, 17] were found overlapping one another, in a configuration that attracted the attention of the archaeologists. It is assumed that all the objects in the assemblage were purposefully deposited in such a manner.

Like those from Pirika 1 [see 6–15], the points from Mikoshiba represent a type of implement from the Late Paleolithic period, which was followed by microliths or microblades. Before the bow and arrow were introduced around 10,500

B.C., people hunted by throwing spears with attached stone points. In some areas, such as Hokkaidō, for example, stone spearheads remained in use until the fifth or sixth century A.D., when they were replaced by the bow and arrow.

Stone adzes recovered from Mikoshiba are large and include both polished [18, 19] and chipped [20, 21] types. The partially polished adz, called the Mikoshiba-type stone adz, is one of the diagnostic artifacts that help archaeologists identify a site as Late Paleolithic. Objects that appear to be the stone cores from which blade tools were produced were also found [24, 25]. The scarcity of stone flakes, which are removed in making the tools, suggests that Mikoshiba was not the site of original manufacture.

Edge-polished adzes have been discovered mainly in northeastern

Japan and are of the same types as those distributed in eastern Siberia. Wooden handles to which the adzes were hafted have recently been recovered from waterlogged sites. The handles indicate that the tools were meant to be held in the hand as gouging implements in woodworking. Over the course of the succeeding Jōmon period, the roughly made stone adzes were gradually reduced in size.

This important group of stone artifacts suggests that cultural exchange existed between the Asian continent and the Japanese islands immediately before the beginning of pottery making in Japan. Artifacts from Mikoshiba are indispensable in identifying the transitional lithic phase between the Paleolithic and Jōmon periods.

DOI TAKASHI

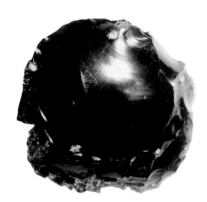

26, 27 BACKED BLADES

Late Paleolithic period,
ca. 17,000 B.C.
Excavated at Sugikubo,
Nagano Prefecture
Stone
Nojiriko Museum, Shinano
Township, Nagano Prefecture

26
3¼ × ¾ × ⅛ in.
(8.3 × 1.8 × 0.4 cm)

27
3½ × ⅝ × ¼ in.
(9.0 × 1.5 × 0.7 cm)

Backed blades appeared around twenty thousand years ago and remained in use as versatile cutting tools for a longer period than other stone artifacts of the Paleolithic period. One of the most universally produced stone tools of the Paleolithic culture throughout Japan, except in Hokkaidō, the backed blade also displays local characteristics. A precise technique was used to detach the blades from their stone cores: the tip and bottom were slightly blunted to form an elegant willow-leaf shape. Such blades are identified as the Sugikubo type in the Chūbu region of central Japan

and the Higashiyama type in the Tōhoku region of northeastern Honshū.

The backed blade made of longitudinal flakes—the Moro type, named after a site in the Kantō Plain, near Tokyo [see 28, 29]—is distributed throughout the Chūbu, Kantō, and Kyūshū regions. Another type of backed blade, made of short, side-blow, wing-shaped flakes—the Kou type [see 30, 31]—has been found throughout the Chūgoku and Kansai regions in Osaka Prefecture.

DOI TAKASHI

Late Paleolithic period,
ca. 17,000 B.C.
Excavated at Sunagawa,
Saitama Prefecture
Stone
Meiji University Museum of
Archaeology, Tokyo

28
3¼ × ¾ × ³⁄₁₆ in.
(8.3 × 2.0 × 0.5 cm)

29
2⅝ × ¾ × ¼ in.
(6.6 × 1.9 × 0.7 cm)

These so-called Moro-type knives are commonly made of obsidian, chert (resembling flint), or shale, which were worked to form longitudinal flakes. Although named after a site in Tokyo, the Moro-type backed blade is also found in the Kyūshū area, where the same materials were used.

Shaped by an elaborate technique, the flake was blunted obliquely to leave the blade and point sharp. Among stone tools, the Moro-type backed blade is assumed to be most similar to a modern knife. In Japa-

nese, backed blades are referred to as "knife-shaped stone implements." Some archaeologists believe that they were used simply for cutting and slicing; others argue that they were attached to the top or side of a wooden haft as a spear tip. Most likely, the backed blades were all-purpose tools for cutting and piercing.

DOI TAKASHI

Late Paleolithic period,
ca. 17,000 B.C.
Excavated at Kou, Osaka Prefecture
Stone
Senpoku Archaeological Museum,
Sakai City, Osaka Prefecture

30
3 × 1¼ × ½ in.
(7.8 × 3.2 × 1.1 cm)

31
2⅛ × ¾ × ⅜ in.
(5.4 × 2.1 × 0.9 cm)

A particular backed blade, named for specimens from the Kou site, Osaka Prefecture, is called the Kou-type knife, and the sites in which they are found belong to the Kou-type knife culture. The tools of the Kou assemblage include horizontally flaked cores, wing-shaped flakes, and knife-shaped stone implements, typical forms from western Japan. The major distinctions between knives found in eastern and western Japan derive from the flaking technique used to shape the blade, depending on the type of stone available. In eastern Japan, where obsidian, chert, and shale were available,

Moro- and Sugikubo-type knives were made by removing flakes longitudinally from the core and then retouching the flakes. The Kou-type knives—used for piercing as well as cutting—were made with the side-blow technique, appropriate for andesite material, which was found in western Japan. Settlements of the Kou-type knife culture have recently been located throughout western Japan, indicating that the people of the Paleolithic period who used the Kou-type knife lived in localized, defined territories.

DOI TAKASHI

3

JŌMON PERIOD

10,500–400 B.C.

Jōmon culture was born of the need for people to lead a stable life in the temperate forests (Nishida 1989, 66–70). The living patterns of the Paleolithic period were transformed and broadened to foster a semisedentary existence based on hunting a wider range of animals. In comparison with the people of the Paleolithic, those of the Jōmon expanded their range of tools, increased their knowledge of the environment, and entered into new ecological relationships. In their intensive practice of hunting and gathering and ambivalence toward cultivation, the Jōmon differed from some contemporaneous peoples in Asia such as the inhabitants of the Yellow and Yangzi river regions in China. The Jōmon were the first Japanese people to use traps and the bow and arrow. They also dramatically expanded the use of ocean resources and the processing of certain foods such as nuts.

The Jōmon period is named for a type of pottery in which the surface decoration was formed by impressing cords into the clay before it was completely hard. Although Jōmon clay vessels and figures as well as stone artifacts were collected from at least the eighteenth century A.D., it was only with the advent of radiocarbon dating after World War II that the relatively great age of the Jōmon was comprehended. The Jōmon period is unusual for its enormous time span of roughly ten thousand years. In many parts of the world a sequence of several very different cultures, characterized by innovations in subsistence patterns and toolmaking, is found in a parallel time range. As we shall see, Jōmon culture actually consists of several regional and temporal subperiods.

The Jōmon period is sometimes identified as "Neolithic" on the basis of its pottery and polished stone tools and is compared with the "Siberian Neolithic," a term used by Soviet archaeologists. Other archaeologists, however, reserve "Neolithic" for cultivating or food-producing societies rather than those based on hunting and gathering. Jōmon people, who knew how to cultivate certain plants including rice by the first millennium B.C., relied most heavily on hunting, fishing, and gathering. Their way of life was actually closer to that of Mesolithic peoples, such as the Natufian people of West Asia or the hunting and fishing tribes of the Pacific Northwest of North America, than to Neolithic cultivators.

Archaeologists have classified Jōmon pottery into many styles and cultural regions, which seem to indicate different subcultural groups (for Jōmon sites, see fig. 6). The word "Jōmon" (cord-mark decoration or motif) does not apply to all types of vessels made throughout the Jōmon period but is instead a broad term embracing different subcultures (Fujimoto 1983, 12). Subsistence patterns, however, manifest a basic

Deep vessel [44]

structure sharply different from those of the earlier Paleolithic hunters and gatherers or the later Yayoi agriculturists. It is appropriate, therefore, to consider the Jōmon period as encompassing a large, loosely integrated cultural complex.

Pottery appears to have been the main focus of Jōmon artistic expression, although woodcarving may also have been of great significance, judging from the few surviving examples of dugout canoes, substantial structures for communal activities, and large sculptures. Clay figures and ornaments were also made in abundance. Recently discovered lacquered objects from the Jōmon period demonstrate a mastery of complex craft techniques and the development of a sophisticated aesthetic.

Jōmon villages consisted of a small group of semisubterranean, or partially underground, pit houses supported by interior posts and covered

0   50   100   150   200   miles

50   150   250   kilometers

N

with thatched roofs that extended to the ground. Horticulture of a range of plants was introduced to the Japanese islands before 5000 B.C., and sophisticated techniques were developed for collecting and storing wild plant material.

The Jōmon people created a wide range of ornaments and ritual objects that attest to a vigorous ceremonial life. These include elaborately carved clay ear ornaments, stone and clay talismans, stone rods, and bronze swordlike objects. The Jōmon culture left ritual circles with standing stones, extensive ceremonial areas paved with stones, under which burial pits have been found, and in a few notable cases mounded communal cemeteries.

Despite differences in their way of life from the Japanese culture known from written history, the Jōmon people are related in several ways to the Japanese people of today. At least some Jōmon groups spoke a language ancestral to modern Japanese after 5000 B.C., and although later migrants entered Japan from Korea and China after the Jōmon period, the Jōmon people, themselves a composite of people from southern China and Siberia, contributed substantially to the modern Japanese population.

Were the Jōmon people Japanese? The Japanese language did not arise at once but rather through a series of migrations over a long period. Judging from glottochronology, speakers of the Japanese language must have first appeared in Japan between 5000 and 3000 B.C.[1] How can we recognize the advent of a new spoken language from the archaeological record? Nowhere are languages marked unequivocally by specific kinds of artifacts. Speakers of the same language may use entirely different kinds of artifacts, or speakers of different languages may share the same technology or styles of artifacts. It has proven extremely difficult to recognize the appearance of proto-Japanese language in Japan.

Did the Jōmon people look like the modern Japanese? Earlier theories suggested that the Jōmon people were the Ainu, who were eventually pushed back from central Japan into Hokkaidō and northern Tōhoku by the modern Japanese beginning in the Yayoi period. There is little doubt that the people who left the spectacular Jōmon remains of northern Honshū and southern Hokkaidō were distant ancestors of the Ainu. The Jōmon people were physically and ethnically diverse, and the Ainu one group among many who lived in Japan during the Jōmon period.

Crossing land bridges and spreading throughout the islands, the earliest human populations apparently came to Japan from eastern and southeastern Asia near the end of the Pleistocene, by at least thirty thousand years ago (fig. 7). Around fourteen thousand years ago, populations from northeastern Asia migrated to Japan via Hokkaidō; during the Jōmon period Mongoloid populations from Neolithic and Bronze Age cultures came to Japan from northeastern Asia. Intensive rice-cultivating people also entered western Japan from Korea around 400 B.C. Thus, throughout the entire Jōmon period, populations from more than one location in eastern Asia were arriving in Japan (Kokuritsu Kagaku Hakubutsukan 1988).

What did the Jōmon people contribute to later Japanese society? Until recently the Jōmon were considered marginal to modern Japanese culture, which was thought to have begun with the irrigation of rice

Figure 7
Entry routes of ancient humans into Japan.

1 By the beginning of the final period of the Pleistocene, more than thirty thousand years ago, people from East and Southeast Asia arrived in Japan.

2 Their descendants crossed land bridges and moved throughout the Japanese islands.

3 At the end of the Pleistocene, about fourteen thousand years ago, populations from the northeast migrated to Japan, affecting the physical make up of the Jōmon people in a gradient from northeast to southwest.

4–7 In the Jōmon period (10,500–400 B.C.), Mongoloid populations arrived from Northeast Asia (4) and from what is now northeastern China and Korea.

5–6 Rice-cultivating peoples from China (6) also entered Japan. The relationship of the groups is not clear, but one group of descendants of these Northeast and East Asian peoples is known to have entered western Japan at the beginning of the Yayoi period (400 B.C.–A.D. 250).

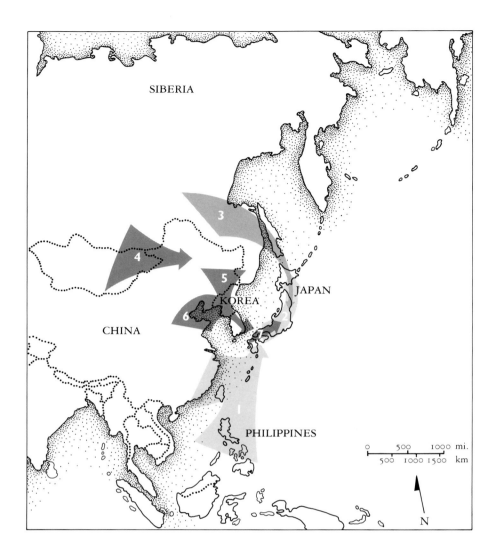

during the Yayoi. It now seems more likely that the Jōmon knowledge of cultivating, storing, and processing plant materials including rice was an important factor that led to the later rapid adoption of irrigated rice cultivation and was also the basis for the development of mountainside slash-and-burn cultivation, which was of great significance to traditional Japanese agriculture (Sasaki Kōmei 1986, 209). The subsistence patterns of mountain people in general, including the collection of wild foods and processing of nuts into starch, have been important in rural Japanese life to the present day.

Moreover, the Jōmon tradition of low-fired ceramics, which entails a preference for earthy colors, rich textures, and surface effects, seems to be preserved in Japanese aesthetics as a parallel to the more formal, symmetrical shapes and regular decorative patterns that often came from the Asian continent. Glimpses into religious practices of the Jōmon may reflect either ancient themes that began in the Jōmon and continued into more recent times or the worldview of the present projected onto the past.

Chronology

The Jōmon period is divided into six phases of unequal length. A fundamental change occurred in the Early Jōmon, with the appearance of pit houses and stabilized settlements. People had previously moved frequently, living in impermanent camps in the manner of Paleolithic hunters. From the Early Jōmon, for sixty-five hundred years or about three hundred generations, the technological pattern was set, with little subsequent change (Nishida 1989, 75–78).

Archaeologists have identified peaks of Jōmon cultural intensity by studying ceramic decoration, site size, and ritual activity. The first peak occurred in the Middle Jōmon with the appearance of Katsusaka, Sori, and Umataka pottery types from the mountain basin region and adjacent valleys of Nagano and the nearby Kantō Plain of central Japan. The second occurred in the Late and Final Jōmon with the Kamegaoka culture and Angyō and Ōbora pottery types of the Tōhoku region of northeastern Honshū.

The Economic Base: Hunters, Gatherers, Cultivators

Two great environmental zones gradually emerged at the end of the Pleistocene with the amelioration of the Asian continental climate: the broadleaf deciduous forest of northeastern Japan, in which dominate nut-bearing trees such as *nara* (*Quercus serrata*), and the broadleaf evergreen forest of southwestern Japan, in which is common the evergreen oaklike tree *shii* (*Castanea crenata*). Jōmon sites are far more numerous in the deciduous zone than in the evergreen. Beech trees, important elements of the broadleaf deciduous forest, reached their maximum distribution in the Early and Middle Jōmon (Fujimoto 1988, 24). As climate began to cool at the beginning of the Late Jōmon, the number of Jōmon sites decreased.

Jōmon culture extended from Hokkaidō to Okinawa, taking different forms in the outlying regions. In Hokkaidō it was particularly concentrated in the south, which supported the same kind of beech forests as those of the Tōhoku region in northern Honshū. The high achievements of the Epi-Jōmon culture of Hokkaidō are represented by a collection of exquisite bone and antler artifacts [93–102]. At each period of the Jōmon, however, interaction with the Asian mainland is evident.

Regional variation within the Jōmon food base was strong. At the northern tip of Honshū the cold current, the Oyashio, brought in rich marine life. Salmon and the related steelhead, which do not migrate to the sea, were important resources, especially in northeastern Japan. Bays along the Sea of Japan and also in the Chiba region provided shellfish. The Nittano site, which yielded abundant faunal remains, appears to have been a coastal settlement occupied over several seasons during the Early and Middle Jōmon; fish were caught in the shallow, brackish water along the shore of Izumi Bay. As the sea level regressed in the Middle Jōmon, the people of Nittano exploited the lower reaches of a nearby stream that flowed into the sea.[2]

The most important food items came from the mountain slopes and basins of Nagano, where deer, wild plants, and probably small river fish flourished. Several imposing mountain ranges converge on that region, providing well-watered slopes and valleys with an abundance of forests and rivers. The large bays and estuaries of western Kyūshū provided many kinds of shellfish. Judging from analyses of artifact assemblages, groups living in northeastern Japan seem to have been generally more specialized in hunting while groups in the southwest were occupied with plant gathering (Akazawa & Maeyama 1986).

Nuts were important foods in both the northeast and southwest, particularly for rendering starch and thereby producing flour. A vital source of carbohydrates, starch obtained from the kernels could be stored for long periods (Watanabe Makoto 1975). The discovery of abundant remains of charred nut trees and uncarbonized nuts in environments where nuts would not be plentiful without human intervention suggests that they were cultivated.[3]

In addition to regional variation, the Japanese environment was characterized by temporal changes (Tsukada 1986). While several episodes took place between the warming trends at the end of the Pleistocene and end of the Jōmon period, the most significant occurred from 5000 to 2000 B.C., when mean temperatures rose by several degrees.[4] Around 4500 B.C. broadleaf evergreen trees are known to have increased rapidly, which suggests that the climate was warmer than before (Yasuda 1984, 404). During that time habitats such as the Nagano region supported large populations, indicating that food resources were particularly abundant. In addition, sea levels rose dramatically around 4,000 B.C., reaching a maximum of about 16⅜ feet (5 m) higher than those of today. While the rise reduced the land area, the length of the shoreline expanded greatly, thereby increasing available marine food resources (Akazawa 1986). In the Final Jōmon, around 900 B.C., a distinct cooling trend appears to have been linked to a population decline.

A distinctive variant of Jōmon culture flourished in the Ryūkyū Islands. There the resources of tropical lagoons were utilized, together with the nuts of evergreen oaks (Ryūkyū Archaeological Research Team 1981). Judging from nail-impressed pottery found in the radiocarbon-dated Agaribaru site, initial contacts from Kyūshū were made around 5000 B.C. Shards of other Jōmon pottery types, such as Early Jōmon Sobata, Late Jōmon Ichiki, and Final Jōmon Yusu, have been found in Okinawa. Local pottery, while recognizably different from Kyūshū ceramics, shows influence from Kyūshū (Okinawa Kōkogaku Kyōkai 1978; Miyagi & Takamiya 1983). The subsistence and ritual patterns, however, reveal adaptation to local conditions. Findings of arrowheads, indicative of hunting, have been slight, and no figures or ritual tools have been recovered. Instead, the emphasis seems to have been placed on processing plant foods. The Okinawan people also made distinctive decorative objects of bone.

Tools of Fishing, Hunting, Gathering

While some innovations in the Jōmon tool kit occurred during the period, most archaeologists emphasize the stability of the subsistence pattern once it was set (Nishida 1989, 16, 17). Many types of tools were used to obtain, process, and store food.

Jōmon people utilized a wide variety of plants and animals in a generalized rather than specialized pattern. Their activities were distinctly seasonal, with a peak of food resources in the fall with the nut harvest, deer and wild boar hunting, and salmon runs. Large amounts of food, particularly nuts, were stored in pits.

Arrows tipped with small triangular stone points and bows made of maple, oak, or a yewlike tree and bound with cherry bark were used to hunt deer, wild boar, bear, monkey, birds, and probably fish. The bows were as long as 51 to 55 inches (130–140 cm). The typical arrowhead has a concave base and is often made of obsidian or other dense volcanic material. Some archaeologists believe that poison was used on arrow tips in later times in northeastern Asia; there is, however, no archaeological proof that it was adopted by the Jōmon people. The double-curved bow was probably in use by the end of the Jōmon (Gekkan Bunkazai Hakkutsu 1990a, 34), and spears were abundant in the Initial Jōmon. From the Early to Final Jōmon, in areas where finds of spears are scarce, it is thought that trapping was probably well developed.[5] An object that appears to be a deer caller has also been recovered.[6]

Dogs, which have been found carefully buried, were greatly important for hunting; in at least one case the burial contained a very old dog (Suzuki Michinosuke 1981, 51). Pointed wooden digging sticks, chipped stone adzes, and sharpened antlers all appear to have been tools for digging roots and bulbs. Polished stone adzes were used to fashion and finish wooden tools and parts of structures.

Fishnet sinkers were frequently employed, and the remains of weirs have been located. While fish traps have not been recognized, basketry fragments found in numerous sites suggest that they were common. Harpoons are abundant in northern Kyūshū and along the coast of the Sea of Japan and near Sendai Bay in Tōhoku. The toggle harpoon, also found in other regions of the North Pacific, was attached to a separate line to retrieve the animal after the harpoon was released from its shaft. Fishing spears and fishhooks were also used, the latter ¾ to 3⅞ inches (2–10 cm) long.

An important tool for subsistence and local transportation was the dugout canoe. From the Torihama Shell Mound in Fukui Prefecture, dating to the Initial and Early Jōmon, around 7500–3500 B.C., a canoe and paddle were found.[7] It is estimated that the canoe could carry 1,100 pounds (500 kg). With its shallow draft, the canoe would have been particularly useful in the upper reaches of rivers.

In addition to the relatively wide range of food-procuring tools, the Jōmon people developed a set of tools to process food, including mortars and pestles; ceramic containers for boiling, steaming, and storage; wooden containers, some lacquered; stone knives with flaked edges; and probably dippers, ladles, and scoops (Nishida 1989, 4–17). Scrapers were used to prepare hides and fashion small tools.

For cooking meat, stone knives and fire were the only "tools" utilized. The preparation of starch required pottery vessels, large quantities of water, mortars and pestles, mats for drying the starch, and storage areas. Starch preparation is generally a complex process involving specialized sites, a range of utensils, and several stages of activity.

Tools of Cultivation

One of the great debates surrounding archaeology in the 1960s concerned cultivation during the Jōmon period. The discovery of charred breadlike material from Idojiri in Nagano Prefecture, datable to approximately

2500 B.C., and from other Jōmon sites appears to be evidence of some kind of grain. In fact, seeds of the beefsteak plant (*Perilla*), which is of the same genus as the condiment *shiso,* have been found in the charred cakes. The size and stability of Middle Jōmon settlements in Nagano and high quality of crafts such as pottery led archaeologists to conclude that agriculture may have been practiced.

Because Japanese archaeology has been based primarily on historical rather than comparative sources, few studies of hunters and gatherers of temperate forests have been available to Japanese scholars in their search for analogies to the Jōmon data. Studies of comparable cultures indicate that hunters and gatherers in regions such as the Pacific Northwest of North America lived in stable settlements and created specialized crafts without necessarily relying on an agricultural base.

It is now clear that Jōmon people cultivated a number of plants at an early date (ca. 5000 B.C.) but that the cultivated plants were not their main source of food. Such plants included bottle gourds (*Lagenaria siceraria*), beans (*Vigna angularis*), the condiments *shiso* and *egoma, asa* (hemp, *Cannabis sativum*), mulberry, colza, and burdock (*Arctium*).[8] *Shiso* and *egoma* are native to broadleaf evergreen forests of Asia. Peach seeds have also been found from Early Jōmon marine sites (now under water) in Nagasaki Prefecture.[9] These plants, none native to Japan, do not need much cultivation but do require natural or artificial forest clearings for abundant light.

In Fukui Prefecture an intensively investigated site has transformed concepts regarding Jōmon subsistence: the Torihama Shell Mound on the southern shore of a brackish lake near Wakasa Bay on the coast of the Sea of Japan. With its wet layers protected by a modern system of pilings to permit intensive stratigraphic examination, the site has been investigated almost continuously since the 1960s. From the Initial Jōmon, Torihama was situated in a beech forest on the edge of the lake and was visited only intermittently. In the Early Jōmon, Torihama was settled more or less continuously.

One hundred different kinds of food resources have been recovered there, including twenty-one species of nuts, thirteen of fish, twelve of mammals (of which deer and wild boar comprise 95 percent), thirty-three kinds of shellfish, and three kinds of tubers. Although not preserved at Torihama, viny tubers such as yams (*Dioscorea japonica*) and *kuzu* (*Pueraria thunbergiana*) are today abundant in the surrounding area and are thought to have been a food resource of the Jōmon inhabitants (Nishida 1989, 18–20). Nuts of beech (*Fagus crenata*), horse chestnut (*Aesculus turbinata*), and walnut (*Juglans mandshurica*) were found in the lower layers of the excavation. They appear to have fallen naturally into the site and do not seem to have been consumed by humans, although the walnuts showed traces of having been eaten by mice. Remains of grasses are rare.

Parts of cultivated plants came from several layers in the Torihama deposit (Sasaki Kōmei 1986, 126–28; Crawford 1987). Beans (tentatively identified), gourds, *shiso, egoma,* and *gobō* (Burdock root) were recovered. *Gobō* is native to southern Siberia. By the Early Jōmon, with the gradually warming climate, the plant environment around Torihama had changed from deciduous to broadleaf evergreen forest. In association with these plant remains were found lacquered objects, including bow fragments, adz handles, flat dishes, and other wooden objects.

Technology

Pottery Making

Simple in technology, complex in decoration, Jōmon vessels evoke universal admiration. Potters marvel at their ingenuity; designers find their originality startling; archaeologists must account for their number and diversity. Japanese museums swell with reconstructed vessels.

Two basic shapes are found among early Jōmon vessels, which were used for boiling food: one with a rounded silhouette and pointed bottom and the other with straight sides sloping inward to a flat bottom (fig. 8). There is a strong possibility that the oldest pottery produced in Japan is undecorated (Kobayashi Tatsuo & Ogawa 1988, 303). Undecorated pottery is found at Ōdairayamamoto in Aomori Prefecture, Ushirono in Ibaraki Prefecture, Maeda Kōchi in Tokyo, and Uwano in Kanagawa Prefecture. Contemporaneous sites in Kyūshū, the Sempukuji and Fukui caves, have yielded pottery with "bean appliqué" (*tōryūmon*) and with linear appliqué (*ryukisenmon*). Another very early form of decoration was achieved with the application of small beads of clay along the rim.

The earliest kinds of pottery are followed by those exhibiting a decorative technique called "thumbnail impression," with rows of sharp indentations (*tsumegatamon*). While the potter may have used a fingernail to make the desired marks, usually a piece of bamboo or split stick was used. During the Incipient Jōmon, pottery spread throughout Honshū but did not enter Hokkaidō. Thumbnail-impressed pottery is found in Okinawa at sites such as Toguchi Agaribaru (layer 4) but dates only to around 5000 B.C. It is not clear whether life at the beginning of the Incipient Jōmon had changed much beyond the Paleolithic. Pottery of the Incipient period is remarkably scarce and was probably in limited, inefficient use. Cord marking (fig. 9) over the entire surface (*ōatsu jōmon*) or cord rouletting (*kaiten jōmon*), with a collarlike rim and flat base, appeared on vessels at the end of the Incipient Jōmon.

During the Initial Jōmon twisted cords or cord-wrapped sticks were also used to decorate pottery. Decoration created by the latter is called *yori itomon*. Either the end or the length of a piece of twisted cord was pressed into the clay. The cord could also be rolled over the surface of the vessel. In some cases multiple cords were intertwined. Twisted in different directions or knotted, they produced great variation in decoration. Rouletting, a technique in which a cord or stick is rocked back and forth across the vessel surface, was also used. Sometimes the impressions were blurred by dragging the implement across the clay.

In central and western Japan, twisted-cord decorated pottery was followed by carved-stick decoration (*oshigatamon*) in which a carved stick was rolled over the surface of the vessel. In southern Kyūshū, at the end of the Initial Jōmon, cord-impressed pottery was succeeded by vessels with shell impressions and a decorated, flat collar (Kobayashi Tatsuo 1979, 55). Pottery ornamented with shell impressions and with grooving (*kaigara chinsenmon*) has been found in northern Hokkaidō and Tōhoku.

Figure 8
Jōmon vessel shapes. Vessel types
became increasingly varied through
time.

Incipient

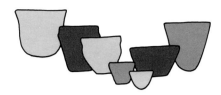

Initial

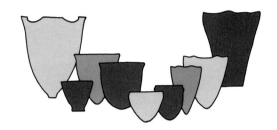

Early

Middle

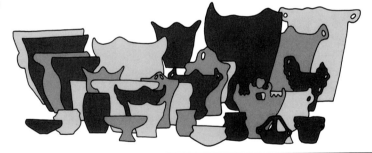

Late

Final

```
o    5    10  in. (approx.)
    10   20   cm  (approx.)
```

New types of ceremonial artifacts, such as figures, earrings, and bracelets, marked the beginning of a distinct social pattern in the Early Jōmon. A leading Jōmon specialist, Kobayashi Tatsuo (1988a), has suggested that ceremonial artifacts and pottery distinguish the Jōmon from other nonagricultural North Pacific cultures with similar utilitarian stone tools.

Twisted-cord decoration remained popular during the Early Jōmon period, particularly from the Kantō region to Hokkaidō and Tōhoku. Made of strands of plant fiber, the cord is less than $\frac{1}{16}$ inch (2 mm) thick. Typical shapes recovered there are deep, straight-sided jars and vessels with richly textured surfaces having twill (*ayasugimon*) or feather (*ujōjōmon*) patterns. Magnificent cylindrical vessels of the Entō type (named after the Japanese term for cylinder) persisted in the region until the midpoint of the Middle Jōmon, around 2000 B.C. Later examples have rim projections, which must be derived from the more sculptured forms of the Kantō region.

Vessels distinguished by wavy rims and pouring spouts and used for food service and other purposes appeared in the Kantō region at the beginning of the Early Jōmon. Narrow-necked jars, shallow bowls, and jars with flaring mouths were also introduced. A florescence of hand-modeled rim decoration is also evident in ceramics dating to the end of the Early Jōmon in the Kantō region. The trend toward more complex decoration and modeling can be seen in the Kinki region of western Honshū and in southern Tōhoku in the north. The Sobata type—a distinctive round-bottomed vessel with a wide mouth and broad, incised linear decoration—appears in Kyūshū and is found throughout the Ryūkyū Islands from Tanegashima in Kagoshima Prefecture to Okinawa. Sobata-type vessels contain fragments of steatite that were deliberately mixed with the clay paste; consequently they are thought to be related to the Geometric or Comb Pattern Pottery of Korea.[10] The distinguished Yale scholar of prehistoric migrations, Irving Rouse (1986, 77–79), has suggested that Sobata-type pottery signals the arrival of the first speakers of the Japanese language from Korea.

There is no doubt that the Middle Jōmon represents one of the great apogees in prehistoric art. New vessel forms in the Middle Jōmon include some that are thought to have been hanging lamps and pots with raised feet and perforated bases. Other new shapes include rare effigies of natural objects, such as shells or fish, and drumlike, wide-bellied pots with holes that may have been used to fasten a skin tympanum. One of the leading specialists on Jōmon food plants and animals, Watanabe Makoto (1984), has proposed that these vessels were used to make wine from wild fruit. If so, the holes that enable the escape of gas in fermentation, according to Watanabe, were unsuitable for fastening a tympanum. Such vessels are concentrated in Yamanashi Prefecture, a modern wine-making region.

In the same region ceramic decoration became dramatically three-dimensional. Sculptured rims with overhanging projections and open-work are hallmarks of the vessel types Katsusaka, Sori, and Umataka. The surface decoration of these pots, applied when the clay was leather-hard, consumed more time than the construction of the vessel. The great "flame-style" vessels of the Niigata region rely on cutting and incising

Figure 9
Jōmon pottery decoration
made by impressing cords or
sticks onto a clay surface
(each utensil appears to the
left of an individual
pattern).

1–6 Patterns made by different
types of twisted cords.
7, 8 Feather patterns (*ujō jōmon*)
made by cords twisted in
different directions and
joined together.
9, 10 Patterns made by two
entwined twisted cords.
11–14 Patterns made by knotted
and twisted cords (*musu-
bime jōmon*).
15 Patterns made by braided or
plaited cord.
16–18 Impressions made by a
stick wrapped with twisted
cord (*yori itomon*).

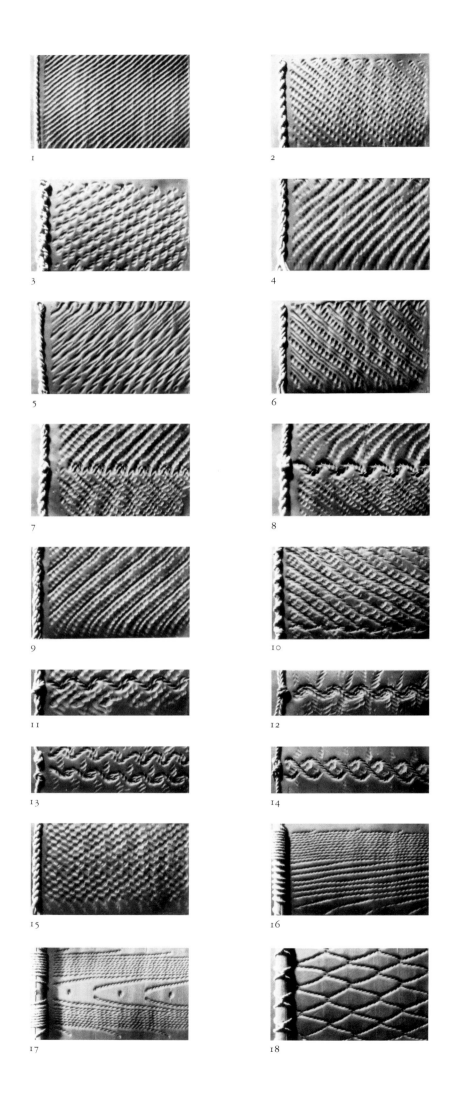

to give the impression of applied strips. Their built-up rims epitomize the exuberance of the most dramatic Jōmon ceramic decoration [47–51].

Major changes took place in the design and application of decorative patterns, which range from bands of images to compartmentalized motifs separated by ridges. The zones appear to be superficially symmetrical but are, in fact, irregular, as if perfect symmetry was to be avoided. While ceramic decoration in western Japan is quite interesting, it remains flat, with virtually no projections or sculptured relief. Although cord-marked vessels have been found in Kyūshū in the Middle Jōmon period, the technique was never popular there.

Pottery of the Late and Final Jōmon is less obviously flamboyant than pottery of the Middle Jōmon. Late Jōmon ceramics are made of a dense clay paste. The typical form of the deep cylindrical jar persisted; some vessels display no burn marks, however, which suggests that they may have been used for holding water instead of for cooking. New types of decoration included erased cord marking (*surikeshi*) in which the cord marking was applied and then partially rubbed out to leave a smooth surface. These vessels were a distinctive innovation of eastern Japan in the Late and Final Jōmon periods. Food vessels, including shallow bowls, plates, and footed jars, must have served ceremonial functions. An analysis of vessel shapes from Ishigami in Saitama Prefecture highlights the relative proportion of different vessel shapes from a single site (fig. 10).

In a fascinating book delineating the practical uses and ritual significance of Jōmon pottery, Sahara Makoto (1979, 27–30) has suggested that some small shallow bowls (*asabachi*) may have been used for serving food that was eaten with the fingers; the modern counterpart of the deep cylindrical shape is the typical Japanese cooking pot (*nabe*). In the Final Jōmon of the Tōhoku region, footed vessels appear to have been set in the fire. These vessels represent progenitors of the modern Japanese ceramics that are used for food cooked in front of guests (*nabemono ryōri*).

The Final Jōmon is known for Kamegaoka-style ceramics [60, 83], centered in Aomori Prefecture in the Tōhoku region. In contrast with earlier forms, the smaller vessels common to Kamegaoka suggest the emergence of new rituals. Low plates with exterior surfaces decorated with curvilinear carving and erased cord marking and lacquered interiors have been found; the fine, regular cord marking contrasts strikingly with the carving. Plates are small enough to contain single servings, although individuals most likely did not have their own personal eating vessels. Sahara (1979, 18) has contended that food was eaten communally during the Jōmon period, although his supposition cannot be confirmed directly from the context in which the pottery has been found.

The form of shallow vessels with raised feet (*takatsuki*), often with openwork, and spouted pouring vessels (*dobin*) suggests their use for ceremonial display. The pouring vessel's spout is set exceptionally low on the shoulder. Since the *dobin* could not contain much liquid without overflowing, the pot may have had a social rather than a purely practical use. Kamegaoka ceramics are famous for the application of lacquer to the entire surface. Red, black, and brown lacquer decoration enhanced the durability of the objects and also made them waterproof.

The Late Jōmon people in the Kantō region developed reduction-fired, polished black pottery. The technique later appeared in Kyūshū

Figure 10
Distribution in a single site of Late Jōmon (1500–1000 B.C.) vessel shapes, representing 494 specimens recovered from the Ishigami Shell Mound, Saitama Prefecture.

Shallow Jars: 3.6%

11 vessels: 2.2%   6 vessels: 1.2%   1 vessel: 0.2%

Footed Jars: 1.6%

7 vessels: 1.4%   1 vessel: 0.2%

Deep Jars: 94.4%

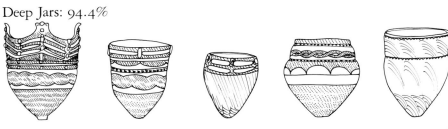

32 vessels: 6.5%   36 vessels: 7.3%   39 vessels: 7.9%   34 vessels: 6.9%   321 vessels: 65%

Spouted Vessels: 0.4%

2 vessels: 0.4%

during the Late and Final Jōmon in the making of simply decorated low bowls. In fact, pottery decoration in Kyūshū almost ceased at that time. The final type of decoration in northern Kyūshū, which consisted of a raised band (*tottaimon*), formed a smooth transition to the pottery of the succeeding Yayoi culture. Polished black ceramics are also found in the Kamegaoka culture. In some cases it appears that Jōmon potters actually added crushed iron material to the clay or mixed clay with organic material (Sahara 1979, 70).

The Late and Final Jōmon witnessed the production of some unusual vessel types, including squared, basket-shaped containers and double-spouted forms. Totally plain vessels used for the production of salt are known from coastal regions such as Ibaraki Prefecture, northeast of Tokyo (Sahara 1979, 55).

Only a few archaeologists have attempted to draw general conclusions about early Japanese ceramics. Kobayashi (Kobayashi Tatsuo & Ogawa 1988) has distinguished four major shifts in the overall decoration. In the first two thousand years of production, which he called the "Image Period," the decorative patterns of the Incipient Jōmon, the latest of which was cord marking, evolved. During the second period, coinciding with the Early Jōmon and termed the "Period of Establishing Independence," new surface treatments emerged on the basic vessel forms: Decorative Pattern A, in which the treatment is applied evenly all over the body or in zones, and Decorative Pattern B, in which patterns are applied in more complex zones that may have been created by different techniques. The ceramics of the Period of Establishing Independence shifted from purely utilitarian to elaborately decorated.

Kobayashi has termed the Middle, Late, and Final Jōmon the "Period of Adaptation." The use of pottery expanded beyond the preparation of food, and the decoration changed to a narrative form characterized by internal complexity and an interplay of different registers. The Period of Adaptation is the last stage of innovation in Jōmon ceramics.

Ueno Yoshiya (1987), a scholar investigating the meaning of pottery decoration systems, has described the animated surfaces of Jōmon ceramics as fields of information. During the Initial Jōmon, decoration often completely covered the surfaces of vessels but the amount of information conveyed is not great because the decoration is uniform. In the Early Jōmon, decorative schemes changed. Different ways of organizing motifs arose in the central Japanese Alps in two groups of mountain basins: one in the areas of Itō, Matsumoto, and Suwa and the second in the areas of Nagano, Saku, and Ueda. These valleys form channels for the flow of information. The first set of valleys is connected to the Kantō Plain, while the second follows the Chikuma River, which originates in the Yatsugatake mountain range, the lower slopes of which are densely dotted with Middle Jōmon settlements. This area, in which Jōmon ceramics underwent the most dramatic transformations, lies at the junction of three ecological zones: the deciduous forests of northeastern Japan, the broadleaf evergreen forests of southwestern Japan, and the upland regions of the central mountains. In addition to being an ecotone, this region was the meeting point of different information systems that must have passed through the valleys in their transmission throughout the archipelago. The two separate worlds of the northeast and the southwest were combined in these valleys.

Textile Production

Impressions on pottery and rare samples of preserved textiles provide evidence of Jōmon twining or knitting. It is thought that hemp and ramie fibers were used. At present the most abundant evidence comes from sites along the coast of the Sea of Japan, particularly in Ishikawa Prefecture. The earliest examples date from the Initial Jōmon. Primitive embroidery, in which decoration was outlined with a simple stitch, and the sewing together of layers of cloth for strength have also been noted (Ōzeki 1989).

Lacquer Production

Lacquer production began in the Early Jōmon by 4000 B.C. and quite possibly earlier. Thus far, the Japanese finds of lacquerware are contemporaneous with the lacquered objects recovered from the Neolithic site of Hemudu, Zhejiang Province, in southeastern China. While the major source of lacquer is the sap of *Rhus verniciflua,* a tree native to China, closely related species are indigenous to Japan. At present the archaeological record indicates that the use of lacquer was more advanced and diverse in Japan than in China at that early date (Suzuki Kimio 1988, 32). Microscopic analysis has shown, for example, that multiple layers were applied to Jōmon objects, in some cases, black over red. While Suzuki Kimio of Keio University, Tokyo, is convinced that the lacquer tradition developed indigenously, it may have been introduced to Japan from southern China before 5000 B.C. together with a number of very old cultivated plants, such as beans and gourds, found in the Torihama Shell Mound.

The use of lacquer is a multistage process, involving the slitting of the bark of the tree and collecting the sap from early summer to mid-fall, as we know from the study of Japanese traditional lacquer. The lacquer is applied in many coats. The sophistication of the technique attests to the great experience of the Jōmon people in the use of plant resources.

Archaeological specimens show us that lacquer was applied to a wide range of utensils, including wooden bowls, plates, cups, combs, ornaments, and bows. It was also applied to clay vessels and earrings, woven baskets, and bone objects. Red and black pigments were used, the red produced by adding to natural lacquer the minerals hematite or cinnabar, and the black, by the addition of naturally occurring iron or fine carbon.

The first discoveries, in 1926, of Jōmon lacquer came from a Final Jōmon site, the peat layers of Korekawa in Aomori Prefecture. Objects included a remarkable decorated wooden bow [84], sword, bracelets, earrings, and deep and shallow bowls. The sophisticated artistry of these objects convinced some scholars that the end of the Jōmon period in the Tōhoku region might have been as late as the Kamakura period (1185–1333), since it was thought that lacquer had reached Japan after the arrival of Buddhism. Thus the lacquer finds of Korekawa were initially dated from the sixth to thirteen centuries A.D. Now it is clear that lacquer technology dates to at least 4000 B.C.

Early Jōmon sites such as Torihama in Fukui Prefecture and Yoneizumi in Ishikawa Prefecture have yielded decorative combs fashioned of small branches of *Callicarpa japonica* (*murasaki shikibu*) that were sewn together with transverse pieces. The back of the comb was covered with a mixture of sawdust, shavings, and lacquer. Yoneizumi also yielded twined plant-fiber textiles, which were used to strain the lacquer.

Settlements

Archaeologists are able to unearth house and food remains, tools, and ritual objects. The challenge is to determine how the finds were related in the organization of everyday life in ancient Japan. Did families share tools or cooperate in food preparation? How many people lived in a village at one time? Were individual villages self-sufficient?

Most Jōmon villages consisted of only a few houses. Although dozens of house pits may be found in a single archaeological site, only a few houses may have been occupied at one time. By dividing pottery styles into finely differentiated subtypes, specialists have found that only a few houses share the same subtype, an indication that they were the only dwellings occupied at a particular time (Habu 1988). Middle Jōmon villages, consisting of four or five houses and with a population of about thirty to fifty people, may have been somewhat larger than those of the preceding periods.

Some studies have suggested that even in the largest settlements the villages were temporarily abandoned, which explains the accumulation of black earth in house pits. Critics of that theory state that the dark soil was produced when the house pits were repaired and enlarged (Nishida 1989, 50). Few studies describe settlement patterns over a region rather than for individual sites.

Excavations of the past decade have greatly expanded our knowledge of house types and construction methods of the Jōmon period. At least three dwelling types are known (fig. 11): semisubterranean houses, houses built on the surface of the ground, and houses constructed with posts set in the ground. The simplest form, the houses set on the ground, cannot easily be detected archaeologically except through scatters of artifacts.[11] They may have been used for temporary shelter, especially in hunting camps.

The most common type of Jōmon house was the semisubterranean pit dwelling. The use of so-called pit houses was most common in northeastern Japan, whereas villages in western Japan were composed of surface dwellings with the poles converging to a peak. In the earliest form of pit house, common in the Initial and Early Jōmon, the posts were set in the bottom of the pit. Found in Hokkaidō and Tōhoku, that type may have proved unsatisfactory because water from the sloping roof would flow into the pit. Early builders may have avoided that problem by piling earth over the roof out to the pit's edges. The average area of a pit house has been estimated to be about 215 square feet (20 sq m; Suzuki Kimio 1988, 104), but examples as large as 754 square feet (70 sq m) are known from the Initial Jōmon. Other forms of pit houses had upright walls with an overhanging roof. Thatched roofs were developed on pit houses at the end of the Initial Jōmon, around 5000 B.C.

At the end of the Early Jōmon some extremely large structures as big as 1,080 square feet (100 sq m; Miyamoto 1988, 92, 93) were surrounded by a vertical outer set of posts in a small trench and constructed of woven branches covered with mud. Many large structures lacked hearths and are therefore not considered to have been used as residences. Later examples, however, have a row of hearths and central storage pits. Some large structures were near stone-paved areas, as if the houses may have had a ceremonial function (Miyamoto 1988). By the Middle Jōmon very large structures, the largest more than 2,153 square feet (200 sq m; Miyamoto 1988, 94), were constructed all over eastern Japan. A village usually had only one such centrally located structure. Elevated buildings,

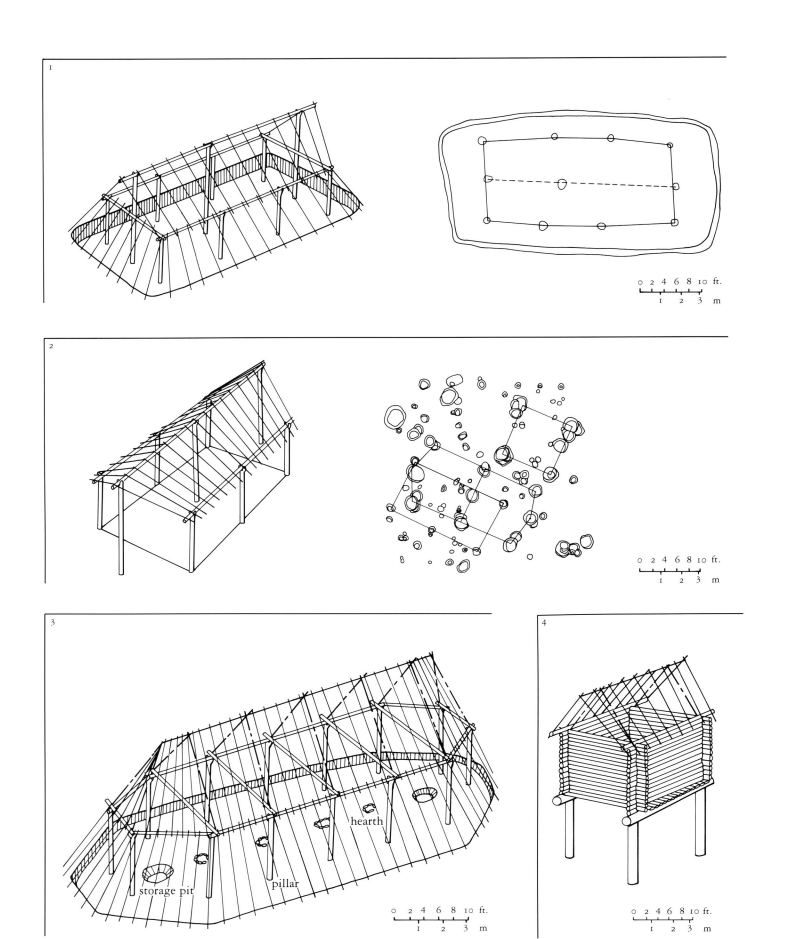

Figure 11
Variations in Jōmon structures.

1 *Left,* hypothetical reconstruction
  of an Early Jōmon (5000–2500
  B.C.) pit house with internal
  posts; *right,* plan showing postholes and pit foundation as
  excavated. Dwelling 155, Naka-
  sone 2 site, Iwate Prefecture.
2 *Left,* hypothetical reconstruction
  of the upper framework of a
  Middle Jōmon (2500–1500 B.C.)
  structure built with postholes
  dug into the ground; *right,* plan
  of excavated postholes. Nishida
  site, Iwate Prefecture.
3 Hypothetical reconstruction of a
  large communal Middle Jōmon
  structure with central hearth and
  storage pits; 56 feet (17 m)
  long. Dwelling 2, Fudōdō site,
  Toyama Prefecture.
4 Reconstruction of an elevated
  storage structure. Nishida site,
  Iwate Prefecture.

thought to be all-purpose storehouses, have been found near the central community house. It was previously believed that this type of elevated construction was not practiced until the Yayoi period.

Since some villages consisted of only a few houses, Nishida Masaki (1989), a cultural ecologist, has concluded that cooperative groups were extremely small and that most tasks were undertaken by single house-holds, with the exception of the building of houses and canoes. These small Jōmon communities had a low ratio of producers to consumers. With their dispersed resources and limited ecological capability, Jōmon people could not sustain the large populations necessary to control vast territories. Nishida Masaki (1989, 33) has calculated that it would require fifteen to twenty days for one person to dig a pit foundation and fifty to one hundred days to construct a house. One or two families probably contributed labor to construct each dwelling.

While many Jōmon villages were small, some exceptionally dense sites of the Middle Jōmon on the southern slopes of Mount Yatsugatake in Nagano Prefecture and in adjoining Yamanashi Prefecture have yielded more than one hundred dwellings. Some twenty houses may have been occupied at one time.

Jōmon villages were often divided into two spatially distinct groups of houses. Ōyu in Akita Prefecture contains two groups of stone circles, about 328 feet (100 m) apart, which mark burials. Kobayashi and others have pointed out that similarly organized Jōmon communities must have been composed of two social groups who intermarried, a circumstance that could occur only in large settlements.

Other unmistakable signs of larger networks of creative activity and cooperation are also evident. Ten large posts split from logs of the edible chestnut tree (*Castanea crenata*), each weighing between 1,100 and 1,760 pounds (500–800 kg), have been discovered in a circular arrangement at the Chikamori site in Kanazawa, Ishikawa Prefecture. The ends of the logs are perforated for ease in hauling. Another circle of large wooden posts was found at Yoneizumi, 1¼ miles (2 km) away (Mori 1989a, 78). Considerable coordinated labor would have been required to form the circles of posts.

Communal burials and fish weirs are further evidence of Late Jōmon intervillage cooperation. Communal burials placed beneath a central area surrounded by an outer ring-shaped mound have been found in Hok-kaidō. The most famous is the Kiusu site (Ikawa-Smith 1989; Nishida 1989, 36). Some of its burial areas have grave pits dug in and outside an encircling earthwork.[12] In addition to personal ornaments, lacquered wooden tools and perforated beads have been recovered there. Ikawa-Smith has interpreted the circular embankment surrounding the common grave site as a symbolic expression of social cohesion.

In the late 1970s, during reconnaissance for the construction of a dam site at Shidanai in Morioka City, Iwate Prefecture, a series of waterlogged deposits was uncovered (fig. 12). In addition to a group of houses be-longing to the Late and Final Jōmon periods, the wooden posts of a fish weir consisting of a long line of stakes leading to a round pen and an attached holding area were found.[13] Excavators also located an old wash-ing place: a foot-smoothed riverbank with associated wooden objects, spouted vessels, and a lacquered comb.[14]

Figure 12
Wooden sculpture of anthropo-
morphic form, Late or Final Jōmon
period (1500–400 B.C.), 25⅝
inches (65 cm) long. Shidanai site,
Iwate Prefecture.

Intervillage exchange of special materials available only in circumscribed localities bound villages together over long distances. Obsidian
was traded from Kōzushima, about 31 miles (50 km) from the tip of Izu
Peninsula, while crystal from Gumma Prefecture was bartered from
Shimokita Peninsula, at the extreme north of Honshū, to Kii Peninsula,
south of Osaka. Exchange networks of pottery have also been identified
on the basis of extremely close similarities of decoration in pottery found
at distant sites. Pottery from Torihama, on the coast of the Sea of Japan,
for example, is extremely similar to vessels found in the Kitashirakawa
site in Kyoto Prefecture, some 44 miles (70 km) distant across a range of
low mountains. Shell bracelets were exchanged throughout the Kantō
Plain (Watanabe Hitoshi 1990, 100), and hematite, a red mineral
pigment, and sanukite were also traded over long distances. Natural
asphalt, used for decoration and as an adhesive, spanned distances in central and northeastern Japan (Mori 1989a, 118). Nishida Masaki (1989,
21) has noted that special kinds of fish such as red sea bream—although
not staples in the diet of island people—were carried as far as 31 miles
(50 km) from the coast to inland cave sites. With the introduction of salt
production in the Final Jōmon, intervillage exchange of salt and preserved foods probably increased.

Burials

Jōmon people generally buried their dead in simple pits dug in the
ground. Exceptions are jar burials, which were used for infants. In the
Kantō and Nagano regions the custom of burying children in jars under
the entrance of a house began in the Middle Jōmon period and spread
to nearby areas during the Late Jōmon. Jars also seem to have been
buried as religious offerings between houses in Middle Jōmon villages
on the slopes of Mount Yatsugatake. Bones are poorly preserved in the
acidic soils of Japan, and simple interments are therefore difficult to
recognize. The few cemeteries that have yielded large collections of skeletons are usually in sandy soil or shell middens. Without grave goods,
skeletal remains, or special burial facilities, it is difficult to distinguish
between Jōmon burial pits and simple storage pits.

In recent years wide-area excavations and soil analyses have confirmed
the presence of disintegrated bone, thereby enhancing our understanding
of Jōmon cemeteries. Burials have been identified by such signs as adzes
(which were occasionally used as grave offerings), bone ornaments, ceramics, stone rods, red coloring in the soil, and groups of small stones or
stone pavements above the burial areas. Piles of animal bones and the
remains of small fires have also been found on grave surfaces.

A basic burial pattern extending from the Middle to the Final Jōmon
in eastern Japan has been recognized (Suzuki Kimio 1988, 121–27). Burials were localized beneath the central open space of the village; around
the open space were the remains of dwellings and storage pits. Forming
circular zones, the burials were clustered in family groups and inter-
spersed with postholes that are thought to have been left by funerary
structures. It is significant that the burial area is an integral part of the
village, as if all villagers, living and deceased, were believed to occupy
one world (Suzuki Kimio 1988, 124). The Jōmon burial pattern contrasts

sharply with that of the later Yayoi people, who buried their dead outside the village. It is also different from that of the Ainu people of Hokkaidō, where several independent villages maintained a common burial site distant from the villages.

Social Organization

With small, dispersed hamlets and cooperative family groups, Jōmon society would appear to have existed at a small scale with an egalitarian social organization. There are hints, however, that the archaeological record may be distorting our perception. After years of comparative study of hunters and gatherers worldwide, Watanabe Hitoshi (1990), a renowned cultural anthropologist who has studied hunting and gathering peoples of all periods, has concluded that the Jōmon people had a hierarchical society, in the manner of other groups such as the people of the Northwest Pacific Coast of America. He uses the term "stratified" to discuss Jōmon social relations and states that people of chiefly rank monopolized certain high-status activities, such as bear and other large-animal hunting. Bear-hunting involves complex technology as well as ritual. Evidence of specialized bear-hunting sites has been found in Nagano and Gumma prefectures.

Although Watanabe's argument is based almost entirely on analogy rather than from testing patterns of archaeological data and his use of the term "stratification" might be better understood to mean "ranked," his assessment of the complexity of Jōmon society seems reasonable, in comparative perspective.[15] Particularly in central and eastern Japan, Jōmon society appears to have achieved a higher level of complexity than previously recognized. In southwestern Japan, however, few cultural traits indicate such complexity. Our view of Jōmon society may be transformed if we compare the Jōmon archaeological record with that of the Pacific Northwest rather than with the ethnographic record.[16]

When wild resources are particularly abundant and reliable, elite groups gain control of the areas where the resources are processed and develop into a chiefly class with many prerogatives. Through positive feedback the rich become ever more powerful, unless the resource supply collapses. It appears that in Japan no single resource yielded a preponderance of food. Consequently, the elite did not tightly control specific food supplies. Thus, despite signs of ranking, we do not see the same degree of monopolization of resources or chiefly control as are evident in the most elaborate chiefdoms of the Pacific Northwest, where salmon was the primary resource.

Fishing of tuna (*maguro*) and swordfish was another elite activity. High-status groups commanded access to the resources of remote habitats in the mountains and deep sea. (Among stratified hunters and gatherers in general, there is a division of labor in which elite male hunters from families who maintain access to distant habitats engage in highly specialized operations.) In each community some males, like elderly women and children, did not hunt large mammals or certain types of fish.

Elite Jōmon families also sponsored the production of prestigious items, which, according to Watanabe, include Katsusaka-type pottery of the Middle Jōmon. This has yet to be demonstrated by actual archaeological data, such as the excavation of vessels from larger-than-average houses or in special disposal areas. Although in many comparable societies women make vessels and may have produced Jōmon ceramics (Kobayashi Tatsuo 1979; Pearson 1990b), Watanabe proposes that men created the most elaborate Jōmon vessels, since men produce valuable objects in most sedentary hunter-gatherer societies.[17]

According to Watanabe, other objects that may have been produced or circulated under elite sponsorship include semiprecious stone pendants and bracelets of bivalve shells that originally came from the Izu Islands but have been found in the Kantō and Tōhoku regions. Watanabe Hitoshi (1990, 100) has noted that compared to other shell bracelets, limpet shell (ōtsutanoha [Penepatella]) bracelets are always extremely scarce. Another domain of elite activity is the construction of large wooden structures. There are no comparable examples of buildings of similar scale except among Pacific Northwest hunters and gatherers.[18]

Continued population growth during the Middle Jōmon in central Japan and the Final Jōmon in the Tōhoku region of northern Japan seems to have led to reduced mobility, larger communities, and greater specialization. A more circumscribed subsistence area generally leads to increased group identity, manifested in greater stylistic diversity among artifacts associated with specific groups. Moreover, group boundaries may be maintained by exchange and conflict (Price 1981, 81). This model of hunter-gatherer social complexity accounts for the proliferation of distinctive pottery styles and forms during peak periods of Jōmon population.

Rituals

While many scholars have proposed that the Jōmon people conceptualized their world as magical, Nishida Masaki (1989, 78) has most succinctly articulated the notion by stating that Jōmon society did not focus on maximizing productivity but on enriching social and ritual life. Jōmon people expanded their spiritual world and adapted to their stable existence with elaborate rituals and magic. By settling for relatively long periods in one place, they continued to live near abandoned houses, grave markers, and ritual areas and to experience a different sense of time and history from their mobile Paleolithic forebears.

At the Early Jōmon site of Mawaki in Ishikawa Prefecture a wooden pole 16⅜ feet (5 m) long, the upper half of which has been carved, was found lying in a concentration of several hundred dolphin skulls and other fish and animal bones. The site may have been used for the ritual disposal of dolphin skulls, a practice possibly related to the modern, recorded beliefs of the Ainu people and Siberian tribes. They believed that the head of an animal retained its spirit, which, through the ritual disposal of the animal's remains, would return to the world, bringing food in the form of an animal of the same species (Ōtsuka 1988, 130). The preparation and execution of the large carved wooden pole at Mawaki must have involved the cooperation of several small communities.

In addition to hunting rites, the Jōmon people also practiced rituals to mark critical transitions in life. They celebrated puberty, marriage, remarriage, and possibly the death of parents through ritual tooth ablation (usually the removal of canines and incisors). In addition, the incisor teeth are sometimes found to contain filed notches. In an often-quoted study, the archaeologist Harunari Hideji (1986) has postulated that people born in a community practiced different forms of tooth extraction than those who moved into it and that different patterns of postmarital residence could be ascertained by plotting burials by sex, type of extraction, and location in the cemetery.

Ritual Objects. Since much of Jōmon creative energy was expressed in fired clay objects, archaeologists have been afforded glimpses of a vigorous ceremonial and artistic life that is not well represented for other hunters and gatherers who did not use pottery. Stone and wooden ritual objects also have been retrieved from Jōmon sites.

The interpretation of the meaning of artifacts is always difficult. Two kinds of analogies can be drawn: The first is a comparative analogy, constructed by searching for comparable artifacts or behavior among the peoples of northeastern Asia such as the Ainu or Siberian tribes, whose way of life is generally similar to that of the Jōmon, or the Pacific Northwest American tribes. The second is the use of a historical analogy, in which patterns in later periods of Japanese culture provide clues to the interpretation of the Jōmon.

A vigorous tradition of figural image making is one of the major features of Jōmon culture. The earliest examples are the incised pebbles found in Kamikuroiwa Rock Shelter, Ehime Prefecture [61]. Dating to the Incipient Jōmon, they appear to depict a figure with long hair and minimal clothing. Later types of figures occur in a wide variety of styles, from small triangles devoid of arms and legs to large standing figures 19⅝ inches (50 cm) high. A few unusual larger clay sculptures, such as the remarkable figure from Chobonaino [64], have also been found. Some of the most uncommon forms are limited to a single river valley. The stylistic distinctiveness of the Middle and Late Jōmon, detected not only in figures but also in other aspects of ritual, reflects the rise of a local group identity.

The standing figural type originated in the Japanese Alps during the Middle Jōmon. By the end of the Middle Jōmon, figures were fewer in the Chūbu and Kantō regions. In the Late Jōmon, three new types appeared: those with heart-shaped faces, crescent eyebrows, or pointed heads. Another late type, found in the Kantō Plain, is characterized by a hornlike headdress. A remarkable, recently discovered seated figure with clasped hands [63] typifies a small group of seated, three-dimensional clay sculptures.

One of the most imposing types is the hollow "snow-goggle" figure of the Late and Final Jōmon in the Tōhoku region. Most have crown-like headdresses. Decoration consists of an opening at the navel and spirals and *surikeshi* cord marking, which may represent tattooing. Snow-goggle figures are associated with the Kamegaoka complex [65].

The distribution of Jōmon clay figures varies. Some sites appear to have many more than others. While a handful have been found in burials, clay figures are most commonly recovered from dumps or are broken and scattered. It is unusual to find them intact. They may have been used in curing rituals in which the figures received the illness or misfortune of an individual and were then broken to eliminate the source of suffering (Pearson 1990b, 23). This interpretation alludes to the custom of dispelling illness through the *hitogata* (human doll). The name of an illness or misfortune is written on a thin, wooden figure that is then placed in a stream or ditch to be washed away. Such effigies have been found in the eighth-century A.D. Heijō Palace in Nara.

One of the most remarkable instances of the scattering of fragmentary figures is evident at Shakadō in Yamanashi Prefecture, a huge Middle Jōmon settlement. The five-acre (2 hectare) excavated area yielded 1,145 figures and the remains of 172 houses. Many fragments were found in huge pottery dumps near habitation sites (Yamanashi Ken 1986, 1987). Intensive research has disclosed that fragments of only fifteen figures could be reassembled, even with pieces recovered from distances as far apart as 262½ feet (80 m). It has been suggested that the wide deposition of figures was deliberate and ritually significant, but this interpretation does not shed light on every case (Yamanashi Ken 1986, 1987, 2: 275, 276). At the Tanabatake site in Chino City, Nagano Prefecture, an exceptionally large female figure was found intact in a pit in the middle of the central burial area of a large settlement. It is not clear why the figure was buried in that manner.

Stone figures are also known, the earliest being the incised pebbles from Kamikuroiwa. The most common type, however, is made of white stone in a form resembling the snow-goggle clay figures. The center of distribution of white stone figures in the Tōhoku region is Mabuchi River Valley. A specialist in Jōmon stone artifacts, Inano Yūsuke (1983) has cautioned against regarding the stone figure as simply a copy of a clay figure since it is white whereas the clay figures are usually polished black. Stone figures lack the crown worn by the snow-goggle figures and occur in a variety of sizes, including some that are much larger than the clay specimens.

Small, triangular clay objects have also been recovered. They are most common in central Japan and date from the Middle to Final Jōmon. Most are abstract, although a few are realistic representations of human forms. Interpretations of the objects vary; they may be ornaments for clothing or hold religious significance (Kaneko 1983). Other Jōmon clay creations include wedge-shaped decorative objects—found in Niigata, Toyama, and Yamagata prefectures in Middle and Late Jōmon sites (Kojima 1983)—and perforated decorated spheres, which may have been used as weights—located only in eastern Toyama, western Niigata, and northern Nagano prefectures (Kojima 1983).

Possibly no artifact has stimulated the imagination more than the "crowns" made of stone or clay found in eastern Japan in regions in the mountainous interior. A phallic protuberance extends from one side of a small stone crescent in the crown. Three basic interpretations of the crowns' function cite their use in daily life as weapons, head protectors, or food graters; their ritual use at the time of burial, possibly as phallic emblems; and their change in status from everyday to ritual object, perhaps as a pounding implement. A detailed study of a carefully chosen sample might eliminate postulations that cite their use in bizarre behaviors.

Stone rods, found from Middle to Final Jōmon sites, particularly in regions bordering the central mountains of eastern Japan and the Kantō Plain, are widely believed to have been used in ritual. They are often found inside houses, buried under the floor or near the hearth, which suggests their use in household rituals. In later Jōmon contexts stone rods are often buried outside the house, perhaps signifying their use in village rituals (Yamamoto Teruhisa 1983).

Polished stone swords and knives have been found in Final Jōmon sites in Hokkaidō and Tōhoku. They are believed to be ritual objects based on the Chinese bronze halberd of the mid to late Shang dynasty (1700–1050 B.C.; Nomura 1983). Elaborately shaped rods found in southern Hokkaidō and Tōhoku are thought to have been used to kill fish or as ceremonial weapons. Large, beautifully polished stone adzes appear to have had ritual rather than practical use.

Perhaps one of the most fascinating types of ornaments created by the Jōmon people were earrings. Early Jōmon earrings are shaped like flat slit rings, to be fitted over perforated earlobes. The same shape is found in Neolithic burials near the coast of China. Although these earrings are usually made of stone, pottery specimens have also been found. Judging from their depictions on some figures, spool-shaped ear ornaments were inserted in the lobe during the Middle Jōmon period (Takayama 1965). The shape changed in the Final Jōmon to that of a pulley (Esaka 1983, 71). Lacquered specimens from Korekawa are carved and colored. The distribution of Early Jōmon slit-ring forms is centered in the Kantō Plain, while later forms are most common in the Chūbu, Kantō, and northern Tōhoku regions. It is not clear whether both sexes wore earrings. Sahara Makoto (1987a, 217) has noted that in a small sample of burial remains with adequate skeletal preservation, a high proportion of females were found to have worn earrings, while many males wore V-shaped decorated bone objects. The distribution, however, was by no means exclusive.

Suzuki Kimio (1988, 128) has postulated that when a Jōmon youth was about ten years old, a hole would be opened in the earlobe, then enlarged in graded steps. A study of the distribution of ear ornaments from five sites from the Late and Final Jōmon suggests that the spools can be grouped into four sizes, ranging up to five inches (12.8 cm) in diameter. A group of exquisitely carved and colored clay ear ornaments was found in a large house at Chiamigaito in Gumma Prefecture [70–74]. Their delicacy suggests that they were produced by skilled artists.

Transition to the Yayoi Period

Dryland rice cultivation on upland slopes in Kyūshū probably began by 1000 B.C. (Crawford 1987, 27). It is assumed that rice was introduced to Japan from Korea, where it was known as early as 1500 B.C. (Pearson 1982, 24). In the Final Jōmon of Kyūshū, similarities with Korean cultures can be recognized in plain clay vessels with simple horizontal ridges and other pottery forms (Pearson 1976, 328). Carbonized rice grains, barley, and beans have been recovered from the Late Jōmon deposits at Kuwagaishimo, Kyoto Prefecture.

By 400 B.C. a new culture, the Yayoi, appeared in Kyūshū. It was characterized by irrigated rice cultivation, plain pottery, polished stone tools, metal weapons and mirrors, glass beads, and shallow, semisubterranean pit dwellings with a circular plan. The Yayoi culture rapidly spread north, from Kyūshū to the Kinai region. At the same time, Yayoi colonies were established at several points along the coast of the Sea of Japan, including the northern tip of Honshū, where rice was present as early as the second or third century B.C.

What was the relationship between the waning hunting and gathering culture and the new agricultural culture? What happened to communities as colonists impinged on their territories? Various possible scenarios have been proposed, but no rigorous tests of the postulations have been completed (Crawford 1987, 10). Watanabe Hitoshi (1986) has proposed that elderly men who no longer were strong enough to hunt experimented with plant cultivation, thereby providing the transition to cultivation. Akazawa Takeru (1986) has suggested that Jōmon coastal fishing communities would have been the most conservative and that inland groups, living in the broadleaf evergreen forest zone with a generalized subsistence economy, would have been the first Jōmon communities to adopt cultivation. Sasaki Kōmei (1986), a cultural geographer who studies shifting agriculture, believes that Jōmon communities in the broadleaf evergreen forest zone already had some marginal experience with cultivation, an important factor in the transition. Sasaki also has proposed that the lure of the metal weapons and mirrors of the Yayoi people must have been a major factor in adopting cultivation. New prestige items would have created the kinds of high expectations that occur in cargo cults, in which the advent of a foreign superior culture, by dramatically raising expectations of the benefits from a new way of life, profoundly affects an indigenous culture.[19]

Jōmon culture was not submerged by Yayoi culture. Nishida Masaki has emphasized that the waning of the Jōmon culture involved the collapse of a particular worldview and not simply a change in subsistence and technology. The decision to adopt a new subsistence pattern requiring intensive labor may have been motivated by a desire to emulate the customs of new groups of rice farmers who had access to superior technology. Such social factors must have been preeminent, since there seems to be no indication of food shortage or population pressure.

Jōmon culture contributed to Yayoi lowland subsistence, and Jōmon methods persisted in the agricultural life of the mountain inhabitants of Japan, who played an important role in gathering all kinds of natural resources and in making a lasting impression on the development of Japanese aesthetics.

Summary

The technological and artistic achievements of the Jōmon period were made possible by the use of rich forest and coastal food resources, which became particularly abundant after the Post-Pleistocene climatic optimum (5000–2000 B.C.). By the Early Jōmon an effective set of tools and practices for hunting, gathering, and processing animal and plant foods was established.

In the Early and Middle Jōmon, regional pottery styles diversified, each becoming distinct. We have much to learn about the social and practical uses of Jōmon vessels, particularly since they are rarely found in their original context, as distinct from discard or disposal. It would be difficult to believe, however, that their flamboyant decoration was not for public display or to reinforce regional boundaries. For instance, major ethnic divisions are indicated by the cylindrical pottery of the Tōhoku region, the sculptured rim vessel styles of the Kantō Plain, and the polished, plain vessels of the Kyūshū region. Kobayashi Tatsuo (1979, 70) has proposed other divisions as well.

While the production of the finest vessels may have been sponsored by high-ranking people, such vessels seem to have marked group rather than family or individual distinctions. Other cooperative projects, including the construction of large ceremonial houses, earthworks, stone circles, and fish weirs, may indicate the existence of loosely integrated tribes, members of which came together for ceremonial occasions. These may have taken place at sites where numerous discarded pottery figures have been found.

Perhaps in the future it will be possible, based on pottery distribution, to distinguish "rich" from "poor" villages. At present, social ranking seems fluid and shifting, with an emphasis on ceremonial activities. Different tribal groups exchanged special pottery vessels and stone materials. Burial patterns, at such sites as Nishida in Iwate Prefecture, are communal, as expected in societies with a medium degree of ranking.

Although social ranking was present during the Jōmon period, no superordinate chiefs appear to have emerged. The model of resource management suggests that no single food dominated the Jōmon subsistence economy, as did salmon in societies of the Pacific Northwest, thereby allowing high-ranking families to control the flow of the most important kinds of food. Although many analogies can be drawn between Northwest Coast and Jōmon societies, there are important social differences as well.

Notes

1. It is possible that the emergence of a Japanese-speaking people is associated with Early Jōmon Sobata-type pottery in Kyūshū, but the occurrence of a prototype of Sobata pottery at an appropriate date in Korea, the source of the proto-Japanese language, has not been unquestionably confirmed (Rouse 1986, 88, 102).

   Glottochronology is a linguistic means of dating the splits between languages by studying the rate of replacement of basic vocabulary items with noncognatic forms. In some cases it is estimated that about 17 percent of the basic vocabulary of any language changes in one thousand years.

2. Akazawa Takeru (1980) has postulated that the area exploited by the villagers, including the stream, estuary, and bay, was about 6¼ miles (10 km) in radius.

3. Cultivation of chestnuts and walnuts is thought to be a solution to apparent resource scarcity (Crawford 1987, 14; Nishida 1989). It is still not clear, however, whether all the nut remains were left over from food preparation.

4. The mean temperatures rose by 3.5 to 5.4 degrees Fahrenheit (2 to 3 degrees Centigrade; Sakaguchi 1983; Tsukada 1986, 51).

5. Various types of traps probably were used for small animals, judging from holes measuring up to 3¼ feet (1 m) deep (Sahara 1987a, 130).

6. The deer caller was recovered from Saga Shell Mound in Nagasaki Prefecture. Nishida Masaki (1989, 7), who mentions this object, does not date it to a specific period within the Jōmon.

7. The canoe is 23 feet (7 m) long and 11¾ inches (30 cm) deep.

8. *Shiso* and *egoma* are varieties of *Perilla frutescens*. Used today as a lacquer thinner, *egoma* seeds were ground to produce an oil.

9. There is no consensus whether buckwheat (*Fagopyrum*) was cultivated in the Jōmon period. Pollen grains of buckwheat have been recovered from bogs and Jōmon sites of different ages (Crawford 1987, 34).

10. The Geometric or Comb Pattern Pottery of the Korean peninsula lasted from around 5000 B.C. to around 1500 B.C. in the north and around 1000 B.C. in the south, when it was replaced by a soft orange pottery called Plain Coarse Pottery. Deep vessels with simple patterns of incised decoration and pointed bottoms were typical. Geometric Pottery is closest in shape and decoration to Sobata pottery of the Early Jōmon in Kyūshū.

11. Some scatters seem to indicate the presence of raised eating areas associated with pit houses.

12. The largest of fourteen earthwork enclosures at Kiusu has an outer diameter of 246 feet (75 m), an inside diameter of 111½ feet (34 m), and a mound 17¾ feet (5 m) high. Ōtani Toshizō (1983, 48–50) has estimated that the largest burial mound at Kiusu contained about 106,000 cubic feet (3,000 cu m) of soil, which could have been moved by twenty-five people in roughly 125 days if one person handled 35 cubic feet (1 cu m) of fill per day.

13. The Shidanai site yielded a circular stone pavement, roughly 279 to 328 feet (85–100 m) in diameter, covering a total of eight hundred grave pits in about ten groups, each about 33 feet (10 m) in diameter. The waterlogged deposit yielded pottery, stone tools, food remains, and a red lacquered wooden club. In it were also found a life-sized clay human head, with decorations on the cheeks and forehead and perforations along the jaw for the attachment of a beard [62]. Another find was a wooden sculpture 25⅝ inches (65 cm) long (see fig. 12).

14. The remains of wooden grave posts and figures were also found (Iwate Ken 1982).

15. Ranked society is thought to have begun in the Marpole phase (ca. 500 B.C.) of the Gulf of Georgia region of British Columbia, Canada (Fladmark 1982, 112). The surviving markers of this hierarchical society—distinguished by particular styles of polished stone tools, bone ornaments, projectile points, and stone beads—are woodworking tools associated with the production of plank houses and ornaments known from ethnographic sources to be associated with high status. Both are indirect indications of a ranked society. Other markers, such as the production of works of art from wood, are known from a few waterlogged sites in which wooden objects are better preserved. The surviving archaeological remains in the Gulf of Georgia region probably reveal less differentiation than the record for the cultural peaks of the Jōmon period. In comparison, the archaeological record of the Jōmon people is beginning to display clearer signs of complexity.

Testing patterns of archaeological data begin with a model of prehistoric behavior that may be constructed by extrapolating from historical accounts or accounts of the same region from a later period or by studying living societies from different parts of the world. Archaeological criteria linking the model to the archaeological remains are devised, and the model (or more simply a detailed notion of life in the past) is checked to see if it conforms to the original expectation. Selected hypotheses may be used instead of a model.

16. The ethnographic record is created by observing a culture while its members are living, through participation, interviews, photographs, etc.

17. This conclusion does not agree with that of others who think that all potters in the Jōmon were women.

18. Watanabe Hitoshi has suggested that the buildings may be comparable to the wooden henges of Neolithic Britain. Those structures, however, were produced by agriculturalists rather than by hunter-gatherers.

19. A cargo cult is a religious cult noted in the islands of the western Pacific in which foreigners were thought to bring fabulous treasure in the form of advanced technology.

NISHIDA

KOBAYASHI TATSUO

Dating to the Middle Jōmon period, Nishida lies on the western bank of the Kitakami River, which flows north to south in the center of Iwate Prefecture in northeastern Honshū (fig. 13).[1] Excavations were conducted there from April 1975 to December 1977 before construction began on the Tōhoku Shinkansen Railway Line, completed in 1982.

Sixty percent of the Nishida settlement, including its center, was excavated, thus providing a nearly total picture of the site. Structural remains included 35 pit dwellings, 192 graves, more than 1,450 postholes, and 129 storage pits. A large amount of pottery, various types of stone artifacts, and clay figures were also unearthed.

The settlement pattern was organized in concentric circles, with groups of grave pits occupying the center and forming a circular cemetery slightly elongated to the east and west.[2] Fourteen graves were concentrated in the inner ring. Although not excavated completely, the outer ring probably contained about 195 grave pits.

Each burial pit was oval or rectangular with rounded corners and ranged in diameter from 1⅝ to 6⅝ feet (0.5–2.0 m), probably corresponding to the size of the children or adults buried in each pit. In general, the long axis of each pit was oriented radially toward the center of the burial area. Eight subgroups, each including about ten graves, faced in the same direction without overlap. The pattern implies that the circular cemetery area had originally been divided. A jadeite pendant was found from a grave pit located at the southern edge; no other grave goods were recovered. Although the pits did not contain human bones, the shape of the pits and presence of the pendant suggest that the pits were graves.

The more than 1,450 postholes surrounding the circular burial area were within a zone spanning 39⅜ to 49¼ feet (12–15 m) wide.[3] The postholes were larger than those of typical structures dating to the same period. Assuming that each structure had four to nine posts, more than fifty-eight units could be identified; these units, arranged in ten groups, each consisted of three to nine structures. Within each group—but not between groups—were overlapping structures. The ten groups seem to have been restricted within predetermined boundaries.

Thirty-five pit dwellings were found outside the zone of structures with large postholes. Accounting for the unexcavated portions of the site, both to the east and west, one could probably count one hundred houses in all. Located in the northern corner of the dwelling area, where the pit houses were found, was a concentration of what are assumed to be storage

Figure 13
Plan of pits and features of the
Nishida site, Iwate Prefecture. *Left,*
diagram of excavated site; *facing
page,* aerial view.

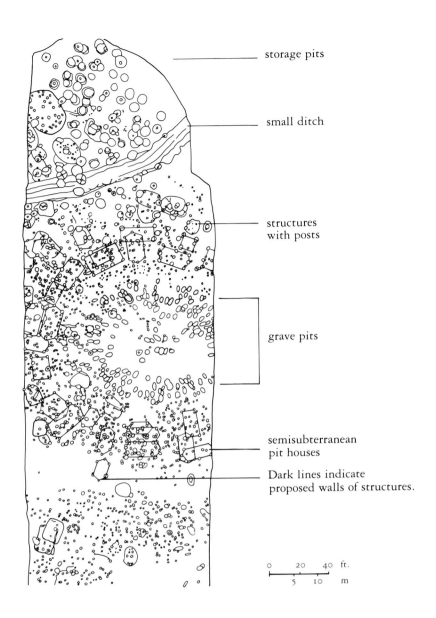

storage pits

small ditch

structures
with posts

grave pits

semisubterranean
pit houses

Dark lines indicate
proposed walls of structures.

0   20   40   ft.

5   10   m

pits. Of the typical flask shape, with a narrow opening and wide bottom,
they often contained clay vessels, both complete and broken.

Nishida shares some characteristics with typical Jōmon settlements.
The prototypical Jōmon settlement consisted of pit houses arranged
in a circle surrounding a central open space. Well-known examples are
Minamibori Shell Mound in Yokohama, an Early Jōmon site that yielded
a large mortar, and Togariishi in Nagano Prefecture, a Middle Jōmon
site noted for a large pit located in the central open space and a deep
ceramic bowl recovered there. These sites contain a central, open space in
which were held social activities. Nishida is one of the first types to
have a grave area in the central space surrounded by structures with posts.

Was Nishida an exceptional settlement type during the Jōmon period?
The Ōyu stone circle, a site dating to the beginning of the Late Jōmon,
is noteworthy by comparison. A recent survey of Ōyu disclosed groups
of structures with posts surrounding the outer circumference of a stone
circle. Moreover, pit dwellings and storage pits were scattered outside
the area of the structures with posts. These features are quite similar
to the concentric plan of Nishida, if one considers the Ōyu stone circle
to be the counterpart of the Nishida grave pits, suggesting that Ōyu
followed the pattern of Nishida.

The organization represented by Nishida seems to have continued as the typical settlement pattern in the north in the Tōhoku region. The inclusion of the grave area within the settlement, which reinforced the coexistence of the living and the dead, discloses aspects of Jōmon life. Structures with posts in the middle area—between the graves at the center and the pit dwellings in the outer ring—might also have served to link the worlds of the living and the dead.

Notes

1. Located at the center of a terrace about 33 feet (10 m) above the river, Nishida sits at an elevation 334¾ feet (102 m) above sea level.

2. Most pits were located within an inner circle 75½ to 98½ feet (23–30 m) in diameter and an outer ring 91⅞ to 101¾ feet (28–31 m) in diameter.

3. The postholes were 19⅝ to 27½ inches (50–70 cm) in diameter and 19 to 39⅜ inches (50–100 cm) in depth.

Middle Jōmon period
(2500–1500 B.C)
Excavated at Tanabatake,
Nagano Prefecture
Stone
Chino City Education Commission,
Nagano Prefecture

32
Arrowhead
¾ × ½ × ⅛ in.
(2.1 × 1.3 × 0.3 cm)

33
Arrowhead
¾ × ½ × ⅛ in.
(2.1 × 1.1 × 0.2 cm)

34
Arrowhead
¾ × ⅝ × ¼ in.
(2.1 × 1.6 × 0.6 cm)

35
Arrowhead
⅞ × ½ × 1⁄16 in.
(2.3 × 1.3 × 0.3 cm)

36
Arrowhead
¾ × ⅝ × ⅛ in.
(2.0 × 1.7 × 0.2 cm)

37
Tanged scraper
1¼ × 1⅞ × ¼ in.
(3.1 × 4.7 × 0.6 cm)

38
Tanged scraper
1 × 1¾ × ¼ in.
(2.6 × 4.6 × 0.6 cm)

39
Arrowhead
1¼ × ⅝ × ⅛ in.
(3.3 × 1.5 × 0.4 cm)

40
Arrowhead
1½ × ¾ × ⅛ in.
(3.8 × 2.1 × 0.4 cm)

41
Ax
4¾ × 2⅜ × 1⅛ in.
(12.0 × 6.0 × 2.8 cm)

42
Grinding stone
3¾ × 3 in.
(9.5 × 7.6 cm)

43
Mortar
15⅛ × 12⅜ × 5⅛ in.
(38.6 × 31.5 × 13.0 cm)

Arrowheads [32–36]

Arrowheads [39, 40]

Ax [41]

Tanged scrapers [37, 38]

These artifacts are representative of the stone tools of the Middle Jōmon period. During that time specific areas within a settlement were selected for festive and ritual occasions and as residences and grave sites. Detailed research on the carbonized food remains found at Middle Jōmon sites indicates that subsistence was not based solely on deliberate food cultivation but also relied on meat, fish, and nuts obtained by hunting and gathering. Archaeologists consider that the harmonious balance of a stabilized food supply and a dependent population was relatively well maintained. It is assumed that the average family had six members and that thirty to fifty people formed a village.

Although the Jōmon people ate a variety of foods, including animal and plant protein, their diet was nevertheless vulnerable to climatic and environmental changes. From a nutritional study of human bones, it is assumed that a person with an average lifespan of thirty-five years experienced four or five periods of extreme hunger in his or her lifetime.

Arrowheads—possibly with a lethal poison such as *torikabuto* (*Aconitum chinensis Sieb*) smeared on the tips—were used for hunting deer and wild boar. The angle of penetration of arrowheads found lodged in animal bones indicates that hunters waited in treetops by the side of animal trails to shoot their prey. There is also evidence of large-scale hunting with pits, traps, and dogs. In areas where fish were abundant, stone arrowheads were used for fishing.

The tanged scrapers [37, 38] would have been used in a manner similar to present-day field knives. The scrapers have a knob on top, assumed to be used to thread a cord attached to the waist so that the knife would be handy for cutting up a carcass.

Axes [41] were used from the beginning of the Jōmon period. Their principal function was for felling trees, but they were also used to shape or repair house posts or beams, dig pit dwellings, and harvest edible bulbs. Adzes are of two types: chipped or elaborately polished.

Grinding stones and mortars [42, 43] were used together to crush bulbs or grind nuts to make flour. At this time a technique of blanching or leaching to rid the nuts of their harsh taste had been developed. The results of a recent analysis of carbonized remains found on a mortar indicate that the Jōmon people ground meat on a mortar to make a kind of patty (mostly of wild boar and deer). Other foods eaten include biscuits, meat stew, dried fish, and shellfish.

DOI TAKASHI

Grinding stone and mortar [42, 43]

Incipient Jōmon period
(10,500–8000 B.C.)
Excavated at Omotedate,
Aomori Prefecture
Earthenware
Height 11¾ in. (30.0 cm);
diameter 10 in. (25.5 cm)
Aomori Prefectural Museum,
Aomori City

The first pottery made in Japan
is said to have originated when a
leather container was coated with
clay. The oldest earthenware vessels excavated in Japan, dating
around twelve thousand years ago,
are either plain or decorated with
linear relief.

The deep earthenware vessels
from Omotedate in Aomori Prefecture represent the decorated form.
This well-proportioned vessel with
pointed bottom was embellished
when the clay was soft; the surface
clay was then squeezed into ridges.
The vessel's mouth turns out gently,
and vertical incisions on the lip ac-
cent the otherwise simple shape.
The curve of the rim is similar to
that of a bark basket. Earthenware
vessels of this type have sometimes
been found in association with microblades, which were used late in
the Paleolithic period.

The first pottery made in Japan
is no doubt among the oldest of the
world's prehistoric cultures. The
origin of the pottery, however, has
been intensely debated. Some archaeologists consider that pottery originated independently in Japan,
while others insist that it came from
eastern Siberia. The theory of diffusion from Siberia is related to the
fact that the microlithic culture culminating at the end of the Paleolithic period was based on the Asian
continent. No pottery found on the
continent, however, has yet been
scientifically determined to be older
than the Japanese type with linear
relief design. Research concerning
the origins of Jōmon pottery is not
only essential to an understanding
of Japanese archaeology but also is
important for solving questions
regarding the overall development
of prehistoric culture throughout
eastern Asia.

HARADA MASAYUKI

Incipient Jōmon period
(10,500–8000 B.C.)
Excavated at Muroya Cave,
Niigata Prefecture
Earthenware
Height 9¼ (23.5 cm); max.
diameter 7¾ in. (19.7 cm)
Nagaoka Municipal Museum of
Science, Niigata Prefecture

The Jōmon period is named for pottery decoration made by rolling twisted cord on the clay surface of a vessel. The various methods of twisting cord and applying it with skill produced many beautiful pieces. Other decorative techniques, which predate the distinctive cord marking, are found on pottery vessels believed to be the oldest in Japan. Such decoration includes appliqués of clay bands and impressions made with fingernails or split bamboo sticks. A thin cord, called the "extra-added" cord, was wound around a thicker cord, and the two were rouletted over the clay surface of this vessel. This technique was applied only to the upper area, not below the constriction.[1]

This flat-rimmed vessel, with a slightly constricted mouth and shoulder, is the oldest known spouted vessel. The liquid contained in the vessel could be transferred through the spout to another container.

Jōmon pottery is generally considered to have been used for cooking and boiling meat, shellfish, nuts, and vegetables. It is interesting to find a spouted vessel from such an early period, when clay vessels had just appeared. The spouted vessel disappeared for a time, later to reappear as a bowl with a pouring lip. By the end of the Jōmon period, after many transformations, vessels with spouts were used for special purposes, such as to serve wine.

DOI TAKASHI

1. Measuring ⅜ by ⁵⁄₁₆ inches (0.95 × 0.8 cm), the spout is attached about ¾ inches (2.0 cm) below the rim.

Early Jōmon period
(5000–2500 B.C.)
Excavated at Itoimiyamae, Gumma
Prefecture
Earthenware
Height 11⅜ in. (29.0 cm); max.
diameter 13¾ in. (35.0 cm)
Gumma Prefectural Archaeological
Research Center, Kitatachibana
Village

The vessel's overall shape is slim and elegant, with a large mouth, gently curving body, and relatively small bottom. The decoration was incised with a pointed stick or split bamboo tool, then stick- and button-shaped pieces of clay were attached to the surface for further embellishment. Semicircular clay coils were arranged symmetrically around the mouth rim, with straight, stick-shaped clay coils at the center. Within each space defined with semicircular clay coils is a button-shaped piece of clay, looking like a human face. Seven such images appear on this vessel rim. Some archaeologists believe these semicircular clay decorations represent shells. The application of shell or human-face motifs eventually led to the elaborate decorations on the rims of "flame-style" earthenware [see 47–51].

DOI TAKASHI

Middle Jōmon period
(2500–1500 B.C.)
Excavated at Umataka, Niigata
Prefecture
Earthenware
Height 11⅝ in. (29.5 cm); max.
diameter 11¾ in. (30.0 cm)
Collection of Kondō Atsuho
Important Cultural Property

The decoration of flame-style vessels was formed by adding clay strips to the rim. This magnificent pottery vessel, found more than fifty years ago, typifies the Jōmon style and technique. Dating to the Middle Jōmon period, when the most creative Jōmon designs were established, it exemplifies a common form of flame-style pottery. Modern-day artists greatly admire the flame style as an expression of the archetypal Japanese aesthetic.

More than fifty vessels of this type have been found along the coast of the Sea of Japan. Other areas of Japan yield different types of ancient pottery with beautiful forms and imaginative designs, yet none is comparable in the dexterity and decorative mastery embodied in flame-style pottery. This vessel, decorated with raised clay bands and applied spiral patterns to create a sophisticated effect, represents the form and decoration of vessels from Umataka, Niigata Prefecture.

DOI TAKASHI

Middle Jōmon period
(2500–1500 B.C.)
Excavated at Umataka, Niigata
Prefecture
Earthenware
Nagaoka Municipal Museum of
Science, Niigata Prefecture

48
"Cockscomb type" deep bowl
Height 12¾ in. (32.5 cm); max.
diameter 13 in. (33.0 cm)

49
"Jeweled-crown type" deep bowl
Height 11¾ in. (29.9 cm); max.
diameter 8¼ in. (21.0 cm)

The decoration on the vessels discussed in catalogue entries 47 and 48 resemble a cockscomb and are, therefore, called "cockscomb type" (*keikangata*). The decoration on the vessel with four elaborate protuberances [49] looks like a crown, from which is derived the term "jeweled-crown type" (*ōkangata*).

The crown-type flame-style earthenware has higher protuberances and simpler decoration than the cockscomb type. The spare elegance of the crown type ware contrasts with the grandiose complexity of the cockscomb type.

The openwork protuberances and linear relief of spirals and arabesques covering both vessels demonstrate the extreme artistic sensibility and commanding spirit of the Jōmon people. Before many vessels of this kind were unearthed, archaeologists often assumed them to be ritual wares. Since they have been found in increasing numbers, with soot adhered to them, the vessels are now thought to have been practical wares for daily use.

DOI TAKASHI

Middle Jōmon period
(2500–1500 B.C.)
Excavated at Sasayama, Niigata
Prefecture
Earthenware
Tōkamachi Municipal Museum,
Niigata Prefecture
Important Cultural Property

50
Height 18¼ in. (46.5 cm);
max. diameter 16½ in. (42.0 cm)

51
Height 13½ in. (34.5 cm);
max. diameter 13 in. (33.0 cm)

The repetition of a coil decoration encircling the rim between the four cockscomblike protuberances of these two vessels follows the basic technique of flame-style pottery. The soot and carbonized materials that were found adhered to the inside of the vessels indicate that the pots were used as daily utensils.

Flame-style vessels did not suddenly appear in the Shinano River Basin of Niigata Prefecture. Rather, over hundreds of years the forms, designs, and techniques of pottery were passed down and improved upon before the exuberant flame style was achieved. Over time, the protuberances assumed rounder and softer shapes, finally evolving as spirals on the upper parts of the vessels.

For a prehistoric society to have produced a perfected work of art such as flame-style earthenware, a balance between population density and stabilized food supply must have been maintained. Advances in processing edible plants in the mountainous areas and efficiently organized fishing and shell-collecting practices along the coast resulted in the achievement of such a harmonious balance, as witnessed by the deposition of enormous shell mounds.

DOI TAKASHI

52, 53 DEEP VESSELS

Middle Jōmon period
(2500–1500 B.C.)
Excavated at Tsunagi, Iwate
Prefecture
Earthenware
Morioka City Education Commission, Iwate Prefecture; on deposit at Iwate Prefectural Museum, Morioka City
Important Cultural Property

52
Height 19¾ in. (50.2 cm);
max. diameter 12 in. (30.4 cm)

53
Height 17⅝ in. (44.8 cm);
max. diameter 12⅛ in. (31.0 cm)

During the Middle Jōmon period in the Tōhoku region Daigi-type pottery became popular. The form is characterized by swirling clay spirals applied onto a cord-marked background, as in these two vessels. Both have an undulating rim that is slightly curved inward and a deep, tall body decorated with small and large spirals branching from vertical ridges.

Seven vessels in all, including these two, were found as a group

lying upside down in a large pit at Tsunagi, Iwate Prefecture. It has been suggested that they were probably used for the burial of human remains and that the small hole piercing the bottom of each vessel was made as a passage through which the deceased's soul could be released. For a dead child, two jars with bottoms removed were put together as a burial container.

In the Middle Jōmon, pottery styles proliferated and differences in technique became more pronounced. For example, the protuberances on the rims of Daigi-type vessels occur mostly in threes or odd numbers, whereas rim elaboration on Katsu-saka-type vessels from the Chūbu and Kantō regions and the Umataka flame-style type from the Shin'etsu region were based on units of four or even numbers.

Jōmon culture, which embraced all Japan, has often been broadly discussed as a uniform culture of hunters and gatherers centered in the broadleaf evergreen forest. But distinct regional styles of pottery were developed. Recent research on the pottery types of individual areas has revealed a large variation in the group identity of people living in different areas.

HARADA MASAYUKI

Middle Jōmon period
(2500–1500 B.C.)
Excavated at Kaido, Nagano
Prefecture
Earthenware
Height 17¼ in. (43.8 cm); max.
diameter 12⅛ in. (30.8 cm)
Okaya City Education Commission,
Nagano Prefecture
Important Cultural Property

Many archaeological sites have been found at the foot of the Japanese Alps and the Akaishi Mountains in central Honshū. Among these, the Kaido site, Nagano Prefecture—located on the northern shore of Lake Suwa, a typical inland lake of Japan—was a large settlement of the Middle Jōmon period.

During the excavation of Kaido, this vessel, lying mouth down and crushed, was found near the center of a pit dwelling. Its rim is curved strongly inward and its body waisted like a gourd, that is, expanded and defined near the bottom. Of particular interest is a realistically modeled human face attached to the edge of the rim and facing outward. With a joyful expression, it appears to be talking.

In general, Jōmon vessels are decorated with an astonishing variety of geometric motifs, and the few that have representational images such as human faces are not of high quality. As a rare example, this vessel is considered important in representing the physical features of the Jōmon people. The spiral decoration at the back of the head may depict the Jōmon hairstyle; sometimes the hair is styled in the shape of a snake, which was respected as a god who commanded earthly existence. A few vessels displaying a face and having attached handles have been found, mostly among Katsusaka-type pottery. The faces are invariably turned inward, as if the image is watching the stored foods in the vessel. Katsusaka-type vessels were often decorated with abstract motifs of frogs, centipedes, and flying fish. These features suggest to some archaeologists the possibility of belief in an earth deity.

By examining numerous Chūbu sites and considering the abundance of artifacts, pottery forms, and size of settlements, it can be assumed that Middle Jōmon people supported primitive cultivation and the management of chestnuts and cereals while they also pursued simple hunting and gathering activities.

HARADA MASAYUKI

Middle Jōmon period
(2500–1500 B.C.)
Excavated at Bōgaito,
Gumma Prefecture
Earthenware
Height 13¾ in. (35.0 cm); max.
diameter 11 in. (28.0 cm)
Gumma Prefectural Archaeological
Research Center,
Kitatachibana Village
Important Cultural Property

Vessels with two protuberances opposite each other at the rim—one large and one small—characterize the pottery of a certain period in the Middle Jōmon. A human face is depicted on the larger protuberance on some vessels [see 54].

This vessel was elaborately fashioned with more than three methods of decoration. Clay strips were applied at the center of the large rhomboid protuberance to create a circular decoration. The body below the shoulder of the vessel is divided: sinuous decoration snakes

around the upper portion and a spiral design encircles the lower part. Deeply carved triangular shapes occupy spaces outlined by the main decoration.

Although similar vessels have frequently been discovered from sites of the Middle Jōmon period around Tokyo, an elaborately decorated specimen such as this is rare. While flame-style vessels are found near the Sea of Japan, this vessel is characteristic of the area from the Chūbu Mountains to the Pacific.

DOI TAKASHI

Final Jōmon period
(1000–400 B.C.)
Excavated at Korekawa, Aomori
Prefecture
Hachinohe City Education Commission, Aomori Prefecture
Important Cultural Property

56
Jar with spout
Lacquered earthenware
Height 3 in. (7.5 cm); max.
diameter 4⅝ in. (11.9 cm)

57
Jar with constricted neck
Lacquered earthenware
Height 3 in. (7.7 cm); max.
diameter 5 in. (12.8 cm)

58
Bowl
Earthenware
Height 3⅜ in. (8.5 cm); max.
diameter 5⅜ in. (13.8 cm)

59
Vessel with pedestal
Earthenware
Height 3 in (7.9 cm); max.
diameter 4¼ in. (10.9 cm)

Vessels began to vary during the Final Jōmon period as they diverged from earlier deep, narrow shapes. Various forms appropriate for containing liquid or piling up pieces of food suggest that cooking methods had become more diverse. At the same time, vessels became smaller, indicating that each family member used individual pots and no longer shared food from a common container. Further, small vessels and those of particular shapes seem to have been reserved for ritual occasions, such as for an initiation or wedding.

The Kamegaoka and Korekawa sites in Aomori Prefecture are typical of the Final Jōmon. Many elaborately created vessels of the Kamegaoka culture—either painted with red lacquer or finely polished, for example—can be regarded as ancient examples of high-quality craftwork (*kōgei*). Some vessels made in northern Japan were found in the Osaka area, more than six hundred miles (1000 km) south of Kamegaoka, indicating that vessels were transported as objects of exchange. Vessel surfaces often exhibit the same carved designs found on Final Jōmon hunting tools made of bone and antler.

Lacquer that is well preserved after more than two thousand years is evidence that the lacquered earthenware vessels and wooden objects found in low-lying damp ground were protected by anaerobic conditions in which the soil was neutral, in contrast to the poor preservation of artifacts in acidic soil.

DOI TAKASHI

Final Jōmon period
(1000–400 B.C.)
Excavated at Kamegaoka, Aomori
Prefecture
Earthenware
Height 9⅝ in. (24.5 cm); max.
diameter 9⅜ in. (24.0 cm)
Tatsuuma Archaeological Museum,
Nishinomiya City, Hyōgo Prefecture
Former collection of Kudō Yūryū
Important Cultural Property

Kamegaoka is located in northwestern Japan in Aomori Prefecture in a low-lying area where the Tsugaru Peninsula curves slightly around Tsugaru Bay. Writers and amateur archaeologists have visited Kamegaoka to collect artifacts since the Edo period (A.D. 1615–1868).

This spouted vessel is widest at the shoulder. The mouth rim is constricted twice, and the surface is a finely polished lustrous black. The narrow, protruding spout slants upward from the middle of the body. Consecutive incised lines define the lip; cord marks decorate the body, except those areas defined by semicircular grooves. The knotlike projections around the neck and body are characteristic of designs from the Tōhoku region in the Late Jōmon period. Archaeologists call these vessels "knot-attached" pottery.

The original cord marks of the grooved areas have been smoothed over, a technique that was common during the Late and Final Jōmon periods. Spouted earthenware vessels, like the example from Muroya Cave in Niigata Prefecture [see 45], existed in the Initial Jōmon, but it was not until the Late and Final Jōmon that the particular shape became more common. The well-defined and symmetrical designs enhance the elegant shape.

HARADA MASAYUKI

Incipient Jōmon period
(10,500–8000 B.C.)
Excavated at Kamikuroiwa Rock
Shelter, Ehime Prefecture
Stone
1¾ × ⅞ in. (4.5 × 2.4 cm)
National Museum of Japanese History, Sakura City, Chiba Prefecture

The fine lines incised on this flat pebble represent a woman's hair, breasts, and straw skirt. Made around the beginning of the Jōmon period, this piece, popularly called the Venus of Kamikuroiwa, was found among one of the oldest pottery assemblages in Japan. In its representation of a woman, it shares attributes with other early figures found worldwide dating to the Paleolithic period.

Lines incised on the back of the pebble include an X-shape motif. The figural design is distinct in lacking facial features. Clay figures of the Initial Jōmon period were also initially without facial features, which has led some archaeologists to trace the origins of figural representation in Japan to these engraved pebbles. Other scholars argue, however, that the restricted location of the pebbles precludes the possibility that they were a precursor of clay figures. As the oldest examples in Japan to express human features, they are nevertheless valuable creations.

On the surface of the pebble, an unclear triangular design appears on the obverse, in the area corresponding to the straw skirt. The fine, unintelligible lines indicate that many attempts were made at incising. The repeated engraving, probably for correction, is found on similar kinds of incised pebbles.

Altogether, nine pebbles with fine, incised lines were recovered from Kamikuroiwa Rock Shelter in Ehime Prefecture; none was found from other sites of the same period. The incised pebbles were probably created independently for a particular ritual connected to the Kamikuroiwa site. This Venus figure is believed to have been used in prayers for fecundity.

DOI TAKASHI

Late Jōmon period
(1500–1000 B.C.)
Excavated at Shidanai, Iwate
Prefecture
Earthenware
9¾ × 8¾ in. (25.0 × 22.3 cm)
Agency for Cultural Affairs, Government of Japan, Tokyo; on deposit
at Iwate Prefectural Museum,
Morioka City
Important Cultural Property

Clay figures (*dogū*) were used on ritual occasions during the Jōmon period. Their origins can be traced to the Initial Jōmon period. The early figures were small, flat plaques without clearly defined facial expressions. From the Middle Jōmon period the figures become bigger, assume a standing posture, and have facial details.

This head, found broken into more than ten pieces, was probably once part of a burial. Even though it is hollow, it seems to have been made from one piece of clay. Except for some small fragments, possibly belonging to the hand and leg, no parts of the figure below the neck were found. Intact, the entire figure would be more than 3¼ feet (1 m) long.

A raised, narrow belt above the eyebrows encircles the head, and a raised band defines the area extending from the cheeks to the upper jaw. The same technique of indicating facial features is often observed on clay figures of the Late Jōmon period in the Tōhoku region. The Tōhoku figures are assumed to represent people wearing wooden masks. Perhaps the herringbone incisions applied vertically to the cheek on this example indicate mask decorations. Small holes piercing the top of the head and lower jaw have led some archaeologists to assume that feathers were inserted into the holes, as was the custom of Northwest Coast American tribes. The realistically carved ears, nose, and mouth recall an example in clay unearthed from Hatten in Iwate Prefecture.

The Shidanai site in Iwate Prefecture, where this specimen was discovered, extended over the terraces of a mountainous riverbank, and its dwelling clusters were spread widely in a circle. The settlement contained clearly defined groups of grave pits. The abundant and varied excavated artifacts include a large quantity of ceramics, stone implements, and even a carved object similar to a totem pole.

HARADA MASAYUKI

63 FIGURE

Late Jōmon period
(1500–1000 B.C.)
Excavated at Kazahari 1, Aomori
Prefecture
Earthenware
7¾ × 5⅝ × 6 in.
(19.8 × 14.2 × 15.2 cm)
Hachinohe City Education
Commission, Aomori Prefecture

The clay figure assumes a praying position with hands held in front and knees drawn up. A clay ridge on the slightly tilted face delineates the nose and prominent eyebrows. A small strip of rolled clay with fine punctures encircles the oval mouth. The facial expression resembles that of the head from Shidanai {see 62}. Two incised clay strips ring the neck and may indicate a necklace. Grooved, curvilinear patterns and fine cord marking decorate the body.

Figures in this particular posture, which archaeologists call "pose figures," have been unearthed only from Late Jōmon sites in the Tōhoku region and are extremely rare. The hands are displayed in different positions in relation to the drawn-up knees; sometimes they are clasped around the knees or sometimes an elbow rests in the palm of the opposite hand. The poses may be related to the religious attitudes of the Jōmon people.

Among such figures, fingers and toes vary in number from three to eight; on each hand of this clay figure are six fingers. Did the Jōmon people overlook the actual number? By comparison, units in the decoration of Jōmon vessels were carried out precisely. The contradiction is interesting.

Originally lacking a left foot, this figure was found as if it were crouching on the floor of a pit dwelling near a wall. When the missing left foot was later unearthed, the whole body could be perfectly restored.[1]

The archaeologists who unearthed the figure found a thick coat of natural asphalt smeared on the broken section of the left foot. Apparently the people who lived in the Jōmon dwelling had repaired the figure by reattaching the foot and then continued to venerate it. Although most Jōmon figures were deliberately broken and buried after a ritual, some rare examples, such as this, may have been treated in a different manner.

HARADA MASAYUKI

1. The foot was retrieved from a location about 8⅛ inches (20.7 cm) from the main figure.

64 FIGURE

Final Jōmon period
(1000–400 B.C.)
Excavated at Chobonaino, Hokkaidō
Earthenware
17 × 8 in. (43.0 × 20.2 cm)
Minami Kayabe Township Education Commission, Hokkaidō
Important Cultural Property

Clay figures with distinct regional styles were developed during the Jōmon period. In eastern Japan, for example, large figures with exaggerated facial features and abstract characteristics were made in the Late Jōmon. The style, with larger, hollow figures, continued into the Final Jōmon. This large, hollow clay figure underwent various stylistic changes, finally developing into a container for a deceased child in the beginning of the Yayoi period. This example from Chobonaino in Hokkaidō is the largest to be found among the rare, very large figures.

Small ridges decorate the slightly tilted, expressive head, and narrow clay coils define the eyes, mouth, and eyebrows. The punctures around the jaw line may depict the stubble of a beard. The body is well proportioned, with wide, straight shoulders, small waist, and long, full legs. Just below the shoulders, centered on the breasts, large engraved circles are part of a complicated design of triangles, circles, and straight lines. This particular pattern is generally observed on pottery vessels of the Final Jōmon. It was later adopted by the Ainu people of Hokkaidō in their ethnic costumes. A slight bulge in the abdomen, perhaps suggestive of an early stage of pregnancy, together with an engraved line called the "lifeline," may indicate the figure's special purpose for use in a ritual associated with fertility or childbearing.

During the Jōmon period, communal rites became increasingly complex, and distinct funerary rituals were developed. Secondary-burial rituals eventually evolved, particularly in eastern Japan.

HARADA MASAYUKI

65 FIGURE

Final Jōmon period
(1000–400 B.C.)
Excavated at Kamegaoka,
Aomori Prefecture
Earthenware
13½ × 9⅞ × 3⅝ in.
(34.3 × 25.2 × 9.4 cm)
Tokyo National Museum
Important Cultural Property

The large bulges on the face are commonly assumed to depict goggles made of bone or wood, similar to those used as eye protection by the Inuit people of North America. This specimen typifies the goggled clay figures found near Kamegaoka-type vessels [see 60]. Such objects are dated primarily to the early half of the Final Jōmon period in the Tōhoku region.

The large, broad-shouldered body is missing the left leg. The hairstyle modeled in openwork achieves the effect of a crown. Jōmon clay figures were deliberately broken in ceremonial rituals, so it is quite rare to find a figure that can be restored to its complete shape.

HARADA MASAYUKI

Early Jōmon period
(5000–2500 B.C.)
Excavated at Negoyadai,
Tochigi Prefecture
Stone
Utsunomiya City Education
Commission, Tochigi Prefecture
Important Cultural Property

Top row:

66
1¾ × 2 × ³⁄₁₆ in.
(4.4 × 5.1 × 0.5 cm)

67
1⅝ × 2 × ³⁄₁₆ in.
(4.2 × 5.2 × 0.5 cm)

Bottom row:

68
2⅛ × 2⅜ × ³⁄₁₆ in.
(5.4 × 6.1 × 0.5 cm)

69
2¼ × 2⅜ × ⅛ in.
(5.9 × 6.2 × 0.4 cm)

Jōmon people decorated various parts of the body, including the head, ears, neck, arms, wrists, and ankles. Ornaments were made from many kinds of materials: stone, teeth, wood, tusk, antler, and clay. Slit earrings were fashioned from flat, circular pieces of soft stone for easy crafting. Serpentine and soapstone were favored, particularly in green, blue, milky white, and brown. To make an earring, a hole was pierced at the stone's center, from which a slit was opened toward the outer edge then finished with elaborate polishing; the edge of an earlobe went through the slit to the central perforation.

Earrings are often found in burial excavations among skeletal remains on either side of the skull. Slit-stone earrings have been unearthed from sites all over Japan dating through the Jōmon period. Production sites, found in Nagano, Niigata, and Toyama prefectures, seem to have met the demand for ornaments from various areas of Japan.

Slit-stone earrings resemble *jue,* the ancient Chinese jade rings with a cut-out segment. In fact, the Chinese character for *jue* represents the Japanese word for this kind of earring. Opinions diverge regarding the earring's origin. One theory holds that the style of earring came originally from China; another theory is that it developed independently in Japan.

KAWAGOE SHUN'ICHI

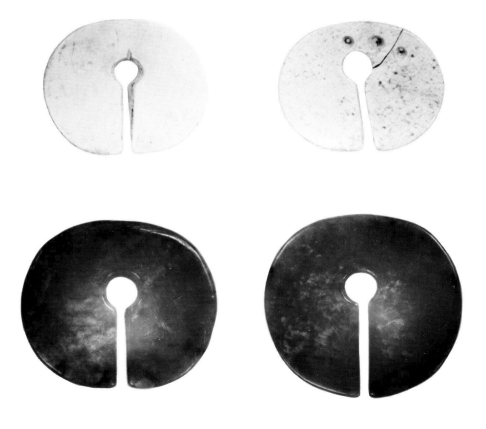

Final Jōmon period
(1000–400 B.C.)
Excavated at Chiamigaito,
Gumma Prefecture
Painted earthenware
Kiryū City Education Commission,
Gumma Prefecture
Important Cultural Property

Top row:

70
Thickness ⅞ in. (2.3 cm);
diameter 3⅛ in. (8.0 cm)

71
Thickness 1⅛ in. (2.9 cm);
diameter 3⅝ in. (9.3 cm)

72
Thickness 1⅜ in. (3.5 cm);
diameter 3⅜ in. (8.6 cm)

Bottom row:

73
Thickness 1 in. (2.5 cm);
diameter 2 in. (5.2 cm)

74
Thickness ⅞ in. (2.3 cm);
diameter 3⅛ in. (8.0 cm)

To decorate one's body beautifully has perhaps been an innate desire of all human beings throughout history. Small stone beads have been found even from Paleolithic sites in Japan. During the more than eight thousand years of the Jōmon period, many kinds of stone, clay, tusk, and antler ornaments were produced. Among them, pottery ear ornaments, which became especially popular during the Final Jōmon in the Kantō Plain, were the most exquisite. No other ornaments are comparable in their refined design.

Earthenware ear ornaments from Chiamigaito in Gumma Prefecture are made of selected clay, with the large outer circle and connecting portions decorated with intricate carving. Well-proportioned, thin shapes were achieved, and red pigment was applied to enhance their beauty.

At Chiamigaito more than one thousand small and medium-sized ear ornaments were discovered in a confined area, which suggests that it may have been a workshop. Only certain sites among the many of the Final Jōmon have yielded hundreds of ear ornaments. In addition to Chiamigaito, the other sites include Kayano in Gumma Prefecture; Kofukasaku in Saitama Prefecture; and Ōhana in Nagano Prefecture. The specificity of their locations suggests that ear ornaments were made as a specialized craft as early as the Jōmon period by people who lived in certain limited settlements. It is interesting, moreover, that common or astonishingly similar design elements are found from sites hundreds of miles apart. Perhaps the Jōmon artists who were competitively developing their skills in the craft were in much closer contact with each other than we would imagine. Such exchange would allow artists to acquire information for making larger and more exquisite ear ornaments. Even though neither class differentiation nor full-time occupational specialization seems to have existed during the Jōmon period, specialized workers began to emerge at that time.

HARADA MASAYUKI

Early Jōmon period
(5000–2500 B.C.)
Excavated at Uwahaba,
Akita Prefecture
Stone
Akita Prefectural Museum,
Akita City
Important Cultural Property

75
23¾ × 3⅜ × ⅞ in.
(60.2 × 8.5 × 2.2 cm)

76
19⅝ × 2 × 1¾ in.
(49.8 × 5.0 × 4.4 cm)

The technique of making polished stone tools was first adopted in Japan during the Late Paleolithic period. From the Early Jōmon, completely polished stone tools were produced. The material used was a fine green tuff, cut by abrading with a sawtooth-edged stone object to make a long, flat piece, which was then finished by grinding. The technique came to be applied as well to stone earrings or beads. An elaborate procedure requiring extreme patience, the method became obsolete by the Middle Jōmon. Jōmon technological development was not, therefore, simply a smooth and gradual progression.

Four stone adzes, including these two, accidentally found during road construction, were unearthed as a set; rescuers had no way of discerning the exact conditions of the find. Artifacts scattered nearby, however, date to the Early Jōmon period and are assumed to be contemporaneous with the adzes.

Such large examples of polished stone adzes are quite rare in Japan, but similar specimens have been found as grave goods in communal Neolithic graves in Korea.[1] The Korean adzes are thought to have been treasured objects rather than ordinary tools for daily use. Accordingly, the large stone adzes from Uwahaba in Akita Prefecture may also have been made as special artifacts.

HARADA MASAYUKI

1. Some measure 7⅞ to 11¾ inches (20–30 cm) long, while others are as large as 19⅝ inches (50 cm).

Middle Jōmon period
(2500–1500 B.C.)
Excavated at Kamasuyashiki [77]
and Chōjayashiki [78],
Iwate Prefecture
Stone
Iwate Prefectural Archaeological
Research Center, Tonan Village

77
13¾ × 7 × 1 in.
(35.0 × 18.0 × 2.5 cm)

78
12⅜ × 5½ × 1 in.
(31.5 × 14.0 × 2.5 cm)

In Japan the so-called Chinese broad blade refers to an artifact with a curved blade that was used in China. Around two hundred years ago Kinouchi Sekitei, a specialist of stones, gave that name to stone implements unearthed in Hokkaidō. Some sixty specimens of the type have been found in Japan.[1]

The use of the Chinese blade-shaped objects is debated by archaeologists, many of whom hold the view that they were utilitarian—either weapons or clubs used for salmon and trout fishing. The theory that they were devoted to practical use is unlikely, however, since so few are known. All are made of stone except for one, which is made of whale bone. Their distribution is limited to southern Hokkaidō and northern Tōhoku, and

they were made during a defined period during the Middle Jōmon. Blade-shaped objects with a bump near the handle [77] are thought to be older than those without a bump [78].

No apparent prototype for these objects has been found in Japan; it is generally assumed, therefore, that the prototype came either from the Asian continent or the North Pacific. Broad bladed stone objects began to disappear soon after the appearance of sword-shaped stone objects [see 79].

DOI TAKASHI

1. The blades are about 12 inches (30.0 cm) long.

Final Jōmon period
(1000–400 B.C.)
Excavated at Satsukari, Hokkaidō
Stone
14 × 1½ × ⅜ in.
(35.8 × 3.8 × 1.0 cm)
Hokkaidō Historical Museum,
Sapporo

During the Late and Final Jōmon periods the Jōmon cultural pattern was stabilized and cultural and intellectual patterns became increasing complex. Large numbers of artifacts embodying the spiritual world of the Jōmon people, such as clay figures, stone tools, and sword-shaped objects, were produced.

In eastern Japan in the Final Jōmon period, sword-shaped objects made of hard shale superseded stone rods or batons, which had developed in the Middle Jōmon and later. The blade was slightly curved, and the top of the handle was decorated with the spiral pattern often seen on contemporaneous earthenware vessels.

Opinions concerning the prototype of the sword-shaped stone objects vary, with the most probable assumption being that the objects were fashioned to imitate bronze artifacts from the Asian continent. During the Final Jōmon period, when the sword-shaped objects were being produced in Japan, the Shang and Zhou cultures were flourishing in China. The bronze knife, an element of the Chinese bronze culture, was brought into Japan, and through its imitation a new Japanese artifact was developed. Similar instances of

emulation of Chinese artifacts are evident in Japanese prehistory; these include the Chinese-style broad bladed objects of the Middle Jōmon period [see 77, 78] as well as the stone adz with side projections and double-edged stone club or sword of the Yayoi period. Only one bronze artifact originally from China—a bronze knife from Misakiyama, Yamagata Prefecture—has ever been found in a Japanese prehistoric site. Although it was not recovered in a formal excavation, circumstantial evidence of contact does exist. Glass beads of undisputed Chinese origin were found at Kamegaoka in Aomori Prefecture, and a tripod earthenware vessel, which looks like an imitation of a bronze ware, was excavated from Imazu in Aomori Prefecture. It is almost certain that some artifacts came from the Asian continent to the coast of the Sea of Japan in the Tōhoku region during the Late and Final Jōmon periods.

This sword-shaped stone object from Satsukari in Hokkaidō is an excellent example in which the original shape of the imported object was adapted as a Jōmon implement.

HARADA MASAYUKI

Final Jōmon period
(1000–400 B.C.)
Excavated at Misawa 1, Hokkaidō
Stone
15⅜ × 1½ × 1¼ in.
(39.0 × 3.8 × 3.1 cm)
Hokkaidō Education Commission,
Sapporo; on deposit at Chitose City
Education Commission, Hokkaidō

Like earthenware figures, bar-shaped stone rods were typical religious artifacts of the Jōmon period. It is assumed that they embodied sexual symbolism in primitive religious rituals. Although the contents of the ceremonies are not fully clear, it is highly likely that prayers to nature spirits were offered for abundant harvests and fecundity.

During the Late and Final Jōmon period, stone rods made for ritual occasions became longer and slimmer, with a finer shape, knobbed ends, and sculpturally embellished heads. Two different forms emerged: the bar-shaped stone rod represented by this object and the sword-shaped object with flattened body.

The archaeological context of this type of stone object also changed over the Jōmon period. Originally used in religious rites as phallic symbols, toward the end of the Jōmon they became more abstract and were added to burial assemblages.

Misawa 1, Hokkaidō, is a group burial site dating to the end of the Final Jōmon period. This specimen was recovered from a grave pit there, where it had been placed as an offering. Five or six horizontal notches are incised deeply on both ends of the rod. The central part expands slightly; the traces of pecking and numerous perpendicular striations were probably produced in finishing the object. The strongly projected head symbolizing the male organ is separated from the shaft by a hoop decorated with circles and engravings.

Bar-shaped rods and sword-shaped objects with flattened bodies disappeared at the beginning of the Yayoi period, as Jōmon religious rituals were gradually replaced during the transition from Jōmon to Yayoi society. Fundamental changes in subsistence, from hunting and gathering among the Jōmon to farming among the Yayoi, greatly influenced societal rituals.

HARADA MASAYUKI

Middle Jōmon period
(2500–1500 B.C.)
Excavated at Ōzakai Cave,
Toyama Prefecture
Stone
Length 37⅜ in. (95.0 cm)
Tokyo University Museum

A few small bar-shaped stone clubs with no clear decoration engraved on them emerged during the Early Jōmon. The many bar-shaped stone clubs of the Middle Jōmon period, however, are large.[1] In most clubs the phallic shape is expressed by a simple enlargement at the end of an elongated shaft without the elaborate carving that is seen in this example. Similarly detailed examples existed only in a limited area along the coast of the Sea of Japan, centered in Ishikawa and Toyama prefectures and including neighboring Gifu and Nagano prefectures.

The decoration on the rod can be interpreted as symbolizing the male and female principles. Open expressions of sex were related to religion in Jōmon culture. Japanese native religion, rooted in nature worship but transformed by the introduction of rice cultivation, gradually developed into Shinto. This particularly elaborate bar-shaped stone rod from Ōzakai Cave in Toyama Prefecture manifests an element of the Jōmon culture that was later also expressed in Shinto.

HARADA MASAYUKI

1. The largest known to date, 6½ feet (2 m) long, was excavated in Nagano Prefecture.

Early Jōmon period
(5000–2500 B.C.)
Excavated at Ondashi,
Yamagata Prefecture
Lacquered earthenware
Height 6⅛ in. (15.5 cm);
diameter 9¼ in. (23.6 cm)
Agency for Cultural Affairs,
Government of Japan, Tokyo; on
deposit at Yamagata Prefectural
Museum, Yamagata City

Jōmon lacquer production is well
known from specimens unearthed
from sites dating mainly to the Final
Jōmon period, such as Kamegaoka
[see 83] and Korekawa. Quite recently, however, it has been found
that lacquer making was well established in the Early Jōmon, thousands of years earlier than previously
known. Two sites—Ondashi and
the Torihama Shell Mound—have
yielded lacquered pottery vessels
of the Early Jōmon period. Perfect
specimens have been found only
in Ondashi.

The gentle bulge in the middle
of this vessel curves down to a
stepped, round bottom. A line of
small circular holes surrounds the
sharply inward-turning mouth rim.
The vessel is undercoated with red
lacquer, over which a bold design of
spiral motifs has been painted in
black lacquer.

A few earthenware vessels dating
to the latter half of the Early Jōmon
have been unearthed from sites in
the Chūbu region. Rimmed with
a series of holes, the vessels are assumed to have played a special role
in ritual celebrations. In the Tōhoku
region this particular type of clay
vessel was painted with lacquer, the
most advanced decorative technique
available at that time. This outstanding specimen is evidence that
lacquerwork in Japan during the
Jōmon period was not inferior to
that of Neolithic China and that
it had existed for as long, with
unique designs and techniques.

A similar lacquer technique was
applied to wooden bows [see 84].
Although most lacquered objects
have perished, those that have survived indicate that Jōmon lacquer-
wares added vivid color to daily
existence.

HARADA MASAYUKI

Final Jōmon period
(1000–400 B.C.)
Excavated at Kamegaoka,
Aomori Prefecture
Lacquered earthenware
Diameter 8 in. (20.5 cm)
Aomori Prefectural Museum,
Aomori City

A complex wavy motif in red and black lacquer decorates the inside of this shallow bowl. Lacquerware techniques were already quite advanced in the Early Jōmon period [see 82], but the process was further developed during the Late and Final Jōmon. Recent excavations have yielded a woven cloth for filtering lacquer fluid and a stick to incise the tree trunk to collect the sap used to make lacquer. Lacquered objects include bamboo baskets; earthenware vessels; wooden containers, combs, bracelets, and earrings; and ornamental swords.

Recent developments in the scientific analysis of lacquered objects together with reconstructions of ancient processes of lacquering reveal clearly that undercoating was the norm during the Jōmon period. In a technique nearly identical to modern practice, ancient designs were painted with red lacquer. Lacquer was applied not only to enhance the beauty of the vessel but also to waterproof the low-fired ceramic.

HARADA MASAYUKI

Final Jōmon period
(1000–400 B.C.)
Excavated at Korekawa,
Aomori Prefecture
Lacquered wood
Length 50 in. (127.0 cm)
Hachinohe City Education
Commission, Aomori Prefecture
Important Cultural Property

In the Jōmon period, when living patterns were adapted to forest conditions, wood, together with clay and stone, was extensively used for crafts. The humid, warm climate of Japan, however, has almost completely destroyed the objects made of wood and other organic materials. In rare cases peat layers from low-lying damp sites have yielded wooden objects in astonishingly complete condition. The Kamegaoka and Korekawa sites of the Final Jōmon period, the former known for clay figures with goggles [see 65], are situated in low-lying damp areas and are outstanding for the objects that have been preserved. Artifacts recovered from Korekawa, including this bow, are abundant and varied. Thousands of earthenware vessels, stone tools, and wooden objects, such as containers and combs, have also been found there.

To make the bow, a single piece of wood was scraped and its two ends were rounded and decorated in relief. The central portion of the sheath was flattened, and the two extremities were perforated at regular intervals. The whole bow was then painted with red lacquer and carefully finished.

Stone arrowheads from Incipient Jōmon sites suggest that the bow and arrow had replaced the throwing spear by that time. Remains of bows, however, have been found only in Early Jōmon sites such as the Tori-hama Shell Mound. The bows are small, unpainted, and made of wood.

A few bows, apart from those used in hunting, were made for rituals in the Final Jōmon period. Although they were longer than the bows of earlier periods, they are nevertheless small compared to those developed later during the Kofun period.

HARADA MASAYUKI

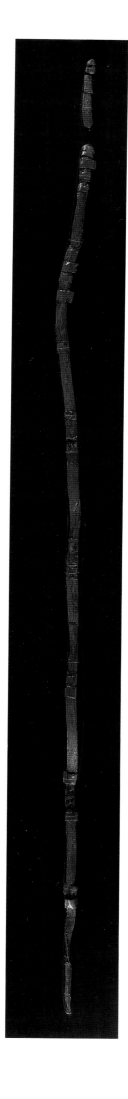

Final Jōmon period
(1000–400 B.C.)
Excavated at Numazu Shell Mound,
Miyagi Prefecture
Antler
Tōhoku University Archaeological
Research Laboratory, Sendai City,
Miyagi Prefecture
Important Cultural Property

85
Harpoon head
5⅞ × ¾ × ¼ in.
(15.0 × 2.0 × 0.6 cm)

86
Harpoon head
5⅜ × ¾ × ⅜ in.
(13.8 × 2.1 × 1.1 cm)

87
Harpoon head
4⅜ × ¾ × ¼ in.
(12.5 × 2.0 × 0.9 cm)

88
Fishhook
2⅝ × ⅞ × ⅛ in.
(6.7 × 2.3 × 0.5 cm)

89
Fishhook
2¼ × 1 × ¼ in.
(6.0 × 2.7 × 0.7 cm)

90
Toggle harpoon head
4¼ × 1⅝ × 1 in.
(11.0 × 4.2 × 2.8 cm)

91
Toggle harpoon head
4⅛ × 1½ × ¾ in.
(10.5 × 3.8 × 2.1 cm)

92
Toggle harpoon head
4¼ × 1⅜ × ⅝ in.
(10.7 × 3.5 × 1.8 cm)

These specimens represent the bone and antler implements discovered in the shell mounds of coastal Japan. Near the coast of the Tōhoku region in northern Honshū, where the cold Kuril and warm Kuroshio currents come together, a great number of fish are found. Fishing tools of bone and antler made in the Jōmon period greatly varied in size and function and reflect the Jōmon people's abundant knowledge of fish. In Japan's earliest documents, written thirteen hundred years ago, more than one hundred kinds of fish are identified.

One type of harpoon head was fixed on the tip of a wooden stick for spearing fish [85–87]. The barbs for preventing fish from escaping from the hook are cleverly made. Notches were carved at the base of the harpoon for hafting the harpoon to the shaft; sometimes an adhesive such as natural asphalt was applied. Another type of detachable harpoon head, sharply pointed at the tip, was socketed to a shaft [90–92]. A stone arrowhead, effective for catching large fish, was sometimes used instead. As soon as a harpoon hit a fish, the arrowhead detached from the shaft.

Fishhooks were of two types: one with a barb, the other without [88, 89]. The form of fishhook is identical to present-day Japanese fishhooks made of iron. For making harpoons the Jōmon artisan selected a relatively straight portion of the middle of a deer's leg; the fishhook was made of deer antler.

DOI TAKASHI

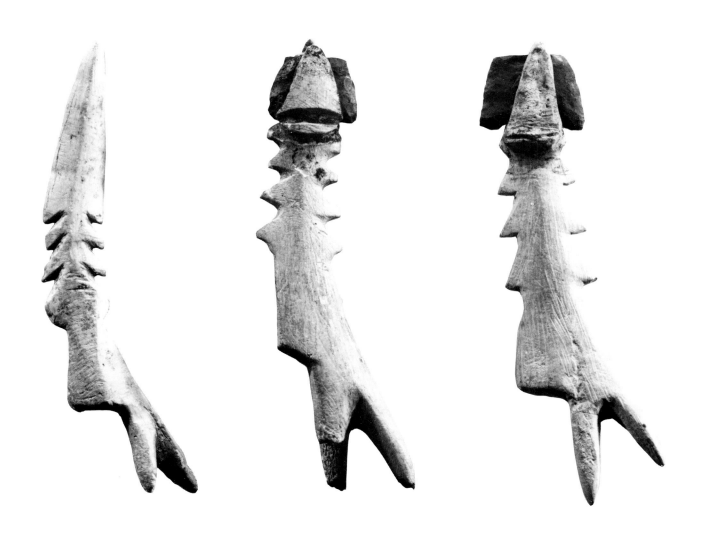

4

YAYOI PERIOD

400 B.C.–A.D. 250

Excavation in 1884 at a site in Yayoi-chō, a district of Tokyo, yielded a type of pottery very different from Jōmon pottery and led to the definition of a new period of Japanese prehistory, the Yayoi (fig. 14).

The immediate distinguishing feature of the Yayoi culture is its reddish orange, smooth pottery. Together with the pottery, bronze and iron artifacts appeared for the first time with the introduction of ironworking, bronze casting, glassmaking, weaving, and advanced methods of woodworking. Moreover, the beginnings of agriculture, which transformed the earlier subsistence economy based on hunting and gathering, have been confirmed in discoveries of rice grains as well as actual ditches and fields. The early center of Yayoi culture lay across the Tsushima Strait from Korea, in northwestern Kyūshū, where rice-paddy cultivation appeared as early as 400 B.C.

For many years the dramatic differences distinguishing the Yayoi from the preceding Jōmon period were thought to indicate a massive migration from Korea to Japan. Evidence of immigration from the Korean peninsula includes changes in styles of pottery and stone tools and differences in human skeletons. Today, however, the beginning of the Yayoi is viewed as a complex process of migration and local adaptation. It is apparent that cultural innovations were integrated with Jōmon practices so that Yayoi culture was by no means a wholesale importation from the Asian continent.

The introduction of agricultural food cultivation into Japan provided expanded sources of energy for enlarged social systems, and around 300 B.C. a hierarchical form of social organization took shape. Over the relatively brief period of around six hundred years large networks of exchange and visible symbols of power, such as earthworks to enclose communities, were created.

Yayoi burial forms expressed a new system of beliefs and a transformed social order in which local chiefs competed for access to luxury items imported from the Asian continent. Arranged in well-defined cemeteries, some burials more elaborately prepared than others contain grave offerings of weapons and ornaments. The burial goods indicate that certain individuals had social and ritual power. Ownership of coveted items marked the owners' high status and probably helped consolidate local confederacies.

Interaction took place among various parts of Japan, from Kyūshū to southern Hokkaidō, and exchange networks penetrated far into the Ryūkyū Islands. In this way chiefs secured weapons, ornaments, including precious bracelets of tropical shell, and ritual objects such as

Jar with pedestal and
constricted neck [135]

mirrors. Even more complex burials in northern Kyūshū (fig. 15), the Kinai region, and Okayama Prefecture suggest that by the third century A.D. confederacies of chiefs circulated rare objects as badges of alliance and power. Ample evidence also reveals that chiefs warred against one another. Warfare spread throughout Japan, perhaps in cycles; villages were heavily fortified and alliances were formed to protect exchange systems from disruption.

In the Middle Yayoi period the center of power shifted from northern Kyūshū to the Kinai region, centered around Nara. Confirmation for the shift can be found in the wealth of burials and the amount of energy expended on them. By the third century A.D. a group of powerful chiefs in the Kinai region dominated Yayoi society and would form the economic and social basis for developments in the later Kofun period.

Figure 14
Yayoi sites mentioned in the text.

1 Minami Shimpo
2 Ōtsuka
3 Asahi
4 Toro
5 Koshinohara
6 Shibagahara
7 Tsubai Ōtsukayama
8 Higashinara
9 Kitoragawa
10 Nishiura
11 Karako-Kagi
12 Kamei
13 Ikegami
14 Sakuragaoka
15 Tamatsu Tanaka
16 Kōjindani
17 Miyayama
18 Mine
19 Tatetsuki
20 Doigahama
21 Tateiwa
22 Shiganoshima
23 Akatsuka
24 Yoshitake-takagi
25 Itazuke
26 Hirabaru
27 Nanaita
28 Kemidani
29 Futatsukayama
30 Yoshinogari
31 Nabatake

Chronology

The chronological definition of the Yayoi period depends on the criteria employed. By 500–400 B.C. or possibly earlier, rice-paddy cultivation was established in Kyūshū; if one chooses subsistence and living patterns as markers for the beginning of the Yayoi, the date should be set before 300 B.C., which was until recently the traditional date for the beginning of the Yayoi. According to the new system, the period before 300 B.C. is called Initial Yayoi (Hudson 1990, 65). If one uses artifactual criteria, such as the appearance of reddish orange, porous utilitarian pottery, the date could be slightly later, although the transition from Final Jōmon to Yayoi pottery types is not clearly demarcated.

The accepted chronology for Yayoi is loosely based on historical correlations with events in China and on the cross dating of Chinese mirrors and Korean bronze artifacts and pottery. A precise temporal ordering is problematic, however, because the period is brief and relatively recent; radiocarbon assessments are therefore imprecise.[1] Moreover, the Korean comparative sequence remains inexact (Uno 1988).

The beginning of the Yayoi period and the migration of east Asian populations are thought to be related to disturbances in China during the Warring States period. Korean bronze objects were probably imported to Japan around 200 B.C., during the Early Yayoi, while Chinese mirrors appeared in Japan from the Middle Yayoi. In the Late Yayoi, Chinese mirrors of the Eastern Han and Three Kingdoms period appeared in Japan.

Recent discoveries have changed conceptions about the close of the Yayoi period, which seems to have occurred by the mid-third century A.D. By that time keyhole-shaped burial mounds in the style of the Kofun period were constructed in the Kinai region and Yayoi pottery was beginning a transition to the reddish *haji* pottery characteristic of the Early Kofun. The transition from Middle to Late took place slightly earlier in Kyūshū (ca. A.D. 100) than in the Kinai region (ca. A.D. 200; Barnes 1983, 322).

The scale of human migration via Korea from the Asian continent at the onset of the Yayoi period is a subject of scholarly debate. From human skeletal data, it seems most likely that a considerable population arrived and that sporadic migration continued long after the Yayoi period. Skeletal material contrasts with that of the earlier Jōmon people.[2] Two physical types seem to have coexisted in Kyūshū during the Yayoi.

The relationship of Jōmon to Yayoi people has been conceptualized differently depending on the types of analyses employed. According to some scholars, the Yayoi population represents a replacement of the Jōmon population (Howells 1986); statistically the two groups are seen to have no relationship. Others have proposed a hybridization process, in which the modern Japanese people developed gradually through the mixing of Jōmon people with Asian continental migrants beginning in the Yayoi onward (Hanihara 1986). This premise seems to best fit the cultural data, which discloses a process of acculturation. Another theory maintains that Jōmon people evolved into Yayoi, Kofun, and present-day Japanese populations with minimal immigration. The latter theory tends to contradict later historical evidence of migration during the

Figure 15
Middle Yayoi (100 B.C.–A.D. 100) chiefdoms in northern Kyūshū (shaded areas). Numbered locations indicate sites of elaborate burials for individuals of high rank.

Thin lines indicate elevations (328 ft.; 100 m).

1 Imagawa
2 Shikabu
3 Sakurababa
4 Kuriomuta
5 Ukikunden
6 Mikumo
7 Ihara
8 Arita
9 Yoshitake
10 Shiganoshima
11 Hie
12 Itazuke
13 Sugu Okamoto
14 Tateiwa Hotta
15 Futsukaichimine
16 Higashiodamine
17 Kuriyama
18 Mitsueiden
19 Yoshinogari
20 Futatsukayama

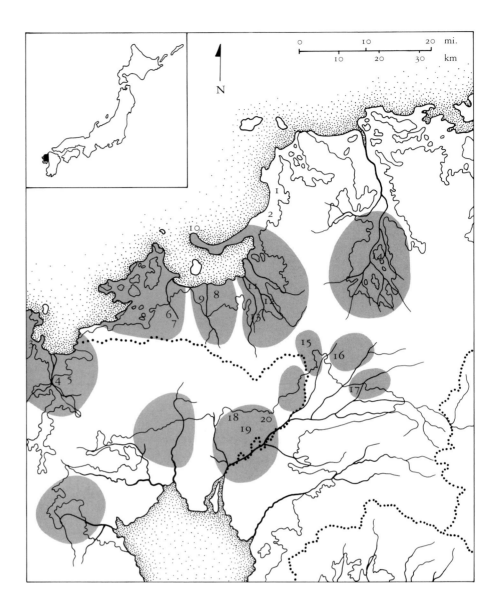

Kofun period and also runs counter to the cultural record of the Yayoi period. Migration from the continent is a historical fact; the degree of its impact is still debated (Hudson 1990, 66).

The spread of Yayoi culture was gradual. Building on knowledge of rice cultivation and other forms of horticulture extending far back into the Jōmon, Initial Yayoi people in Kyūshū began to live in agricultural villages based on intensive rice-paddy cultivation around 500–400 B.C.

From 300 to 200 B.C., Yayoi culture spread rapidly from northwestern Kyūshū through western Japan as far as the area around Nagoya. Evidence for that movement is in the uniform distribution of the Early Yayoi Ongagawa pottery type throughout the region. The dispersion confirms that the Inland Sea served as a primary channel of communication from Kyūshū to the Kinai region and beyond. Ideas spread quickly through the area not only in the Yayoi but also in later times.

From Nagoya into eastern Honshū the route of diffusion followed rivers and mountain passes; communication was especially rapid along the coast of the Sea of Japan. Yayoi culture seems, in fact, to have influenced the northern Tōhoku region before the Kantō and southern Tōhoku, judging from the discovery of early agricultural sites such as paddy fields dating to the Final Jōmon and Initial Yayoi in Aomori and Miyagi prefectures (Sahara 1987b, 236; Hudson 1990, 70).

During the Yayoi period the cultures of Hokkaidō and Okinawa diverged from those of the main islands of Honshū, Shikoku, and Kyūshū. The Epi-Jōmon culture existed in Hokkaidō from two thousand to twelve hundred years ago. In the latter half of the Epi-Jōmon, surface decoration on pottery disappeared, marking the end of the great Jōmon tradition.[3] A major form of Epi-Jōmon pottery, the Esan type, resembles the Final Jōmon Ōbora pottery of Tōhoku and also bears a close relationship with the Yayoi pottery of Tōhoku (Fujimoto 1988, 31).

Epi-Jōmon settlements, which have not been found in large number, are composed of round semisubterranean houses. Burials occurred in ring-shaped communal cemeteries, with abundant pottery offerings, the occasional piece having been traded from Tōhoku communities of the Yayoi people. The Epi-Jōmon interacted with the agricultural Yayoi populations to their south and were aware of cultivated plants, but plant cultivation seems to have remained peripheral to their way of life (Crawford & Takamiya 1990, 907).

Several hundred Yayoi pottery shards typical of northern Kyūshū have been recovered from Okinawa. It is thought that an exchange network supplying the chiefs of northern Kyūshū with shell bracelets from Okinawa in the Ryūkyū Islands brought the pottery in return but that Okinawa remained distinct from Kyūshū in its lack of bronze prestige items and absence of rice cultivation. By the end of the Yayoi period the exchange of shells disappeared and shells were replicated in bronze whorl-shaped ornaments (*tomoegata;* Pearson 1990a).

The Economic Base: Sedentary Agriculture

Jōmon people practiced horticulture for millennia, and their knowledge contributed substantially to the development of cultivation on a larger scale in the Yayoi. Crops grown by Yayoi farmers included rice, barnyard and foxtail millet, barley, wheat, buckwheat, hemp, *shiso, azuki* bean, soybean, pea, melon, peach, apricot, plum, and pear. Millet, grown in areas unsuitable for rice, particularly in northeastern Japan, may have been of great significance (Hudson 1990, 76–78). Domesticated fruit trees, which were not known to Jōmon cultivators, were notable imports from Neolithic China.

By the Final Jōmon, rice paddies had been constructed in a number of locations in Kyūshū. Stone agricultural tools were recovered from the Final Jōmon site of Nabatake, Saga Prefecture. Based on the composition of the stone material, some tools are considered to have been imported from the Korean peninsula. In addition, a wooden rake for smoothing rice paddies was recovered (Sahara 1987b, 42). Pollen studies indicate that rice was grown in a number of sites across Japan by twenty-five hundred years ago (Akazawa 1982, 160–63). Late Jōmon rice impressions on pottery, carbonized barley grains, and phytoliths of rice plants have been identified from both Late and Final Jōmon sites. Initial Yayoi sites dating before 300 B.C. are found not only in Kyūshū but also along the Inland Sea.

While it has long been assumed that rice cultivation spread to Japan from southern China via the Korean peninsula, some scholars suggest that a northern route via the Shandong and Liaodong peninsulas and Korea may have been followed. That rice grains from Final Jōmon and Early Yayoi sites appear to be smaller than those from the Hemudu site of China's Zhejiang Province suggests that the relationship is not very direct (Sahara 1989). Rice grains, which have been preserved through a slow oxidation process known as carbonization, demonstrate that early rice was relatively short-grained [106, 107].

Although it was once thought that rice was sown in natural marshes in early Yayoi cultivation, it is now known that paddy fields were developed from the beginning of the period. Ancient fields, with rows of rice-plant stumps, reveal evidence of dense transplanting that appears to have been accomplished by individual members of a cooperative group (Sahara 1987a, 246). Some villages were situated in low-lying areas near the fields. In northern Kyūshū in particular, Yayoi villages and fields occupied areas that are still used today as paddy fields, while upland areas have yielded cemeteries.

The cultivation of rice, a tropical crop, reached its worldwide northern limit in Japan. The annual cycle of rice growing throughout the monsoon world of eastern Asia has a particular rhythm and a spiritual as well as technological dimension. Through the introduction of this non-native food plant to Japan, a new way of life was created. Cultural anthropologists have noted that common themes—festivals, deities, symbols, social forms—unite Japan with Korea, southern China, and Southeast Asia. Moreover, rice culture linked Japan to other regions of eastern Asia before the advent of Buddhism and the adoption of Asian continental learning.

Irrigation systems of various types developed in the Yayoi. The Early Yayoi Itazuke site in Fukuoka, northern Kyūshū, yielded a series of paddies at least 98⅜ by 32¾ feet (30 × 10 m), surrounded by earth embankments held in place with wooden planks and stakes. Along one side of the field was a watercourse with a sluice for filling or draining the field.[4] At the Late Yayoi site of Makimuku in Nara Prefecture, a ditch appears to have joined two streams (Tsude 1988, 112).[5]

Evidence of animal domestication is extremely limited. Until recently most scholars believed that there were no domesticated animals in Japan during the Yayoi period, although they are known on the Korean peninsula. It now appears that they were introduced during the Yayoi period (Hudson & Barnes 1991). Bones of domesticated pig have been recovered from Yoshinogari in Saga Prefecture (Sahara, Takashima, & Nishitani 1989); other sites in Ōita and Saga prefectures have also yielded skulls of fully domesticated pigs.[6] The period of experimentation in pig domestication in Japan seems to have been drastically shorter than that of other regions.

Chickens were introduced to Japan in the Yayoi but were kept as sacred birds. They were not used as food until after the Edo period. Remains of a domesticated cow have been found in the Late Yayoi site of Toro, Shizuoka Prefecture (Aikens & Higuchi 1982, 235). It is commonly thought that in the fifth and sixth centuries horses and cows were introduced as beasts of burden but not as sources for food. In historic times the Japanese people did not consume the blood or internal organs of animals nor did they castrate animals or humans or use human or animal blood in religious ritual (Sahara 1989). The path of animal domestication in Japan followed a different trajectory from that in the Old World.

Cultivation Tools

Stone (chipped and polished), wood, and iron tools formed the basis of Yayoi production. Bone utensils were no doubt also used, although they have not been recovered in great numbers.

The Yayoi stone-tool assemblage contained two components: chipped-stone arrowheads and knives deriving from the Jōmon period and polished-stone tools based on Chinese prototypes, which came through Korea. The latter included a tree-felling ax, two types of woodworking adzes, and a stone reaping knife (Sahara 1987b, 37).[7] As far as can be determined from the archaeological record, iron sickles had replaced stone reaping knives by the Late Yayoi (Hudson 1990, 86). Stone awls were also used in the Early Yayoi, later to be replaced by iron tools. Jōmon stone mortars (*ishisara*) and spoonlike knives (*ishisaji*) disappeared. Yayoi production of stone tools seems to have been localized and controlled by elites.[8]

Technology

Textile Production

The discovery of spindle whorls indicates that spinning was practiced in the Yayoi period. According to studies of excavated cocoons, sericulture was brought to Japan during the Yayoi period from south-central China but was limited to Kyūshū until the Kofun period. The export of sericulture techniques from China was prohibited during the Yayoi period, so non-Chinese were likely responsible for bringing the cocoons to Kyūshū. Cocoons of Korean origin were used from the Middle Yayoi, after the establishment in 108 B.C. of the Lelang Garrison on the Korean peninsula (Hudson & Barnes 1991). Once the art of weaving linen and silk was introduced to Japan, it developed in a different manner from Chinese weaving (Kuraku 1989a, 24).

Fragments of linen were found attached to a dagger from Burial Jar 1002 of the Yoshinogari mound burial. The linen is made from hemp rather than ramie, of similar fineness to modern shirts and handkerchiefs (Hudson & Barnes 1991).

Glass and Stone Production

From the Early Yayoi, glass products were imported, and by the Middle Yayoi, domestic production had begun from raw material thought to have been imported from Lelang. At first the raw material was lead glass, from which comma-shaped beads (*magatama*) and tubular beads were fashioned.

The molds—open or two-sided—for casting *magatama* were either stone or clay. Beads were also made from long, tubular forms that were cut into sections. Groups of houses at sites such as Hyakkengawa Imadani in Okayama Prefecture appear to have been part of a community of craft specialists.[9] The Higashinara site in Osaka Prefecture yielded not only the sandstone mold of a bronze bell [124] but also a mold for making many glass *magatama* at one time (Kuraku 1989a, 27).

Glass disks (*heki*), symbols of high prestige in China, were imported to Japan. In China these broad circular disks with a central perforation and small bumps on the surface were made in imitation of jade symbols of authority dating to the Neolithic period.

Stone ornaments, which had been produced in the Jōmon period, became more important in the Yayoi. Nephrite comma-shaped beads as well as other beads and pendants had been made from the Late and Final Jōmon. Manufacturing sites on the shores of Lake Biwa and in the San'in and Hokuriku areas range from small, family production areas to larger-scale processing centers.[10]

Woodworking

The adoption of metal tools permitted the use of hard, durable woods that had not previously been workable. Waterlogged sites have yielded an abundance of wooden vessels from the Yayoi period. Containers were fashioned by scooping out a cylindrical section of a tree trunk and adding a flat bottom. Lugs on the containers permitted the lids to be tied down. Circular, oval, rectangular, and square vessels, with covers and small feet, were also produced. The wooden vessels were often made in sections held together by mortise and tenon joints. Many wooden serving dishes, particularly elevated bowls, were created. These were sometimes made in several parts and finished by attaching them to a turntable and trimming them with iron chisels while they turned. It is assumed that a primitive lathe, with a shaft rotated by a person who pulled on a cord wound around it, first in one direction and then in the reverse, was used by the Yayoi people. Laboratory assessment of a specimen preserved in the Minami Shimpo site in Kanazawa, Ishikawa Prefecture, of *keyaki* wood (*Zelkova serrata*) demonstrated that its manufacture was so uniform that it must have been done with a wheel (Kuraku 1989b, 98).

Other objects of wood include a remarkable crownlike hair ornament from the Middle Yayoi site of Kamei, Osaka Prefecture; fragments of a carved wooden lacquer shield; and carved wooden birds that are said to have been spirit messengers. The ritual role of birds is prominent among other rice-growing cultures in China and Korea.

Wooden agricultural tools recovered during the late 1940s in excavations of the Toro site include two-piece hoes with the blades fitted at oblique angles to the handle, hoes with forked ends, blades that may have been used in plows, spade fragments, and pick heads (Aikens & Higuchi 1982, 236). Examples of wooden agricultural tools, preserved in waterlogged deposits, were also found [103–5].

Fundamental changes took place in ceramics with the shift to a new type of subsistence and social order brought about by the arrival of immigrants from the Asian continent. At the same time, many characteristics of Late and Final Jōmon pottery persisted during the Yayoi period, particularly in northeastern Japan.

The classification of Yayoi pottery differs from that for Jōmon pottery in that five periods of Yayoi pottery have been established exclusive of the Initial Yayoi to account for the entire Yayoi period of approximately six hundred years. As noted earlier, the Initial Yayoi lasted from 400 to 300 B.C. Period I lasted two hundred years (300–100 B.C.), whereas the others were each about one hundred years. The five-period system is used for Kyūshū and the Kinai region. In northeastern Japan, however, Yayoi pottery is assigned type-site names (as can be seen in the pottery types identified in fig. 16) in the same manner as Jōmon pottery (Barnes 1983, 322).

In general, Yayoi ceramics of Kyūshū and the Kinai region sharply contrast with the elaborately sculptured forms of the Middle Jōmon vessels from central Japan (fig. 16). Many Yayoi vessels appear at first glance to lack decoration of any kind, and their shapes are smooth and formal compared to most Jōmon vessels.

In decoration and shape Jōmon and Yayoi ceramics share some characteristics. The pattern of innovations and continuities in method of manufacture, form and use, and decoration suggest that new people and ideas flowed into Japan but did not completely submerge the Jōmon population. While Yayoi ceramics differ in shape and color from those of the Jōmon, their technology does not represent a complete break with the past. The firing temperature, 1100 to 1470 degrees Fahrenheit (600–800 degrees Centigrade), was about the same as that for Jōmon vessels, and it is thought that many Yayoi vessels were fired in open stacks. In Kyūshū, however, where Asian continental innovations took hold first, ventilated pit kilns were used.

The exterior surfaces of Yayoi ceramics were treated with surface burnishing, paddling, shaving, scraping with a piece of wood (leaving a characteristic scoured surface), and smoothing with a wet cloth. The vessel interior was also scraped or smoothed.

While the symmetrical form and in some cases the large size of Yayoi vessels give the impression that they were shaped on a wheel, it is now known that even the very large vessels were made from stacked bands of clay in a fashion that was also used in making the pottery of the Korean peninsula. From the Middle Yayoi, vessels were often decorated or paddled on a revolving turntable (Barnes 1990a, 32, 34). The use of a carved wooden paddle and an anvil, which was sometimes a smooth pebble, has also been documented; the carved paddles were used to create an intricate surface decoration of fine lines or circular patterns. Paddled or stamped pottery developed in the Geometric Tradition of the Warring States period in China and later spread to Korea in the soft, gray pottery of the Proto-Three Kingdoms period.[11] Paddling, which compacts and thereby increases the surface area of a vessel and probably its thermal

Early	Middle	Late

Tōhoku

| | Minami Oyama | Tennōsan |

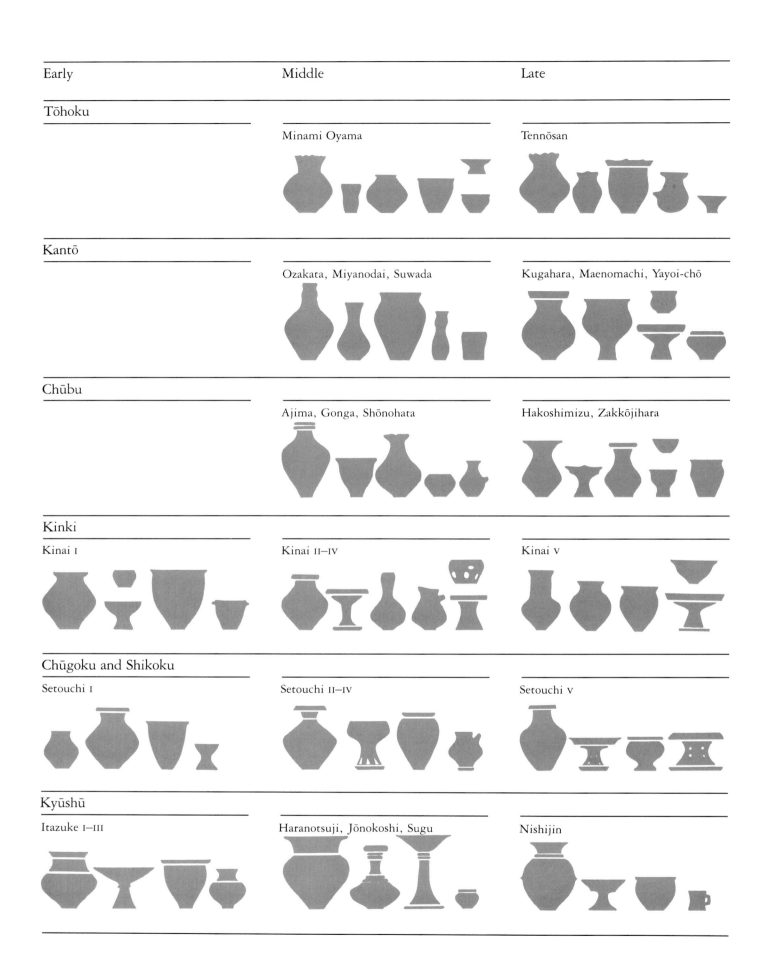

Kantō

| | Ozakata, Miyanodai, Suwada | Kugahara, Maenomachi, Yayoi-chō |

Chūbu

| | Ajima, Gonga, Shōnohata | Hakoshimizu, Zakkōjihara |

Kinki

| Kinai I | Kinai II–IV | Kinai V |

Chūgoku and Shikoku

| Setouchi I | Setouchi II–IV | Setouchi V |

Kyūshū

| Itazuke I–III | Haranotsuji, Jōnokoshi, Sugu | Nishijin |

Figure 16
Yayoi pottery types organized
chronologically and by region.

conductivity, made the pots less likely to crack or break with changes in temperature during firing.

In western Japan, in the geometric decorative repertoire, incised patterns, comb patterns, raised bands, and punctates were common. The raised band is a carryover from the Final Jōmon motif of raised-band decoration (*tottaimon*), created by sculpting or applying a rolled coil to the surface. In eastern Japan, zoned cord marking, a continuation from the Jōmon technique called *surikeshi*, patterned paddling, incised geometric patterns, and appliqué were popular. The exuberant tradition of eastern Japanese Jōmon ceramics persisted through the Yayoi period with the application of Jōmon decorative techniques to Yayoi vessel forms.

The basic shapes or functional types of Yayoi pottery reflected social change. Large storage jars, derived from the Plain Coarse Pottery culture of the Korean peninsula, and traditional Jōmon-style deep cooking pots assumed importance.[12] In Jōmon assemblages 80 percent of the recovered vessels are deep cooking vessels, whereas in the Yayoi assemblages 70 percent are for storage and cooking and 30 percent are for serving food and liquid. Cooking vessels were typically wide mouthed, measuring about 11¾ inches (30 cm) high and holding about 1⅞ to 2⅛ gallons (7–8 liters). Usually the upper part of the vessel is heavily blackened. Large examples, which were not blackened, however, may have been used for storing water, either buried or kept inside the house. In some cases the cooking vessels were set on a tripod support, apparently for more efficient cooking. In western Japan two-tiered steamers were used to boil or steam rice. An improvised steamer may have been made by perforating the bottom of a small, wide-mouthed jar (*kame*) and setting it on top of another cooking vessel. The perforated vessels have blackened exteriors, however, which seem to argue against that hypothesis (Kuraku 1989b, 96). In northeastern Japan the two-tiered steamer was not adopted, suggesting that another grain, perhaps millet, may have been an important staple.

Yayoi serving vessels became distinct from cooking vessels. Bowls, pedestals (*takatsuki*), and plates were used for serving food. Footed pedestals, often shaped to imitate wooden objects, are particularly striking. A basic East Asian form found in a number of Chinese Neolithic cultures from about 5000 to 1700 B.C., footed pedestals first appeared in Japan during the Final Jōmon of northern Honshū. Usually low and decorated with openwork, they differ from those of the Yayoi period, which are often tall, plain, and austere. Perhaps the footed pedestal was introduced twice into Japan, to distinct areas and from different Asian continental sources.

Jars with narrow mouths and long or short necks were used for storing water for daily use and for food, such as rice, cereals, beans, nuts, or shells. Pitcherlike jars with handles were produced during the Middle Yayoi period in the Kinai region. Jars (*takotsubo*) about 3⅞ inches (10 cm) high, cylindrical, with a round bottom, and perforated near the mouth to hold a rope, were used for catching small octopus. Having entered a dark empty vessel for refuge, the octopus could be simply lifted to the surface, a practice used to the present day. *Takotsubo* are extensively distributed in the Osaka Bay and the Inland Sea regions from Period III sites (A.D. 1–100; Kuraku 1989b, 97). In the Inland Sea region clay vessels were also used for making salt. Such vessels are roughly fashioned, with a small foot and flaring sides, which extend to a height of about 7⅞ inches (20 cm).

Ritual vessels were an essential feature of Yayoi ceramics. In the Early Yayoi, miniature copies of vessels for everyday use appear to have been used for ceremonies. Beginning in the Middle Yayoi, distinct forms, often beautifully decorated, were created for ritual use; they reached a peak in Period V (A.D. 200–250). The forms used for graveside rituals in northern Kyūshū, polished and painted in red with cinnabar, were particularly distinctive. Elevated pedestals, which approached 3¼ feet (1 m) in height, were especially impressive. Some had geometric patterns of burnished decoration visible only from certain angles. Patterns created with red slip containing iron oxide were polished when dry with a blunt stylus or pebble (Barnes 1990a, 31). Polishing can be seen on ceremonial vessels of the Korean Plain Coarse Pottery culture and on the fourth-century B.C. Zhongshan burial ceramics of Hebei Province in China.[13] At Itazuke, offerings of pottery were found at drains and irrigation catchment areas; offerings of polished red vessels had been placed near rows of stakes in rice paddies. Ritual vessels have also been found in large ditches and wells in the Kinai region.

An important type of burial jar, 15¾ to 27½ inches (40–70 cm) high, with a narrow neck, sometimes decorated with a three-dimensional human face just below the lip, is thought to be a container for human bones in a secondary burial. It has also been suggested that these human-faced jars were used to protect cemeteries or contain seeds (Barnes 1990a). Yayoi figures are exceptionally rare. In western Japan a small number of remarkable figures, either of human form or "violin" shape with indented sides, have been found. Some bear stamped decoration. Since they were recovered in house remains, they are thought to have been individual talismans (Barnes 1990a, 31).

Except for the production by men of large, heavy burial jars, pottery making probably remained a women's task (Kuraku 1989b, 106). In the Kinai region during the Late Yayoi, abstract geometric marks called *kigō* are sometimes found on vessels, usually near the shoulder (Barnes 1990a, 36). Thought to be the owner's marks, they were incised into the vessels before firing. Thus each household or social group may not have been self-sufficient in the production of vessels, which were being made by specialized craftspeople. Further evidence of changes in pottery production from household to workshop may be seen in the standardized vessel sizes and shapes of Late Yayoi vessels from the Kinai region.

A number of stylistic trends can be seen in Yayoi ceramics, the finest of which were used for burials and other ceremonial occasions. Two contrasting groups of Yayoi ceramics developed, the first from Kyūshū [125–30] and the second from the Nagoya region [131–36]. In Kyūshū the earliest Yayoi pottery, the Itazuke type, displayed simple forms of both narrow- and wide-mouthed jars and footed pedestals. Outer vessel surfaces are plain and often polished; small vessels are sometimes decorated with painting. Also from Kyūshū, the Sugu type of the Middle Yayoi includes burnished ware, often decorated with only a few bands. Late Yayoi ceramics feature ceremonial motifs of concentric arcs made by shell impressions on plain, red, or black surfaces.

In the Kinai region Middle Yayoi pottery was comb-decorated or incised with images of animals, fish, birds, raised granaries, and boats. With the exception of incised dragons—a Chinese motif that may have been reserved for decorating water or rice-wine vessels—drawn decoration disappeared during the Late Yayoi (Barnes 1990a, 36). At the same time, the Nagoya region was distinctive for its "palace style" beautifully colored and polished redware, which early twentieth-century scholars named after the Mycenaean ceramics of Knossos. Also during the Late Yayoi the Okayama region became famous for elaborately decorated cylindrical jar pedestals with cut-out sections and exquisitely incised curvilinear decorations [148]. These large ceremonial pedestals, which were placed on the surfaces of the burial mounds, are the prototypes of the cylindrical *haniwa* grave ceramics of the Kofun period.

Decoration is abundant on the shoulders of vessels from the Kantō Plain. In the northern regions of Tōhoku and particularly in Aomori, elegantly shaped, thin-walled ceramics with cord marking and incising are found. Footed vessels from northern Honshū, with their undulating rims and round forms, retain a Jōmon flavor (Seki 1985).

Metalworking

Yayoi bronze goods consisted of weapons (swords, spearheads, and halberds), mirrors, bells, and ornaments (bracelets and shell replicas). All these items, even the sharp, narrow-bladed weapons, had ceremonial significance. Mark Hudson (1990, 82), a research student at the University of Tokyo, has stated that the context of early metallurgy in Japan is one of trade and tribute. In receiving weapons from powerful chiefs, lesser chiefs and warriors participated in ceremonies of allegiance. The weapons are thought to have been important in ceremonial display as well.

Significant local production using melted-down artifacts or raw material imported from the Asian continent began only during the Middle Yayoi. Locally produced objects were most likely ceremonial— wide-bladed weapons or large, ornate bells, for example.

Bronze weapons were cast in two-piece stone molds, the sockets formed by inserting a clay plug. Other objects cast in stone molds were bracelets and ornaments. Bronze bells (*dōtaku*) were initially made in reusable sandstone molds; ten castings from the same mold have sometimes been found. Clay molds, which allowed for finer detail, were eventually produced. These required more labor overall than the stone molds since the sandstone, relatively easy to carve, could be reused, whereas the clay molds could be used for only one casting (Kuraku 1989a, 20).

Lead-isotope analysis has persuaded researchers to determine that from the Yayoi to the Kofun periods three kinds of lead (already incorporated into bronze) were imported to Japan from the Asian continent and Korean peninsula.[14] The material for the narrow daggers and fine-line mirrors came from southern Korea, possibly the Ch'ungch'ŏng region. Mirrors of the Western Han dynasty came from northern China, possibly Shaanxi Province. Those of the Eastern Han dynasty and Three Kingdoms period came from central and southern China. All the mirrors have different lead-isotope ratios from those found in metal from Japanese sources.

Bronze objects produced in Japan during the Yayoi period were made with raw material from Korea and northern China. In the Kofun period, metal from central and southern China was used; in the seventh century A.D., Japanese raw material was used for such objects as the bronze pipe of the Mizuochi water clock (Iwanaga 1989).[15]

Lead-isotope analysis clarifies the origin only of the lead in bronze; no effective method has been found to trace the origin of copper and tin. While Middle Yayoi *dōtaku* have inconsistent lead-isotope ratios, which may indicate the mixing of metals from different sources, Late Yayoi *dōtaku* display a consistent lead-isotope ratio that would support the conclusion that ingots of mixed copper, tin, and lead were imported from a specific region on the Asian continent. About four hundred bells have been recovered so far. These would have required a total of about 5,965 pounds (2,705 kg) of copper (Mori 1989b, 149, 150). Indigenous deposits of copper appear not to have been mined until the mid-seventh century A.D. (Hudson 1990, 86). Mori Kōichi, a senior archaeologist specializing in the Yayoi and Kofun periods, asserts that the mixing of different local copper sources could confuse the results of analyses, and he does not accept the results of lead-isotope testing that date the beginning of Japanese mining to the mid-seventh century. He has noted that many of the most prominent finds of *dōtaku* in the Kinai and Sea of Japan region are near copper mines known in recent times.

Bronze was a precious commodity to the Yayoi people. Bronze replicas of whorl-shaped *Harpago* shells and shell bracelets of *Laevistrombus,* worn by high-status people in Kyūshū, were made in stone molds. In the Late Yayoi, people substituted one precious medium for another by copying the shell prototypes in bronze (Pearson 1990a, 919).

Although iron was introduced into Japan slightly earlier than bronze, it was used primarily for utilitarian objects. Weapons, such as the daggers buried with Yayoi elite, are bronze rather than steel or iron. Most of the twenty-eight hundred iron pieces found to date are from the late third century A.D. from northern Kyūshū (Hudson 1990, 84). As in the Early Kofun, raw iron material was imported from Korea and some smelting was done in Japan. In Kyūshū, ironworking began in the Middle Yayoi. By the Late Yayoi, stone reaping knives were no longer used, having been replaced by iron sickles (Tsude 1988, 111).

Settlements

Excavation of entire Yayoi settlements provides important information on community structure. Villages consisted of a cluster of houses, work areas, and storage facilities, which were large pits during the Early and Middle Yayoi and elevated storehouses in the Late Yayoi. Excavated about 20 inches (50 cm) into the soil, houses were generally semisubterranean and circular, oval, or rectangular with rounded corners. A central hearth was typical; large postholes inside a structure supported the roof.

The Toro site has yielded detailed information on house construction (Aikens & Higuchi 1982, 231–34). The village was flooded, suddenly abandoned, and remained in waterlogged condition until its excavation. Oval to squarish in shape, the houses were built directly on the ground. Deep postholes positioned in a square pattern in the center of the house had been dug for the posts that supported the roof. A clay-lined fire pit was located in the middle of the house. Around the edge of the living floor was a bench about 12 inches (30 cm) high and 40 inches (1 m) wide, faced with flat panel boards held in place by stakes. The lower walls of the house extended to the ground along the outer edge of the bench. While most houses appear to have been constructed of poles and thatch, others had a long, low wall of vertically set wooden planks. Doors facing south were set with a flat board for an entrance step.

The size of recovered Yayoi settlements varies from 5 acres (2 hectares), represented by the Ōtsuka site in Kanagawa Prefecture, to 69 acres (28 hectares) at the Karako-Kagi site in Nara Prefecture (Nara Kenritsu 1989, 22). Fortification, in the form of ditches, moats, and palisades, was an essential element of most villages. There appear to have been cycles of moat construction, and from the stylistic dating of the ceramics found in the moats, it seems that peaks of moat building in northern Kyūshū occurred in the first half of the Early Yayoi, latter half of the Middle Yayoi, and middle of the Late Yayoi. In the Kinai region, moats were constructed on a different cycle.[16] In most cases the moat was associated with a series of earth embankments and constructed on an imposing scale. One at Karako-Kagi was 36 feet (11 m) wide and 6½ feet (2 m) deep.

Other sites seem to reveal periods of peace and trade between villages and regions. The Tamatsu Tanaka site in Hyōgo Prefecture, which began in the Early Yayoi and developed in the Middle Yayoi, lies between two small rivers and covers 61¾ acres (25 hectares). Evidence of exotic raw materials for stone reaping knives and beads as well as unusual pottery vessels and bronze weapons indicates that the inhabitants were involved in long-distance exchange along the Inland Sea (Nara Kenritsu 1989, 24).

Karako-Kagi, the site that yielded carbonized rice grains {106, 107}, attests to the ascendance of the Kinai region during the Middle Yayoi period. Karako began as a central settlement surrounded by smaller communities, each with its own moat. Not until the middle of the Middle Yayoi was a large encircling moat constructed around the entire area. The inner moat was 32¾ feet (10 m) wide, and the outer moat about 14¾ feet (4.5 m) wide. In scale the system rivals the moat organization found around Japanese castles of later times. It is thought that Karako was the hub of an exchange network for pottery from the Owari region near Nagoya at the head of Ise Bay to the Kibi region of Okayama Prefecture. Pottery vessels from Karako-Kagi are incised with motifs of deer and human figures as well as elevated storehouses, boats, and other subjects that may have been important in ceremonies. The inhabitants of Karako were likely raising captured wild boar as well as cultivating, hunting, and fishing (Nara Kenritsu 1989, 28).

The largest Yayoi settlement discovered to date is Asahi in Aichi Prefecture. It is situated on the Owari Plain, now far inland, but it originally enjoyed favorable access to the sea. Including the cemetery, the site covers 173 to 198 acres (70–80 hectares). From the end of the Early Yayoi to the beginning of the Middle Yayoi, Asahi was a center of local exchange. A large moated precinct, 112 by 78¾ feet (34 × 24 m), was constructed in the early part of the Middle Yayoi, while another moat, 115 feet (35 m) long, was built in the latter half of the Middle Yayoi. It appears that an elite social group emerged quickly and possessed power comparable to that of elite groups in Kyūshū.

Melvin Aikens, professor of anthropology at the University of Oregon, and Higuchi Takayasu, director of the Nara Prefectural Kashihara Archaeological Research Institute, have described several other Yayoi settlements (Aikens & Higuchi 1982, 199–241). The Ōtsuka site in Kanagawa Prefecture, located on a low hill, yielded ninety late Middle Yayoi structures in an area of about 5 acres (2 hectares) surrounded by a ditch and a possible outer earthwork. Small single-family dwellings seem to have been distributed in three clusters, each with two particularly large dwellings and elevated storehouses. A total of thirty structures may have been occupied at any one time (Aikens & Higuchi 1982, 241).

Burials

Although their relationships are not always clear, several forms of burial occurred in the Yayoi: simple earth-pit burial, primary jar burial, secondary jar burial, stone-coffin burial, and stone-lined pit burial. The social significance of the variations has not been investigated thoroughly. Bone or other organic materials survive poorly in the acidic soils of Japan; without knowledge of age, sex, trauma, nutrition, and cause of death, it is difficult to link burial customs to social organization.

At Itazuke, adults were buried in wooden coffins and children in ceramic jars. Wooden coffin burial, ultimately of Chinese origin, was also used by the Korean elite at that time. It is possible, but not probable, that Yayoi jar burial may have been a continuation of a custom from the Late and Final Jōmon in which most such burials were for young or unborn children.

By the beginning of the Middle Yayoi, northern Kyūshū had developed a burial system independent from other parts of Asia. Adults in Kyūshū were buried in large undecorated ceramic burial jars, which resemble the Kimhae jars of the southeastern Korean peninsula. The absence of grave goods in the majority of cases indicates that the custom was not limited to the highest elite. Extremely large plain vessels with simple decoration such as an applied ridge were used for primary burial. Typically two jars were placed horizontally in the ground, mouth to mouth. The deceased individual, in flexed position, was put in one jar; the other jar was placed in the ground adjacent to the first. Occasionally a single jar was used, with a flat stone for a cover. On rare occasions the jars were painted black on the inside and outside, as at Yoshinogari, or red on the inside.[17] Some portion of the population, presumably of lower status, judging from the absence of grave goods, was buried in simple earth pits. These burials are difficult to discern in excavation owing to the poor preservation of bone.

The burial system using wooden coffins prevailed in the Kinki region. It is possible that Asian continental practices such as burial in wooden coffins bypassed the northern Kyūshū region and were adapted directly in the Nara area. In the Yayoi practice of secondary burial, bones were exhumed sometime after the initial burial, then washed, occasionally painted with red ocher, and placed in jars. The jars were then buried, often collectively, in large pits, some of which were surrounded by moats

(Saitō 1983, 322). Bones were sometimes crushed and placed in the vessels, accompanied at times with beads (Hudson 1990, 86).

Archaeologists in the 1960s recognized a distinct burial form, a rectangular-shaped mound with small ditches along the sides that are not joined at the corners. For lack of a more descriptive term, this burial form has come to be known as the "moated precinct." Containing from five to fifteen or more burials, thought to be family graves, they usually occur in clusters of ten to thirty. The earliest examples are found in the Kinai region and date to the middle of the Early Yayoi. During the Middle Yayoi the moated-precinct burial was adopted in the Kantō Plain, where it replaced secondary jar burials. The form spread northward to the Tōhoku region in the Late Yayoi and was not used in Kyūshū until the Kofun period.

Other types of mound burials were constructed for powerful chiefs and their families. The earliest example occurs at the Mine site in Fukuoka Prefecture, which dates to the first half of the Early Yayoi. The mound is about 59 feet (18 m) long, 42⅝ feet (13 m) wide, and 3¼ feet (1 m) high. By the Middle Yayoi a mound twice that size, the largest Yayoi mound burial known, was built at Yoshinogari (Hudson 1990).[18]

The Late Yayoi mound of Tatetsuki in Okayama Prefecture provides an important example of the scale of burial facilities for paramount chiefs (Kondō 1986). The burial mound was 141 feet (43 m) wide and 14¾ feet (4.5 m) high and had two earthen projections.[19] Inside the rectangular wooden chamber was a wooden coffin 6½ feet (2 m) long. An exceptional amount of cinnabar, some 66 pounds (30 kg), was spread in the coffin.[20]

The projections attached to the Tatetsuki mound may represent the origins of the triangular or rectangular front mound of the keyhole-shaped burials of the Kofun period: the manner of placing the jars and pedestals on top of the mounds is also similar to the pattern of offerings for the later keyhole-shaped mounds. The types of personal burial offerings—swords, beads, and in some cases mirrors—in Yayoi elite burials also anticipate the burial practices of the Kofun period.

The recently discovered Shibagahara burial mound from the Yamashiro region north of Kyoto spans the chronological boundary between the Yayoi and Kofun periods. A small keyhole-shaped mound, it is thought to be a chief's tomb, constructed shortly before the Tsubai Ōtsukayama Kofun.[21] Of particular interest were the shards of four Shōnai-type narrow-necked jars on the surface of the mound, together with an elevated pedestal. On the basis of the ceramics, the archaeologists dated the mound to the third century A.D. (Kyoto Furitsu 1987, 4–7).

The Yayoi period marked the first appearance in Japan of differences in wealth that were most clearly manifested in contrasting burial practices, in variation in the size and complexity of burial facilities, and in the types and quantity of grave goods. Such distinctions are not well corroborated in other aspects of social life such as residential architecture. Certain individuals or families were buried in segregated facilities, in large mounds or moated precincts, with objects obtained through long-distance trade, such as shell bracelets, Chinese bronze mirrors, or bronze weapons. Shell bracelets exchanged from Okinawa to Kyūshū played an important role in marking status distinctions. The most precious were *gohōra* (*Tricornis latissimus Linne*) bracelets [141] found in burials only on the right arms of a few males, who may possibly have been religious specialists (Pearson 1990a).[22] Other objects, such as glass beads or bronze ornaments, were locally produced. Although elite burials all required great amounts of labor and resources (termed "energy expenditure" by anthropologists) and elaborate preparation, forms of burial mounds varied during the Yayoi period in comparison with those of the subsequent Kofun period, suggesting that the centralized regulation of social customs was not yet well developed.

Analysis of grave goods from cemeteries of different periods during the Yayoi does not indicate enduring unification or regional centers of power in the valleys or river-drainage systems of northern Kyūshū. In other words, the greatest concentrations of wealth in burials, which actually consisted of small numbers of objects, did not remain at the same site for more than one subperiod within the Early, Middle, or Late Yayoi (Stark 1989). This finding suggests fluidity in the concentration of power.[23]

In the Yayoi period in Kyūshū only a few individuals in each cemetery were buried with grave goods. Since the total number of burials is often omitted in discussions of grave goods, it is difficult to ascertain the relative proportion of individuals of high rank to commoners. It can be noted, however, that of the hundreds or thousands of burials at the Yoshinogari site, only a few individuals were buried in the main mound with grave goods.

The burial ritual for the Yayoi elite stressed the importance of precious magical objects of exotic materials. The beliefs underlying the burial practices are difficult to grasp but seem to center on symbolic weapons and ritual regalia. Evidence suggests that food receptacles for feasting and drinking may have been deposited outside the grave.

Ritual Metalwork. The creation of *dōtaku* bells in Japan marks a distinctive phase of the Yayoi period. The prototype is a small Korean horse bell. While some small *dōtaku* have been found in Kyūshū, the greatest concentration is in the region of the Inland Sea. It has been proposed that this region was characterized by rituals involving bronze bells, while the northern Kyūshū region favored the use of bronze weapons. Bronze regalia are thought to have been communal property rather than the exclusive possessions of elite persons.

Dōtaku are found buried, often in caches, in isolated places and are virtually never discovered in dwellings or refuse. It is thought that their ritual power made it impossible to dispose of them near human settlements; hence, they never occur as grave offerings. The shape of the *dōtaku* is that of a truncated cone, with a flange extending lengthwise along the sides and across the top of the body. The top of the flange is perforated for suspension of a tongue or clapper. The sound of the *dōtaku* is described as rattling (Aikens & Higuchi 1982, 218).

The decoration of the *dōtaku* is often laid out in registers consisting of depictions of seasonal activities such as hunting, fishing, or hulling rice [121]. Other patterns may be geometric. Deer are the most common among animal motifs, followed by wild boar and long-legged shorebirds. Less common are spiders, praying mantis, frogs, lizards, crabs, monkeys, and dogs. Later styles developed elaborate flanges and attached circular ornaments.

Figure 17
Sixteen bronze weapons and six
dōtaku bells found at the Kōjindani
site, Shimane Prefecture. The
discovery of weapons and *dōtaku* at
the same site confirms that they
were used together in Yayoi rituals.

A spectacular cache of bronze objects was excavated in 1984 and 1985
at Kōjindani in Shimane Prefecture on Honshū (fig. 17). The site is
located on a valley hillside near Lake Shinji along the coast of the Sea of
Japan, a region previously thought to be remote from major centers of
Yayoi culture.[24] A total of 358 bronze daggers, all set on edge next
to one another, six bronze bells, and sixteen bronze halberds were
found (Piggott 1989). While caches of bronze weapons and bells have
been previously recovered in other parts of Kyūshū and the Kinai
region, the size of the Kōjindani find has no parallel.[25] The discovery
of both *dōtaku* and weapons at Kōjindani confirms that they were used
together in rituals.

The bronze daggers were of a medium-wide type originally made
in northern Kyūshū but later more dispersed. It is thought that the
daggers and *dōtaku* were produced locally but that the halberds were
from northern Kyūshū and brought to the Izumo region of eastern
Shimane Prefecture.

Many archaeologists have attempted to explain the Kōjindani cache.
Theories range from considering it as a temporary hiding place to pre-
suming it was a ritual site, the latter hypothesis supported by the symmetrical disposition of the bronzes. The caches may have been assembled
in preparation for power struggles between Izumo and the Kibi region
or in light of the encroaching power of Kinai rulers (Terasawa 1989).

Mirrors were not manufactured in Japan in large quantities until the Kofun period. They are circular with cast-relief decoration on the back. Most are of Chinese style, said to have been imported via the Korean peninsula, from the Chinese Han dynasty garrisons such as Lelang and Taebang in west-central Korea.

Mirrors of the Western Han dynasty have been found in Kyūshū, while those of the Eastern Han of the so-called TLV type and petaloid decoration (*naikōkamonkyō*) are found in the Kinai region as well. A group of three mirrors from Futatsukayama in Saga Prefecture include an early example of Japanese manufacture with an imitation Chinese inscription [151].

One particular mirror type dating to the third century A.D. is of great interest to archaeologists. A triangular-rimmed mirror with a pattern of deities and animals, it is the so-called *sankakuen shinjū kyō,* the "triangular-rimmed mirror with deities and animals." About three hundred mirrors of this type have been found in Japan. Miyazaki Ichisada (1988), the foremost Japanese historian of China, has proposed that the triangular-rimmed type might have been made in Taebang. Wang Zhongshu (1981) of the Institute of Archaeology, Beijing, has proposed that the triangular-rimmed mirrors were made in Japan by artisans from the southern Chinese state of Wu. One of his reasons for assuming a non-Chinese origin for the mirrors is the presence of what he believed to be the umbrella pine motif, which occupies the space between the seated human figures. Niiro Izumi (1989, 152) of Okayama University has demonstrated, however, that the motif represents a tiered standard of the type seen on the walls of tombs of the Korean kingdom of Koguryŏ. Such standards were conferred sparingly on surrounding polities at the end of the Han dynasty to acknowledge relationships with subordinate kings. Did the Japanese understand the Chinese symbols well enough to manipulate them on mirrors of their own manufacture, or were they made in China to bestow on Japanese rulers? With each new study concerning the mirrors, the potential for exploring political relationships increases.

At the end of the Yayoi period, copies of Chinese mirrors were made in southern Korea and Japan [150, 51]. About 150 of these, each smaller than 3⅜ inches (10 cm) in diameter, have so far been found in Japanese sites.

Social Organization: War and Confederation

The preoccupation with metal blades as symbols of status and magic that is seen in Yayoi Japan was common among cultures located in the periphery of the great centers of metal production, both in Europe and eastern Asia (Nakamura 1989, 37). Bronze daggers, descendants of originals from northeastern China and the Korean peninsula, were symbols of high office among Kyūshū chiefs. Their use also spread to the Kinai region, where they were less numerous.

Warfare is considered to have been a major feature of Yayoi society. The causes of this warfare are not completely clear. Expanding agricultural populations may have required more land, especially that suitable for rice cultivation. Not all archaeologists agree, however, that rice was the most important food source for the Yayoi people. Population pressure on land resources cannot, therefore, be convincingly demonstrated without careful study of the ratios of land to sites and their estimated population. Melvin Aikens and Higuchi Takayasu (1982, 225, 226) have proposed that sites were abandoned and their populations dislocated owing to flooding caused by higher sea levels around the Middle Yayoi. They contend that competition from the dispossessed communities led to warfare. While alluvial clay layers in the low-lying sites near Osaka seem to indicate this kind of flooding, it is not clear whether the situation was so widespread as to be a major factor in the rise of warfare. Shifts in power relations among chiefs may have been more important factors than pressure on food resources. Competition for access to trade routes and goods may also have led to warfare.[26] Most likely, both social competition and environmental and subsistence factors may have worked together to bring about the need for defense.

In societies in which warfare occurs regularly, confederacies are usually important. Archaeologists have proposed that Chinese mirrors of the triangular-rimmed type were symbols of alliances centered around the Kinai region in the third century A.D. In a ground-breaking study linking the distribution of mirrors to social organization, Professor Kobayashi Yukio of the University of Kyoto discovered a network of relationships among tombs sharing mirrors cast from the same mold (Kobayashi Yukio 1961). Further fieldwork since the 1960s has extended his study. Tsubai Ōtsukayama burial mound in Kyoto Prefecture yielded more than thirty-six mirrors of all types, thirty-three of which were of a triangular-rimmed type. Within this type, mirrors from the same molds have been found in many mounds.[27] The distribution of burial mounds containing mirrors from the same mold as those found in Tsubai Ōtsukayama extends from Chiba and Gumma prefectures in the east to Nagano and Tottori prefectures in central Japan and Fukuoka and Saga prefectures in the west. In addition, the distribution of locally made mirrors (as distinct from those produced in China) also provides some interesting patterns.[28]

Kobayashi Yukio (1961, 193) has also noted that the outlying burial mounds such as Haraguchi in Fukuoka Prefecture and Akatsuka in Ōita Prefecture—which yielded mirrors cast from the same molds as those from Tsubai Ōtsukayama—are the earliest type of burial mound in each region. He speculated that the local chiefs were tied into a political network probably centered on Tsubai Ōtsukayama before the appearance of burial mounds. The area under the control of these great chiefs was probably the terminus of a water route connecting the Yayoi center of power and the Inland Sea via the Yodo and Kizu rivers.

The distribution pattern of related mirrors is material evidence of an exchange network between central powers and outlying chiefs. The large-scale tombs of the third century A.D. as well as the concentration of prestige goods may indicate the rise of a centralized power in the general Kinai region, the locus of later Japanese state development. It is difficult to break this trend into the Yayoi and Kofun periods, when it is part of the same political process. Many writers place the Tsubai-Ōtsukayama site in the Kofun period rather than in the Yayoi period. It is not possible to date the mirrors exactly, in the absence of dated Chinese prototypes.

The Historical Record

Yayoi Japan is mentioned in three Chinese documents: *Hou Han shu* (Records of the Later Han Dynasty); *Dongyi zhuan* (Record of the Eastern Barbarians), a section of the *Wei zhi* (Annals of the State of Wei); and *Han shu* (Records of the Han Dynasty).

The *Hou Han shu* was not written until A.D. 445. The chronicle mentions the conferring in A.D. 57 of a gold seal by the Han Emperor Guangwu (r. A.D. 25–57) to a chief of northern Kyūshū. A seal inscribed with the Chinese characters *"Han Wo Nu guowang"* ("King [of the] state of Nu of Wo, [vassal] of Han") was found in 1784 in a grave on Shiga-noshima, an island mear Fukuoka in Kyūshū. The *Hou Han shu* also details a tribute mission from Wo, as Japan was called by the Chinese, to China in A.D. 57 and 107.

Of the three documents, the *Wei zhi* is the most informative. Based on a no-longer-extant historical work, the *Wei shu* (written in A.D. 266), the *Wei zhi* was completed in A.D. 297 by Chen Shou (A.D. 233–97), a Chinese official of the Western Jin dynasty. The *Wei zhi* briefly describes life in Japan during the Yayoi period. The following passage is from the *Wei zhi:*

The people of Wa [Wo] dwell in the middle of the ocean on the mountainous islands southeast of [the prefecture of] Taifang. They formerly comprised more than one hundred commanderies. During the Han dynasty [Wa envoys] appeared at the court; today, thirty of their communities maintain intercourse [with us] through envoys and scribes. . . .

The country [of Yamatai] formerly had a man as ruler. For some seventy or eighty years after that there were disturbances and warfare. Thereupon the people agreed upon a woman for their ruler. Her name was Himiko. She occupied herself with magic and sorcery, bewitching the people. Though mature in age, she remained unmarried. She had a younger brother who assisted her in ruling the country. After she became the ruler, there were few who saw her. She had one thousand women as attendants, but only one man. He served her food and drink and acted as a medium of communication. She resided in a palace surrounded by towers and stockades, with armed guards in a state of constant vigilance [Tsunoda & Goodrich 1951, 8, 13].

Gina Lee Barnes (1983, 160), a Cambridge University archaeologist who specializes in ancient Japanese state development, has cautioned that "care must be taken in reading these Chinese descriptions for they exhibit the tendency of any sophisticated society to interpret simpler social systems in terms of their own sophisticated organizations." In addition to the problem of interpreting the description of simpler political systems as written by participants in a more complex system, we also must consider the specific effect of Chinese political culture and the Chinese worldview. The Chinese sought well-defined pathways of authority and regulation of markets and may have assumed the existence of such in Japan where the economic system was not so complex.

Both archaeological evidence and the Chinese writings indicate that Yayoi Japan was in contact with China and Korea, but the supraordinate role of Yamatai (the term used in the Chinese records) is not apparent from the archaeological record. Barnes (1983, 160) has pointed out that "both the archaeological record and the Chinese documents concur on the structure of Japanese society in the third century as a number of polities integrated by trade conducted between economically specialized villages and regulated by common agricultural rites involving ceremonial use of imported bronze mirrors and locally produced bronze bells and weapons."

Summary

Increased agricultural productivity, based primarily on irrigated rice cultivation, provided a firm economic base for social transformation during the Yayoi period. By the third century small-scale chiefdoms in northern Kyūshū were superseded by larger, centralized chiefdoms in the Kinai region. The rich documentation provided by Yayoi archaeology offers a unique picture of political change spanning six centuries.

Yayoi villages display increased storage capacity, with communal storage facilities such as pit dwellings and raised warehouses. Although high social rank was marked by segregated tombs and grave offerings, those distinctions were limited to small numbers of people. Compared to other chiefly societies, status differentiation was slight. Social delineations have not yet been recognized in Yayoi residential structures. Yayoi ritual life is distinguished by the use of bells and weapons. Objects of daily use in ancient China, mirrors assumed magical significance in Japan. Female rulers were also distinctive to Japan.

Historical sources mention that the Wa people, who inhabited coastal Korea as well as Japan, went to the Chinese court to gain political and economic favors. The chronicles state that chiefs coordinated long-distance trade of bronze and glass objects and sponsored craft specialization in glass, textiles, woodworking, and pottery.

The interaction of the Yayoi people with the Epi-Jōmon cultures in Hokkaidō and with Okinawa is the first instance in which Japanese society of the heartland maintained relations with the simpler societies of the outlying regions.

Notes

1. Radiocarbon dates, like all products of statistical procedure, are subject to a range of error. This range, one standard deviation of the count of radioactive particles given off by the specimen, brackets the date by about one or two centuries and is dependent on a number of factors. There is one chance in three that the date falls outside the range of the standard deviation. Radiocarbon dating thus gives a range, not a precise date, and is less useful for dating short periods of time.

2. The Jōmon people tended to be quite short, with the average height of a male being about 5⅛ feet (156 cm) toward the end of the period. The limb bones were robust, muscle attachments well developed, and the face wide and square. The Yayoi population was taller, with the average male height about 5¼ feet (160 cm), the bone structure lighter, and the face longer.

3. While Yayoi ceramics sometimes display complex surface decoration, produced by the use of combs or paddles, the decor is less sculptural than that of Jōmon pottery. The surface decoration of Yayoi ceramics in northeastern Japan follows the tradition of Jōmon ceramics, with the use of cord marking and simple incising. Jōmon ceramics are outstanding in their display of decorated, textured surfaces.

4. The sluice is 6½ feet (2 m) wide and 3¼ feet (1 m) deep.

5. The ditch is 426½ feet (130 m) long, 16½ feet (5 m) wide, and 3¼ feet (1 m) deep.

6. From the Ikegami site near Osaka a high percentage of sixty wild-boar skulls were of young animals, suggesting that they may have been in an initial stage of domestication (Sahara 1987a, 134; Kōmoto 1989).

7. Microscopic studies of the edges of polished-stone reaping knives indicate that the cutting of plant stems, which contain silica, were used to polish the stone.

8. Large bifacial axes used for felling trees or splitting wood were made of hard basalt quarried from Iwayama and Nokoshima mountains in Fukuoka Prefecture. The axes are distributed widely in Fukuoka, eastern Ōita, and Saga prefectures. Tateiwa in Iizuka City, Fukuoka, may have been a center of production of stone reaping knives (Mori 1989a, 143).

9. Almost 4½ pounds (2 kg) of discarded glass was recovered in Hyakkengawa houses.

10. The San'in area comprises northern Kyoto and Hyōgo prefectures as well as Tottori and Shimane prefectures. Hokuriku consists of Fukui, Ishikawa, Niigata, and Toyama prefectures.

11. Chinese ceramics of the Warring States period were hard, gray vessels. They were made by beating clay over an anvil with a paddle carved with geometric motifs to produce a surface with a regular geometric stamped decoration. In the Proto-Three Kingdoms period in Korea a soft, gray tilelike pottery has been identified. It is thought to be ancestral to the hard, gray stoneware of the Three Kingdoms period, which was taken into Japan from Korea in the fifth century A.D.

12. The relatively hard, brown earthenware of the Comb Pattern period in Korea was replaced by Plain Coarse Pottery as early as 1500 B.C. in the northern part of the Korean peninsula and 1000 B.C. in the south. This pottery, which broke easily, was orange in color and very soft and coarse. It is somewhat similar to the Yayoi pottery of Japan in its paste, color, and consistency.

13. Wares made of soft clay, either gray or burnished black, possibly made to imitate metal, were found in the fourth-century B.C. tombs of the Zhongshan royalty, in Hebei, northern China. In some cases it appears that metallic paints were applied and then polished to produce decorative effects.

14. Lead-isotope analysis is used to examine the ratios of different isotopes of lead, which are characteristic and unchanging for each geographic source of lead ore. The ratio does not change even in the process of alloying.

15. Mabuchi Hisaō, Hirao Yoshimitsu, and Masaki Nishida (1985) have concluded that the earliest bronze objects made in Japan were fashioned from melted-down, narrow-bladed bronze daggers from Korea; later the raw metal was imported to Japan. It is possible, however, that the Japanese also recycled Han dynasty bronze artifacts. From the Late Yayoi period ingots of copper, tin, and lead, made in China for export, were available throughout western Japan.

   A drawback to Mabuchi's conclusions is that lead-isotope analysis measures lead, not copper, which allows the possibility that native copper might have been mixed with the imported lead or bronze. Other researchers have suggested that local copper from Japan was mixed with imported lead.

16. In the Kinai region, moats were constructed at the end of the Early Yayoi, middle of the Middle Yayoi, end of the Middle Yayoi, and middle of the Late Yayoi (Nara Kenritsu 1989, 20).

17. At Tateiwa in northern Kyūshū the inside of one burial jar was painted with red lacquer.

18. Yoshinogari (discussed in this publication by Sahara Makoto, 154–57) contained the remains of 350 structures and two thousand burials that yielded more than three hundred preserved skeletons.

19. Two rows of standing stones, 3¼ to 6½ feet (1–2 m) high, separated by a band of gravel fill, encircled the mound. The primary burial lay in the center of the mound in a pit 29½ feet (9.0 m) long, 18 feet (5.5 m) wide, and 6 feet (1.8 m) deep.

20. The wooden chamber was 11½ by 4⅞ feet (3.5 × 1.5 m). Near the head of the coffin was a necklace of one jade *magatama,* seventeen jasper cylindrical beads, and one agate bead. An iron sword was placed at the individual's right side, together with several hundred small jasper cylindrical beads and small glass beads. A platform composed of a thick layer of pebbles covered the coffin. From the pebbles were recovered fragments of a unique clay female figure, with incised decoration around the neck representing two *magatama,* a large stone sculpture with a curvilinear incised pattern, and a substantial amount of ceremonial pottery. Two other wooden coffins, poorly furnished and without grave goods, were recovered elsewhere in the mound. They are thought to be burials made after the primary burial.

21. The mound is 69 feet (21 m) long and 11⅛ feet (3.4 m) high. The burial, in a vertical pit with wooden coffin, was accompanied by a mirror, an extremely rare third-century A.D. example of the four-animal, four-nipple type (most are from the fifth century), two shell-shaped bronze bracelets, eight jadeite *magatama,* 187 pipe-shaped beads of jasper, an iron plane, and eight iron needles. Above the coffin was one unidentifiable piece of iron.

22. Other ornaments included shell rings and necklaces, such as the examples from the Doigahama cemetery, Yamaguchi Prefecture [141–45]. The *gohōra,* or *Tricornis,* are tropical snaillike creatures with shells about eight inches (20.3 cm) long.

23. It is important to keep in mind that during the Yayoi period changes in burial customs could affect the range and quantity of burial goods so that the relationship of the number of burial goods to one's exact position in a political hierarchy was not constant.

24. Two steps were cut into the slope of the valley. In the lower step a rectangular pit was excavated, and in it 358 daggers were placed in four rows of 34, 111, 120, and 93, from west to east. It is thought that the swords had been bound in seven groups of forty to sixty each and that the binding cords had decomposed. Directly on top of the daggers was a layer of black soil that may be the remains of a cloth covering. Over the dark layer was a layer of pale yellow earth, pebbles, and clay, followed by yellowish brown clay. Three pits on the upper terrace and one on the lower terrace may indicate the existence of some solid structural covering. About twenty-three feet (7 m) from this cache, at the same elevation, was a second pit, slightly smaller than the former, containing sixteen halberds set on edge with tips and sockets alternating on the east side and six bronze bells on the west side. Pale yellow clay soil covered the objects to form a mound.

25. The Sakuragaoka find in Hyōgo Prefecture, for instance, contained a cache of fourteen bronze bells, while three different locations at the foot of Mount Ōiwa, Koshinohara, and Yasu-gun in Shiga Prefecture yielded one, nine, and thirteen bells respectively (Sahara 1987a, 281). One Sakuragaoka bell has a flowing-water pattern, another features partitioned panels depicting seasonal activities [121, 122].

26. Anthropological archaeologists have identified competition among chiefs and their families as an important factor in primitive warfare. As in any society, elites compete for intangible badges of no commercial value and followers align themselves with these powerful people. Warfare takes place when trade routes are blocked or threatened. Some writers have referred to the "prestige-goods economy" (Frankenstein & Rowlands 1978) to describe the circulation of rare, nonutilitarian goods to elite members of political alliances, while others have termed this phenomenon the "wealth or valuable-goods economy" (Helms 1979, 1988).

27. Thirty-six were of the triangular-rimmed type, of which twenty-nine were made from common molds. Four subtypes of mirrors were shared by forty-one tombs located over a wide area of Japan; these tombs contained a total of fifty-seven mirrors.

28. Several keyhole-shaped mounds in the Kyoto region, dating to the third century A.D. and belonging to the transition between the Yayoi and Kofun periods, yielded mirrors of local manufacture that share molds with mirrors found in Aichi, Okayama, Saga, Shiga, and Shimane prefectures, evidence that suggests a second set of relationships (Kyoto Furitsu 1987).

YOSHINOGARI: THE WORLD OF THE WEI DYNASTY ANNALS

SAHARA MAKOTO

From 1986 to 1989, before construction of an industrial complex, the Saga Prefectural Education Commission excavated Yoshinogari (fig. 18). Excavations yielded data that clarified aspects of the center of one of the Yayoi chiefdoms mentioned in the *Wei zhi*.

It is recorded in this third-century Chinese chronicle that sometime between A.D. 170 and 180 the thirty chiefdoms of Wa were at war with one another. When Queen Himiko of Yamatai in Wa gained control, fighting subsided. The result was a united chiefdom with Himiko as the supreme ruler. The residence of Himiko is said to have included a palace, watchtower, and earthen wall with rows of palings. In A.D. 239, Himiko sent an envoy to the Wei emperor in China, and she was subsequently given the title Xin Wei Wo Wang (literally, "Monarch of the Wa, Friendly to Wei").[1] It was reported that when she died, she was buried in an elaborately large funerary mound. Since the *Wei zhi* is, in part, archaeologically accurate, dubious, and idealized, the description of Himiko's residence, therefore, was not assumed reliable until recently, when archaeological discoveries at Yoshinogari confirmed the existence of such buildings.

Many long, low hills stretch to the south from the Seburi mountain range, which runs east to west, marking the northern boundary of the Saga Plain in Kyūshū. Yoshinogari is located on one of those hills, 66 feet (20 m) above sea level.[2] The southern limit of the Saga Plain is the Ariake Sea. At present, Yoshinogari is slightly more than 6¼ miles (10 km) from the coast; during the Yayoi period, it would have been a mere 3 to 3¾ miles (5–6 km) from the coast.

Yoshinogari was occupied over several centuries. Excavations have revealed that around the fourth to third century B.C. a rice-farming population came to live in Yoshinogari. It was surrounded by a dry moat, from which pig bones have been recovered. Outside this moat was a bronze-casting workshop. Archaeologists found dagger molds, together with broken pieces of a spearhead mold, a mold for a decorative fixture for a shield (a bronze whorl plaque with a central boss), and a tin fragment.

In the first century B.C. an area of Yoshinogari was surrounded by a large dry outer moat with a V-shaped cross section.[3] A village dating from the first century B.C. to the first century A.D. was located in the southern half of the area surrounded by the outer moat. A burial mound was located in the northernmost area.[4] The mound was constructed with hardened layers of pounded earth.

An important discovery was that the outer moat was left open at two points, to the southwest and northeast of the mound, providing an entrance and exit to the elite burial area. In particular, the southwest entrance served as an approach to the mound for the populace. Many ritual vessels were found by the side of the access path, suggesting that people of several villages under the control of Yoshinogari were obliged to come there to pay their respects. The chiefdom's authority is also reflected in the Chinese historical annals by the use of the term *"guo,"* meaning "country," to describe Yoshinogari.

Six jar burials were discovered during the excavation of the burial mound. Inside the mound a large jar 4¼ feet (1.3 m) or more in height had been placed in each pit before the deceased was put in the jar. A second jar was positioned mouth to mouth against the first. Five jars contained bronze daggers and numerous cylindrical blue glass beads (fig. 19). About twenty jar burials seem to have been arranged within the mound, which was for several decades the resting place for the elite of Yoshinogari.

Altogether, two thousand jar burials and 330 pit graves were discovered at Yoshinogari. The jar burials were located in several places besides the mound. In a common pattern at the site, two rows of jar burials— located 13⅛ to 16½ feet (4–5 m) apart and extending for 656 to 1,640 feet (200–500 m)—were discovered inside and outside the outer moat. More than three hundred skeletons were found. Their osteological characteristics demonstrate that the people of Yoshinogari were not descen-

Figure 18
Yoshinogari site, Saga Prefecture. Excavators uncovered a moated, fortified settlement with watchtowers, storehouses, a large cemetery, and a large burial mound for elite individuals. The site is shown after excavation and reconstruction of main buildings (*right*). Modern protective structures have been built over some features.

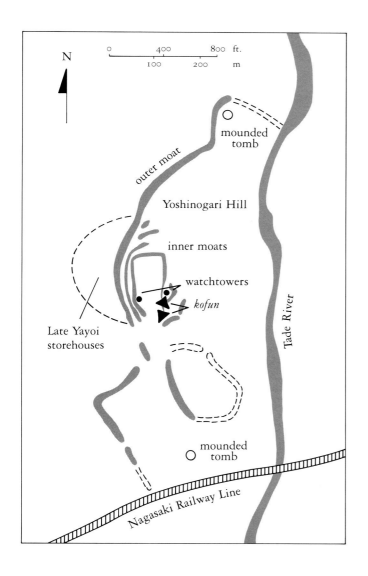

Figure 19
Glass beads and bronze dagger
[146,147] recovered from Yoshinogari, pictured as originally found
by excavators in a large earthenware
burial jar (now shattered).

dants of Jōmon populations but were of Asian continental origin. Victims of battles, such as individuals whose skulls are missing or, in one example, with twelve arrowheads piercing the bone, can be identified. Fragments of silk, hemp, and hair have been recovered from the jar burials.

An inner moat constructed in the second to third century A.D. surrounded the central portion of the area defined by the outer moat.[5] Within the inner moat about one hundred pit dwellings were found. C-shaped protuberances in certain parts of the inner moat attracted the attention of excavators. Postholes arranged immediately inside the protuberances are assumed to be watchtower remains. Soil that had spilled into the inner moat suggests that earth had been piled outside the moat to form a defensive wall. Rows of palings erected on the earthen wall, together with the evidence of watchtowers, recall battle descriptions in the *Wei zhi*. Within the inner moat was an elevated structure surrounded by a ditch 3¼ feet (1 m) wide and forming a square 65½ feet (20 m) on each side. Some archaeologists assume this to have been a palace.

To the west of the outer moat were nearly fifty elevated storage houses.[6] These were much larger than the average storehouses of the Yayoi period, which were about half as long. The Yoshinogari storage facilities were quite imposing and of appropriate size to store harvested rice, which was collected as taxes by the chiefdom (fig. 20).

The elaborately built burial mound, earthen walls with palings, and large storage houses indicate that Yoshinogari was the center of a chiefdom contemporaneous with Yamatai, the chiefdom described in the *Wei zhi*. Some people have even surmised that Yoshinogari and Yamatai were the same place.

Interim restoration at Yoshinogari has been completed on several structures and earthen walls with palings in preparation for the creation of a full-scale archaeological park. The Japanese people have a great interest in Yoshinogari. Over the time span of eighteen months, ending in January 1991, 3.6 million people visited the site. In the spring of 1991 the Japanese government designated Yoshinogari as a special historic site.

Notes

1. The dates of the Wei dynasty are A.D. 220–65.

2. Yoshinogari was a large village more than 656 feet (200 m) from north to south and 393¾ to 525 feet (120–160 m) from east to west.

3. The area was 14 acres (35 hectares), spanning more than ⅝ miles (1 km) from north to south and 984 to 2,297 feet (300–700 m) from east to west. The moat was 19¾ to 23 feet (6–7 m) wide and 11½ feet (3.5 m) deep in the well-preserved portions.

4. The burial mound was 131¼ feet (40 m) from north to south and 85¼ feet (26 m) from east to west and 14¾ feet (4.5 m) in original height.

5. The outer moat is 492 feet (150 m) from north to south and 230 to 262½ feet (70–80 m) from east to west.

6. The houses were 19¾ to 23 feet (6–7 m) long.

Figure 20
Reconstruction of storage structures at Yoshinogari, a site that yielded the remains of some 330 pit graves and 2,000 jar burials.

Epi-Jōmon culture;
ca. Late Yayoi period
(A.D. 100–250)
Excavated at Usu 10, Hokkaidō
Sapporo Medical University,
Hokkaidō

93
Spearhead
Antler
8½ × ⅞ in. (21.5 × 2.2 cm)

94
Spearhead
Antler
7⅝ × ¾ in. (19.5 × 2.0 cm)

95
Harpoon head
Antler
6½ × 1 in. (16.7 × 2.5 cm)

96
Harpoon head
Antler
4¾ × ¾ in. (12.3 × 1.9 cm)

97
Toggle harpoon head
Antler
4⅜ × 1⅝ in. (11.2 × 4.2 cm)

98
Toggle harpoon head
Antler
5¾ × 1³⁄₁₆ in. (14.5 × 3.0 cm)

99
Toggle harpoon head
Antler
4⅛ × 1½ in. (10.6 × 3.7 cm)

100
Toggle harpoon head
Antler
4 × ⅞ in. (10.4 × 2.3 cm)

101
Fishhook container
Bone
5⅛ × ¾ in. (13.0 × 2.0 cm)

102
Spatula with bear design
Antler
9⅜ × 2 in. (23.8 × 5.0 cm)

Around 400 B.C. the technique of rice-paddy cultivation was introduced to Kyūshū from the Asian continent. Previously based on hunting and gathering, the society quickly became agricultural. The diffusion of rice cultivation was rapid, presumably reaching the northern Tōhoku region within several decades. At roughly the same time, bronze objects, such as weapons, mirrors, and other ritual goods—symbolizing the powerful elite who controlled land and trade—were introduced to Japan.

In Hokkaidō, meanwhile, where climatic conditions were inappropriate for rice cultivation, hunting and gathering continued to be practiced. Owing to the extremely different circumstances existing in Hokkaidō at the time, the culture there is called Epi-Jōmon. Initially concurrent with the Yayoi period in Honshū in the south, the Epi-Jōmon continued well beyond the Yayoi period in Hokkaidō. The end of the culture corresponds with the founding in A.D. 710 of the Heijō capital in Nara. In the mid-eighth century it evolved into a new culture, called Satsumon.

The swallow-tailed toggle harpoon [98], a type of rotating harpoon, is a typical implement of the Epi-Jōmon culture. Over time, harpoon heads [99, 100] became more elaborate and refined. Only a few reliable examples of associated metal artifacts have been documented, but traces of the use of metal tools for shaping bone or antler implements are known. The implements were made mostly of the leg bones and antlers of the Ezo deer.

Usu 10 site is located about 328 feet (100 m) inland on an island off the coast of Hokkaidō. Human settlements have not been confirmed there. Most artifacts from the site are considered to have been specially made as burial goods.

DOI TAKASHI

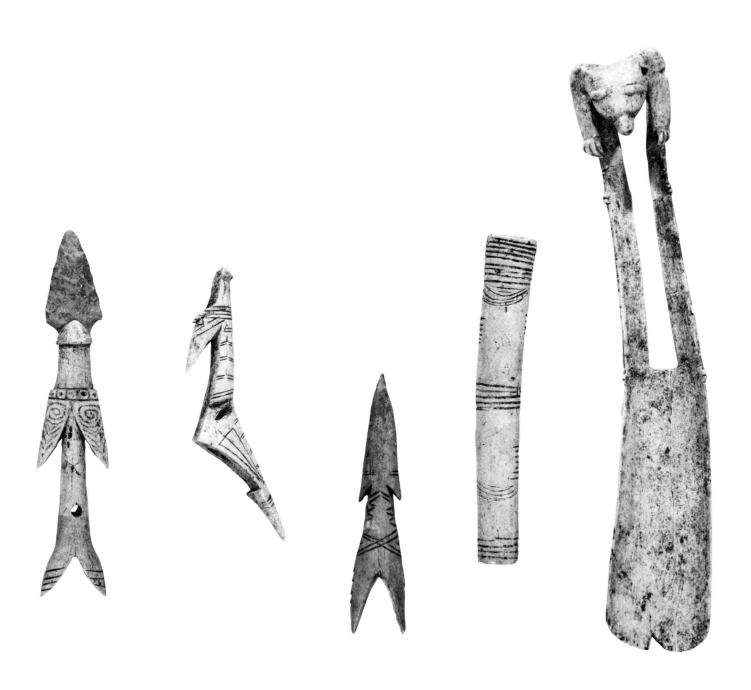

Early-Late Yayoi period
(300 B.C.–A.D. 250)
Excavated at Kitoragawa,
Osaka Prefecture
Wood
Higashi Osaka Municipal Museum,
Osaka Prefecture

103
Pestle
40⅜ × 2¾ in. (102.6 × 7.0 cm)

104
Spade
Length 45 in. (114.5 cm); blade
width 6⅝ in. (16.9 cm)

105
Hoe
Length 39⅝ in. (100.6 cm);
blade width 8½ in. (21.8 cm)

From the introduction of rice-paddy
cultivation in Japan the hoe and spade
were used as a set. Many wooden agricultural tools have been found
all over Japan, and Kitoragawa,
Osaka Prefecture, is particularly
known for its Yayoi cultivation tools.

Two kinds of hoes have been recovered at this site: a narrow-blade

[105] and wide-blade hoe. From
these basic types, variations—such
as a hoe with a round blade or a
blade divided into three segments—
were used for specific functions. Hoes
were made separately and attached
to the handles.

The handles and blades of spades
[104], however, were made in one
piece. It was not until the Kofun
period that iron blades replaced
wooden blades and were attached to
wooden handles of hoes and spades.
The introduction of iron increased
the efficiency of the tools.

Pestles were used to pound rice.
Depictions on bronze bells often
illustrate how the pestles were utilized. The example excavated from
Kitoragawa is elaborately made with
incised decoration [103].

TANABE IKUO

Early-Late Yayoi period
(300 B.C.–A.D. 250)
Excavated at Karako-Kagi,
Nara Prefecture
Tawaramoto Township Education
Commission, Nara Prefecture

106, 107
Carbonized hulled and unhulled rice
Not measured

108
Reaping knife
Stone
4⅞ × 1⅝ × ¼ in.
(12.5 × 4.3 × 0.7 cm)

109
Reaping knife
Stone
5¼ × 2⅛ × ⅜ in.
(13.3 × 5.4 × 1.0 cm)

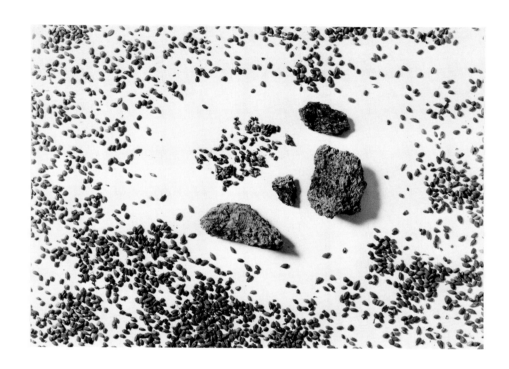

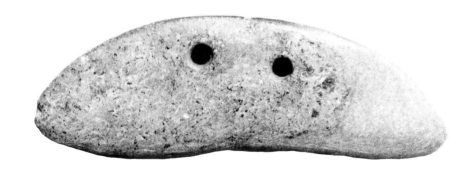

110
Arrowhead
Stone
2¼ × 1 × ¼ in.
(5.9 × 2.5 × 0.6 cm)

111
Arrowhead
Stone
2 × 1⅛ × ³⁄₁₆ in.
(5.3 × 2.8 × 0.5 cm)

112
Arrowhead
Stone
2½ × ⅝ × ¼ in.
(6.4 × 1.7 × 0.6 cm)

113
Adz
Stone
3⅛ × ⅜ × ⅜ in.
(7.9 × 1.0 × 0.9 cm)

114
Double-edged sword
with knob
Stone
7½ × 1¼ × ½ in.
(19.2 × 3.4 × 1.4 cm)

115
Ax
Stone
5¼ × 2¾ × 1⅞ in.
(13.3 × 7.0 × 4.8 cm)

116
Awl
Stone
3 × 1¼ × ½ in.
(7.7 × 3.1 × 1.4 cm)

117
Awl
Stone
1⅞ × 2½ × ⁵⁄₁₆ in.
(4.8 × 6.4 × 0.8 cm)

118
Spear
Stone
6⅜ × 1¹⁄₁₆ × ½ in.
(16.3 × 2.7 × 1.4 cm)

119
Spindle whorl
Stone
Thickness ⅜ in. (0.9 cm);
diameter 1½ in. (3.9 cm)

120
Spindle whorl
Antler
Thickness ¼ in. (0.6 cm);
diameter 2⅜ in. (6.0 cm)

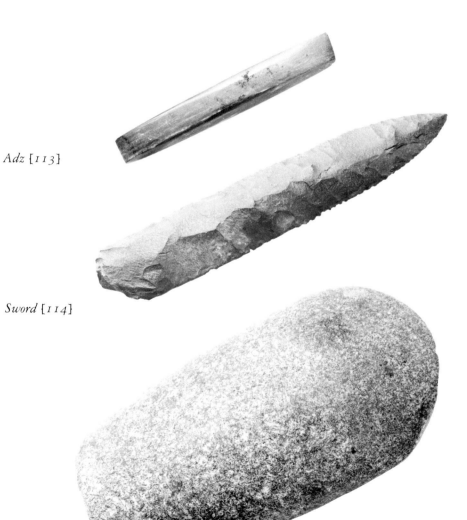

Adz {*113*}

Sword {*114*}

Ax {*115*}

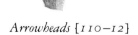

Arrowheads {*110–12*}

Rice-husk impressions on the bottom of earthenware vessels were the first indirect evidence of a Japanese society based on agriculture. Carbonized rice grains were found subsequently to further substantiate the existence of early agriculture.

During the Yayoi period bronze and iron artifacts began to be used, influenced by Asian continental practices. Although stone tools were still employed for many purposes, the kinds of stone tools and their applications had changed from the days of Jōmon hunting and gathering. In particular, major transfor-mations appeared in polished stone tools, typified by the artifacts unearthed from Karako-Kagi in Nara Prefecture, a site in the Kinki region, a center of Yayoi culture.

The most common Yayoi agricultural tool was a stone reaping knife for cutting the heads of rice plants [108]. The long, oval piece has a blade on one edge and pierced holes on the other for insertion of a rope. Most blades were made by polishing. Stone tools for craftwork, such as awls and polished axes and adzes, were also developed. Two kinds of woodworking tools were made: an ax for splitting wood and an adz for scraping. Spindle whorls for spinning thread were made of stone [119] or deer antler [120].

Stone arrowheads became larger, with an increased potential to serve as weapons in an agricultural society that had to face battles [110–12]. A stone arrowhead stuck into a human bone was discovered from the Yayoi site of Doigahama, Yamaguchi Prefecture. Stone spears and double-edged stone clubs (sometimes called stone swords) with one-handle knobs [114] were other weapons of the Yayoi people.

TANABE IKUO

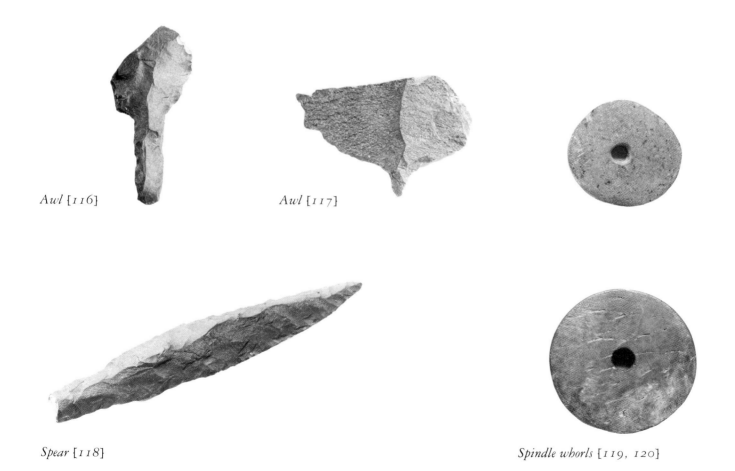

Awl [116]

Awl [117]

Spear [118]

Spindle whorls [119, 120]

Middle Yayoi period
(100 B.C.–A.D. 100)
Excavated at Sakuragaoka,
Hyōgo Prefecture
Bronze
Kobe City Museum,
Hyōgo Prefecture
National Treasure

121
15½ × 8¾ in.
(39.3 × 22.2 cm)

122
16⅝ × 10¼ in.
(42.4 × 26.1 cm)

The original purpose of the bronze bell (dōtaku) was to make a sound when hit with a stick or clapper. The prototype for the Japanese bronze bell is assumed to have come from Korea. The earliest dōtaku are relatively thick and small, with the area for suspending the bell sturdily constructed. In general, the later bells are larger and thinner and the area for suspension is decorated with a flat attachment. Some display geo-

metric designs; others, including these, have naturalistic motifs, such as images of deer, animals found near water (crabs, dragonflies, turtles, frogs, snakes), and human figures fishing or pounding in a mortar. The heads of people shown hunting or fishing are indicated by round shapes (assumed to represent men), whereas the heads of individuals pounding mortars are triangular (assumed to be women). Scenes of fishing, hunting, and harvesting were depicted to represent the wish of the people for success in these endeavors. Such images indicate the importance of the bells as ceremonial objects in village harvest rituals.

About four hundred bronze bells dating from the end of the Early Yayoi through the Late Yayoi periods have been found in a wide area from northern Kyūshū to central Honshū. Most bronze bells have been unearthed singly, with some exceptional multiple finds. These two, discovered from Sakuragaoka in Hyōgo Prefecture, were found among fourteen bronze bells and seven bronze halberds. It is thought that during the Late Yayoi political and ritual power became more concentrated and individually held ritual objects were collected in one place for centralized management.

MORIMITSU TOSHIHIKO

Late Yayoi Period
(A.D. 100–250)
Excavated at Nishiura, Osaka
Prefecture
Bronze
35¼ × 16¾ in.
(89.6 × 42.7 cm)
Agency for Cultural Affairs,
Government of Japan, Tokyo; on
deposit at Habikino City Education
Commission, Osaka Prefecture
Important Cultural Property

This *dōtaku* was found during the renovation of an elementary school in 1977. Bronze bells are often recovered accidentally; this was, however, one of the rare finds in which archaeologists were able to ascertain the original context of the bell.

It had been buried at a forty-five-degree angle in a hole 25½ inches (65 cm) wide and 13⅝ inches (35 cm) deep. No structure relating to the bell was found. The bell was sealed tightly in clay soil, completely removed from organic material. There was, therefore, no sign of green weathering or patination, the surface being a radiant gold color when it was first exposed.

The handle and flangelike decoration have sawtooth and herringbone patterns. Nine earlike protuberances with spirals are attached to the outer rim of the flange. Thick, convex lines mark the crossed bands on the body of the bell.

The handle is flat, with excessive decoration, and the lack of evidence that the bell was hit from inside suggests that the bell was made only for viewing. This example belongs, therefore, to a stage near the end of the development of the bells, representing a bell "to see" rather than "to hear."

This specimen is much larger than the Sakuragaoka bells [see 121, 122]. When it was found, sand was still attached to the inside, indicating that the inner mold was made of sand. The casting was generally successful, resulting in clearly delineated decoration. The metallic composition of this bell is 87.29 percent copper, 5.6 percent lead, and 4.31 percent tin.

TANABE IKUO

167   Yayoi Period

Middle Yayoi period
(100 B.C.–A.D. 100)
Excavated at Higashinara, Ibaraki
City, Osaka Prefecture
Stone
17⅛ × 11⅜ in. (43.5 × 29.0 cm)
Agency for Cultural Affairs,
Government of Japan, Tokyo; on
deposit at Ibaraki City Education
Commission, Osaka Prefecture
Important Cultural Property

An inner mold and a two-piece outer mold were needed to cast a bronze bell. This example is one part of the outer mold for a bronze bell of the Middle Yayoi period that was decorated with a flowing-water pattern [see 122]. The mold is made of fine volcanic tuff, and its outer surface is roughly shaped. The inside, where the mold was in contact with the metal, is finely polished and blackened by exposure to heat.[1]

A sketch of the decoration seems to have been drawn on the mold before the final pattern was created. Four independent spiral patterns and a series of spirals are found on the outer area for suspension; the inner side is undecorated. A saw-tooth design embellishes both ends of the body, and bands of spiral motifs divide the central portion into four zones. A flowing-water motif is found on each zone. Attached fin-like pieces exhibit a pair of ornamental ears at three locations on each side of the bell. The upper portion of the bell is so worn that it is impossible to detect a decorative pattern.

Besides this piece more than five pairs of bronze bell molds, more than two pairs of clay molds for bronze halberds, and two pairs of molds for *magatama* were discovered at Higashinara, which was assumed to be a workshop. The discovery of stone molds for bronze bells has caused archaeologists to modify the previous assumption that all molds for bronze bells were made of clay.

KAWAGOE SHUN'ICHI

1. According to the chronological classification of bronze bells into types numbered I to IV, a bell made from this mold belongs to type II and would be about 12¾ inches (32.5 cm) high and about 6¾ inches (17.0 cm) wide. Currently no bells made from this mold have been recovered.

169 Yayoi Period

Middle Yayoi period
(100 B.C.–A.D. 100)
Excavated at Nanaita,
Fukuoka Prefecture
Painted earthenware
Yasu Township Education Commission, Fukuoka Prefecture; on
deposit at Prefectural Amagi
Museum

Clockwise from upper left:

125
Pedestal
Height 20⅞ in. (53.0 cm);
bottom diameter 14³⁄₁₆ (36.0 cm)

126
Jug
Height 15⅞ in. (40.5 cm); mouth
diameter 13¾ in. (35.0 cm)

127
Jar
Height 12 in. (30.4 cm); mouth
diameter 14⅛ in. (36.0 cm)

128
Bowl with pedestal
Height 10⅜ in. (26.5 cm); mouth
diameter 9⅜ in. (24.0 cm)

129
Bowl with pedestal
Height 9⅜ in. (24.0 cm); mouth
diameter 7⅜ in. (18.8 cm)

130
Jar with lid
Height 10 in. (25.5 cm); mouth
diameter 8 in. (20.3 cm)

During the Middle Yayoi, refined
earthenware vessels were created in
northern Kyūshū, which, like the
Kinki region in western Honshū,
was a center of Yayoi culture. Vessels became simpler, with precise
curves and polished surfaces elaborately finished with a spatula. Except
for a few raised bands, the decorations used in previous periods
were abandoned.

Sacred vessels, painted red with
iron oxide over the entire surface,
are particularly beautiful. Certain
requirements may have determined
the combination of vessel forms in
a set, since similar groupings have
been unearthed from almost every
site of the Middle Yayoi period.
Earthenware vessels from Nanaita
in Fukuoka Prefecture are outstanding in their shape and coloring.

The Nanaita settlement supported more than two hundred
houses and survived from the Yayoi
to the Kofun period. A graveyard
containing about fifty jar burials was
located on the east side of the site.
Most of the painted red vessels were
discovered in an L-shaped ditch surrounding the cemetery. Perhaps
burial rites were held in the corner
of the communal graveyard and vividly colored vessels were significant
for those occasions.

TANABE IKUO

Middle Yayoi period
(100 B.C.–A.D. 100)
Excavated at Asahi, Aichi Prefecture
Painted earthenware
Aichi Prefectural Kiyosu Kaigara-
yama Shell Mound Museum, Kiyosu
Township

131
Bowl with pedestal
Height 8⅞ in. (22.6 cm); max.
diameter 9 in. (23.4 cm)

132
Bowl with pedestal
Height 7 in. (17.7 cm); max.
diameter 4¾ in. (12.0 cm)

131

132

133
Jar with constricted neck
Height 9⅜ in. (23.7 cm); max.
diameter 7⅞ in. (20.1 cm)

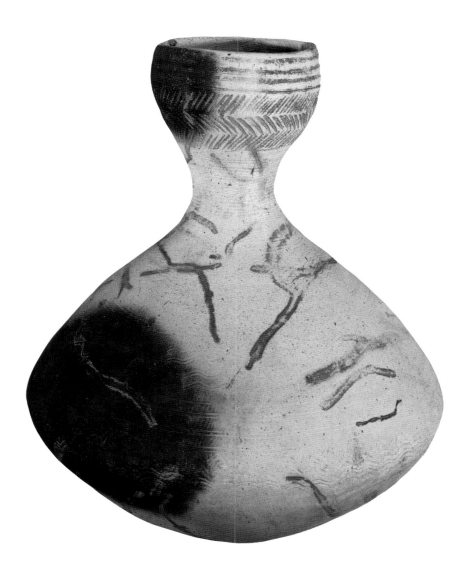

134
Jar with constricted neck
Height 11¾ in. (29.9 cm); max.
diameter 8⅜ in. (21.2 cm)

135
Jar with pedestal and
constricted neck
Height 14¼ in. (36.2 cm); max.
diameter 11⅜ in. (29.1 cm)

136
Jar with pedestal
Height 10½ in. (26.7 cm); max.
diameter 5⅛ in. (13.0 cm)

Elaborate vessels painted red with iron oxide became popular in the Tōkai area. Their refined shapes are customarily defined as "palace style."

The palace-style vessels exhibited here are from Asahi in Aichi Prefecture, a large settlement that included a shell mound located at the center of a large plain formed by the Kiso and Nagara rivers. The damp, low-lying area was fertile and supported rice-paddy cultivation. An adjacent, slightly elevated sandy area is assumed to have offered the most favorable location for a Yayoi settlement. Together with the northern part of Kyūshū and the Kinki region, the Tōkai area, including the Asahi site, became a center of advanced Yayoi culture.

Among the large number of vessels found at Asahi, palace-style vessels are few and seem to have been used for particular occasions such as agricultural rites. In particular, the bowl [131] and jar [135] with pedestals share certain characteristics that suggest their use as vessels for containing food or offerings for the gods. The vaselike jar with a short pedestal [136] also indicates a specialized function, quite apart from that of utilitarian vessels.

The assembled vessels, refined and aesthetic creations, convey not only the sensitivity of the Yayoi people but also the importance of their vessels as ritual objects.

HARADA MASAYUKI

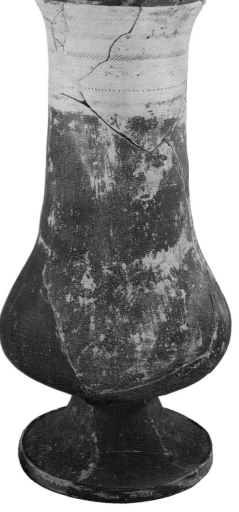

Middle Yayoi period
(100 B.C.–A.D. 100)
Excavated at Kemidani, Saga
Prefecture
Bronze
Agency for Cultural Affairs, Government of Japan, Tokyo; on deposit at
Saga Prefectural Museum, Saga City
Important Cultural Property

137
32¾ × 3⅜ in.
(83.4 × 8.5 cm)

138
33 × 3¾ in.
(83.8 × 9.6 cm)

139
33 × 3⅞ in.
(83.7 × 9.7 cm)

Twelve bronze spearheads, including these three, were accidentally discovered in a deep valley among the hills of Saga Prefecture in northern Kyūshū. According to the excavation report, the bronze spearheads were arranged neatly with alternately crossed blades pointing upward in a square hole of about 5 feet (1.5 m) on each side. It was assumed that they were originally contained in a box that has since completely deteriorated. No other remains or structures have been found nearby. Only under special circumstances would bronze spearheads have been buried without other artifacts. Their context is similar to that of the bronze bells from western Japan [see 121–23] and suggests their special use for a community ritual.

All the unearthed spearheads are large and about the same size. The wide blade and rounded tip indicate that the they were not used as weapons. The blades were filed from several directions to form a finely abraded herringbone pattern. The pattern on the blade would have created a glittering effect in certain lighting conditions. The luminous appearance would have awed the commoners of the Yayoi period who were not familiar with metal artifacts.

TANABE IKUO

Early Yayoi period
(300–100 B.C.)
Excavated at Yoshitake-takagi,
Fukuoka Prefecture
Necklace, jasper; approx. length
11¾ in. (30.0 cm)
Ornament, jadeite; 1⅝ × 1 in.
(4.1 × 2.5 cm)
Agency for Cultural Affairs,
Government of Japan, Tokyo; on
deposit at Fukuoka Municipal
Museum
Important Cultural Property

Personal adornments, such as comma-shaped beads (*magatama*) of colored stones, became increasingly more elaborate during the Late and Final Jōmon. Ornaments were worn for cultic or spiritual purposes—to prevent mishaps, fortify the wearer in the face of hazards, or bear evil in place of the wearer.

During the Yayoi period, when the agricultural society became stabilized and class differentiation increased, only a few people could obtain and wear ornaments made of valuable jasper or other stones. From the more than twelve hundred jar and wooden coffin burials at Yoshitake-takagi in Fukuoka Prefecture, only a few contained grave goods. Among the burial objects indicating social differentiation were bronze mirrors, daggers, halberds, and socketed spearheads as well as ornaments fashioned of jade, jasper, or other rare stones. These symbols of power became increasingly diverse and ornate.

TANABE IKUO

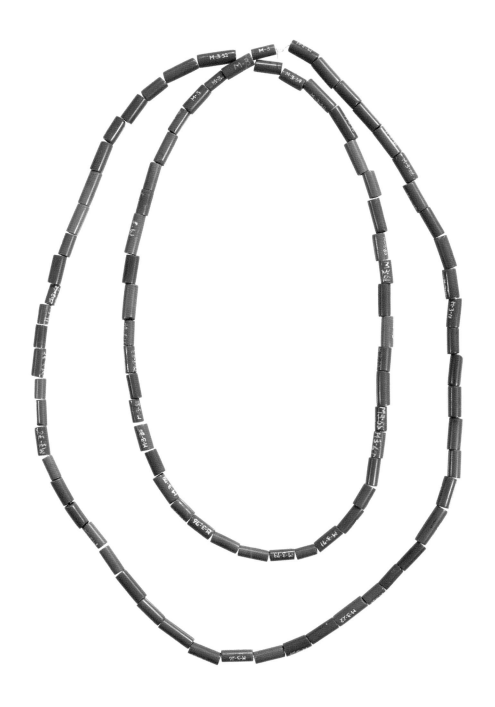

Yayoi period, 2d century B.C.–
1st century A.D.
Excavated at Doigahama,
Yamaguchi Prefecture
Shell
Hōhoku Township Education Commission, Yamaguchi Prefecture

141
Bracelet
Depth 2½ in. (6.5 cm);
diameter 5⅝ in. (14.5 cm)

142
Bracelet
Depth 1⅝ in. (4.3 cm);
diameter 3⅜ in. (8.5 cm)

143
Bracelet
Depth 3/16 in. (0.5 cm);
diameter 1⅞ in. (4.7 cm)

144
Necklace
Approx. length 9¾ in. (25 cm)

145
Ring
Depth ¾ in. (2 cm);
diameter 1 in. (2.5 cm)

Ornaments made in the Yayoi period had three distinct origins: they were inherited from the Jōmon tradition, adapted from the Asian continent, or invented by the Yayoi people. Bracelets made of shells from the seas south of Japan originated in the Yayoi culture.

In making shell bracelets, artisans used bivalves, vertically or horizontally cut large spiral gastropod shells, or univalve limpets. Two bracelets in this group [141, 142] were made of a horizontally cut piece of *gohōra* (*Tricornis latissimus Linne*), a large spiral shell from the region extending from Amami Ōshima to the Okinawa Islands.

An important feature of shell bracelets of the horizontally cut type is that only one bracelet can be made from a single shell. This same type of shell bracelet was unearthed from the right wrist of the skeleton of a mature male. Since a large bracelet worn on the right wrist would impede manual labor, it is assumed that the wearer was either a magician, spirit medium, or powerful village leader. Bracelets for women were made of horizontally cut pieces of shell. In the Kofun period, shell bracelets for men were fashioned of green agate and became important ritual objects.

Shell rings were made of a horizontally cut cone shell (*Conus geographus*). While some are ornamented with triangular protuberances, others have a plain, circular shape. This example [145] was found in association with a male, but some have been found with females.

As many as several hundred small shell disks have been found scattered around buried skeletons at other sites. It is highly probable that the disks were strung together with stone cylindrical beads to make a necklace or bracelet or were stitched to clothing for decoration. The Doigahama site, which has yielded a large number of burials, is located in coastal sand dunes and dates to the Early and Middle Yayoi.

KAWAGOE SHUN'ICHI

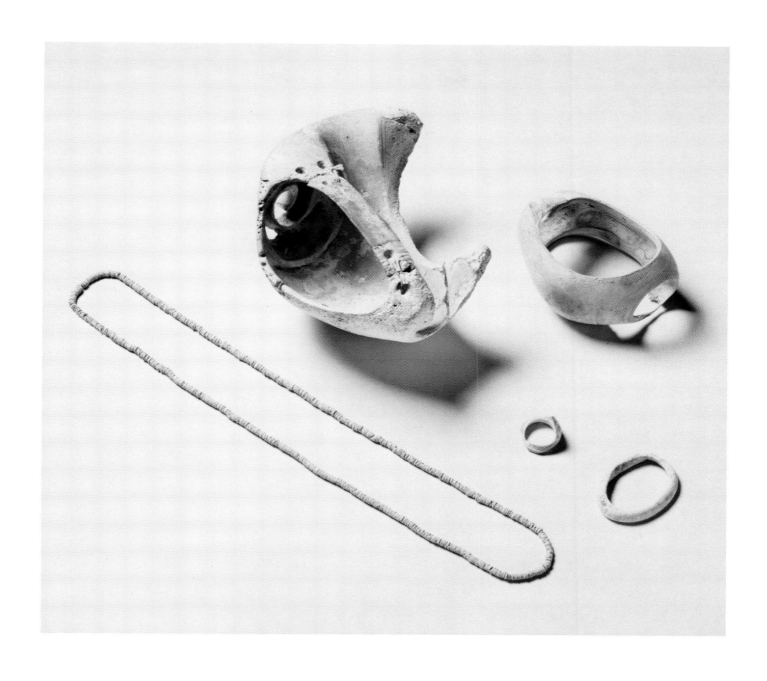

Yayoi period, 1st century B.C.
Excavated at Yoshinogari,
Saga Prefecture
Agency for Cultural Affairs,
Goverment of Japan, Tokyo; on de-
posit at Saga Prefectural Museum,
Saga City
Important Cultural Property

146
Beads
Glass
Length, range, ⅝–2⅝ in.
(1.8–6.7 cm)

147
Dagger
Bronze
17⅝ × 7¼ in. (44.8 × 18.3 cm)

This bronze dagger was found together with glass cylindrical beads in the central jar coffin in the large burial mound discovered at the Yoshinogari site. About twenty individuals are assumed to have been buried in the mound that is datable to the first century B.C. Partial excavation revealed bronze daggers in five of six jar burials. The dagger's hilt and blade were cast in one piece, which differentiates it from the usual type made by assembling separately cast pieces. The top of the hilt is decorated. This example is only the fourth specimen of one-piece casting found thus far in Japan. Although scholars have looked to the Korean peninsula for the origins of the Japanese bronze dagger, there is no clear evidence that one-piece casting was practiced there. This dagger is assumed, therefore, to have been made in Japan.

Beads are the most beautiful among the ancient Japanese glass products, including those excavated from Yayoi and Kofun period sites as well as those housed in the mid eighth-century Shōsōin Repository in Nara. Traces of wire coated with mud remain around the glass of the Yoshinogari examples. Large and small beads were combined to make a peaked headdress. Beads of similar quality have been found in Hapsŏng-ni, Ch'ungch'ŏng Province, in Korea, and Changsha, Hunan Province, in China.

KAWAGOE SHUN'ICHI

181   Yayoi Period

Late Yayoi period (A.D. 100–250)
Excavated at Miyayama, Sōja City,
Okayama Prefecture
Earthenware
Height 37 1/16 in. (94.2 cm); max.
diameter 17 1/2 in. (44.5 cm)
Okayama Prefectural Museum,
Okayama City

From around the second to the first century B.C., people were buried in jar coffins in a common graveyard near their village. As observed at Yoshinogari [see 146, 147], some jars contained grave goods, such as bronze daggers and mirrors and jade objects, although most were without grave offerings. People of higher status were buried in the same kinds of jars and graveyards as commoners.

By the second and third centuries A.D., however, a large grave area was separated from the common graveyard, signifying the emergence of a powerful elite. The offering jar and its pedestal became bigger and thicker in proportion to the increased size of the elite grave mounds. Clusters of keyhole-shaped mounds developed in the Okayama area and the use of distinctive clay pedestals on top of the mounds likewise are manifestations of power.

Narrow clay coils applied to the surface of the cylindrical portions of this pedestal separate decorative areas. Portions were then alternately ornamented with openwork and a surrounding circular design, leaving an undecorated area in between.

Over time the shape of this type of pedestal lost its flaring bottom and was replaced by a cylindrical image or *haniwa* form. Like the cylindrical *entō haniwa,* the pedestal possessed a special significance and distinct purpose as a funerary object in the burial regalia of an important individual.

KAWAGOE SHUN'ICHI

Excavated at Futatsukayama,
Saga Prefecture
Bronze
Saga Prefectural Museum, Saga City
Important Cultural Property

149
Mirror with circular pattern
China; Western Han dynasty,
1st century B.C.
Diameter 6¼ in. (15.9 cm); depth
¼ in. (0.7 cm)

150
Mirror with whorl design
Korea; Lelang Garrison
(108 B.C.–A.D. 343)
Diameter 2¼ in (5.7 cm); depth
⅛ in. (0.3 cm)

151
Mirror
Japan; Late Yayoi period
(A.D. 100–250)
Diameter 3⅝ in. (9.2 cm); depth
³⁄₁₆ in. (0.5 cm)

The bronze mirrors found in Japan in sites dating to the Yayoi period include those made in China during the Warring States period and the Han dynasty, those manufactured in the northern part of the Korean peninsula, and those produced in Japan in imitation of Han mirrors.

The outer ring of the Chinese mirror [149] is inscribed with twenty-nine characters recounting the story of Qu Yuan, a politician of the Chu state, in which a misunderstanding led to his suicide. Made in imitation of a Han mirror but of inferior quality, the Japanese mirror is inscribed with characters that have been reduced to a decorative pattern [151]. The mirror from Korea is also an imitation of a Han mirror [150]. A mirror made from the same mold was unearthed in Korea from Ŏŭn-dong, Yŏngch'ŏn, Kyŏngsang Prov-

ince, which suggests that this mirror [150] was made in Korea and brought to Japan.

Futatsukayama in Saga Prefecture is a Yayoi cemetery where as many as 250 jar burials and box-shaped wood-plank coffins have been discovered. The burials are divided into four or five groups but since the grave sites do not differ much in size, it is assumed to be a cemetery for commoners. Some graves, however, had burial offerings such as bronze mirrors and iron weapons and tools, indicating the beginning of status differentiation. By the Late Yayoi the chief of a village was buried in an individual burial area isolated by a surrounding ditch, a configuration that later developed into the *kofun* (mounded tomb).

MORIMITSU TOSHIHIKO

Late Yayoi period, 3d century A.D.
Excavated at Hirabaru,
Fukuoka Prefecture
Bronze
Diameter 18¼ in. (46.5 cm)
Agency for Cultural Affairs, Government of Japan, Tokyo; on deposit at Maebaru Township Education Commission, Fukuoka Prefecture
Important Cultural Property

This specimen is one of many bronze mirrors unearthed from the square, moated burial precinct of Hirabaru in Fukuoka Prefecture. The mirror is one of the largest so far unearthed in Japan. The knob base is decorated with eight petals or arcs, surrounded by nine concentric circles. The outer rim is flat. Three other mirrors made from the same mold were also discovered at the Hirabaru site and are assumed to have been made in Japan.

The site is estimated to date to the end of the Yayoi period.[1] The main mound structure was located almost at the burial precinct's center. Archaeologists were astonished to unearth a large number of mirrors, deliberately broken, from the four corners of the grave pit.[2] Included in the find were thirty-nine mirrors. Guardian spirits are represented on thirty-two mirrors, which are related to Chinese TLV mirrors, named for the shapes of their geo-metric motifs: a central square surrounded by a space with T-, L-, and V-shaped motifs. Another Chinese mirror recovered at Hirabaru is decorated with four dragons. Of the six other mirrors with floral patterns, the four largest were made in Japan, the other two in China.

The overwhelming abundance of TLV mirrors is common in the jar burials of the Yayoi period, but large Japanese mirrors are quite unusual. They have been found only at the Hirabaru site, which archaeologists consider to be extremely important in understanding the transition from the Yayoi to the Kofun period.

KAWAHARA SUMIYUKI

1. The site is 59 feet (18 m) from east to west and 46 feet (14 m) from north to south. The surrounding moat is 6½ feet (2 m) wide.

2. The grave pit is 14¾ feet (4.5 m) from east to west and 11¾ feet (3.6 m) from north to south.

5

KOFUN PERIOD

A.D. 250–600

Chinese dynastic annals provide glimpses into Yayoi life but contribute few details concerning Japan in the following period, the Kofun. The period takes its name from the mounded earth tombs, *kofun,* that first appeared in the third century in the Kinai region. They lasted there until the late sixth century, when large earth-mounded tombs were no longer considered an appropriate form of burial according to the beliefs of Buddhism, which was introduced to Japan in the first half of the sixth century. In the Kantō and Tōhoku regions, affected much later than the Kinai region by Buddhism and Asian continental practices, the custom of constructing *kofun* lasted until the end of the seventh century (fig. 21).

Built for elite members of society, *kofun* objectified shifting centers of power. In areas around Osaka and in Gumma, Kyūshū, and Okayama prefectures, the great tombs are prominent features even today. Their slopes, now densely wooded, and placid moats are vivid reminders of an age of contending great chiefs and the emergence of Japan's imperial line.

Reserved for the most important leaders and their families until the Late Kofun period, when they were used for commoners as well, the tombs have yielded special funerary ceramics of two kinds. Inside the tombs, hard, gray ware (*sue*), made in Japan from the early fifth century, was used to hold offerings of food and drink. On the tops and sides of the tomb mounds, in locally distinctive arrangements, figures of soft, orange earthenware, termed *haniwa,* were placed in honor of the dead.

Grave offerings changed from a predominance of religious and ritual objects in the Early Kofun to an emphasis on military weapons and horse gear in the Late Kofun. Beyond their significance as symbols of power and wealth, the specific meaning of individual grave offerings is difficult to interpret. Japanese *kofun* bring to mind the burials in large tumuli elsewhere throughout Eurasia of paramount chiefs or kings and their role in warfare and confederacies. These concentrations of burial objects provide anthropologists with a means of discerning social and political relationships, since it is assumed that the most powerful people monopolized the sources of precious objects and bestowed them on equals or subordinates.

While the tombs and their contents have overshadowed other archaeological finds of the Kofun time span, new discoveries of settlements, agricultural fields buried under volcanic ash, and workshops for the production of ceramics and beads afford glimpses of everyday Kofun life. While many details are unclear at present, it appears that by the late fifth century in the Nara Basin a full-fledged state called Yamato, named after the region in which it arose, had begun. A hierarchy of offices—

Haniwa quiver [166]

controlled by a centralized authority, which directed the distribution of salt, iron, and prestige objects, such as mirrors and large ceremonial swords—and intensive agricultural productivity—through the conversion of forests to agricultural land—developed during the period.

Chronology

Unlike the Jōmon and Yayoi periods, the Kofun period is named for a type of tomb rather than a characteristic ceramic ware. Field archaeologists use *haji,* the soft, reddish utilitarian ware that developed from Yayoi ceramics in the third century, as a chronological indicator for *kofun* culture in a manner comparable to Jōmon and Yayoi ceramics for their

Figure 21
Kofun sites mentioned in the text.

1 Kuroimine
2 Mitsudera
3 Tsukamawari
4 Watanuki Kannonyama
5 Akabori Chausuyama
6 Funazuka
7 Ōhiyama
8 Kaki
9 Haraguchi
10 Shiraishi Inariyama
11 Sakitama Inariyama
12 Inaridai 1
13 Iwazu 1
14 Ishiyama
15 Tsubai Ōtsukayama
16 Mount Miwa
17 Imakiyama
18 Shin'ike
19 Taita Chausuyama
20 Shikinzan
21 Tsudōshiroyama
22 Fujinoki
23 Isonokami
24 Miyayama
25 Samida Takarazuka
26 Shinyama
27 Yufunesaka 2
28 Nagase Takahama
29 Iwada 14
30 Tsukinowa
31 Nagakoshi
32 Okinoshima
33 Iwatoyama
34 Etafunayama

respective periods; but *haji* ceramics persisted long after the creation
of mounded tombs and are therefore not reliable markers for the end of
kofun culture.

Until recently the beginning of the Kofun period was set at A.D.
300. The undeniable existence, however, of large third-century tombs,
stylistically distinct from those of the preceding Yayoi, has persuaded
archaeologists to push back the Kofun dates.

The period is divided into Early (A.D. 250–400), Middle (A.D. 400–
500), and Late (A.D. 500–600; later in remote areas). Time distinctions
within the Kofun are based on cross dating. Curation, by which objects
are kept as heirlooms and not buried until long after their introduction,
may account for a time lag factor. Chinese mirrors, iron and bronze
gear, sword handles, and *sue* ware have been studied in this regard. In
addition, lists of kings exist from later historical records but are not
considered reliable before A.D. 500. Further, tombs thought to belong to
members of the imperial line have not been excavated and the identity
of their owners is based on conjecture. Broad dating, within a century,
seems to be reasonable, given the uncertainties that face archaeologists.
The closing date assigned to the Kofun period thus varies from around
A.D. 600 in the Kinai region to A.D. 700 in the remote areas of the
Kantō Plain.

Hokkaidō

Contemporaneous with the Kofun period in Honshū and Kyūshū was the
Ezo culture, sometimes called Satsumon, in Hokkaidō. The distinctive
traits of the Ezo people are physical, linguistic, and ethnological. The
Ezo practiced agriculture in Tōhoku, growing barley, wheat, millet, and
beans. They generally resisted the people from Yamato, although they
may have been allies at some times, judging from grave finds of Yamato
items such as sword handles. Commoners' houses in Hokkaidō are similar
to dwellings in the Kantō and Tōhoku regions of the Kofun period. *Sue*
ware was traded from the Tōhoku region. Fujimoto Tsuyoshi (1988),
a specialist in Jōmon studies and the archaeology of Hokkaidō, has
contrasted the northern culture of Hokkaidō, based on hunting and
gathering, with the rice-cultivating, hierarchical societies of central
Japan. Gary Crawford of the University of Toronto and Hiroto Takamiya
(1990) of the University of California, Los Angeles, who are studying
ancient plant foods, have noted, however, that the subsistence pattern
of the north included a cultivation system based on plants such as barley,
wheat, beans, and other crops. The northern culture thus possesses a
pattern of cultivation distinctive from that of the central or Yamato
culture and is not simply a culture of riverine hunters and gatherers.

Okinawa

Whereas Kofun period tumuli were built in southern Kyūshū, particularly in Miyazaki Prefecture, burial practices did not affect the customs maintained on the Ryūkyū Islands, which are thought to have
remained outside the wet rice-cultivation system of the main islands.
Sue ware was made on Tokunoshima and traded to Okinawa after A.D.

1000, but it was not until at least A.D. 1100 that local chiefdoms emerged, culminating in state-level organization at the end of the fourteenth century (Pearson n.d.).

The Economic Base

The Kofun period was a time of intensive overseas trade. Ships traveled frequently from Osaka Bay through the Inland Sea to Kyūshū and Korea. A large port in Kawachi, now part of Osaka, at the mouth of the Yamato River, served as an important terminus.[1] Great *kofun* constructed near the shore were visible from the sea, and warehouses or naval bases have been found at strategic locations, such as Wakayama, located at a narrow point on the entry to Osaka Bay. Overseas routes, which also ran from ports along the Sea of Japan, were linked to the Silk Roads of the Asian mainland (Miyazaki 1988).

Technology

Major improvements in agricultural production occurred during the fifth and sixth centuries with profound effects. New agricultural tools reached Japan from the Korean peninsula, providing a transition to modern Japanese agricultural tools (Kurosaki 1989, 61). It is not clear from the archaeological record, however, how common the tools were or how much impact they had on overall production.

The first innovation was the step plow, which appeared at the end of the Yayoi period and spread rapidly northward from Kyūshū to Tōhoku. As with other agricultural tools, the plow was initially made of oak. In the fourth century an iron bit was attached to it. Its wide blade of 7⅞ to 11¾ inches (20–30 cm) in length could be used for several cultivating functions, and it had a special attachment with which to squeeze sticky mud from the blade (Kurosaki 1989, 62). Cultivating tools made of iron have also been found from dwelling sites and burials.

In the fifth century a new type of iron blade was developed to sheath the end of the wooden hoe. U-shaped, with a width of about 5⅞ inches (15 cm), it seems to have been useful in upland soils. Iron forms of the Yayoi stone reaping knife were also utilized, as were curved iron sickles. A horse-drawn wooden cultivating tool, similar to a large rake, found in the Kaki site in Fukuoka Prefecture, is thought to have been used to prepare rice fields and gather hay for cows. Skeletal cow remains have been found in the ash-covered Kuroimine site in Komochi Village, Gumma Prefecture (Kurosaki 1989, 64, 65). Since dry upland areas could be opened up with iron tools, the proliferation of iron agricultural tools can serve as a kind of index of dry-land development.

The Kofun period was also a time of great change in rice paddies. Ancient rice fields have been found preserved under volcanic ash in Gumma Prefecture; discoveries have revealed their outlines as well as the marks left by plows as they dragged dark topsoil into the subsoil. Fields were divided into sections by low dividing ridges (*aze*), with small fields grouped into larger units separated by higher dividing paths.

Fourth-century systems in Gumma Prefecture seem to have allowed water to overflow from one field to another over the small ridges. Water conduits, already known in the Yayoi site of Itazuke, were developed in the fifth century to divert water from one group of fields to another. Large-scale canals, which carried water across diluvial terraces, were built in the Middle and Late Kofun, whereas Yayoi fields had been limited to bottomlands and low terraces. The Furuichi ditch in Osaka Prefecture was 66 feet (20 m) wide and 16 feet (5 m) deep at its maximum and extended 1¼ miles (2.1 km). Systems of land allotments, recognized through gridded field boundaries, appear to have been undertaken in the sixth century by regional chieftains. That field systems are not all aligned in the same direction in relation to north is construed as evidence that they were not governed by one authority. Tsude Hiroshi (1989a, 44), who has studied the Kofun period and the emergence of state power, has suggested that extensive land clearance in the Kofun period created the need for land reorganization in the Nara period.

As well as telling us about death and burial rituals of the Kofun period, the archaeological record also elucidates the organization of craft specialists and their attachment to the rulers and powerful chiefs. The archaeology of craft production provides insight into the ways objects are made and indicates how ancient society was organized to supply and distribute goods and services. Full-time craft specialization in Japan arose during the Kofun period. It took different forms, depending on the goods produced and their history.

Bead Production

An indigenous specialty that can be traced to the Jōmon period—the making of beads from semiprecious stones such as nephrite, crystal, and jasper—was an important prehistoric artistic endeavor. Teramura Mitsuharu (1980), an authority on Kofun period craft production, has postulated three phases of bead production coinciding with the Early, Middle, and Late Kofun. In the Early Kofun the major products were stone ornaments for burial offerings, including three kinds of bracelets and several types of beads, such as green tuff or a jasperlike stone. Primary production centers were the Hokuriku and the Kantō, outside the area of Early Kofun mounded-tomb construction. Gina Lee Barnes (1987, 96–98; 1988, 258–64) has noted that manufacturing sites in the Early Kofun period were peripheral to the centers of power and that precious objects reached the elite through long-distance trading networks. In the individual villages where the remains of beadmaking have been found, artisans were members of nonspecialized communities. Only one village entirely devoted to beadmaking is known.

In the Middle Kofun, beadmaking was reorganized and different kinds of artifacts were produced in imitation of objects to be used as ritual grave offerings. Production sites, which came to comprise entire specialized communities, were grouped in three regions, the Hokuriku, Kantō, and San'in. All were located within the sphere of Kofun culture as defined by the presence of keyhole-shaped mounds. Beadmaking was integrated directly into the Yamato economic exchange system, and beads were produced for ritual specialists rather than political rulers. Bead production indicates that political and ritual roles were separated at the top of society, whereas they had previously been assumed by the same individuals.

The discovery of beadmaking sites dating to the Late Kofun in the Kinai region, far from sources of raw materials, suggests that workshops were set up near the patron consumers. The raw materials, rather than the finished products, were transported to the production sites. Barnes (1987, 98) has mentioned that in addition to the remains of beadmaking, iron slag as well as unfinished hilts and scabbards have been recovered from the Furu area in the western Yamato Basin.

Stone-Coffin Production

All the large keyhole-shaped mounds of the fifth century were equipped with stone coffins resembling storage chests and assembled from slabs of stone. They were manufactured from Tatsuyama tuff or rhyolite quarried from a single source in northern Hyōgo Prefecture. One can hypothesize that a single group of stonemasons was responsible for the manufacture of the coffins. Stonemasons probably transported their half-finished products, both sarcophagi and ceiling rocks for tomb chambers, to the site of tomb construction and finished them there.

Production of the house-shaped stone coffin, which succeeded the assembled stone coffin, was decentralized in the sixth century. Five new production centers of house-shaped stone coffins in the Kinai, each producing stylistically distinct products, appeared in the sixth century. Wada Seigo (1986, 362) of Ritsumeikan University, Kyoto, has postulated that powerful families in the Kinai region organized their own groups of masons to produce house-shaped coffins.

At the end of the sixth or beginning of the seventh century, two types of stone coffins, the southern Yamato and the Harima, predominated. Other types that had originated in the previous period never spread beyond their area of origin, and most were discontinued by the early seventh century. The popularity of the two new types of coffins is linked to new stoneworking techniques, the consolidation of power in the Yamato state, and the centralization and regulation of burial customs, which accompanied the spread of Buddhist culture (Wada 1986, 362).

Haniwa *Production*

Shin'ike—a *haniwa* production site dating to the fifth and sixth centuries with kilns, workshops, and workers' houses—was recovered late in 1989 near Takatsuki City, Osaka Prefecture. Three kilns and three workshops date to the mid-fifth century, while eighteen kilns are attributed to the sixth century.[2] *Haniwa* shards from the site match those from the nearby Taita Chausuyama Kofun and Imakiyama Kofun—both thought to be the tomb of Emperor Keitai (r. A.D. 507–31). That *haniwa* for imperial tombs were produced at Shin'ike means that the site was definitely occupied by state-controlled members of the occupational group (*be*) who made *haniwa* (Gekkan Bunkazai Hakkutsu 1990d, 88).

Weapons and Horse-Gear Production

Japanese iron production may have begun in the fifth century, but evidence for it is not clear until the second half of the sixth century (Ogawa

1990). The pig iron that was produced was suitable for forging. In addition, iron ingots from the fifth century, which upon analysis have been shown to come from Korea or China, appear in the mounds. Their weight corresponds to an ancient Chinese system of measures in which the larger specimens are twenty times the weight of the small ones. Iron was used not only for producing weapons, armor, and agricultural tools but also as a medium of exchange. The supply routes of raw iron were of great concern to the rulers of the Kinai region and to chiefs under their control who regulated its distribution. Political and exchange relationships with southern Korea were particularly significant, since that area was a major source of iron (Tsude 1989b, 49).

Swords and armor were important to the elite of the Kofun period. Whereas Yayoi warriors favored bronze weapons, the hallmark of the Kofun period was iron weaponry. Usually the sword blade was wrought separately from the handle, which might be fashioned in bronze or silver and gilded.

The historian Egami Namio has proposed that Japan was invaded via Korea in the fifth century by horse-riding nomads from northeastern Asia who established a ruling dynasty (Ledyard 1983a). While that theory has not gained wide acceptance, it is true that horse gear such as saddles and stirrups appears rather suddenly in elite tombs of the late fourth and fifth centuries. Since small horse bells have been found in Late Yayoi sites in Kyūshū, it is possible that horseback riding began in the late third century. The first horse bits found in Japan date, however, from the late fourth to the early fifth century in Kyūshū.

In the first half of the fifth century new forms of horse gear appeared in Osaka and Shiga prefectures. Over the next half-century horse gear became more common and the custom of horseback riding spread to eastern Japan in Gumma, Shizuoka, and Yamanashi prefectures. It was not until the first quarter of the sixth century, however, that horse gear began to be produced in Japan (Sakamoto 1985).

Several components comprised a set of horse gear. An iron bit, joined in the middle, passed through the horse's mouth. It often had decorated cheekpieces such as those shown on the Tsukamawari horse [164]. The saddle had an upright front and rear portion; the saddlebows [155] were often richly embellished and their gilt-bronze decoration [156] was fitted over a wooden frame. Hanging from the side of the saddle were mudguards and stirrups, both iron-ring and pocket-shaped types. A bell hung at the horse's neck, and from the straps that extended from the saddle over the rump of the horse was a series of ornaments, the elaboration of which varied according to the status of the owner. Pendant flank ornaments, jingle bells, and strap fixtures with upright metal tassels were also part of the gear (Kidder 1985, 98, 99).

The gilt-bronze saddle decorations of the Fujinoki tumulus in Nara Prefecture reflect the highest level of East Asian metalworking of the late sixth century and demonstrate Japan's cultural ties with the continent. The recently restored ornamental gilt-bronze saddlebow and cantle from the Fujinoki Kofun [155] are of great significance in expanding our knowledge of sixth-century Japan. The motifs indicate that some Japanese were gaining fluency with Asian continental patterns and symbols in the Late Kofun period, before the flood of ideas and images in the seventh century. The decoration on the saddlebow is divided into hexagonal spaces filled with dragons, lions, birds, and a makara (a composite animal-bird form, occasionally represented as a winged sea monster, originating in the religious art of India; Kidder 1990b).

Settlements

A unique mirror was found in 1881 in Samida Takarazuka Kofun in Nara in association with a mirror cast from the same mold as one of the Tsubai Ōtsukayama Kofun mirrors. Four different kinds of dwellings are represented on the Samida Takarazuka mirror [153]: a pit house, a ground-level house, an elevated house, and an elevated storehouse. The house built at ground level had a boarded floor, a feature that is almost impossible to recover archaeologically. In the Kinai region, near the central polity of Yamato, villages of high-status people comprised elevated houses with verandas and elaborate roof lines, elevated store-houses, and long stables for cows and horses. Villages of local chiefs elsewhere in Japan contained large houses built on the ground, such as those found at Mitsudera 1, while smaller villages, some moated, were occupied by agricultural communities (fig. 22).[3] Clustered villages also existed, but a dispersed pattern of small hamlets seems to have pre-dominated (Barnes 1988, 242).

Elite Residences

Dwelling sites of the Kofun period reflect similar status differentiation as that of the tombs. Long before actual house remains were uncovered, *haniwa* representing houses (fig. 23) and depictions of houses on sword handles and mirrors indicated the range of styles in domestic architecture. Since the discovery of Mitsudera 1 site in 1981, a series of elite residences entirely separate from the hamlets of commoners has been exca-

Figure 22
Kofun period structures, villages, and hamlets. Kofun period villages consisted of five types of structures: *a,* elevated elite houses, *b,* elevated storehouses, *c,* large houses built on the ground, *d,* small structures for specialized tasks such as craft production, *e,* semisubterranean pit houses, *f,* sheds for livestock.

Villages of high-status people closely connected to the central power of the Kinai region contained structures shown in number 1. Local settlements such as Mitsudera, Gumma Prefecture, are represented in number 2. The structures comprising wealthy farmers' dispersed hamlets are illustrated in number 3, while commoner farmers' hamlets took the form of those represented in numbers 4 and 5.

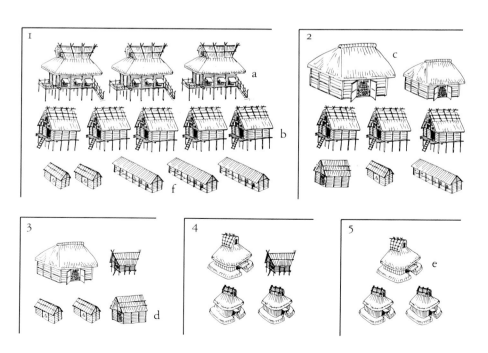

Figure 23
Reconstruction of arrangement of
house-shaped *haniwa* on top of
the Akabori Chausuyama Kofun,
Gumma Prefecture, first half fifth
century; the *haniwa* in the center
is 21 inches (53.2 cm) high. Such
haniwa may have served as dwellings
for the spirit of the deceased and
as public statements of status and
privilege.

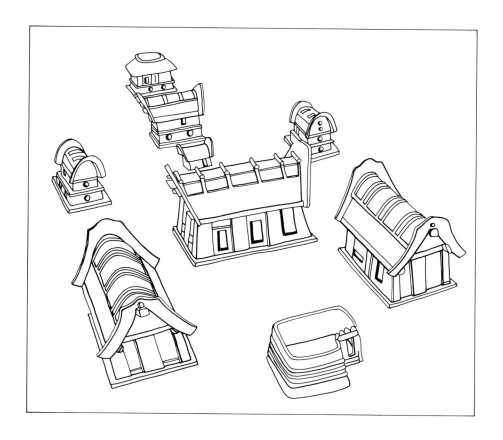

vated. The pattern of dispersed settlement did not lead automatically
to the growth of towns nor to the rise of cities. The elite instead continued until the seventh century to shift their residences and palaces,
establishing with each change a symmetrical palace-administrative center.
The pattern is different from that of West Asia, for instance, where
densely populated sites were known by 3500 B.C.

The arrangement of house-shaped *haniwa* on the summits of large
tombs gives some idea of the power and wealth of the families who built
the tombs. The *haniwa* represent elite houses built on flat foundations
and not commoners' pit dwellings. It was thought that the spirit of the
deceased resided temporarily in these houses before leaving for the other-
world. Professor Ogasawara Yoshihiko of Shiga University, Ōtsu, has
studied the styles and arrangements of houses of four large tombs of the
first half of the fifth century (Ogasawara 1985)—Akabori Chausuyama
and Shiraishi Inariyama in Gumma Prefecture, Nagase Takahama in
Tottori Prefecture, and Tsukinowa in Okayama Prefecture. At the summit
of Akabori Chausuyama were a main hall, two residences, two barns,
and two storehouses. A fencelike *haniwa,* with square, central openings,
has been reinterpreted as a Chinese-style gate. The most common arrangement was a large house placed in the center, flanked by smaller
houses and storehouses. The relative importance of the buildings can be
determined by the degree of elaboration of the roof and its beams or
ridges. In front of the houses was an open space for ritual and political
gatherings. The house arrangement is the same as that adopted in
seventh-century palaces such as Fujiwara. Since this type of configuration
is not seen in villages of the Yayoi or Kofun periods, it was most likely
introduced from China (Ogasawara 1985, 33).

Kofun villages do not differ in their level of technology from those of the Yayoi, although the number of terraced sites increased, indicating an expansion in agriculture. A settlement was composed of several groups of houses situated around an open area about 131¼ feet (40 m) in diameter. Small groups of people cooperated in rice cultivation and other production tasks as well as social activities. While houses were replaced occasionally, their locations persist from period to period, suggesting that the small groups were in fact cooperative work groups (*kyōdōtai*). Barnes (1988) has termed the dwellings—which are rectangular with semisubterranean floors, interior posts, and an interior fireplace along one side—"quadrangular pit dwellings." In the Late Kofun period the fireplace was replaced by a clay hearth, constructed against a side wall at floor level, with a flue to the outside. This kind of fireplace, which can be seen in the Chinese pottery tomb figures of the Han dynasty, probably came to Japan in the fifth century with the arrival of potters from Korea who specialized in manufacturing *sue*-ware pottery. Some Late Kofun villagers lived in houses at ground level, with large posts dug into the ground. This more advanced type of residence first appeared in western Japan and the Kinai region, where political power was concentrated (Ogasawara 1989, 94). Late Kofun villages with access to irrigated rice fields apparently grew larger, while those based on dry fields became smaller.

In Gumma Prefecture a number of Kofun period villages have been found well preserved under thick layers of volcanic ash. Both semisubterranean houses and those built on the surface have been discovered. Many had sod roofs.

Religious Sites

In addition to the chiefly rituals of succession, many other religious ceremonies give us some idea of the organizing principles of the Kofun culture. Remote mountain plateaus and passes as well as some islands were thought to be the residences of the gods (*kami*), according to beliefs that persist in the Shinto religion. Sacred places were venerated by offerings of stone, metal, and ceramic objects; and ceremonies were held there to propitiate the gods of the sea.

Okinoshima, off the coast of Kyūshū, was an island shrine in the Sea of Japan dedicated to the safe passage of voyagers. From the second half of the fourth to the ninth century, offerings were placed in the island's various cliffs and crags, which were regarded as seats of the gods. Bronze mirrors, horse trappings, gilt-bronze fittings, and other rare objects were deposited under overhanging rocks, while *sue* ware and soapstone effigies of humans, horses, and boats were found on open sites. Okinoshima is one of the most mysterious of sacred places. At present, the Munakata Shrine in northern Kyūshū controls access to the island; women are forbidden to enter it and few visitors are permitted.

Twenty-one bronze mirrors, semiprecious objects, and swords were found at site 17. Bracelets of talc stone and halberds were discovered at another site. The objects, identical to those found in the large *kofun* in the Kinai region but dissimilar to those from the local burials, indicate that the ceremonies for overseas safety must have been controlled directly by the distant Yamato authority. Ceremonies at Okinoshima ended in the ninth century with the cessation of tributary expeditions to China (*kentōshi;* Iwasaki 1984, 127).

At the foot of Mount Miwa on the eastern edge of the Nara Basin, votive offerings of elaborate *magatama* beads, *haji* ceramics, wooden bird-shaped vessels, weaving implements, and ceremonial staffs have been found. The veneration of the mountain suggests that Shinto beliefs and practices were observed in the fourth century. Votive offerings were the same as those used in high-status burials.

Rituals for water gods have been inferred from offerings of pottery, bronze arrowheads, mirrors, swords, talc replicas, and jewels found in ditches, such as at Nagakoshi in Hyōgo Prefecture, or associated with stone-paved ritual sites. Other paved sites, with offerings of *sue*-ware pottery, talc replicas, and iron objects, are thought to have been used for agricultural rituals. Talc-stone replicas found in ritual sites usually include mirrors, swords, and jewels, whereas those from *kofun* are knife blades and jewels. The three treasures of Shinto—mirrors, swords, and jewels—seem to have symbolized subordination of chiefs to the central ruler. In the account of the visit to Kyūshū by Emperor Chūai (dates unknown) in the *Nihon shoki* (Chronicles of Japan), Chief Kuma-wani welcomes the emperor with branches of the *sakaki* (*Cleyera*) tree decorated with mirrors, swords, and jewels (Iwasaki 1984, 134–40), a ritual derived from the ceremony for welcoming the gods.

Kofun

The hallmark of the Kofun period is the *zempōkōenfun,* a burial tumulus with a round rear mound attached to a rectilinear front mound. The distinctive form, which looks like an old-fashioned keyhole, is thought by some to have come from Korea, where prototypes have been found both in the south (Tsude 1989c, 28) and north (Gekkan Bunkazai Hak-kutsu 1990a). South Chinese tombs of the Eastern Han are also thought to be possible prototypes (Tsude 1989c, 31). Chinese technical knowl-edge is evident in the use of stamped earth to make the mounds and in the engineering skills required to lay out symmetrical circles and other shapes. Japanese Yayoi tombs also provide convincing models for keyhole *kofun.* The rectangular front of the keyhole mound may be an extension of the corner of the Yayoi rectangular mound, added to connect the sur-rounding terrain and isolated burial sanctuary. Alternatively, it may have developed from the pathways leading to Yayoi burial mounds and elabo-rated into a ceremonial area.

Much excavation of the Kofun period has been devoted to tombs, and their changes from century to century have been delineated. In the Early Kofun, mounds were placed on the brow of a slope to take advan-tage of the terrain and make the mound look larger or to incorporate natural slopes and hillocks within the mound itself. In the Middle Kofun the flat top of a plateau or terrace was more commonly chosen. Many of the most imposing tombs were located on level, arable land, as if to enhance the status of the occupant and kin by appropriating productive land for the glorification of the ruler's ancestors. In the Late Kofun the

Figure 24
Fujinoki sarcophagus, Nara
Prefecture. *Right,* contents
of the stone sarcophagus
with lid removed, as originally found by excavators;
left, diagram illustrating
placement of the contents.

1–3 Mirror
   4 Hollow beads
   5 Silver decorative
     attachments
   6 Dagger
7–10 Long sword
  11 Gilt-bronze crown
  12 Sword pommel decoration
     (*miwadama*)
  13 Earring
14, 15 Gilt-bronze shoes
  16 Bronze broad belt

foot of a mountain slope was preferred. In the succeeding Asuka period the most favored position was the thickest and widest part of the mountain, facing south.

Major changes took place in the location of the burial within the mound and in access routes to it. The Late Kofun horizontal chamber with a passage and side entrance allowed for the serial burial of family members whose coffins were placed in the corridor. While multiple burials occurred in earlier mounds, the important difference was the open, horizontal chamber. Such open chambers first appeared in the mid-fifth century in Kyūshū with interiors that were sometimes incised and painted. At first the open chamber was only large enough for the burial, but the coffin later sat in a large open area with space for grave goods.

During the Kofun period the Japanese were committed to a style of burial having certain salient features. Elite status was symbolized by the size of an earthen *kofun* and its isolation from settlements. Surrounding moats or structures and offerings on the mound surfaces, meant to be seen by the living, were important ritual aspects. The interment of

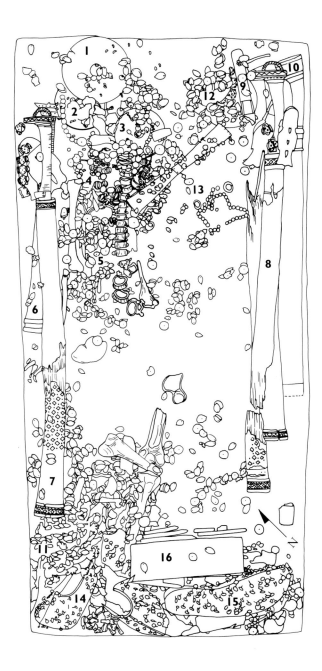

Figure 25
Corridor-style tomb chamber of
Fujinoki, with burial goods placed
in front of the sarcophagus (for
several of these *sue*-ware vessels, see
entries 170–76).

the elite involved one or more coffins, plus a chamber or compartment
for grave offerings, which were protective and magical objects rather
than utilitarian items.

The use of coffins and concept of a burial chamber came to Japan from
China. Two types of wooden coffins were manufactured in the Early
Kofun: the hollowed-out and the split-log types. Examples of small,
split-log coffins date to the end of the Yayoi period; the predominant type
from the Kofun period is long, from 13⅛ to 26¼ feet (4–8 m). Stone
coffins, either hollowed-out or boat-shaped, were used in addition to
a type made of assembled pieces. The multipiece chest-shaped stone coffin
appeared with the construction of huge tombs in the Kinai region
during the Middle Kofun; the house-shaped stone coffin was created in
the Late Kofun and early Asuka period. The symbolism of house or
lineage seems to have been stressed at a time when close kinship among
rulers was important. In some instances, such as at Fujinoki Kofun
(figs. 24, 25), more than one member of an elite "house" was actually
buried in the coffin. Later, during the Asuka period, in Takamatsuzuka
Kofun, coffins of lacquered wood were adopted from the Asian continent.

Many categories of burial objects, such as swords, mirrors, and regalia
(fig. 26), are shared with Korea. But the specific magico-religious configuration of weapons, replicas, and regalia is uniquely Japanese. In

Figure 26
Regalia of paramount chiefs of the Kofun period: *left,* fourth century; *right,* sixth century.

1 Circular jasper head ornament
2 Tubular semiprecious stone beads and curved pendant (*magatama*)
3 Ceremonial jasper staff
4 Long iron sword with cast gilt-bronze ring-shaped handle and silver binding
5 Gilt-bronze decorated crown
6 Gold or gilt-bronze earrings with pendants
7 Necklace of hollow metal beads
8 Long, loop-handled sword
9 Fish-shaped hanging belt ornament
10 Gilt-bronze shoes with spangle decorations

particular, the application of red color and strategic placing of mirrors around the body with the reflecting surfaces facing outward are related to the Japanese concept of fighting evil (*hekijo;* Wada 1989, 116).

Changes in the types of grave goods also reflect a shifting value system. In the Early Kofun the predominance of mirrors, beads, and small replicas of woodworking or agricultural tools gave way in the fifth century to large groups of weapons and horse gear. Throughout the Kofun period, iron, which had complex economic and social significance, remained an element in the grave assemblages.

From the earliest *kofun* of the fourth century, burial goods included various types of imported bronze mirrors. Some were decorated with a square and four deities, some with astronomical patterns, and others with deities, animals, and a distinctive triangular rim [184, 185]. Other types of grave goods included hoe- or wheel-shaped stone bracelets in imitation of the shell bracelets of the Yayoi period and other objects of probable magical use, such as those with the shape of a cane, staff, or bridge (like that used for the Japanese musical instrument, the koto [194, 195]), cylindrical beads, and covered bowls. There were also bronze and iron weapons: arrowheads, swords, daggers, and spearpoints. Agricultural tools included sickles, axes, planes, and knives. Miniature tools, such as knives, gravers, and arrowheads, were also part of the burial assemblage. The emphasis was on the magical nature of grave goods, an extension from Yayoi burial practices.

Around the mid-fourth century ritual objects declined in quality and quantity. Armor made of vertical, horizontal, or triangular metal pieces bound together by leather straps was also buried with the deceased. Helmets and weapons became prominent as burial goods. Large mirrors of Japanese origin replaced imported mirrors.

The great mounds of the fifth century, such as those on the Osaka Plain, contain almost no large mirrors or jasper bracelets; iron weapons and armor, however, are abundant. *Sue*-ceramic vessels replaced covered jasper vessels and *haji*-ceramic vessels typical of earlier burials. Horse gear, such as stirrups, bells, saddle fittings, and special strap ornaments, appears for the first time. Gold and silver belt hooks, waist decorations, and earrings have been found as well. These objects were imported or produced by foreign artisans.

In the sixth century the inclusion of luxury grave goods continued, with *sue*-ware vessels, brilliant gilt-bronzed ornaments such as crowns, earrings, waist decorations, and shoes for people of the highest status. Even swords, daggers, armor, and horse gear were gilded (Okauchi 1986, 143).

Representing the highest stratum of society, the great moated *kofun* capture the imagination. Unfortunately, since they are officially designated as imperial tombs and their excavation is prohibited, we know little about their contents. Extremely large tombs are concentrated in the Kinai region and the Kawachi Plain along the eastern shore of Osaka Bay, with the fifth-century *kofun* by far the largest. In many societies the greatest competitive display is created when a polity is striving to consolidate its power and prestige. The elite observe a number of strategies to maintain and increase power and prestige. In fifth-century Japan, burial ritual seems to have had precedence, perhaps to exalt the power of the corporate group and its ancestors and legitimize claims to authority and control of surrounding territories.

In the Kofun period at least three distinctive burials correspond to different social groups. The great *kofun* of the Kinai and Kawachi regions belonged to the central, highest rulers. The large *kofun* in other regions, including Izumo, Kyūshū, and Okayama, belonged to powerful chiefs. The smallest *kofun* belonged to minor local chiefs.

Far-reaching excavations undertaken all over Japan in the wake of extensive land development have unearthed large numbers of commoners' burials. Commoners did not have the prerogative to erect mounds over their burials. Groups of irregular pits, lacking grave goods or preserved skeletal remains, are believed to be communal cemeteries from the Early and Middle Kofun (Fukunaga 1989, 120). In the late Kofun a large proportion of the population was buried in mounded tombs, which were constructed in immense groups. The richness of grave goods declined. Commoners, however, were still buried in unmarked graves.

The number of burials interred together and the disposition of burials also changed during the Kofun period. From the Early and Middle periods, multiple and sometimes serial burials within the same coffin or within the same mound are found.[4]

201   Kofun Period

The Niizawa Senzuka tumulus group near Nara, which has a huge number of burial mounds in a concentrated area, is said to be the burial ground for the Yamato no Aya family of Chinese-Korean origin, also known as the Sakanoue family (Ōbayashi 1987, 241–86). Tomb 126 of the group yielded a cut-gold plaque possibly attached to a crown— similar to one found in a Xianbei (nomadic tribe) burial mound in northern China—a gold earring with long chains, a unique spiral gold hair ornament coiled around a glass rod, and glass objects probably of Persian origin. The burial mound is an unusual square shape; the alignment of the grave-goods box is perpendicular to the coffin in an arrangement similar to that of the tombs of the Silla capital of Kyŏngju. Unlike most sixth-century burials, many Niizawa Senzuka tombs contain coffins buried directly into the top of the burial mounds instead of in corridor tombs (Nara Kenritsu 1977).

Equally impressive are the huge stone-chambered keyhole-shaped mounds of the Kitano area of Kyoto, which are thought to be tombs of the Hata family, who migrated from Silla. A series of Buddhist temples was later built in the same region (Nagata 1987). Some graves of families from Korea are marked by a miniature earthenware oven (*kamado*) set in the corridor burial chamber. The social anthropologist Ōbayashi Taryō (1987, 241–66) believes this to be a ritual object used by patrilineal groups from the Asian continent.

Burial Ritual

How did the ideology of the chiefs materialize in burial practices? During the long process of burial, ceremonies took place at several junctures. First, the burial site was chosen, cleared, and consecrated. Judging from reports of broken pottery and charcoal on the original ground surface, a dedicatory ceremony was apparently held at the initiation of tomb construction. Next, the mound was constructed by various methods. One was to build an earth embankment around the perimeter of the mound, then fill the central portion. Another was to start with a small mound in the center and add to it. Further construction of the burial chamber proceeded in different ways depending on the type constructed. During the Early and Middle Kofun periods in the Kinai region a vertical pit was used. It was prepared after the construction of the mound, by digging down from the top. In the Late Kofun period a horizontal stone chamber was erected before the mound was built.

The deceased was housed in a separate facility (*mogari*) until the *kofun* was completed. In some cases recovered bones are found to have been bleached, indicating that a body had been kept aboveground before burial. It is not clear how a body was transported to its final resting place. The wooden coffins may initially have been used to transport a body; the development of heavy stone coffins, however, which were finished in their final place, and lacquered coffins, in which the body was placed but not transported, must reflect a change in burial rituals. Matting or textile, remains of which have been found in Yayoi jar burials, may have been used to carry the deceased to the tomb (Wada 1989, 116).

At the time of burial iron oxide or other red color was sometimes scattered over the deceased or the entire burial chamber. A ritual sealing of the coffin took place. In the Early Kofun the coffin was not only underlain by a bed of clay but also sealed by a thick layer of clay after burial. This was the burial method at Ishiyama Kofun in Mie Prefecture [193–209]. In later burials the heavy lid of the stone sarcophagus would be maneuvered into place, perhaps before the roof of the chamber was complete.

Since a person's spirit was believed to be located in the head, the space around the head and shoulders of the deceased was frequently packed with mirrors and other objects. At the time of interment in the tomb, further ceremonies took place. Concurrently or shortly thereafter, *haniwa* figures were placed on top of the mound. It is believed that, in addition to funerary rituals, rites of succession for the new chief were also performed. In many cases this must have been a kind of idealized succession since power transitions were often contested.

Grave Offerings

Haniwa. These low-fired clay sculptures give the most direct impressions of the Kofun period (fig. 27). The emergence of *haniwa* is related to the Late Yayoi and Early Kofun practices of placing vessels in and on graves to enhance their visibility. In Mesuriyama Kofun in Sakurai City, Nara Prefecture, three rows of immense cylinders from 4 to 7⅞ feet (1.2–2.4 m) high were arranged over the burial chamber.

Haniwa were arranged to outline the crest of the knoll of *kofun* in the Kinki area, but in the Kantō region they followed the contours of the mound. The function of cylindrical *haniwa* is not entirely clear. Some scholars have suggested that they defined a sacred boundary, while others propose that they stabilized the outer edge of the mound.

In the Osaka region *haniwa* models of houses, weapons, and ceremonial objects began to appear in the late fourth century. House models were most common in the Kinki area. The distinguished archaeologist and art historian J. Edward Kidder (1990a) has stated that while they may have been retreats for the spirit of the deceased, which hovered near the body for some time after death, they also may have been a public statement of status and privilege. Other forms of *haniwa* include military gear, ceremonial objects, and stringed instruments as well as boats, hoes, and knives.

Human figures were also represented in *haniwa* in the form of elite rulers, warriors, shamans, court attendants, common farmers, and horse attendants. While it seems that the *haniwa* shape was derived from offering vessels and cylinders, it is not clear why the shift was made to representational forms. Considering the amount of Chinese learning that flowed into Japan during the Kofun period, it is difficult to exclude any connection with the vigorous tomb-figure tradition that began in China in the Qin dynasty (221–206 B.C.) and persisted for millennia through the Ming dynasty (A.D. 1644–1911). The excavation of small figures in the fourth- and fifth-century tombs of the Jiangsu and Zhejiang regions has suggested the possibility of diffusion from China (Yang 1984; Yang 1985). The location of tomb figures on the surfaces of

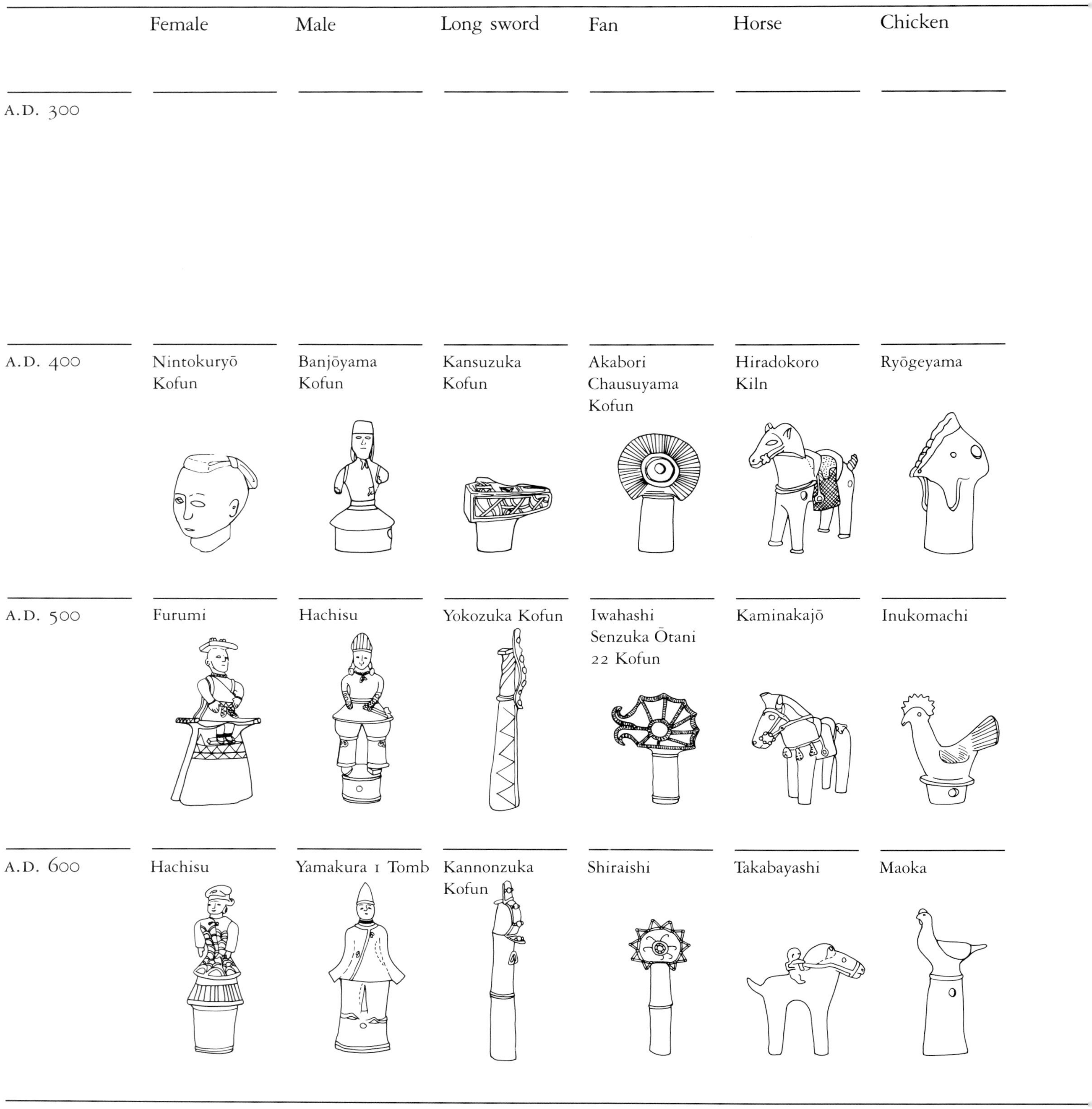

Female	Male	Long sword	Fan	Horse	Chicken

A.D. 300

A.D. 400

Nintokuryō Kofun	Banjōyama Kofun	Kansuzuka Kofun	Akabori Chausuyama Kofun	Hiradokoro Kiln	Ryōgeyama

A.D. 500

Furumi	Hachisu	Yokozuka Kofun	Iwahashi Senzuka Ōtani 22 Kofun	Kaminakajō	Inukomachi

A.D. 600

Hachisu	Yamakura 1 Tomb	Kannonzuka Kofun	Shiraishi	Takabayashi	Maoka

Figure 27
Haniwa forms keyed to sites and arranged chronologically. (For prefecture names, see Index.)

the burial mound remains a distinctive Japanese characteristic. Even that feature, however, could be rooted in the ancient spirit roads of Chinese tombs.

Haniwa representations of animals and birds are characteristic of the Kantō region. Hawks or falcons, sometimes represented with the keeper, provide evidence for the ancient use of these birds in hunting. Chickens are thought to have been kept as ritual birds, their morning crow summoning spirits from the underworld. Swans are represented rather frequently, particularly from the Middle Kofun in the Kinki region.

Waterbird	Fish	Sunshade	Shield	House	Pillow	Stand
Kawarazuka Kofun	Kawarazuka Kofun	Hibasuhimeryō Kofun	Hibasuhimeryō Kofun	Ishiyama Kofun	Tōrōzuka Kofun	Mesuriyama Kofun
Ōjinryō Kofun	Uwanabe Kofun	Hirazuka I Kofun	Miyayama Kofun	Miyayama Kofun	Nekozuka Kofun	Akabori Chausuyama Kofun
Hachimanyama Kofun		Seno Chausuyama Kofun	Ishimi	Imashirozuka Kofun	Ojioka Kofun	
Sakitama	Shiromasu		Hachisu	Akabori mura		

In *haniwa,* a wild pig and a dog often appear as a hunting set, the earliest examples dating to the second half of the fourth century. Deer, including females with their spotted coats rendered by painting, are also represented. Fish, mounted horizontally on tubular stands, were well developed in the southern Kantō region. The famous monkey *haniwa* of the Ōhiyama Kofun in Ibaraki Prefecture is unique (Nara Kenritsu Fūzoku 1990, 49).

Horses are represented in three different *haniwa* forms: with and without decorative trappings and on rare occasions carrying a rider. The large horse from Tsukamawari in Gumma Prefecture (a center of power during the Kofun period) wears the full complement of decorative trappings [164]. Many arrangements of animal *haniwa* appear to be intact, while other *haniwa* were found in the moat in which they had fallen. Some scholars suggest that the animals were arranged to represent the hunting parties in which the dead had participated. It is interesting that such scenes were depicted on the walls of Korean and Chinese tombs of about the same period. Horses may represent wealth, and hunting scenes probably the high status of the deceased.

From the ditches surrounding keyhole-shaped mounds, wooden objects in the same form as *haniwa* have been recovered, indicating that the surface of the tomb was marked with both wooden and earthenware objects. Wooden objects take the form of birds set on posts, shields, and portions of the ritual parasol (*kinugasa*). Recent excavations of Ishizuka Kofun in Sakurai City, Imazato Kurumazuka site in Kyoto Prefecture, and Shijō site in Nara Prefecture have yielded particularly beautiful examples (Nara Kenritsu 1986b, 36; Shiraishi 1990, 40).

The *haniwa* figures from several mounds in the Tsukamawari Kofun group are extraordinary in their characterization of high-status individuals [157–64]. They appear to have been arranged to depict the important ritual ceremonies performed to placate the spirit of the deceased chief who was buried in the tomb and to transfer power to the successor. The images can be seen as representing political legitimization. The standing female figure representing a *miko,* or female shaman, carrying a sword [161] is recognizable by her flat hairstyle, *magatama* necklace, and loose robe (*kesai*). Her cheeks are rouged, probably according to a mourning custom. A kneeling young man, with a braided hairstyle, large gloves with cross straps, and short sword, may be offering condolences [162]. The horse, in full regalia, perhaps belonging to the deceased chief, wears ornamental trappings and bells [164]. At the Tsukamawari tomb site a group of house-shaped *haniwa* was placed on the rear, rounded part of the tomb and around them were placed *haniwa* shields and large swords.

Watanuki Kannonyama Kofun provides a second example of the mounded tombs in Gumma Prefecture (fig. 28). The tomb is a double-moated, keyhole-shaped mound with two tiers on the sides. The burial goods included a Chinese mirror of the same kind as that found in the early sixth-century tomb of King Muryŏng (r. A.D. 501–23) of the Korean kingdom of Paekche as well as a bronze water bottle similar to those from tombs of the Northern Qi dynasty (A.D. 550–57) in China. Watanuki Kannonyama Kofun also yielded a large sword with a gold and silver handle, iron armor, and weapons; gilt-bronze horse gear; and *sue*-ware pottery. At the "neck" of the keyhole, on the flat step, a row of *haniwa* was found.

The arrangement of the *haniwa* on this tomb gives a vivid impression of the burial rites, including the rite of succession of the new chief. Human effigy *haniwa* were placed as though in a procession, led by a male—the new chief—with his hands clasped together as in prayer. Remains showed that the chief buried in the mound wore the same kind of belt with a bell as this *haniwa* figure. Next, a shaman knelt facing him; she and the chief were watched over by another woman. A third

Figure 28
Watanuki Kannonyama Kofun, Gumma Prefecture, a double-moated, two-tiered keyhole-shaped mounded tomb. A row of *haniwa* was found at the "neck" of the keyhole, on the flat step.

woman, carrying a leather bag, continued the line of figures, followed by two men, one in full armor and one armed; a farmhand; then a person carrying a shield. Two representations of shields were found in the row with human figures. Cylindrical *haniwa* continue all around the tomb, except for the end of the trapezoidal portion of the keyhole, where a line of about eight horses and a *haniwa* farmhand was formed. Two house-shaped *haniwa* were found on the summit of the rear burial area and one on the front portion of the tomb.

Another pattern observed on several keyhole-shaped mounds in different parts of the Kantō Plain comprises *haniwa* representing houses on top of the circular front mound and rear projection; a horse and a human figure on the back of the circular mound; and *haniwa* representations of equipment and human figures assembled near the passage to the stone chamber (Nara Kenritsu 1990, 58). The houses on top of the mound may have been resting places for the spirit of the deceased. The human figures near the tomb entrance may also be closely associated with the deceased.

Sue **Ware.** One of the hallmarks of the Kofun period is the production of high-fired, deep gray *sue* ware [170–81]. The color was produced by the introduction of damp foliage into the kiln at the end of firing. Intimately associated with the *kofun* through its use as grave offerings, *sue* ware was also used for utilitarian purposes, such as cooking, serving and displaying food, and storing food and liquids. Of particular interest are the high-pedestaled vessels with miniature pots or cups on the shoulders or along the rim of a supporting base {179}. These vessels, made in the sixth century in major centers such as Aichi, Gifu, and Osaka, may have been used to present offerings of several types of food and drink at one time. Other masterpieces include high-pedestaled vessels with small figures of birds, deer, horses, and men on horseback around the shoulder or along the top of the stand.

Recent excavations confirm that the oldest *sue* ware was made in the Fukuoka region of northern Kyūshū. Korean potters from Paekche are thought to have brought to Japan the technology, which included the tunnel kiln (*anagama*) for high-temperature firing (Kidder 1990a, 41). From there it moved to the Kinai region, where early kilns at Takakura near Suemura, Osaka Prefecture, yield shards of both *haji* and *sue*, which suggests that the kilns were adapting to the production of *sue*. The earliest *sue*, called "pre-Suemura," has been found from several widespread locations in Japan. This early *sue* ware is closest to wares from the Korean kingdoms of Kaya and Paekche.

Sue-ware grave offerings became particularly abundant during the sixth century, with the adoption of the horizontal tomb. Vessels were placed in large numbers in the burial chamber and adjacent corridor. The proliferation of tombs and appearance of clustered tombs in clan cemeteries further increased the need for *sue*-ware vessels (Kidder 1990a). *Sue* ware is not confined, however, to tombs but was a utilitarian ware that continued to be produced and used as late as the fifteenth century (Miwa 1990, 53).

Political Organization

As Reflected by Kofun

The large burial mounds from the end of the third century that mark the beginning of the Kofun period demonstrate continuity as well as innovation. By the end of the Yayoi period large burial mounds, set apart from the burials of commoners, clearly demarcated social ranking. Local chiefs, from Tōhoku to Kyūshū, were allied to a social ranking system under the leadership of a central authority in the Kinai region, symbolized by the adoption of the keyhole-shaped tomb.

In his intensive study of the Kofun of the Kinai region, Hirose Kazuo (1987; 1988) found that as the Kofun period progressed, tombs of local chiefs and powerful regional chiefs became segregated. In the fourth century, during the Early Kofun, the strongest rulers were linked by lineage ties to less powerful chiefs who lived in the same region. Hirose has postulated that two levels of hierarchy became delineated; the upper level of status comprised four large groups of *kofun* in the Kinai region: Furuichi, Mozu, Saki, and Umami. Mounds around these tombs appear to have been constructed by chiefs of the lower rank. In the fifth century, during the Middle Kofun, the construction in the Osaka Plain of great tombs, completely isolated from the tombs of the lower chiefs, indicates a separation of the two levels of society. Examples of the earliest Kofun period tombs are Hashihaka Kofun in Sakurai City and Tsubai Ōtsukayama Kofun near Nara. Their location at the southern end of the Nara Basin indicates that the region was the center of power at the end of the third century.

Ranking within the late third- and early fourth-century polity centered in the Kinai region seems to be borne out by comparisons of the dimensions of *kofun*. The great Hashihaka Kofun is almost precisely three times as large in all major proportions as three major mounds in the region—Itsukahara, Motoinari, and Terado Ōtsuka of Mukō City—suggesting that the pattern of Hashihaka was regularly adhered to in the construction of the subordinate mounds (Sasaki Kenichi 1990, 29).[5]

Bronze mirrors and ritual objects of jasper were recovered from two smaller keyhole-shaped tombs excavated in the late 1940s: Shikinzan in Osaka Prefecture and Ishiyama in Mie Prefecture [183–209]. These objects reflect the burial rituals of the Early Kofun, when miniature tools and weapons, large quantities of iron weapons, and glass beads were buried together with mirrors and ceremonial objects. Neither ceramics nor horse gear have been found in these Early Kofun burials. Both mounds were covered with stones and adorned with *haniwa*.

Ishiyama Kofun exemplifies a relatively small local burial mound, outside the center of the Kinai region and intermediate in political scale. An earthen pit in the top of the circular mound yielded three burials encased in clay. The middle burial was in a long wooden coffin about 26 feet (8 m) long. Outside the coffin were a shield, spear, iron sword, and bronze and iron arrowheads. Three rows of tubular *haniwa* as well as *haniwa* shaped as a house, parasol, wrist guard, and quiver surrounded the tomb.

Shikinzan dates to the fourth century and from it were recovered mirrors and other ritual objects [183–92].[6] The triangular-rimmed mirrors, while not made of the same molds as those from Tsubai Ōtsukayama, are of the same general type, decorated with deities and animals, indicating the existence of several independent sources for the mirrors.

The Shikinzan excavations yielded grave goods from three locations: inside and outside the coffin and on top of the stone chamber. One Chinese mirror was found inside the coffin, together with *magatama* and other beads. Eleven mirrors were found outside the coffin, including a local mirror with *magatama* decoration. Armor, bracelets, tools, arrowheads, sickles, and a plow were recovered. Outside the chamber were sixteen iron swords, twenty-one iron daggers, and an iron plow.

In the mid-fifth century the horizontal stone chamber appeared in the Kinai region in the tombs of the most powerful chiefs. This new type of burial chamber, which originated in Korea and was first adopted in Kyūshū, was prestigious because it displayed knowledge of Asian continental engineering.

As Reflected by Inscribed Swords

One of the greatest contributions to our understanding of fifth-century political relationships lies in the distribution of inscribed iron sword blades. The Seven-Branched Sword held by Isonokami Shrine (the ancestral shrine of the Mononobe family, which was later defeated by the Soga) is said to have been made for the king of Wa by the Korean king of Paekche.[7] It is inscribed in gold inlay with a date of A.D. 369. Only a minute portion of the Japanese population would have been literate at that time.

The discovery in 1988 by X-ray examination of an inscription on an iron sword blade with the characters *ō shi* ("gift of the king") from Inaridai 1 Kofun in Chiba Prefecture seems to indicate that the sword was given to a powerful local chief by a ruler from the Kinai region (Ichihara Shi 1988). Although the sword is not inscribed with a specific date, it appears to belong to the fifth century. Since a personal name is not given in the inscription, it may be that such swords were prepared in advance for bestowal on meritorious persons.

A sword found in Sakitama Inariyama Kofun in Gyōda City, Saitama Prefecture, most likely dating to A.D. 471, does have a personal name, however, and appears to mention patrilineal ancestors (Anazawa & Manome 1986). The Inariyama sword and a sword discovered in Kumamoto Prefecture from Etafunayama Kofun are commemorative swords awarded for service to the central Japanese authority. Niiro Izumi (1989, 156) has suggested that the bestowal of inscribed swords also symbolized the trust held by the Yamato powers for their subordinate regional chiefs.

In the sixth century a different style of sword—long and with decorated pommels—symbolized political relationships. Again, connections with Korea can be seen. A famous gilt-bronze decorated sword with a ring handle depicting a single dragon in side profile, belonging to King Muryŏng of Paekche, has been dated to A.D. 501 or 522. A similar sword has been recovered in Japan from Iwada 14 Kofun in Okayama Prefecture. Was the second example made in Japan, in imitation of the Paekche sword, or was it made in Paekche as a gift to the king or a powerful chief?

Sword handles with ring pommels decorated with twin dragons were produced in Japan and brought from the Asian continent. A fine example was found in Yufunesaka 2 Kofun in Kumano-gun, Kyoto Prefecture (Niiro 1989, 157). The prototype appears to have been made in the Koguryŏ kingdom in northern Korea. Handles of this type are not uncommon, but it is difficult to determine whether they were bestowed by the central power in the Kinai region or obtained independently from the Asian continent. Of impressive proportions, an iron sword with a gilt-bronze pommel [169] comes from Funazuka Kofun in Ibaraki Prefecture, a region of considerable power during the Late Kofun period. The last of the twin-dragon ring-head pommels is found beyond the Kinai region in small tumuli that mark the decline of the mounded-tomb tradition at the beginning of the seventh century.

Social Organization

Most attributes that anthropologists such as Vere Gordon Childe (1942) have assigned to a civilization coalesced during the Kofun period. These elements include high population concentrations, elite administrators supported by agricultural surpluses, taxation and religious tribute, religious and palace architecture, military power, writing, the use of a calendar, craft specialization, and long-distance trade of luxury goods (Tsude 1989b, 49–52).

Tsude (1989a, 25) has referred to the "3-5-7 controversy" concerning the establishment of state organization in Japan. Some archaeologists believe that state-level organization occurred in the third century with the emergence of Queen Himiko and her retainers; for others the threshold was passed in the fifth century with the appearance of three powerful kings, known to historians as the great kings of Wa; and for others the state was not established until the seventh century with the promulgation of the *ritsuryō* legal-code reforms. To infer social organization from fragmentary historical sources and archaeological artifacts is a great challenge. Regardless of scholarly debate concerning the precise thresholds of social change, it is agreed that a series of processes operating at various rates and with different interrelationships occurred throughout the archipelago during the Kofun period.

In the early fifth century the great king of Yamato was simply a primus inter pares who held vague hegemony over similar kingships elsewhere in Japan. Status ranking was clearly defined, but the central political power could not control local production or exchange without the cooperation of chiefs, who were organized in dynamic suballiances based in intermarriage, political-prestige networks, and military confederations. Outlying areas functioned with two levels of chiefs—great chiefs, who formed shifting networks with other regional chiefs; and local chiefs, who controlled small territories, perhaps a day's walk in length.[8] During the first half of the fifth century, two hereditary lines managed to monopolize the kingship of Yamato. The so-called Ōjin-Ricchū-Nintoku dynasty of the fourth to fifth century was not initially an actual dynasty.

The period from the death of Emperor Yūryaku (traditional r. A.D. 457–79) to the ascension of Emperor Kimmei (r. 531/39–71) was a time of struggle and fundamental change. The foremost American historian on this topic, Cornelius Kiley (1973), has referred to the period as the "Keitai-Kimmei disturbances." The reign of Emperor Keitai in the sixth century established a stable national order that was not to change until the late seventh century.

The king was no longer a mere war leader but rather a proprietor of entire agricultural communities, widely distributed in and beyond the Yamato area. Barnes (1988) has estimated that true state organization had been achieved by the early sixth century through the breakup of cellular areas of local autonomy and creation of a continuous political hierarchy replacing the local chiefly hierarchies. At the beginning of the sixth century, under the new dynasty of Keitai, local rulers were gradually reduced to complete submission and a well-articulated court structure, with clear status differentiation and a high degree of occupational specialization, appeared. That process is confirmed by Joan Piggott's interpretation of Izumo protohistory in which rulers of the Izumo region began to send tribute to the Yamato king in the early sixth century (Piggott 1989). The consolidation of power at that time permitted the Yamato court to divide its realm into about 120 administrative units called *kuni*.

By the second half of the sixth century the regional chiefs had all submitted to the Yamato ruler and were dedicated to his or her service. Yamato had advanced toward the Izumo peninsula around A.D. 400 to fortify the region militarily, since it faced the Korean kingdom of Silla. The Kantō and Tōhoku regions began to fall under Yamato control in the fifth century. The Inland Sea region was consolidated by A.D. 550 to maintain a critical navigation route. In Kyūshū the rebellion led by the powerful chief Iwai in which he had allied with Silla was suppressed by Yamato in A.D. 528.[9] Subjugated chiefs, who represented the central Yamato power in local areas, held the status of *kuni no miyatsuko*.[10]

Artisan Groups

In the fifth century there seems to have been an incipient court system dependent on specialized service groups. One group of court functionaries consisted of scribes who were part of the first historically known wave of Korean immigrants into Yamato Japan (Barnes 1987, 87). Local craft specialization already existed. A system of organizing the production of crafts, foodstuffs, and supplies for the imperial family and court of Yamato was formalized in the late fifth century (Kiley 1983, 134). It centered around specialist occupational groups, who had been brought from Korea to make *sue*-ware ceramics, horse gear, and other technically advanced commodities.

These specialist groups (*be*) can be classified as those of craft, subsistence, and attendant service. Early lists include as many as 162 different *be,* but it is not certain whether all were active at one time (Barnes 1987, 91). Members of the *be* came from different sources, depending on the activity. Some were immigrants, some were donated to the Yamato court by regional governors, and some were native residents (Barnes 1987).

In the late fifth century, functionaries in charge of various tasks were organized into 180 *tomo* (such as artisans and technicians), each with an overseer chosen from among other literate foreigners, who, owing to their importance as archivists and clerks, had already acquired *tomo* status. The managers were divided into two groups—*muraji* and *omi,* which were ranked titles in the court hierarchy of officials.[11] These ranked positions were called *kabane.*

During the sixth and early seventh centuries the system of *uji* and *kabane* spread widely throughout the regional aristocracy, subject to control by the central state, Yamato. The *uji* was a corporate group of households forming a single kin unit and sharing a common heritable name. They had become influential in the fifth century among certain client groups serving the Yamato king's household and then assumed importance as regional chiefs who accepted the king's superior authority.[12] Within the group were one or more lineages, the *kabane,* bearing an additional hereditary title, which carried with it eligibility for chieftainship in the *uji. Uji* chiefs with *kabane* titles were entrusted with control of *be* groups. The use of the term "*kabane*" for the system of ranked titles among the *uji* is thought to have come from Paekche in southwestern Korea (Kiley 1983, 134).

Uji chiefs of the late sixth century can be grouped into four main categories: *omi,* regional chiefs of high noble status; *muraji,* a service group of chiefs of high noble status; *tomo no miyatsuko,* petty service chiefs; and *kuni no miyatsuko,* petty regional chiefs. Members of the *omi* class were descendants of rulers of domains located in the Kantō Plain, along the coast of the Sea of Japan, and in Kyūshū, all of which were autonomous when Emperor Keitai came to power in A.D. 507. The *kuni no miyatsuko*'s *uji* members probably never exceeded a few hundred, and their relationship to the vast majority of thousands of inhabitants of the district was political, not hereditary. The *tomo no miyatsuko* became the chief intermediary between the local *be* heads and the Yamato authorities. During much of the sixth century the treasuries seem to have been controlled by the dominant *uji* leaders of the Soga clan.[13]

In addition to the dependent *uji,* who were clearly subordinate to the king, a group of high-ranking clans, some of Korean origin, such as the Heguri, Katsuragi, Ki, and Soga, held independent status. These clans provided royal spouses. They also dispatched members as provincial governors to key food-producing areas and were responsible for producing food for the central court. The Hata clan is thought to have arrived in the early fifth century from Korea. They may have helped introduce new techniques of weaving, sericulture, and metallurgy. Several of the highest-ranking families were descendants of these groups or relatives by marriage. The genealogies of both groups state that they were originally Chinese who had fled to Korea during disturbances in the Warring States period and Han dynasty (Carter 1983a, 125; Carter 1983b, 111; Ōbayashi 1987, 265–80; Mori 1989c, 76).

The flood of immigrant artisans into Yamato during the fifth century is thought to have been the stimulus for the court to extend administrative control over craft production, the elaboration of which probably resulted from many factors. Increased agricultural productivity supplied expanded subsistence necessities, so that more time was available for other specialized activities. Intense competition among chiefs, both local and powerful, stimulated craft production for display and aggrandizement as well as basic utilitarian production to finance luxury goods. The rising central polity of Yamato must have attempted to control the flow of luxury items and restrict the rarest and highest-quality imported items for their own use. They were not completely successful in that endeavor, since Japan had many points of access from the Asian continent.

The proliferation of *tomo* and *be* groups in the household organization of the Yamato royal house resulted in a large and complex administrative structure that made available new and reliable sources of military and agricultural equipment. The system accommodated large numbers of regional leaders in the Yamato area as they took charge of various service units. At the same time, the office of the king—working through intermediaries designated by the central government—was gradually divested of all local administrative activities.

Summary

This discussion of the Kofun period has focused on the concentration of political power in the Kinai region and emergence of the Yamato state at the end of the fifth century. The construction of tombs several times larger than those of the surrounding areas confirms that Yamato rulers controlled resources not only in their own territories but also in neighboring states that had previously been independent. The central powers rewarded the loyal confederates with mirrors in the third century and sword handles and blades in the fifth and sixth centuries. Local chiefs whose ancestors had been independent of Yamato became officials in the new state. Inscriptions on sword blades refer to their new titles. State control is seen in the regulation of burial mound size and in the control of the distribution of iron.

The process of political consolidation is alluded to in a memorial sent in A.D. 478 by Emperor Yūryaku to the Chinese Emperor Shundi (r. A.D. 477–79), a portion of which is quoted here.

Our land is remote and distant; its domains lie far out in the ocean. From time of old our forebears have clad themselves in armor and helmet and gone across the hills and waters, sparing no time for rest. In the east, they conquered fifty-five countries of hairy men; and in the west, they brought to their knees sixty-six countries of various barbarians. Crossing the sea to the north, they subjugated ninety-five countries. The way of the government is to keep harmony and peace; thus order is established in the land [Tsunoda & Goodrich 1951, 23].

Most of our knowledge of the Kofun period is still derived from tombs. Although settlement sites have been excavated and described, we do not know much about the daily life of the Kofun people. Those of high social status lived in more elaborate houses than did the commoners. The dispersed settlement pattern contrasts dramatically with those of China and West Asia and even with that of the Yayoi period, in which permanent, fortified villages were common. It may be that the impermanent construction techniques of Japan exaggerate the smallness and temporary nature of Kofun settlements.

New kinds of tools, tipped with iron, enabled the expansion of agriculture into upland areas, while irrigation in the lowlands permitted higher yields.

Even though there was cultural borrowing from Korea and China as well as substantial migration, the ideology of the Kofun period is distinctive. The cult of mirrors set in tombs, use of red burial coloring, methods of sealing the burials in clay, and the making of *haniwa* figures and placing them on the outside of tombs are all peculiarly Japanese. Japanese *haniwa* represented rulers and priests as well as wild birds and animals, whereas Chinese tomb figures portrayed retainers, militia, musicians, and foreigners. The *haniwa* cult rationalized a type of society much smaller than that of ancient China and was based on events of this world and not of deities in the next. The emphasis on the perfectible world of the present continues to be a distinctive aspect of Japanese culture (Smith 1983, 109).

The Kofun period exemplifies the rise of a secondary civilization, one that borrowed heavily from the advanced states around it yet developed a unique ideology and pattern of regional chiefly networks.

Notes

1. These ports later became silted up and were abandoned.

2. The kilns, roughly 55¾ feet (17 m) long and 4⅝ feet (1.4 m) wide, are dug into the ground surface to a depth of about 24 inches (60 cm). They slope about twenty degrees along a hillside. About fifteen pit houses set in an area of 2½ acres (about 1 hectare) were excavated.

3. Mitsudera site is discussed in this publication in an essay by Shiraishi Taichirō.

4. These findings appear to reflect a consanguine group of people, although the reasons for the variation are not clear (Wada 1989, 117).

5. The front mound of Hashihaka Kofun is 902¼ feet (275 m) long and 492 feet (150 m) wide.

6. Shikinzan is about 328 feet (100 m) long and has a stone chamber 23 feet (7 m) long, 3⅝ feet (1.1 m) wide, and 3⅝ feet (1.1 m) high in the top of the rear circular mound.

7. The term "Wa" may be confusing to the reader. It is the Japanese reading of a Chinese character first used in the Han dynasty records to designate the Japanese. As mentioned in the discussion of the Yayoi period, it was used in the Han dynasty to refer to Queen Himiko, who was called the ruler of the Wa. It is said to refer to the Japanese, but it actually appears to have referred to an ethnic group not only in Japan but also in southern Korea, at a time when the people of this region had no notion of themselves as nation-states. It was used until the late seventh century, after which Chinese records show that the Yamato court adopted "Nihon" as its official name. The term names an ethnic group, not a kingdom. Another character for the word "peace" is also pronounced "*wa*" and is used by the Japanese to designate Japan. In later times, such as the Ming dynasty, the term "*wa*" was used negatively, to refer to the "*wakō*," the pirates who menaced China's coast.

8. In the Kyoto region these smallest units, situated along the edges of the alluvial plain, were 1¼ to 3⅝ miles (1.9–5.8 km) long (Tsude 1990).

9. It is thought that Iwai is buried in Iwatoyama Kofun in Fukuoka Prefecture, which is adorned with stone figures resembling *haniwa*.

10. Some of these people held the rank of *omi*. Their tasks were ministerial, whereas the tasks of the *tomo no miyatsuko* were supervisorial.

11. The *omi*, the highest rank of officials at that time, could provide consorts for the Yamato kings, while the *muraji* could not. The *omi* had independent ancestral deities, who rebelled against the ancestral gods of the royal family (Ōbayashi 1987, 241–67). The *omi* were aristocrats from polities that had previously been independent of the Yamato power and had contended with it. The *muraji* title was given to families whose ancestral gods served the gods of the royal family.

12. Cornelius Kiley (1973) has defined the *uji* as a subject chief and kindred, endowed with hereditary authority to direct the conduct of a designated group of royal subjects in the monarch's service. The *uji* chief enjoys a designated share of royal authority but is utterly subordinate to the king's power. Ōbayashi Taryō (1987, 78) has stated that the organizational basis of the *uji* was primarily political and that they were cognatic until the end of the fifth century; that is, inheritance took place through both the father's and mother's side, creating a large group of kin.

13. Other forms of appropriation, such as the designation of lands and granaries as official domains, had little to do with the *kabane*, but the workers on those lands were referred to as *be*.

TSUBAI ŌTSUKAYAMA: MIRRORS WITHIN A BURIAL MOUND

TANAKA MIGAKU

On March 26, 1953, representatives of the Kyoto Prefectural Education Commission made an urgent telephone request to the Archaeology Department of the University of Kyoto. Bronze mirrors had been unearthed during grading near a railway line. Archaeologists were instantly dispatched to the site to conduct a survey. There, on the slope of a cliff, a pit-style stone chamber had been exposed. Fragments of artifacts from the tomb were scattered in earth, sand, and a mixture of clay and cinnabar that had been dug out and discarded in the grading. Among these were fragments of bronze mirrors. The salvage excavation of the Tsubai Ōtsukayama burial mound, which would become well known to Japanese archaeologists, commenced immediately (fig. 29).

In their survey archaeologists carefully examined the inside of the chamber, collected the disturbed artifacts, questioned the construction workers about the circumstances of the finds, and measured the mound. They found the mound to be a keyhole shape 51 feet (170 m) long. A railway track, constructed in 1894, crossed between the front of the mound and the circular rear portion. The pit-style stone chamber, located near the center of the circular portion, was exposed on the cliff surface alongside the track (figs. 30, 31).[1] Inside the tomb were thirty-six bronze mirrors as well as bronze arrowheads and iron arrowheads, daggers, a helmet, and other burial goods. Most artifacts had already been removed and hidden by those involved in the construction but were later recovered by the police. The excavation was completed in early May, when the last of the mirrors were retrieved. Today the artifacts are housed in the University of Kyoto.

The fame of the Tsubai Ōtsukayama mound derives from its status as one of the oldest keyhole-shaped tombs. In addition, it is valued for the thirty-three mirrors (of the thirty-six altogether) found there of a specific type decorated with deities and animals and having a raised, triangular rim. Like other bronze mirrors excavated from Yayoi and Kofun sites, these were imported from China or made in Japan, except for a few that were produced in Korea. In Yayoi and Kofun Japan, mirrors were considered to be ritual implements endowed with magical properties. Only since the end of the seventh century did the Japanese begin to use mirrors for cosmetic purposes.

More than four thousand mirrors of the Yayoi and Kofun periods have been found to date; of these, one-third were made in China and two-thirds in Japan. The greatest number of the Chinese mirrors, 340 in all, are decorated with deities and sacred animals and have a raised, triangular rim. About 90 percent of this kind of mirror are large, 7¾ to 9¾ inches (20–25 cm) in diameter.

Figure 29
Plan of the Tsubai Ōtsukayama site,
Kyoto Prefecture, one of the oldest
keyhole-shaped tombs dating to
the Early Kofun period (A.D. 250–
400). A railway track, constructed
in 1894, cut through the *kofun,*
between the front of the mound and
circular rear portion.

Why does the mirror with triangular rim and associated decoration
stimulate discussion among archaeologists? During the 1950s a young
scholar, Kobayashi Yukio, availing himself of the finds of the Tsubai
Ōtsukayama mound, developed a theory that the mirrors with raised,
triangular rims and decorated with deities and animals had been given
to Queen Himiko by the emperor of Wei, as mentioned in the *Wei zhi.*
He proposed, moreover, that when tribute was paid by Japanese chiefs to
the Chinese state of Wei and subsequently to its successor state, Jin, the
same type of mirror was given in return by the Chinese emperor. Yamato
rulers, who reigned after the Yamatai, also recognized mirrors as symbols of authority and prestige and used them for expanding their rule.

In examining the context and distribution of these mirrors in Japan,
Kobayashi assumed that a mirror was given to a local chief as a sign
of recognition by a Yamato ruler who made the local chief responsible
for the reorganization of that area. The person buried in the Tsubai
Ōtsukayama mound must have been working for the Yamato polity in
the process of extending its rule, and he or she, as the owner or custodian
of the mirrors, must have possessed great power over political negotiations
with local chiefs from a wide region. Kobayashi's theory is based on
detailed research of the mirrors and examination of the conditions of

Figure 30
Entrance to the stone-lined burial chamber of Tsubai Ōtsukayama, located beneath the circular portion of the mound. Thirty-three mirrors considered to be ritual implements endowed with magical properties were found here.

their excavation. His hypothesis created a new image of ancient Japan dependent on archaeological materials recovered after 1945.

The most crucial counter-argument to Kobayashi's theory holds that the mirrors were neither made in China nor given to Wa by the emperor of Wei because no such mirror has ever been found in China. Critics of Kobayashi's theory assume that most mirrors of this type were made by artisans who migrated to Japan. It is my opinion, however, that these mirrors were produced in China. Why were they found only in Japan? Characteristics of the mirrors, such as standardized size and mass production, suggest that they were manufactured for bestowal. In fact, a large number were made from the same molds. If the Chinese emperors ordered a special type of mirror for presentation to Japanese rulers, it follows that they would be found only in Japan, not China.

Nearly forty years have passed since the discovery at Tsubai Ōtsuka-yama mound of the triangular-rimmed mirrors with deities and animals. The theory proposed by Kobayashi, on the basis of that excavation, still strongly influences research on the establishment of the ancient Japanese state.

Note

1. Its inside dimensions are 23⅛ feet long (7 m) and 9⅞ feet (3 m) high.

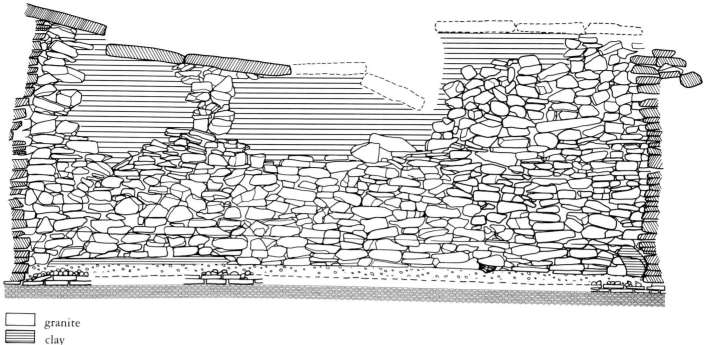

granite
clay
sand
original soil surface

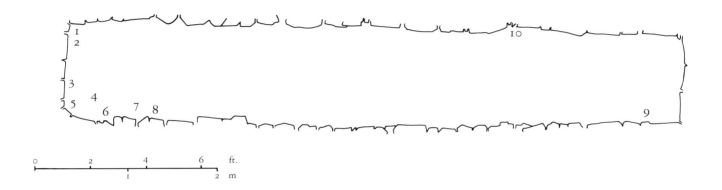

| 0 | | 2 | | 4 | | 6 | | ft. |
| 1 | | 2 | m |

Figure 31
Tsubai Ōtsukayama Kofun.

 Above, elevation showing the burial chamber near the surface of the mound (the dotted lines represent granite slabs on top of the burial chamber); *below,* plan, from above, showing the long burial chamber and location of grave offerings (listed here).

1 Knives
2 Ax
3 Sickle
4 Iron shield
5 Knives
6 Ax
7 Planing tool
8 Ax
9 Triangular-rimmed mirrors with deities and animals
10 TLV mirror

MITSUDERA

SHIRAISHI TAICHIRŌ

Located in western Gumma Prefecture, Mitsudera was the residence of a powerful family in the Kofun period (fig. 32). The site was discovered in 1981 during salvage excavations preceding the construction of the Jōetsu Railway Line. Archaeologists have recently found moated sites with structures assumed to be the residences of powerful local families during the Kofun period. Mitsudera 1 has left the clearest indications of the original structures.

Hodata Tomb Cluster, located about ⅝ of a mile (1 km) northwest of Mitsudera, consists of Futagoyama, Hachimanzuka, and Yakushizuka, three large keyhole-shaped mounds built in succession from the late fifth to the early sixth century. The three mounds are roughly contemporaneous with Mitsudera 1, and the individuals buried there are assumed to have been powerful local figures. These extremely interesting mounds offer archaeologists a chance to study as one unit the residences and burial sites of a local elite.

Both agriculture and warfare began in Japan during the Yayoi period, and many Yayoi settlements in various regions were surrounded by defensive moats. During the Kofun period, however, when large keyhole-shaped mounds were erected, moated settlements were discontinued. In their place came moated elite residences, which signify that the chief, who originally lived in the same settlement with other members of the community, had left the communal site to establish a separate residence. The same process occurred in the segregation of burial facilities

Figure 32
Reconstruction of elite family residences at Mitsudera, Gumma Prefecture, a late fifth- to early sixth-century site.

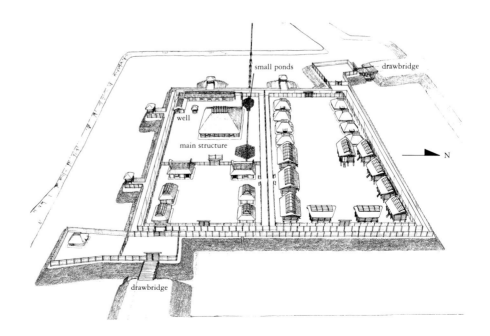

Figure 33
Excavation of paving stones on
the slope of a moat at the Mitsudera site.

and construction of distinctive mounded tombs for the elite. These
developments reflect the birth of a segregated social stratum of power.

The elite residence at Mitsudera I is important in reconstructing
the living patterns of powerful families who erected large keyhole-
shaped mounds of about 328 feet (100 m) long in the Kantō region.
They lived in moated houses, retained surplus products from the villagers, and owned craft workshops requiring high technical skill,
such as metalworking.

The square residential compound at Mitsudera I, about 295 feet
(90 m) to a side, was surrounded by a natural moat created by diverting
the course of the Sarufu River.[1] The bank of the moat in front of the
compound was paved with river stones ranging from head to fist size (fig.
33). Structures enclosed by the moat changed over time. At its most
developed stage, the compound was surrounded by double rows of
palings or fences, inside of which was a row of palings around two blocks,
north and south. Each block, therefore, was surrounded by three
rows of palings.

A large, single-story house, about 46 feet (14 m) to a side, located in
the western part of the block, is assumed to have been the main structure
of the compound. A well with an octagonal roof was located west of
the main central structure. Small ponds, paved with stones and connected
by a ditch running east to west, were located to the northwest and northeast of the main building. The water source was on the western side of the
moat. Finds from the ponds include stone daggers, mirrors, and
miniature *magatama,* which suggest that these were places for rituals
involving water.

Near the northeast corner of the main structure was a small draw-
bridge that gave access to the moat by providing a walkway over the
palings. In addition, an extension into the moat, southwest of the houses,
led to a bridge that crossed the river.

From the house and moat, archaeologists found clay vessels of *haji*
and *sue* wares, miniature ritual objects made of stone and wood, weapons,
and wooden agricultural and weaving tools as well as bellow nozzles,

crucibles, and iron slag used in the manufacture of bronze and iron implements. It is assumed that the complex was occupied for fifty years, from the latter half of the fifth to the early sixth century.

Two pit dwellings were discovered in the northern block, which has been only partially excavated. Since there is no clear evidence for the existence of large structures or storage facilities in the northern block, it is assumed that the block was used for the daily activities of the elite, in contrast with the southern block, which was reserved for festivities and rituals.

It is interesting that half of the Mitsudera 1 residential complex may have been used for rituals, which we assume entailed the use of water for rice-paddy cultivation. Also, a large-scale construction effort was undertaken to divert the course of the Sarufu River to fill the moat surrounding the residences. The master of the large house may have been a priest who controlled water resources and presided over water rituals. Since the Kofun period the word *matsuri-goto* ("ritual affairs") has been used as an alternative term for affairs of state. The word also includes the meaning "to worship the deities," which appropriately describes the role of the chiefs of the Kofun period who were endowed with ritual and political power as the leaders of unified chiefdoms.

Note

1. The moat was 99 to 132 feet (30–40 m) wide and 11½ feet (3.5 m) deep.

KUROIMINE

TSUDE HIROSHI

A farming village of the Late Kofun period, Kuroimine was preserved intact under volcanic ash from a major eruption of Mount
Haruna, located about 12⅜ miles (20 km) west of the site (fig. 34).
Situated at Komochi Village, Gumma Prefecture, Kuroimine is 68¼
miles (110 km) northwest of Tokyo. The settlement occupied an area of
2,038 acres (825 hectares) on a plateau about 820 feet (250 m) above
sea level. Excavations of 20 percent of the site have revealed houses,
storage areas, animal sheds, village enclosures, cultivated land, and
roads, all preserved intact. Full details of the hitherto unknown lives of
the peasants of the Kofun period have been elucidated, and excavations
are ongoing.

The accumulated fall of volcanic pumice and ash was 6½ feet (2 m)
thick. The devastating event, which occurred around the mid-sixth
century, preserved a complete and detailed picture of wooden structures
that otherwise would not have survived later cultivation and other
disturbances. The most recent discoveries include an outer bank about
19⅝ inches (50 cm) high around a pit house, the roof of which was 9⅞
feet (3 m) above the ground (fig. 35). The roof was smeared with a
layer of clay 2 inches (5 cm) thick. In most other sites the structures
(other than pit dwellings) built at ground level had been totally ruined,
leaving only postholes. At Kuroimine, however, the construction of
the walls and roof have remained undamaged under the thick volcanic
ash. Two kinds of small structures with circular floors were built on the

Figure 34
Excavation of the Kuroimine site,
Gumma Prefecture.

Figure 35
Reconstruction of a pit house from
Kuroimine. The surrounding outer
bank of earth served to insulate
the interior.

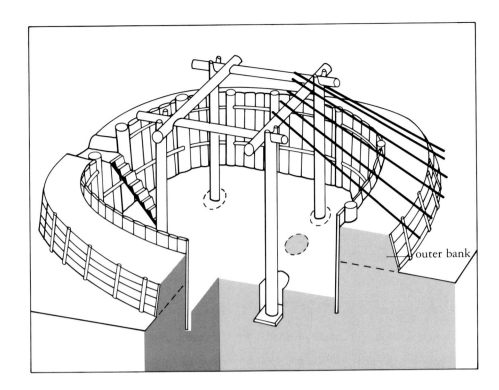

ground. One, having a fire pit inside, is assumed to have been a cooking shed; the other, with an abundance of phytoliths in the soil, may have been a storage area for straw and dried grass.

The most interesting recovered structures are the animal sheds. One, the first cow shed from the Kofun period to have been discovered, has a rectangular plan with five partitions. Analysis of remnant fatty acids indicates that cows were raised and kept in the shed. A brushwood fence surrounding the area occupied by houses, storage facilities, and animal sheds points to the likelihood that these structures comprised a unit.

Upon removal of the volcanic ash the earth surface appeared as it had been in the sixth century, with uneven ridges between the fields creating a beautiful linear pattern. The fields extended to the outside of the residential complex and onto the slopes of the plateau. *Azuki* beans were discovered, as were small cultivated areas within the complex, which may have been private vegetable gardens. The minuteness of the detected particles of plant opal has led some archaeologists to argue, however, that these plots were rice seedbeds. A rice paddy irrigated with water from a river running just below the plateau was also unearthed. The small size of the paddy suggests that cultivation of upland fields was more important than that of lower-elevation areas.

By following compacted soil, excavators were able to trace ancient footpaths (fig. 36). The main path branched out through the village, and smaller paths connected the houses. The enclosure of the residential complex was open to the small paths to create entrances and exits. Such important information enabled archaeologists to follow the villagers' daily activities. Several trees were detected both inside and outside the residential complex, and clay vessels discovered under trees suggest that these were ritual places. Perhaps villagers prayed there for good harvests or protection from disasters or calamities.

The total number of houses is not yet known, but about nine residential units with brushwood fences have been recognized. Eight units with an average size of about 99 by 132 feet (30 × 40 m) were discovered, together with one house complex about twice the average size.

In a residential complex in the western part of the site was a large central house built on the ground, a cooking shed with a circular floor plan, two elevated storage structures, presumably for grain, an animal shed, a storage hut, and a pit house with a brushwood fence (fig. 37). Other housing complexes of similar size did not have storage buildings or animal sheds, indicating that they belonged to people of lower status.

The relationship of ground-level houses and pit houses in the same complex is not clear. Some archaeologists believe that the former was used in summer and the latter in winter. Given the size of a house in an average complex, it is assumed that five to six people, possibly a monogamous family unit, lived in one complex. One may assume that the house of a powerful leader, with storage buildings and cow sheds, was surrounded by smaller house complexes with which it was in a cooperative relationship.

Figure 36
Plan showing features of the eastern sector of Kuroimine.

Figure 37
Plan showing features of the western sector of Kuroimine.

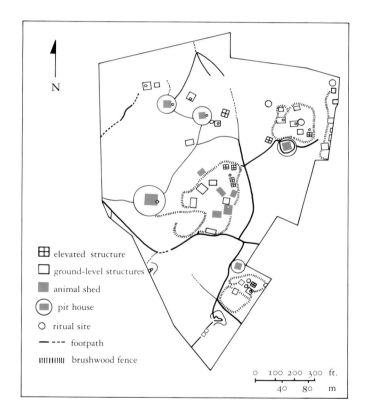

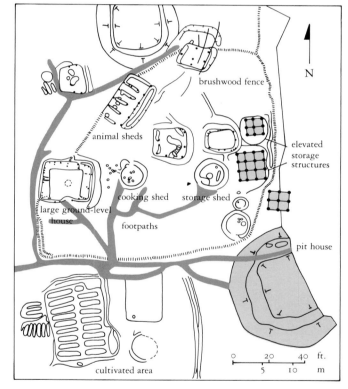

Early Kofun period,
late 4th century
Excavated at Samida Takarazuka
Kofun, Nara Prefecture
Bronze
Diameter 9¼ in. (23.4 cm)
Imperial Household Agency, Tokyo
Reproduced in color, frontispiece

This mirror with a decorative motif composed of houses is unique. Four different houses with thatched roofs in two styles—gambrel and gable—are depicted within the inner zone around the central knob. Gambrel roofs cover the pit dwelling, surface dwelling, and dwelling with raised floor. The gable-roofed building is assumed to be an elevated storage structure. A bird perches on the roof of the pit dwelling, and a tree is planted on each side of the surface dwelling. A ladder is placed on the right side of the house with raised floor, and another ladder leans against the storage building. A balcony, with an open umbrella, is on the left side of the elevated house. A bird perches on the roof of the storage building. Like the pictures on bronze bells or house-shaped *han-*

iwa, the images are highly informative about ancient dwellings.

Samida Takarazuka Kofun in Nara Prefecture, in which this mirror was found, was built on the summit of a hill.[1] Excavations in 1881 unearthed many burial goods, including bronze mirrors, objects of jade and other precious materials, stone bracelets, hoe-shaped jasper bracelets, *tomoegata* ornaments, and bronze arrowheads. In particular, the discovery of as many as thirty-six bronze mirrors of excellent quality was quite rare. Samida Takarazuka is a typical example of a mounded tomb dating to approximately the latter half of the fourth century B.C.

KAWAHARA SUMIYUKI

1. The *kofun* is 367½ feet (112 m) long.

Early Kofun period,
late 4th century
Excavated at Shinyama Kofun,
Nara Prefecture
Bronze
Diameter 11 in. (28.0 cm)
Imperial Household Agency, Tokyo

The decoration of this mirror, consisting of intersecting diagonal and curved lines, is called *chokkomon*. This is one of three mirrors of its kind unearthed from Shinyama Kofun in Nara Prefecture. Two of the three mirrors are decorated with linked arcs. This specimen has a four-petal decoration around the knob, which is surrounded by three concentric zones (four units of intersecting diagonal and curved lines decorate the inner zone); a petaloid pattern is found on the inner zone; and eight units of intersecting diagonal and curved lines enhance the outer zone.

The pattern of intersecting lines was particular to the Kofun period in Japan; it was composed of two straight lines diagonally intersecting, with additional half-arc patterns. The pattern was applied to all

kinds of artifacts, including shell bracelets, quivers, sword decoration, *haniwa,* stone coffins, and slab partitions in the corridor-style stone-chamber tombs. It is generally thought that the decoration was endowed with magical powers.

Shinyama Kofun is a large keyhole-shaped mounded tomb, built sometime in the latter half of the fourth century on the side of a hill.[1] When the site was excavated in 1885, a large quantity of burial goods was discovered at the back of the tomb. Recovered objects include jasper and talc artifacts, gilt-bronze belt clasps, and iron swords. A group of bronze mirrors, thirty-four altogether, made in China and Japan, were part of the grave offerings.

KAWAHARA SUMIYUKI

1. The *kofun* is 450 feet (137 m) long.

Late Kofun period, 6th century
Excavated at Fujinoki Kofun,
Nara Prefecture
Gilt bronze
Agency for Cultural Affairs,
Government of Japan, Tokyo; on
deposit at Nara Prefectural Kashi-
hara Archaeological Research Insti-
tute, Nara
Important Cultural Property

155
Saddlebow 16¼ × 20⅛ in.
(41.2 × 51.2 cm)
Cantle 17⅛ × 22½ in.
(43.6 × 57.2 cm)

Figure 38
Horse trappings of the Kofun
period, as represented in *haniwa*.

1 Decorative plate at end of bit
2 Knob on bit plate of bridle
3 Headstall
4 Metal fittings on straps or at
   strap unions
5 Reins
6 Breast strap
7 Bell
8 Saddle
9 Saddlebow (front of saddle)
10 Cantle (rear of saddle)
11 Decorative fixture with metal
    ornamental plume
12 Crupper
13 Harness pendant
14 Stirrup
15 Mudflaps

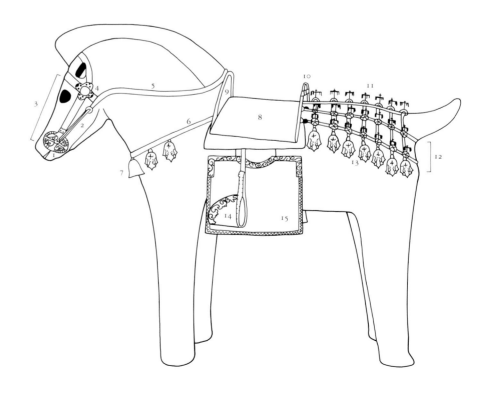

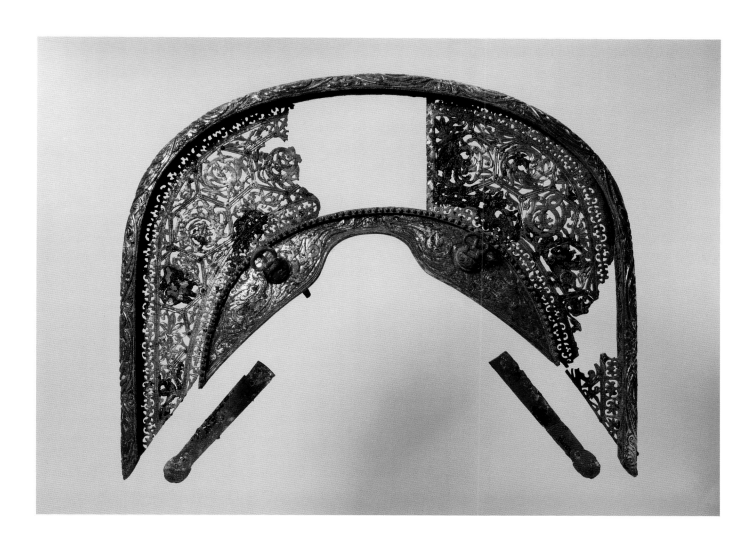

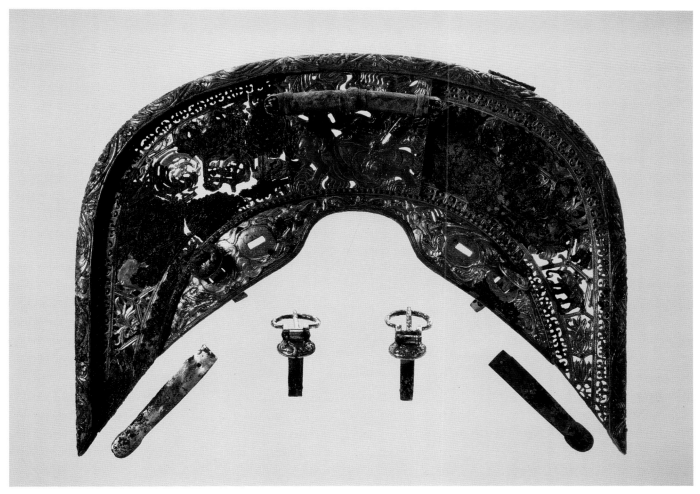

Saddlebow and cantle {155}

156
Ornament 7⅛ × 3⅞ in.
(18.3 × 9.9 cm)

Fujinoki Kofun in Nara Prefecture became suddenly famous in Japan when excavations there from 1985 to 1988 yielded a large number of burial goods of outstanding quality. A circular burial mound, the Fujinoki tomb is thought to date to the second half of the sixth century.[1]

A sarcophagus was placed within the corridor-style stone chamber. Objects recovered there include bronze swords and mirrors, exquisite ornaments, shoes, jade pieces, and clothes. These splendid horse trappings were found outside the sarcophagus (fig. 38). It is assumed that they were not made in Japan but were imported from the Asian continent.

The gilt-bronze saddlebow and cantle [155] were found between the sarcophagus and back wall of the stone chamber, together with other horse trappings. Each consists of a flange and decorative plates. The outer plate (*umi*) of the saddlebow was decorated with an assortment of images, including tiger, phoenix, small bird, dragon, lion, and palmetto pattern on a background of tortoiseshell hexagons. A pair of dragons in relief adorns the inner part of the flange. Phoenix and palmetto patterns are also depicted in relief on the flange.

A gilt-bronze handle is attached at the upper center of the outer plate of the cantle. Each end of the handle is decorated with a hemispherical glass piece. A mysterious figure of a man holding a weapon is seen in slight relief on the outer plate.

Many horse trappings, including a bridle bit, stirrup with hollow, gilt-bronze toe receptacle, metal fittings for mudflaps, strap joiners or unions, and harness pendants, have been excavated. Of particular beauty is a gilt-harness pendant in the shape of a pointed leaf with two phoenixes facing each other [156].

KAWAHARA SUMIYUKI

1. The *kofun* is 158 feet (48 m) wide.

Late Kofun period, 6th century
Earthenware
Agency for Cultural Affairs,
Government of Japan, Tokyo; on
deposit at Gumma Prefectural
History Museum, Maebashi
Important Cultural Property

157
Shield with stand
Excavated at Tsukamawari 3 Kofun,
Gumma Prefecture
49¾ × 15 × 6⅛ in.
(126.4 × 38.0 × 15.5 cm)

158
Seated girl
Excavated at Tsukamawari 3 Kofun,
Gumma Prefecture
27⅛ × 10¾ × 11¾ in.
(69.0 × 27.5 × 30.0 cm)

159
Boy holding a shield
Excavated at Tsukamawari 1 Kofun,
Gumma Prefecture
54½ × 14¾ × 10¾ in.
(138.5 × 37.5 × 27.5 cm)

160
Sword with stand
Excavated at Tsukamawari 4 Kofun,
Gumma Prefecture
60¾ × 4¾ × 5⅞ in.
(154.5 × 12.0 × 15.0 cm)

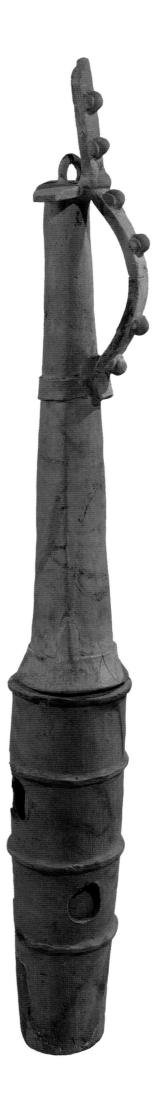

161
Girl with a long sword
Excavated at Tsukamawari 4 Kofun,
Gumma Prefecture
31 × 11⅜ × 10 in.
(78.7 × 29.0 × 25.5 cm)

162
Kneeling boy
Excavated at Tsukamawari 4 Kofun,
Gumma Prefecture
19⅝ × 10⅝ × 15¾ in.
(50.0 × 27.0 × 40.0 cm)

163
Equestrian
Excavated at Tsukamawari 4 Kofun,
Gumma Prefecture
30⅛ × 13 × 9¼ in.
(76.5 × 33.0 × 23.5 cm)

164
Horse
Excavated at Tsukamawari 4 Kofun,
Gumma Prefecture
33½ × 40⅛ × 11¾ in.
(85.0 × 102.0 × 30.0 cm)

From the fifth to the sixth century many kinds of representational *haniwa* were placed on the top and around a *kofun*. The first *haniwa* were in the form of houses, parasols, quivers, shields, helmets, and armor. The custom began in the Kinki region and later spread to the Kantō region. Human and animal figures gradually appeared, and an enormous number and variety of *haniwa* were produced for use on burial mounds.

Haniwa in the form of a house, shield [157], and sword [160] were found atop the circular rear portion of the mound, and human- and horse-figure *haniwa* were lined up on the square terrace at the front (fig. 39). The *haniwa* on the top symbolized the power of the deceased ruler, who was protected with swords and shields. The human-figure *haniwa* on the front represented the funeral ceremony. The procession was led by a girl with a long sword [161], followed by three girls who offer cups, a kneeling boy [162], a horse attendant [163], and a caparisoned horse [164]. They express their grief at the loss of the chief and praise his life and power.

The faces and necks of the human-figure *haniwa* participating in the funeral procession were painted red. Adorned with *magatama* necklaces, bracelets, and bead ornaments, the mourners demonstrate how burial goods were actually worn.

TANABE IKUO

Figure 39
Plan reconstruction of the Tsukamawari 4 Kofun, Gumma Prefecture.
Numbers indicate where individual
haniwa were found by excavators
(for *haniwa* recovered from this site,
see entries 160–64).

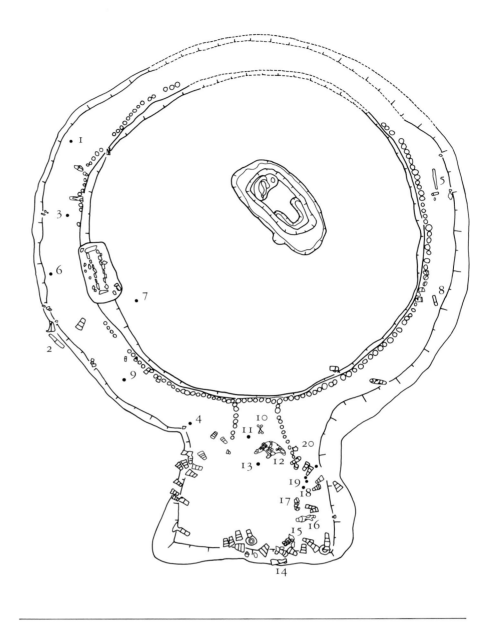

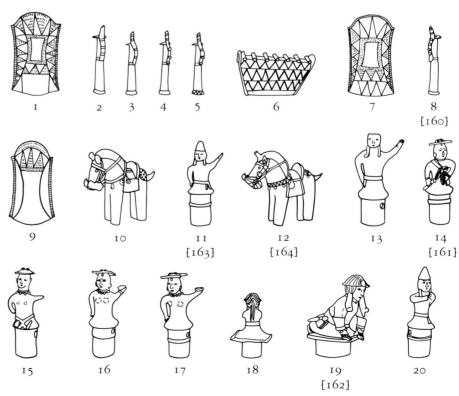

Middle Kofun period,
early 5th century
Excavated at Tsudōshiroyama Kofun,
Fujiidera City, Osaka Prefecture
Earthenware
42¼ × 35 × 22 in.
(107.5 × 89.0 × 56.0 cm)
Fujiidera City Education Commission, Osaka Prefecture

Haniwa in the form of animals appeared around the end of the fourth century. The first creatures depicted included waterfowl, roosters, and fish, but beginning in the fifth century pigs, deer, cows, monkeys, horses, and dogs were added to the repertoire. The most numerous among the bird-shaped *haniwa* are chickens, ducklike fowl, and hawks.[1]

Three waterfowl-shaped *haniwa* were recovered from a square earthen platform constructed in the moat of Tsudōshiroyama Kofun in Fujiidera City, Osaka Prefecture. No other examples of waterbirds placed on this kind of platform (which may have been a sacred precinct where funeral rites were performed) have been found. This specimen is the largest and oldest among the waterfowl-shaped *haniwa* excavated. Since the Yayoi period, waterfowl were considered to be sacred birds that prevented evil and transported the spirit of the deceased.

Tsudōshiroyama Kofun is one of the mounds of the Furuichi Mounded Tomb Cluster located in southern Osaka Prefecture. The cluster includes keyhole-shaped mounded tombs thought to belong to the emperors Ōjin (active late 4th–early 5th century), Chūai (dates unknown), and Ingyō (active mid-5th century). Tsudōshiroyama Kofun is considered to be the oldest keyhole-shaped tomb belonging to an individual having the status of emperor.

MORIMITSU TOSHIHIKO

1. The average bird-shaped *haniwa* is about 20 inches (7.9 cm) high; small baby bird *haniwa* are only three inches (7.6 cm) high.

Middle Kofun period,
1st half 5th century
Excavated at Miyayama Kofun,
Nara Prefecture
Earthenware
57⅞ × 38¾ × 17¼ in.
(147.0 × 98.5 × 44.0 cm)
Nara Prefectural Kashihara Archaeological Research Institute, Nara

Two kinds of quivers were made in
Japan: one was carried on the back
with the arrowheads facing up; the
other was hung around the waist
with the arrows pointing down.
Representing the former type, this
is the largest and most exquisite
quiver-shaped *haniwa* recovered in
Japan.

A box shape with a narrowed top,
the clay quiver is attached to a clay
slab. Thirteen arrowheads in the
form of willow leaves are depicted.
A protective slab is attached from
the arrowhead area. A pattern of
circles on the shoulders of the slab
and spirals on the sides of the lower
end are assumed to represent ropes
for tying the quiver to one's back.
The quiver has several finlike decorations. Intersecting diagonal and
curved lines decorate the quiver
portion, which is divided into four
zones by applied notched and raised
bands.

This *haniwa* and the house-shaped
haniwa [see 167] were unearthed
from the square ritual area at Miyayama Kofun in Gose City, Nara Prefecture. The largest keyhole-shaped
kofun in the southern part of Nara
Basin, Miyayama contained the
tomb of the most powerful individual of the southern Yamato region,
who was buried just beneath the
square ritual area. *Haniwa* in the
form of a quiver, shield, or armor
were placed firmly, facing out, along
the front side of the burial mound,
as if to protect the sacred precinct.

KAWAGOE SHUN'ICHI

Middle Kofun period, 2d half
5th century
Excavated at Miyayama Kofun,
Nara Prefecture
Earthenware
37⅛ × 43¼ × 22¼ in.
(94.5 × 110.0 × 56.5 cm)
Nara Prefectural Kashihara Archaeological Research Institute, Nara

More than five house-shaped *haniwa*
were arranged on a square ceremonial platform over the stone chamber
built at the center of the circular part
of the Miyayama Kofun of the second half of the fifth century. Encircling them in two tiers were a row
of *haniwa* in the form of canopies or
parasols (*kinugasa*) that were held to
shelter people of high rank and a row
of *haniwa* in the forms of shields,
armor, and a quiver [166]. More
than five house-shaped *haniwa*,
which differed in their representations of roof forms, were lined up in
the outermost row. It is unclear
whether the allocation and arrangement of the individual house-shaped
haniwa represent the dwellings of
powerful clan members during their
lifetimes, dwellings in the world
after death, or a place for ceremonies
of succession to the status of the
person buried in the tomb.

This *haniwa* is one of the houses
arranged in a row and is built in two
stories with a gabled roof. The first
level is open with a dirt floor; a large
roof covers the second level. Clay
boards on the roof depict wood
framing to which thatching would
be attached, but there is no indication of thatching. At both ends
of the roof, unusually wide boards
are represented, and the semicircular ends of ridge poles protrude.
Small eaves overhang the edges. Arranged in a wide belt, the pillars,
depicted as square, penetrate the
upper and lower floor. Nearly all
pillars depicted on house-shaped
haniwa and in excavations of buildings are round, so the pillars of this
haniwa may be regarded as a distor-
tion of the actual shape.

KAWAGOE SHUN'ICHI

Late Kofun period,
6th century
Excavation attributed to
Gumma Prefecture
Earthenware
Height 27⅜ in. (69.5 cm)
Nagatoro Museum,
Saitama Prefecture

Leaning back and looking up as if
regarding the tip of his right hand,
this *haniwa* figure adroitly conveys a
dancer's ecstasy while singing and
dancing, presumably at a funeral
ceremony. Among human-figure
haniwa, which most frequently present a frontal view, this example is
unique.

   To form the body and head, clay
coils were piled on top of a cylindrical stand, leaving the figure hollow. The round eyes and wide-open
mouth, with the upper lip slit at
the center, were scooped out with
a spatula; a pyramidal nose was attached to the face to create the
elated facial expression. A round hat
decorated with a series of triangles
is placed on the disproportionately
long head; strands of hair originally
must have been gathered by the ears.
A sash is attached to the waist, and
the lower end of the jacket is simply
indicated.

KAWAGOE SHUN'ICHI

Late Kofun period, 7th century
Excavated at Funazuka Kofun,
Ibaraki Prefecture
Iron and gilt bronze
44⅞ × 4⅝ × ⅞ in.
(114.1 × 11.8 × 2.3 cm)
Diameter of pommel 3¼ in.
(8.5 cm)
Collection of Namegawa Hiroshi;
on deposit at Ibaraki Prefectural
History Museum, Mito

Attached to this iron sword is a gilt-bronze ring pommel decorated in abstract form with two dragonheads facing each other (see detail). A thin gilt-bronze veneer decorated with spirals and circles and engraved with dots covers the hilt and sheath. The sword guard is extremely small. Two fittings for suspension are attached near the mouth of the sheath. The sword would have hung horizontally on a cord from a belt, an indication that the weapon was not used in actual battle.

The original form of the ring-pommel sword is Chinese. People in the Late Yayoi period used an iron sword with a simple pommel attached. The inside of the pommel was first decorated in the Kofun period, and the use of ring-pommel swords was most prevalent from the end of the Middle Kofun period (second half fifth century). It is believed that ring-pommel swords began to be produced in Japan during the later half of the sixth century.

Various kinds of decorated swords were unearthed from mounded tombs in Japan. The ring-pommel sword with the decoration of a dragon or phoenix may have been particularly meaningful. The appearance of such swords seems to correspond to the time when Japanese envoys were dispatched to China by great chiefs of Japan. Swords probably first came to Japan as reciprocal gifts from China. Gradually these kinds of swords came to be produced in Japan and were given to local leaders as symbols of the power of the Yamato court.

MORIMITSU TOSHIHIKO

Detail

Late Kofun period, 6th century
Excavated at Fujinoki Kofun,
Nara Prefecture
High-fired clay
Agency for Cultural Affairs, Government of Japan, Tokyo; on deposit at
Nara Prefectural Kashihara Archaeological Research Institute, Nara
Important Cultural Property

170
Long-necked jar
10⅜ × 6½ in. (26.5 × 16.5 cm)

171
Wine vessel
7¼ × 5⅞ in. (18.5 × 15.0 cm)

172
Bowl with pedestal
7⅞ × 5½ in. (20.1 × 14.0 cm)

173
Bowl with pedestal and lid
10⅜ × 6⅞ in. (26.5 × 17.4 cm)

174
Vessel stand
15⅞ × 10¾ in. (40.5 × 27.3 cm)

175
Jar with pedestal and lid
12⅛ × 6⅜ in. (31.0 × 16.3 cm)

176
Small bowl with pedestal
3¾ × 3⅝ in. (9.6 × 9.2 cm)

High-fired *sue*-ware vessels were introduced to Japan from the Korean peninsula in the early fifth century. Unlike the ceramics of earlier times, *sue* ware required technical specialization and intensive labor. It was manufactured on the wheel, then placed in tunnel kilns with an arching roof (*anagama*) for mass-production firing. Potters received special training to turn pots on the wheel, build low tunnel kilns, collect special clay adapted to high-temperature firing, and supply the kilns with large amounts of fuel.

The production of *sue* ware brought about a tremendous change in pottery making in Japan. A wide variety of vessels was produced, and wares for food became more diversified under the influence of Asian continental practices.

Sue ware was produced all over Japan in the sixth century, and a large amount of *sue* ware was made for use in burials. Particularly in the early sixth century, specialized vessels were made for mounded tombs. It was not unusual for many kinds of *sue* wares, such as bowls, jars, and stands, to be buried as grave goods, as in the Fujinoki Kofun.

TANABE IKUO

Top to bottom [170. 171]   *Left to right* [172–74]   *Top to bottom* {17

Late Kofun period,
2d half 6th century
Excavated at Iwazu 1 Kofun,
Okazaki City, Aichi Prefecture
High-fired clay
Okazaki City Education Commis-
sion, Aichi Prefecture

177
Jar with pedestal and lid
17¼ × 7⅞ in. (44.0 × 20.0 cm)

178
Jar with pedestal and lid with birds
16⅞ × 7⅝ in. (43.0 × 19.5 cm)

179
Jar with pedestal and small cups
13⅜ × 7⅞ in. (34.0 × 20.0 cm)

180
Jar with pedestal and bird and animal decoration
11 × 5½ in. (28.0 × 14.0 cm)

181
Jar with pedestal, lid, and bird and
animal decoration
14⅛ × 5½ in. (36.0 × 13.5 cm)

Iwazu Kofun cluster is located in
Aichi Prefecture, nearly in the center of Japan. Among the six tombs,
tomb 1 is a circular mound about
33 feet (10 m) in diameter. In later
times it was plundered, but one part
of the burial remained in its original
state. The *sue*-ware ceramics recovered there are thought to date to the
second half of the sixth century.

As with *sue* wares from Iwazu 1
Kofun, vessels decorated with human and animal figures were offered
in front of the graves. These *sue*-ware
ceramics are known as "*sue* ware
with attached ornaments" because
animals and birds decorate the upper, spherical part. Among these,
two pieces [180, 181], one missing
a lid [180], are extremely similar
in fabrication, and it is possible that
this set was made to be placed
together in the tomb.

DOI TAKASHI

Middle Kofun period, 5th century
Iron
54¾ × 33½ in.
(139.0 × 85.0 cm)
Isonokami Shrine, Tenri City,
Nara Prefecture; on deposit at
Tokyo National Museum
Important Cultural Property

This is one of two wrought-iron shields that were long ago inherited by Isonokami Shrine in Tenri City, Nara Prefecture. The shrine was dedicated by the powerful Mononobe family, whose base lay in the northern part of the Nara Basin. Members of the family served the Yamato court as military officials during the fifth and sixth centuries. There is no clear record of how the shields came into the possession of the shrine or where they were found.

Iron plaques of various sizes and form, such as trapezoids, rectangles, and L shapes, were assembled to create the geometric decoration on this shield. A wooden frame may have been attached to the back of the shield. The two iron shields from Isonokami Shrine are the only artifacts of their kind known in Japan.

Kofun period shields found as burial goods in mounded tombs or represented as *haniwa* in wall paintings were mostly of the type that were set into the ground as protection from arrows. For its large size and weight, this example was probably set onto the ground. Only a few remaining examples of hand-carried shields exist. Shields buried in mounded tombs were made of lacquer-coated leather braced (or stretched) on a wooden frame. The surface of the shield was decorated with triangles, diamonds, and parallel lines. Shields represented by *haniwa* [157] also have similar designs.

Techniques of assembling wrought-iron plaques by using rivets are similar to the method of making armor in fifth-century Korea and Japan. Since the particular decoration of the shield from Isonokami was found on leather shields from mounded tombs, the Isonokami shield is assumed to date to the fifth century. On the basis of a passage about Emperor Nintoku (active early fifth century) in the *Nihon shoki* in which the Korean state of Koguryō offers tribute to Japan with shields and targets, some archaeologists assume that the Isonokami shield came from abroad.

KAWAGOE SHUN'ICHI

Early Kofun period, 4th century

Excavated at Shikinzan Kofun,
Osaka Prefecture

On deposit at Kyoto University

183

Mirror with beasts and gods

Bronze

Diameter 14⅛ in. (35.8 cm)

184
Mirror with raised, triangular rim
Bronze
Diameter 8¾ in. (22.2 cm)

185
Mirror with raised, triangular rim
Bronze
Diameter 8⅞ in. (22.6 cm)

186
Tubular implement
Bronze
Length 7¾ in. (19.8 cm)

Center row, top to bottom:

187
Hoe-shaped bracelet
Jasper
5⅛ × 3¾ in. (13.0 × 9.4 cm)

188
Hoe-shaped bracelet
Jasper
6½ × 4⅜ in. (16.4 × 11.2 cm)

Top to bottom:

189
Wheel-shaped bracelet
Jasper
5¾ × 4¾ in. (14.5 × 12.0 cm)

190
Comma-shaped bead (*magatama*)
Jadeite
Length 1⅜ in. (3.5 cm)

191
Comma-shaped bead (*magatama*)
Jadeite
Length 1¾ in. (4.5 cm)

192
Spindle whorl
Jasper
Diameter 2¼ in. (5.8 cm)

The construction of large keyhole-shaped mounds during the Kofun period demonstrated the power of the chiefs as well as their spiritual influence and demand for homage. The authority of the chiefs—and their requirements—resulted in changes in the forms of coffins and burial goods. Large split-wood log coffins, different from those of the Yayoi period, were introduced. The burial goods of a tomb included objects bestowed by the Yamato unified powers and the belongings of the deceased as well as offerings and objects made specially for burial. As the quantity and quality of burial goods increased, bronze mirrors were produced in greater number, followed by weapons, armor, production tools, and stone artifacts. The customs and objects that originated in the Kofun period can be observed in Shikinzan Kofun in Osaka Prefecture, a typical mounded tomb of the Early Kofun.

Shikinzan is a keyhole-shaped mound built on the slope of a hill.[1] The mound was paved with stones, and cylindrical *haniwa* were placed on it. The pit-style stone chamber was constructed inside the circular rear portion parallel to the main direction of the mound.[2] Burial goods unearthed at Shikinzan include twelve bronze mirrors [183–85]; tubular bronze implements [186]; wheel- and hoe-shaped jasper bracelets [187–89]; *magatama* beads [190, 191]; shell bracelets; spindle whorls [192]; and numerous iron products, such as cuirass, swords, arrowheads, hoes, adzes, chisels, and planes.

It is interesting to find both shell bracelets and stone replicas of shell bracelets, called hoe-shaped jasper bracelets, side by side. Shell bracelets from the coast of southern Japan first appeared during the Yayoi period. The presence of shell and jasper ornaments together indicates some remaining elements of the Yayoi period in the Early Kofun.

TANABE IKUO

1. The *kofun* is about 328 feet (100 m) long, the rear circular portion is about 250 feet (76 m) wide, and the front portion is about 131 feet (40 m) wide.

2. The stone chamber is 23 feet (7 m) long, 3½ feet (1.1 m) wide, and 4 feet (1.2 m) high.

Early Kofun period, 2d half
4th century
Excavated at Ishiyama Kofun,
Mie Prefecture
On deposit at Kyoto University

193
Staff
Jasper
Height 7⅝ in. (19.5 cm)

194
Koto bridge-shaped object
Stone
3⅛ × 1¾ in. (8.0 × 4.6 cm)

195
Koto bridge-shaped object
Stone
1¼ × 1⅜ in. (3.4 × 3.6 cm)

196
Bracelet
Stone
Diameter 2¾ in. (7.0 cm)

197
Bracelet
Stone
Diameter 3½ in. (9.0 cm)

198
Wheel-shaped bracelet
Jasper
Diameter 5¾ in. (14.8 cm)

199
Hoe-shaped bracelet
Jasper
9 × 5⅜ in. (23.0 × 13.8 cm)

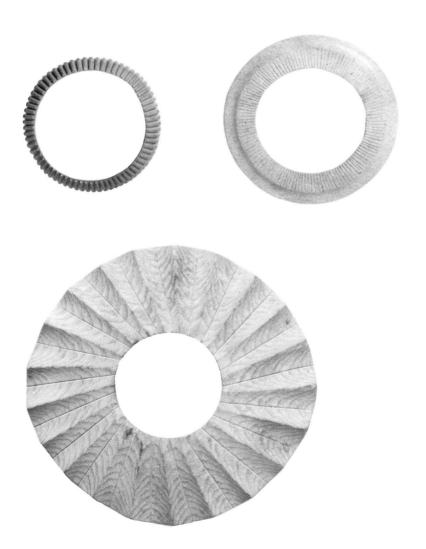

Left to right:

200
Arrowhead
Bronze
2¾ × ¾ in. (7.0 × 2.0 cm)

201
Arrowhead
Stone
3½ × 1 in. (9.0 × 2.9 cm)

202
Arrowhead
Bronze
4⅝ × 1 in. (11.8 × 2.8 cm)

203
Arrowhead
Stone
2⅜ × ¾ in. (6.3 × 2.0 cm)

204
Arrowhead
Stone
2¾ × 1¾ in. (7.1 × 2.0 cm)

Top to bottom:

205
Chisel
Stone
6⅛ × ⅞ in. (15.8 × 2.4 cm)

206
Point plane
Stone
6½ × 1 in. (16.5 × 2.5 cm)

207
Sickle
Stone
4½ × 1¼ in. (11.6 × 3.3 cm)

208
Knife
Stone
4 × 1¼ in. (10.1 × 3.2 cm)

209
Ax
Stone
3¼ × 2⅛ in. (8.2 × 5.5 cm)

A large number of stone artifacts and miniature replicas characterize the grave goods of the Kofun period. The former represent the actual accessories or goods used by the chief, while the latter are miniature tools. Stone artifacts unearthed from Ishiyama Kofun in Mie Prefecture are particularly numerous.

Dating to the second half of the fourth century, Ishiyama is a keyhole-shaped mound built on a hillside. The name Ishiyama ("stone mountain") was derived from the numerous paving stones on the mound.[1] Cylindrical *haniwa* encircled the mound in three rows. They were also arranged on the top of the mound to form a rectangular shape within which were placed representational *haniwa* in forms such as houses, shields, sunshades, and quivers. Between the mound and the front projection, house-shaped *haniwa* were also lined up to form a rectangle (compare with fig. 39).

Bracelets made of jasper [198, 199] imitate the shapes of shell ornaments from the Yayoi period [see 141, 142, 145]. A jasper staff [193] and stone objects resembling koto bridges [194, 195] are considered to have been part of the chief's ceremonial cane. Other objects include stone miniatures of practical implements, such as weapons and armor, as well as tools for agriculture, wine making, and weaving.

TANABE IKUO

1. The mound is about 229¾ feet (120 m) long, the circular rear portion is 230 feet (70 m) wide, and the front projection is 131¼ feet (40 m) wide.

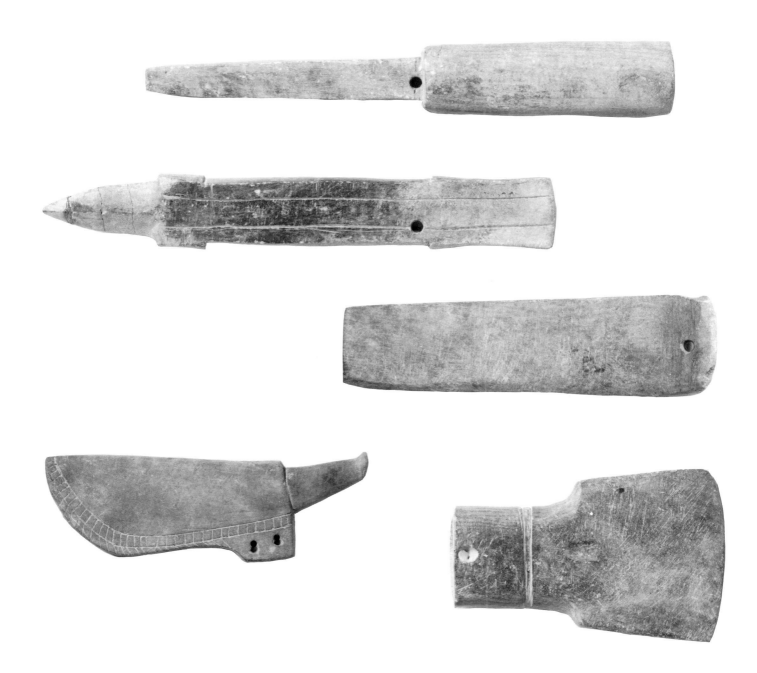

6

ASUKA PERIOD

O ur Lord, sovereign
of the earth's eight corners,
child of the high-shining sun,
founds her great palace
On the fields of Fujii,
of the rough wisteria cloth,
and stands there on the banks
of Haniyasu Pond.

Around her she sees
Yamato's green Kagu Hill
standing lush
towards the Eastern Gate,
a hill of spring,
and this hill, Unebi,
rising newly verdant
towards the Western Gate,
young and fresh,
and Miminashi,
that hill of green sedge,
standing towards the Northern Gate,
superb, like a very god,
and Yoshino Mountain—
beautiful its name—
soaring beyond the Southern Gate
in the distance, among the clouds.

Here in the divine shadows
of high-ruling heaven,
in the divine shadows
of heaven-ruling sun,
may these waters gush forever,
the crystal waters
of her imperial well.

Poem 52 from the *Man'yōshū*
(Levy 1981, 64–66)

Miroku [256]

This poem from the *Man'yōshū* (Anthology of Ten Thousand Leaves), the earliest collection of Japanese poetry, completed in A.D. 759, describes the imperial line of rulers descended from the sun goddess and the great palace of Fujiwara on the wisteria plain, which together symbolize the new social order of the Asuka period.[1]

The Japanese state of Yamato flourished in a ravishingly beautiful corner of the Nara Plain (fig. 40). Occupying a tiny area of only a few square miles and built on an axial plan foreign to Kofun period Japan, Fujiwara Palace in Nara was surrounded by sacred mountains and guarded by Miminashi Peak to the north; the center of the expanding state became the hub of a widespread communication network.

Within roughly 150 years, from A.D. 530 to 680, Japan experienced the introduction of the Buddhist religion; the expansion of literacy and formation of a literate bureaucracy; the introduction of advanced technology, architecture, and specialized knowledge in fields as diverse

Figure 40
Asuka period sites in the Kinai region and Nara Basin mentioned in the text.

The modern city limits of Kyoto, Osaka, and Nara as well as lakes and bays, including two ancient lakes on the Yodo River, are also included. The ancient shoreline of Osaka Bay and the old river course of Yamato River are delineated. Palaces and capitals are identified with rectangles (except for Nara). Thin lines indicate elevations (656 ft.; 200 m).

1 Ōtsu Palace
2 Shikinzan Kofun
3 Tsubai Ōtsukayama Kofun
4 Heijō Capital
5 Ikaruga Palace
6 Fujinoki Kofun
7 Gobōyama 3 Kofun
8 Fujiwara Palace
9 Fujiwara Capital
10 Yakushiji
11 Kiyomigahara Palace
12 Uenomiya Palace
13 Daikandaiji
14 Mizuochi Water Clock
15 Asukadera
16 Kawaradera
17 Itabuki Palace
18 Takamatsuzuka Kofun
19 Asuka Village

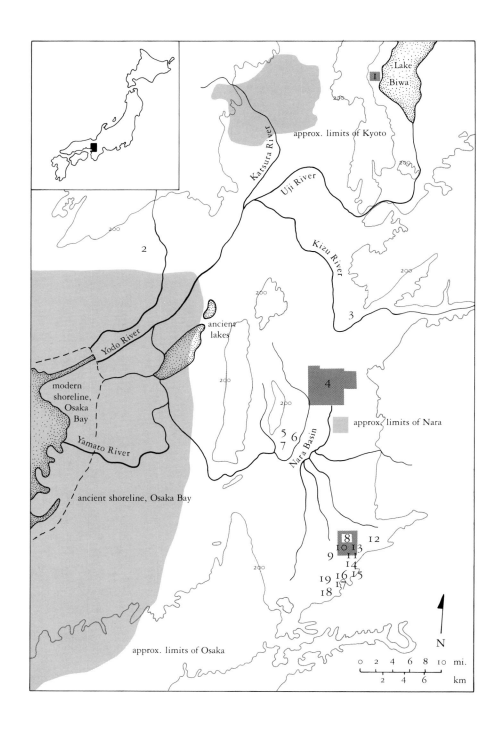

as engineering, politics, and religion; and rapid changes in government organization. Underlying all these innovations was the extension of the power and control of the Yamato state, accompanied by internal struggles and movements for reform and codification. Elite people in the outlying areas whose ancestors had been laid to rest in *kofun* with gilded swords, ceremonial vessels, and comma-shaped jewels were now subject to control by the central state. Status and privileges conferred by the central ruler were necessary to ensure the support of the elite for the Yamato government. These were fascinating times, perhaps much like the Meiji period (A.D. 1868–1912), when Japan was once again "modernized" and the population experienced a series of social and intellectual shocks that ultimately promoted exceedingly high levels of creative energy.

The Asuka period has left extensive archaeological remains, which include palace and residential sites, administrative centers and fortifications, temples, burials, and centers of agriculture and production (fig. 41). Certainly other regions of Japan were interacting with the Asuka region and with the Asian continent; their archaeological record is also of great interest.

Chronology

The Asuka period provides a transition to the Japan that is familiar to us from historical accounts and the culture of East Asian Buddhism. Named for the region near Asuka Village in northern Nara Prefecture, the Asuka period began around the time of the reign of Empress Suiko (r. A.D. 593–628). Historians and archaeologists established the period dates to include changes that first took place in the southern Yamato Plain in the Nara Basin, southeast of Osaka.

A series of important social and political transformations had great impact on everyday life. Ten emperors and four empresses ruled during the Asuka period. Known by posthumous names assigned in the ninth century, they were members of a complex web of close kin, who vied for power among one another, the aristocracy, and the Buddhist clergy (Kidder 1972a, 15). The Japanese nation state was formed in the Asuka region, an area about 1¾ miles (3 km) in each direction. By the end of the period in A.D. 710, a new capital had been built at Heijō in Nara, and the Yamato state structure had undergone several transformations.

The Historical Record

Although numerous brief inscriptions, such as those on sword blades, date from the fifth and sixth centuries, Japanese mastery of the Chinese writing system, as witnessed by the compilation of historical texts, occurred in the Asuka period. During this time extensive documents were written, the most famous being the *Kojiki* (Record of Ancient Matters), *Man'yōshū,* and *Nihon shoki,* all of which were actually published after the end of the period.

Emperor Temmu (r. A.D. 672–86) established a historical commission in A.D. 681 to compile a history to confirm the legitimacy of imperial power and authority. The *Kojiki,* comprising three volumes, was completed in A.D. 712 by Ō no Yasumaro (died A.D. 723).[2] The *Kojiki* provided a national history sanctifying the emperor or empress as head of state.

The *Nihon shoki* was published in thirty volumes in A.D. 720. Tracing the period from the mythological founding of the nation through the reign of the Empress Jitō (r. A.D. 686–97), Emperor Temmu's consort, it draws on a larger number of sources than were used for the *Kojiki*. Because both the *Kojiki* and *Nihon shoki* are composites of earlier historical accounts, myths, and songs, using them to elucidate the archaeological record is a challenging task.

Dating from the end of the Asuka period, household registers (*koseki*), the basis for tax assessment and military conscription, provide detailed insight into everyday life. Household registration may have begun in

Figure 41
Asuka period sites (excluding Kinai region) mentioned in the text.

1 Kanoko
2 Minezaki
3 Sanage
4 Gobōyama
5 Matsuokayama
6 Dazaifu
7 Usa
8 Miharagunga
9 Nachi Mountain
10 Ōkita 24 Tomb

Japan under the supervision of Chinese immigrants as early as A.D. 554. Wooden tablets (*mokkan*) used for recording administrative matters have also been recovered from early palace sites [218–47]. Chinese historical writings, such as the *Sui shu* (History of the Sui Dynasty), compiled beginning in A.D. 629, are also useful for studying seventh-century Japan (Tsunoda & Goodrich 1951, 28–37).

Social Organization

Polygamy was prevalent, and patrilineal succession was the principle in the royal line. Emperor Bidatsu (r. A.D. 572–85) and Empress Suiko were half-brother and -sister, having different mothers. Their sibling marriage, a custom also at the time of the fourth-century emperor Nintoku and his children who reigned in the fifth century, occurred at a historical turning point when royal power became concentrated. In the transition to the *ritsuryō* state, the royal line severed relations with other principal families to enhance its own position. Other cases of royal sibling marriage are known from ancient Egypt, in Peru among the Inca, and from ancient Burma, Hawaii, and Thailand. In cultures where sibling marriage is practiced, rulers are regarded as semidivine; they have the prerogative, therefore, to break the rules followed by commoners. In Japan, offspring of a sibling union did not succeed to the throne. The chief example is Prince Shōtoku (A.D. 574–622), son of Emperor Yōmei (r. A.D. 585–87) and his half-sister, Anahobe no Hashimoto no Himemiko (Ōbayashi 1987, 20–32, 98–104). Sibling marriages ceased in Japan after A.D. 672, probably owing to Chinese influence. In China, individuals with the same surname were not allowed to marry and the patrilineal clan was strongly sanctioned.

The vibrant, shifting life of the Asuka court was kept in constant motion by rapid internal developments and fierce competition from rival elite factions and infusions of people and ideas from the Asian continent. Developments at the center rapidly affected the life of the people in the outlying regions of civilized Japan. New means of creating order were instituted as the process of governing became more complex.

Near the end of the sixth century and in the early seventh century, King Mu (A.D. 600–640), ruler of Paekche in Korea, dispatched to Japan Buddhist monks, temple architects, sculptors, tile makers, and painters. Such arts as calendar making, continental music, and dance were also introduced from Paekche.

In Japan the confrontation of the forceful Soga clan with the imperial household reached a climax in A.D. 592 with the assassination of Emperor Sushun (r. A.D. 587–92) by order of Soga no Umako (died A.D. 626), a commanding member of the Soga clan. Umako's niece, Empress Suiko, succeeded Sushun. Suiko, the third daughter of Emperor Kimmei, was the widow of Emperor Bidatsu, her half-brother. Empress Suiko was the first woman to ascend the throne in Japanese history (Himiko's reign in the third century may be considered protohistoric), although in fact she abstained from politics in favor of her regent, Prince Shōtoku, to whom all powers were delegated. During her reign the supreme authority of the imperial family was established over the chiefs of other families. Moreover, she contacted China as the ruler of an equal sovereign

Figure 42
Plan of Asukadera in Asuka, Nara
Prefecture, the first Buddhist temple
to be built in Japan, between A.D.
588 and 606 (dots represent pillar
bases).

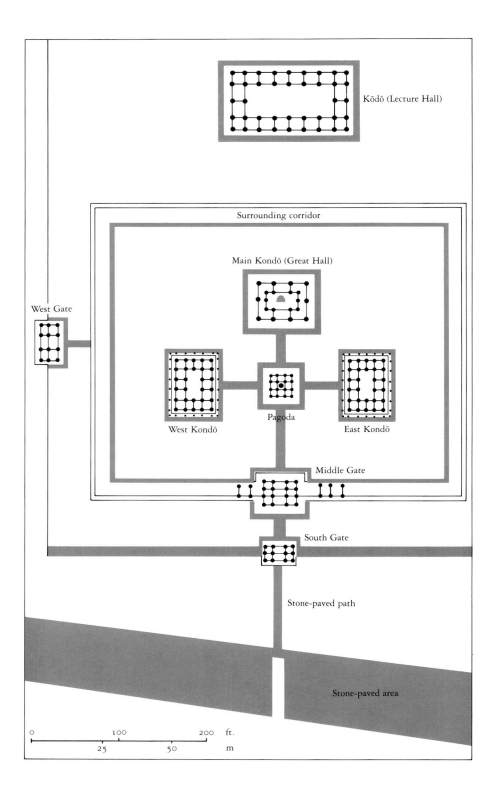

nation (Waida 1976, 328). Both these important steps in the consolidation of state power were symbolized by her use for the first time of the term *tennō* ("emperor").

Prince Shōtoku, who maintained friendly relations with the Korean kingdom of Silla and who favored Buddhism directly, supported the building of the Buddhist temples Asukadera in Asuka (fig. 42), Hōryūji, near present-day Nara, and Shitennōji in present-day Osaka. Shōtoku was a statesman and deeply committed Buddhist who wished to keep religious institutions under state control.

In A.D. 603 the System of Twelve Cap Ranks was initiated, by which hereditary royal attendants were transformed into officials, divided into twelve ranks with distinctive regalia. The system was also modeled after the rank system developed in the Korean kingdoms of Koguryŏ and Paekche. Tribal chieftains in service to the court were ranked individually by the emperor or empress, not by hereditary blood ties. This process connected them individually to the central authority and reduced their attachments to one another. The ideology of an unbroken imperial lineage with its beginning in 660 B.C. was adopted. The date was chosen because it represented twenty-one cycles of sixty years before A.D. 601, when Suiko's consolidation of power constituted the beginning of a new era of Japanese history (Waida 1976, 331). The imperial line, with its heavy emphasis on an unbroken ancestry from the sun goddess, was given supreme legitimacy over other lineages (Kiley 1977, 366).

The Seventeen-Article Constitution was established in A.D. 604. The twelfth article stated that the provincial governors and provincial chieftains (*kuni no miyatsuko*) could not levy their own taxes, since the country had only one sovereign. Government control became increasingly centralized. In the same year, the imperial court adopted the Chinese calendar, which was used until A.D. 690.

In the late seventh century the *kabane* system of ranked positions was displaced by a more bureaucratic form of aristocratic rule. Attempts were made to create a uniform hierarchy of official prestige, and the number of rankings was increased. But in A.D. 684 all *kabane* titles were replaced by a series of eight titles, the highest of which were assumed by the descendants of former rulers. Around A.D. 700 the system was codified so that officials of the fifth rank or below could not be promoted without special decree.

The process of assimilating powerful foreign families demonstrates how the ranking system consolidated the Yamato state and also reveals the enormous contribution made by those families to ancient Yamato society and civilization. By A.D. 684 Korean families that had come to Japan during the fifth and sixth centuries and had been assimilated as important officials were given the rank of *muraji* (*sukune*), equal to the rank held by indigenous powerful families. *Muraji* families actually comprised a group of intermarried Korean families who constructed a consanguine group and related it to a prominent ancestor. Aristocrats from the Korean kingdoms of Koguryŏ and Silla who came to Japan in the second half of the seventh century were not, however, at first allowed to have Japanese names or *kabane* titles. Several generations of service and assimilation were thus important for integration into ancient Japanese society. The *Shinsen shōjiroku*, a listing of genealogies of more than one thousand families having official ranks in the capital and the five central provinces in the early ninth century, contained 324 families of immigrant descent (Carter 1983a).

The Ritsuryō *System*

Fundamental changes in state organization took place in a series of reforms established from A.D. 645 to the end of the seventh century, collectively referred to as the *ritsuryō* system. An immediate cause for reform was the sharp defeat of the Soga, who were resented for their abuse of power. Soga no Iruka was assassinated in A.D. 645 by Prince Naka, later to be Emperor Tenji (r. A.D. 661–72), at an imperial reception for Korean envoys. With the *ritsuryō* system, the introduction of local registration of families, and the establishment of taxation without the mediation of the powerful local chiefs, the centralized government gained more control and the ancient Japanese state became more fully developed (Tsude 1989b, 52).

Both internal and external conditions led to the centralization of state power. Japan had been allied with the Korean kingdoms of Koguryŏ and Paekche against the powers of Tang China (A.D. 618–907) and the Korean state of Silla. The Tang emperor Taizong (r. A.D. 627–50) began hostilities against Koguryŏ in A.D. 631, Paekche fell to Silla in A.D. 662, and Koguryŏ was defeated by an alliance between Silla and Tang China in A.D. 668. With the defeat of Paekche, more than sixty Korean aristocrats came to Japan, where they were provided government ranks in the Yamato state. The influx was an occasion for the Yamato state to absorb new knowledge and technology, thereby gaining strength against Silla and Tang. Constant news of instability on the Korean peninsula and threats to Japanese hegemony spread to Japan and supplied fresh motivation for a Japanese court eager to expand and justify its power (Farris 1985, 11). Emperor Kōtoku (r. A.D. 645–54) sponsored the Taika Reform Edict of A.D. 646—which regulated the positions of officials in the bureaucracy—set up a system of land allotment for peasants, imposed taxes, and drastically restricted the building of mounded tombs.[3] He also increased the number of court ranks from twelve—as instituted by Prince Shōtoku in A.D. 603—to nineteen.

In the late seventh century Japan was troubled by deteriorating internal conditions and the external threat of war against the alliance of Tang China and the Korean state of Silla. The Japanese Empress Saimei (r. A.D. 655–61) went to Kyūshū to direct military activities but died there in A.D. 661; the allied forces of Paekche and the Japanese fleet were destroyed by Silla two years after Saimei's death. To counter an expected attack from Korea, local defenses were constructed in the Kantō Plain and northern Kyūshū at Dazaifu. Emperor Tenji, Saimei's successor, proclaimed a new and more systematic organization for state bureaucracy within six months of the defeat of Paekche. In A.D. 670 he ordered a census that formed the basis for taxation and conscription.

Under Emperor Temmu, Tenji's younger brother, who had defeated Tenji's son in a violent dispute over succession, the number of court ranks was expanded to forty-eight. It is thought that Temmu's palace at Kiyomigahara was the first to have a fully developed set of administrative buildings. Temmu believed that for Japan to survive it must adopt China's system of centralized government. He was impressed that the Korean state of Silla had learned from China and had used that knowledge to free the Korean peninsula from Chinese domination. In A.D. 675 Temmu eliminated hereditary aristocratic control over people and land. He divided up local regional units (*kuni*) and linked them directly to the central bureaucratic administration. By the end of the seventh century about ten thousand officials resided in the capital at Fujiwara (Farris 1985, 15).

In A.D. 702 Emperor Mommu (r. A.D. 697–707) promulgated the Taihō Civil Code, which specified the obligations of officials and the work of various state agencies. Court aristocrats served as provincial governors for a term of six years. The corresponding Taihō Penal Code became the established legal system of the succeeding Nara period.

Buddhism and Local Religion

The introduction of Buddhism during the reign of Emperor Kimmei had major social and political ramifications. Emperor Yōmei, the third ruler after Kimmei, was a Buddhist, as were all his successors. The Soga family, which provided a large number of empresses and emperors, promoted Buddhism, built temples, and supported the clergy and immigrant Korean monks. Four generations of the Soga family served as chief ministers (*omi*) to the imperial court of Yamato. In their official capacity they were strongly linked to Asian continental learning and worked with Korean civil servants to administer the Yamato court. The Soga family waged war against the non-Buddhist Mononobe and Nakatomi families, whom they defeated in A.D. 587. Buddhism became the state religion and almost all major monuments and art forms were made with government support or with the patronage of high-ranking families.

Mahayana Buddhist teaching and art entered Japan from China and Korea (Rosenfield 1983). This mainstream form later gave way to Esoteric, Pure Land, and Zen Buddhism. Mahayana stressed salvation through the worship of a pantheon of deities who protected Buddhist nations and their rulers. The practice of monasticism led to the construction of temples. Monastic compounds provided a quiet retreat where monks and nuns devoted themselves to meditation, study, prayers for the dead, and observance of holy days and ceremonies. In the first decades of the Asuka period some twenty-six temple compounds were built in the Nara-Osaka region. By A.D. 633 forty-six temples in Asuka housed 816 monks and 569 nuns (Kidder 1972a, 93). The copying of the Buddhist sacred texts, known as sutras, began as early as A.D. 677. In the eighth century a network of state-sponsored temples (*kokubunji*) was administered from the Tōdaiji, the central temple in Nara.

Despite the overwhelming devotion to Buddhism as a state religion, evidence of local non-Buddhist beliefs persists in the archaeological record. Small, hand-modeled clay horses deposited in wells and ditches are thought to have been offered at times of drought or flood to placate water spirits. Horses were sacrificed as well, judging from the occurrence of horse bones in similar sites (*Nara Kenritsu Kashihara* 1988, 77). J. Edward Kidder (1985, 108) has mentioned that horse sacrifices at funerals were proscribed in the Taika Reform Edict. He has suggested that it was a northeast Asian custom that came to Japan in the Kofun period.

The Japanese attempted to use Buddhism as protection against disease and sickness. Although seventh-century written records of plagues do not exist, the pattern for the eighth century suggests that virulent epidemics of smallpox and other diseases crossed to Japan from Korea and that Buddhist temple monks and nuns offered prayers and services at those times on behalf of the state. Kidder (1972a, 85) has stated that up to around A.D. 585, people attributed plagues and disasters to vengeful native deities, the Shinto *kami;* thereafter it was believed that calamities were caused by failure to worship the Buddha.

The Archaeological Record

Palaces

Under the fields of Asuka lie numerous monuments, several of which have been excavated. The story of Asuka's creation and maintenance as a national shrine, saved from the ravages of the expansion of the Osaka megalopolis, is a fascinating example of how modern societies define and re-create their individual pasts. A visit to the region, particularly in autumn, with fall foliage and camellia blossoms in chilly copses and fading light across stubble fields, fills the mind with images of the ancient Buddhist capital. A few temples have been preserved as symbols of the transcendental (Kidder 1972a, 61), but the palaces, council chambers, and government bureaus have crumbled to dust.

A series of palace structures, progressing south to north across the Asuka Plain, attest to the growing power of the central court, an increase in the administrative role it played, and the cultural influence of Korea and China in political forms. It was common for rulers to have several palaces and to migrate from one to another. Palaces were moved with each change of emperor and empress and sometimes during the same reign. It is thought that they were located near the lands of the most powerful people of the time. The palaces of the early Asuka period, before Fujiwara was constructed in A.D. 694, were wooden structures without tile roofs or stone bases for columns. Consequently, all that remains are the impressions of wooden posts, particularly if stone floors were absent. Living patterns are therefore difficult to reconstruct.

Among the smaller palace structures excavated to date is Ikaruga Palace built in A.D. 601 by Prince Shōtoku. It consists of two large rectangular buildings oriented north to south and a third that runs east to west and may have been interconnected by a colonnade. Another palace is Itabuki, built for the Empress Saimei in A.D. 642; as the scene of the assassination of Soga no Iruka, it was destroyed in A.D. 655. Itabuki Palace, the name of which refers to its roof of shingle boards, has yielded substantial remains of stone floors and buildings but not roof tiles. Earlier Japanese palaces had thatched roofs. A small pond with a stone-lined watercourse, estimated to be 131 feet (40 m) long, was recovered in 1990 at Uenomiya Palace, where Prince Shōtoku is thought to have lived. It is one of the oldest imperial garden sites of Japan (Gekkan Bunkazai Hakkutsu 1990c).

Following the Taika Reform in the mid-seventh century, larger palaces were constructed. The fully developed palaces of the latter half of the seventh century were rectangular and oriented north to south in Chinese fashion, with the imperial residence set at the extreme north. On entering the palace compound, from the south, one would walk through a forecourt with a pair of buildings, *chōshūden* (imperial assembly halls), facing each other. From there, one passed to the main court around which were four or more (usually twelve) rectangular buildings called *chōdōin* (administrative palace). North of this palace was a small courtyard enclosing one or more buildings called the *daigokuden* (imperial council hall). Finally, a small residential complex outside the cloistered area was known as the *dairi* (imperial residence).

The capitals built before A.D. 694, termed "Japanese style," contained a smaller area for administrative functions than later capitals. Despite the difficulties in tracing structures of this type, the *chōdōin* has been found to be much larger in Fujiwara Palace, which was the capital from A.D. 694 to 710 (Yamamoto Tadanao 1987). The actual state administrative apparatus was located in the *chōshūden* and *daigokuden* (Kidder 1972a, 65). Eight-sided buildings housed the eight ministries; the courtyard was used for ceremonies and other government functions. Within the great rectangle of Fujiwara Palace were two great temples—Daikandaiji and Motoyakushiji—which were planned when the city grid was laid out. The entire area of Fujiwara is estimated to be about 1¾ miles (3 km) north-south and 1¼ miles (2 km) east-west, according to the most widely accepted estimates (fig. 43).[4] The palace, which lay in the northern portion of the city, was roughly 3,032 feet (924 m) east-west by 2,966 feet (904 m) north-south. Emperor Temmu's tomb was constructed in A.D. 687–88 in direct line with the southern extension of the main street of Fujiwara, thereby forming a mandala, a Buddhist diagram of the cosmos. South of the capital rectangle were temples as well as residences for the aristocracy, administrators, and commoners. Main roads led into the capital from different directions.

Wooden tablets or slips (*mokkan*) on which Chinese characters were written in black ink have been recovered from Fujiwara. These could be reused by paring or scraping off the surface. Three types of slips can be distinguished among the thousands recovered from Fujiwara. The first are government documents, records, and correspondence. The second includes information attached to materials that were sent as tributary goods to the capital from outlying districts. The third were used in practicing calligraphy or for casual notes and scribbles.[5]

Figure 43
Reconstruction of Fujiwara Palace administrative center in Nara Prefecture.

1 Imperial council hall
2 Official gate
3 Administrative palace
4 Government offices
5 Middle gate
6 West assembly hall
7 Palace enclosure
8 Main (south) gate
9 East assembly hall

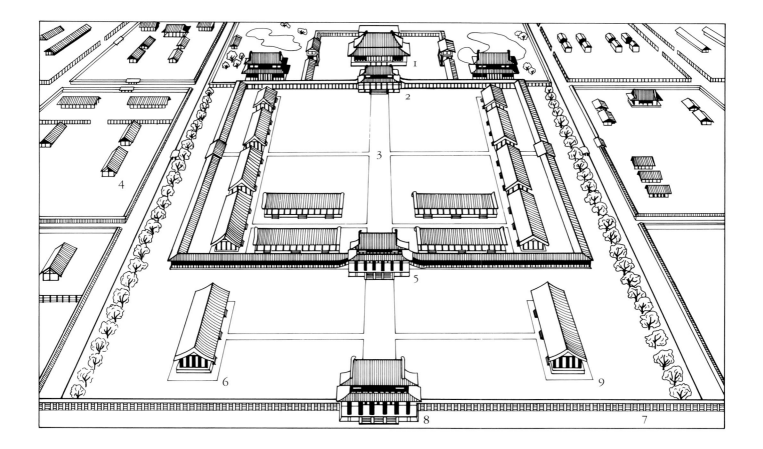

These wooden tablets provide important clues to the urban nature of Fujiwara. The labels and documents refer to government ministries, such as the food-supply office and official winery, which confirm the existence of central government agencies in the palace-government compound. The tags on goods sent to the capital identify tributary goods as offerings to the emperor or empress and also indicate the state of the political reorganization of outlying regions. Although new political administrative units were decreed by the Taika Reform, old units were still active at the end of the seventh century. Officials had passes that allowed them to transport state property from central warehouses to processing areas, the gates of which were named for powerful local families, suggesting that the families controlled checkpoints in the name of the state. The passes often represented the status and occupation of the individual as well as the location of the work (Asuka Shiryōkan 1984). Passes for those who could not write consisted of wooden slips with marks on the sides indicating the position of the joints of the index finger to confirm the identity of the bearer by matching the slip to the bearer's finger.

Aristocrats had borrowed heavily from the Asian continent in introducing changes in clothing, architecture, and consumption, as evidenced by the archaeological record. Imported ceramics, including Chinese three-colored and green-glazed wares of the Tang dynasty, were used in some elite residences. Chinese-style writing utensils have been found at Gobōyama 3 Tomb in Ikaruga-chō, Nara Prefecture. A Chinese ink stone glazed in yellow and green [211] accompanied by a glass brush case was recovered from an earthenware coffin (*Nara Kenritsu Kashihara* 1988, 61). Writing utensils of various types, including ink stones for grinding ink [212, 214], a water dropper [213], and a writing brush [216], convey the importance of literacy in daily life and government activities.

Other palaces were built beyond the Asuka Plain, including Naniwa at the edge of Osaka Bay near the site of Osaka Castle and Ōtsu on the southern shore of Lake Biwa (Kamata 1987).

Temples

A detailed survey of late seventh-century Buddhist temples and kilns conducted in 1983 identified 730 separate sites, the vast majority of which are temples. They range in number from eighty-three in Nara Prefecture to forty-three in all of Kyūshū (mostly in Fukuoka Prefecture) to only ten in the northern Tōhoku region as far north as Miyagi Prefecture. Few sites are located on the coast of the Sea of Japan (Center for Archaeological Operations 1983).

Based ultimately on Chinese forms originally adapted from palace sites, Asuka period temples were likewise rectangular, oriented north to south, and surrounded by some kind of wall or barrier. A mound and a moat enclosed some of the more elaborate structures. On passing through a main gate on the south side, the visitor entered an open space that led to a middle gate, which was set in a surrounding wall protecting the temple's cloister (*garan*). Inside the *garan* was the Kondō, or Great Hall, behind which was the lecture hall. Outside the cloistered nucleus stood a bell tower and a pagoda, a multistoried repository for Buddhist texts or relics. The main hall, the setting for major ceremonies, enclosed the Buddha platform (*butsudan*), symbolizing the sacred mountain on which the Buddha sat. The central Buddha sculpture was flanked by sculptures of bodhisattvas and the Four Heavenly Kings, the guardians of the four cardinal directions. The setting could be enhanced with other sculptures, hangings of metal ornaments and brocades, and canopies suspended over the images (Kidder 1972a, 81).

It was common to bury precious objects at the base of the pagoda. Sixth-century offerings resembled those found in earlier burial mounds. For instance, from the Asukadera, the first temple to be built in Japan, between A.D. 588 and 606 in Nara Prefecture, pagoda offerings included iron armor fragments, horse ornaments and fittings, gilt-bronze earrings, *magatama* ornaments, and pieces of gold and silver foil (Asuka Historical Museum 1978, 98). By the end of the seventh century offerings were Buddhist votive objects rather than adapted pagan grave goods.

In the latter half of the Asuka period bricklike tiles bearing stamped relief depictions of the Buddha attended by two bodhisattvas were made to adorn the interiors of temple halls and pagodas [255].

Sculptures

Asuka artisans mastered the creation of Buddhist representations in wood, stone, clay, hollow and wood-core dry lacquer, copper repoussé, and stone. Gilt-bronze images, easily transported from the Asian continent, predominated as models for Japanese Buddhist sculpture from the time of the first introduction of Buddhist sculpture to Japan until the end of the Nara period in A.D. 794. Representations of seated bodhisattvas in meditation were first popular. They were previously known to us from accidental discoveries, but recent excavations have provided information on their context in temple sites, sutra burial mounds (*kyō-zuka*), and votive sites on mountaintops (*sangaku*).

One example is a fragment of the halo of an image brought to the Yamato no Aya family temple, recently found near the ruins of Hinokuma Temple, Asuka Village. Later examples were made in the Kinai region and carried to outlying temples, such as those in Chiba Prefecture, near Tokyo. The burial of a repoussé Buddha triad in a corridor tomb at Minezaki in Sakura City, Chiba Prefecture, dates to the latter half of the seventh century; it illustrates the assimilation of the new religion in the Kantō region (Kashima 1991). Small and easily portable, Buddha images were ideal vehicles for conveying the ideas of the religion. Bronze images were cast by the lost-wax technique. A wax core was sculpted and then covered with clay to form an outer mold. On heating, the wax melted through channels in the mold, thus forming space for the bronze.

In the Asuka period, statues were made at the request of the local aristocracy, whereas in the Nara period the government was primarily responsible for building temples and granting commissions for images. An office for the construction of temples was established in the eighth century, and Buddhist sculptors were employed as government officials. Thus the sculptors had relatively high social status. Bronze figures of Kannon (seated and standing) convey the archaic serenity of the Asuka style [257, 258]. Buddhist sculptures in clay, fashioned over a wooden armature wrapped with strips of bark, were also produced.

Figure 44
Stone fountain, 7½ feet (2.3 m)
high. Nara National Cultural
Properties Research Institute. Important Cultural Property. The
three-piece fountain may represent
Mount Sumeru, symbolizing the
center of the Buddhist cosmos.

A group of granite sculptures, differing in style and function from earlier *haniwa* and later Buddhist figures, was found in the Asuka region at the beginning of the twentieth century. A large stone sculpture, unearthed near the site of the Asuka Historical Museum, served as a fountain. It has an interior, branched channel for water, which originally poured from the mouth of the female form and from a stemmed drinking cup held up to the mouth of the male. Today the lower part of the cup is missing (Asuka Historical Museum 1978, 21).

Other stone carvings of the same general date from the Asuka region include grotesque figures found at the tomb of the Queen Kibi-hime (active sixth century), a gigantic stone tortoise, and a three-piece monument said to represent Mount Sumeru (symbolizing the center of the Buddhist cosmos), which is also perforated for use as a fountain (fig. 44). The carvings attest to the ability of the Yamato state to recruit large labor forces and specialized technicians to create rare objects for the central authorities. Historical references cite the erection of holy mountain stones for state celebrations. Several such fountains are recorded. One, found near Asukadera, came from a site yielding a series of ditches like those constructed as watercourses in ancient gardens. Of disparate styles, the sculptures bear vague resemblances to Asian continental prototypes. Certain sculpted mountain forms are not unlike those found on Chinese hill censers of the Han dynasty that depict sacred mountains (Kidder 1972a, 148). Similar motifs are also found on a rare "ocean-and-seashore" mirror recovered from the temple Hōryūji (Asuka Historical Museum 1978, 25). These stone figures, some of which appear to emphasize phallic worship and fertility, have unfortunately been moved from their original locations so that their present context yields few clues regarding their original purpose. Early Shinto shrines must have been constructed in Asuka; perhaps these figures were related to them or to local religion, which has been reinterpreted many times over in past centuries.

Roof Tiles

Because clay tiles are less perishable than wooden beams and pillars, we know more about the roofs of some buildings than the structures they adorned. Building plans are only accessible from the patterns of post molds, pits, and pavements found in the ground. Minute variations in the decoration of roof tiles have allowed archaeologists to date stylistic changes and trace patronage relationships among temples sharing identical motifs. Tiles were used for temple roofs in the late sixth century. They were not used for palaces until the late seventh century, when the most important administrative buildings of Fujiwara were tiled.

Two types of unglazed roof tiles were utilized in the Asuka period: convex tiles for the ridges of the roof and slightly wider, intervening concave tiles. Round and curved tiles, with designs on the outward-facing surfaces, ornament row ends. The decoration on the roof-edge tile was usually a lotus image, with different styles of petals derived from Chinese and Korean models. The tiles for Asukadera [249, 250], made by Korean artisans from Paekche, are among the oldest known in Japan. Roof tiles of Kawaradera [251, 252], built in the late seventh century, depict composite, overlapping petals in the style of Tang China. In addition to roof tiles for temples, great numbers of tiles were produced in government workshops administered under the *ritsuryō* system for Fujiwara Palace. Portions of the palace were roofed with cypress bark instead of tiles.

To form roof tiles, clay was paddled over a slightly tapered cylindrical cloth-covered form, which was cut into four vertical sections. The clay piece was then pressed into a mold to form the decoration and joined to another clay piece. In rare cases the decoration on the curved roof-edge tiles was made with a stencil, which would be cut with a knife. Pin marks, evidence that the stencil was pinned down, can be seen on stenciled tiles. Special tiles with fierce, demon faces, called *onigawara,* were set under the ridge ends and at the terminus of the ridges running to the corners of the building.

Ceramics

Haji earthenware continued to be used for everyday purposes during the Asuka period. *Sue* stoneware, which had been restricted to the elite during the fifth and sixth centuries, came to be more common as a utilitarian ware. *Sue* ware was produced in many centers, the largest being the Sanage kilns in Nagoya, which operated from the Late Kofun period to the twelfth century. Kidder (1972a, 40) has reported on a late seventh-century kiln at Sanage, constructed over a ditch, with a barrel-shaped vault of straw-tempered clay.[6]

Three-color lead-glazed ware from China and green-glazed ware from Korea were used for religious and ceremonial functions. In the seventh century, green lead-fluxed glazed bowls, dishes, and tiles were produced near Nara and Osaka with direct technical assistance from Korean potters. For these, the body was fired first, then fired again after glazing, in small, three-sided kilns (Mellott 1990, 62–63).

Tombs

Compared to those of the Kofun period, tombs dating from the beginning of the Asuka period are fewer and are therefore presumed to be limited to people of high status. The outer form of the tombs of the highest aristocrats in Asuka was rectangular, round, or octagonal. The great competing families maintained distinctive burial-mound shapes (Shiraishi 1986, 194). The Soga family, including emperors and empresses and members of the allied Abe family, constructed huge square mounds in the Kinai region. The opposing faction, the Mononobe and Nakatomi families, which included the grandfather of emperors Tenji and Temmu, constructed round *kofun*. In the Tōhoku region and surrounding valleys of the Kantō Plain the great families allied to each faction appear to have maintained distinctive shapes for their burial mounds (Shiraishi 1986, 194). The burial chamber was at the level of the surrounding terrain and often fashioned of huge cut stones. The chamber opened on the side and in some cases included a fired-clay *sue*-like pottery coffin, later examples of which were used for individual burials. The space inside the mound was no longer a wide chamber for multiple burials like those of the Kofun period but rather a small stone chamber resembling a house-shaped stone coffin.

Takamatsuzuka, an exquisite tomb with paintings on interior walls plastered in the Korean and Chinese manner (fig. 45), was discovered in 1972 in Asuka. It is believed to have belonged to a Korean aristocrat serving in Asuka at the time of Empress Jitō and the building of Fujiwara Palace (Inokuma & Watanabe 1984; Kidder 1972b; Suenaga & Inoue 1974). A stellar constellation is depicted on the ceiling. Four men and four women flank the sun and a blue dragon on the east wall. In the group to the south of the dragon, badly damaged, is an individual under a canopy, probably the occupant of the tomb. On the west wall are the moon and a white tiger, again flanked by four male and four female figures. Depicted on the north wall are the tortoise and snake spirits symbolizing the North, which is called the Black Warrior. While the figure on the south wall is lost, it is thought to have been the red phoenix, symbol of the South (Aikens & Higuchi 1982, 285). Grave goods include ornamental Tang-style sword fittings and a Tang Chinese mirror with animals, birds, and grapevine motifs. A black lacquered coffin recovered there displays ornamental gilt-bronze fittings.

Together with the new social and religious order, different forms of burial appeared in Asuka. With the advent of Buddhism and belief in the transience of human life, the custom of burial mounds lost its rationale. From the beginning of the seventh century, tombs were smaller than those of the Kofun period; grave offerings for the upper classes temporarily increased in quality, however. Funerary pillows of precious

Figure 45
Wall painting from Takamatsuzuka, a late seventh-century *kofun* in Nara Prefecture excavated in 1972. The wall paintings are among the earliest paintings in Japan to depict in detail the costumes of elite men and women of the Asuka period (A.D. 600–710).

materials such as amber and glass were used. Coffins of lacquer-coated wood or fabric had exquisite fittings of gilt bronze and appear to have had locks. Swords were set alongside the fully dressed nobles (Nara Kokuritsu Bunkazai 1988).

The early seventh-century custom of burying valuables in graves and practicing ecstatic grieving involving self-mutilation was banned around A.D. 646, with the edicts of the Taika Reform (Kidder 1985, 108). The size and expense of burial mounds had earlier been regulated by sumptuary laws. A unique epitaph cast in Chinese characters on a bronze plaque [248] is dedicated to a high official, Funa no Ōgo, descendant of a foreign immigrant clan, who died in A.D. 641. It reflects an entirely new concept of designating the rank of the individual in a bureaucratic, perhaps less personal, society.

At the time that Empress Jitō was cremated in A.D. 704, bronze vessels similar to those used for votive offerings were used as cinerary urns. Other burial materials include stone, lacquer, glass, wood, *haji* and *sue* wares, and three-colored glazed ceramic. In some cases a few coins were also buried with the dead.

Outside the Asuka region, burial customs followed earlier patterns. Chambers in Kyūshū were excavated into rock faces, while in the Kantō Plain tombs were dug into hard loam.

Settlements

By the middle of the Asuka period about 3.5 to 5 million people lived in the Japanese islands, an enormous number compared to European populations at that time (Farris 1985, 8). Japanese life expectancy was twenty-eight to thirty-three years, which compares favorably with the range of thirty to thirty-five years for people of Renaissance Europe. Most people in Japan lived in dispersed agricultural settlements. The capital at Asuka reached urban proportions during the period, and administrative centers such as Dazaifu in Kyūshū became important government outposts of culture and politics with close ties to the central government.[7]

Rural life of the seventh century is known from historical and archaeological sources. The flat plains of the Yamato Basin today are dotted with irrigation ponds, which suggests that dense, stable populations and intensive cultivation have been present for a long time. (These saucer ponds, however, postdate the Asuka period.) In the Asuka period, water was available from dammed-up valley streams, but water-lifting devices such as waterwheels were not used. Slash-and-burn cultivation was employed and repeatedly banned because it reduced forested areas, and revenues from it could not be easily controlled. Peasants often migrated from their villages to escape taxation and to open up new lands in other, less-developed areas. They also left their land to work on private estates. Historian William Wayne Farris (1985, 144) has referred to a "vicious circle of sparse population and primitive agricultural techniques" that persisted until A.D. 900. Further, urbanized centers of dense population, except for the imperial capitals, did not develop until near the end of the twelfth century. The provincial and administrative centers, such as Dazaifu, contained relatively small populations. Low-level technology meant that state-allotted land could not be kept in perpetual cultivation.

Although still uncommon, iron tools were preferred by cultivators of artificially irrigated soils. Much land under rice cultivation was perpetually swampy and of low productivity.

In the seventh century some of the land around Nara was divided into large standardized tracts about 2,100 feet (642 m) on each side or 102 acres (41 hectares) in area. These large parcels were subdivided for use by peasants, who held their land parcel for life and could not transfer it or pass it on to an heir. Holdings were adjusted every six years so that land was taken from families who had lost members and assigned to new grantees. While some settlements were clustered in productive areas and surrounded by irrigated rice paddies, most agricultural settlements were small hamlets dispersed among dry fields that were not farmed continuously.

Current archaeological excavations are revealing a network of regional centers controlled by the Yamato state. With the threat from the Asian continent in the mid-seventh century, Yamato had moved quickly to fortify and consolidate politically the northern Kyūshū Plain. The Yamato court was mindful that in A.D. 528 the Iwai Rebellion had been created by a coalition between the Korean kingdom of Silla and the paramount chief of Kyūshū.

Earthen ramparts constructed in A.D. 664, in a location at the inland edge of the Fukuoka Plain against the mountains, protected the largest complex west of Asuka—Dazaifu—an administrative center constructed during three separate periods (*Kyūshū Rekishi Shiryōkan* 1986). The earliest construction consisted of wooden posts, while the later two were built on stone foundations. The administrative center consisted of a cluster of buildings, a pair of halls on the east and west sides, and two gates in front.

The plan of Dazaifu follows the general layout of the Yamato palaces. Dazaifu clearly held special status in the Yamato system as a link between the capital and the provinces. Five temples were constructed within the complex, with four more nearby (Kidder 1972a, 50–52). Ōno-shiro, a castle with walls 32¾ feet (10 m) or more in height and 4 miles (6.4 km) in circumference, was constructed on the hilltop behind the site. These fortifications had interior storage structures and water control facilities. Beyond the government buildings was a school or academy, composed of several buildings, one of which yielded exquisite floor tiles decorated with arabesques. In addition, official warehouses contained raw silk and other goods paid as taxes. An open square has been located in the area of the first government buildings. Wooden slips dating to the eighth century, discovered in several locations in Dazaifu, indicate the receipt of tribute from various areas of Kyūshū and also from the northern Ryūkyū Islands.

The mountains east of Fukuoka Plain have yielded defensive stone alignments (*kōgoishi*) thought by some archaeologists to date to the Iwai Rebellion of A.D. 528 and by others to the later seventh century (Takakura & Yokota 1986, 227). At its apogee Dazaifu was a gateway to the Asian continent. In later times it offered safe harbor for those out of favor in the capital. While little remains of the ancient buildings, the place retains a special aura for the modern visitor.

The great Kanzeonji, a temple erected at Dazaifu next to the administrative center, was begun in A.D. 672 by Emperor Tenji as an offering for the repose of the soul of his mother, Empress Saimei. Although the temple was constructed over several decades, the style of the roof tiles suggests that the roof was completed by the end of the seventh century.

Life in the outer regions of the Japanese state is becoming well known through excavations of provincial centers, county seats, administrative offices, and local production sites. In the second half of the seventh century the ancient Japanese state consisted of fifty-eight provinces and three islands; Okinawa and Hokkaidō were not under its political control. The provinces, each with an administrative center, were further divided into five to six hundred counties.

More than ten provincial centers were excavated from 1963 to 1987 (Tanaka 1987, 83). The centers were about 656 to 984 feet (200–300 m) on each side and contained a rectangular compound oriented north-south and demarcated by a moat and an earthen wall capped with roof tiles. In general, the plan of each center consisted of a long building, oriented east-west, at the north side of the compound, and two long buildings running north-south. The buildings surrounding a plaza formed the administrative and ceremonial nucleus. Around these buildings stood the administrative offices where day-to-day government business was carried out. Major administrative buildings in the provincial capitals were constructed with pillars set on foundation stones and roofs covered with tiles. To the local farmer who lived in a pit house, the structures were new and imposing.

More than fifty county seats have been excavated. Unlike the larger provincial centers, they possessed storage facilities for rice, demonstrating that tax was collected at the county instead of provincial level (Tanaka 1987, 86). The county officer's residence was separated from sixth- and seventh-century residential areas and clusters of mounded tombs, indicating that although officials had been appointed from local elites, they had extricated themselves from the age-old system of territorial and blood ties to rule the agricultural population.

County administrative offices, such as the site of Miharagunga in Ogōri City, Fukuoka Prefecture, have also been found. The earliest buildings, dating from the end of the seventh to the early eighth century, consisted of three warehouses, each about 30 by 20⅝ feet (9.2 × 6.3 m), set on wooden posts. It is believed that the county administrators entertained foreign dignitaries in guesthouses and other facilities. The finding of a cache of iron arrowheads is clear evidence that militia were also stationed at the county headquarters.

Early Buddhist temples, similar in style to those of the second half of the seventh century in the Kinai region, have been found at Usa, Ōita Prefecture. Their roof tiles are stylistically comparable to those from Asuka, and baked clay Buddhist plaques have been found in the remains of a tower. Buddhism is thus known to have spread rapidly through western Japan, and Buddhist institutions were in close contact with those in the political center. By around A.D. 700 Buddhism had been introduced to the far southern reaches of Kyūshū.

Kanoko site in Ibaraki Prefecture exemplifies a local craft center and possible military garrison, distinct from provincial and county administrative sites (Tanaka 1987, 86–91). Enclosed by a ditch 328 feet (100 m) long on each side, Kanoko contained twelve elongated pit dwellings and a number of iron-working structures with fire pits, which had nozzles for bellows embedded in their sides. Evidence of a local administration in the form of officials' belt ornaments and ink stones was also recorded, together with iron arrowheads and armor platelets. A rare find of written characters on pieces of paper reused and covered with lacquer to make a lid for a container identified the makers of scabbards and arrowheads.

On the northern frontier are definite records of expansion and conflict between the Yamato state and the Emishi people. Fortifications were built along this frontier in the eighth century. The Emishi in the north and the Hayato people in the extreme south of Kyūshū in Kagoshima Prefecture were important groups living at the edge of the Yamato state. While they were not then subjugated, some members served as guards for the imperial family. The arrival of their missions in the capital is mentioned in the *Nihon shoki* (Kidder 1972a, 148).

Summary

The significant changes of the Asuka period are associated with codification of the state constitution in A.D. 552 and transformation of the status of hereditary attendants into state officials in A.D. 604. It culminated in A.D. 710 in the completion of the symmetrically planned Fujiwara capital, a ceremonial and administrative center that included large Buddhist temples. Changes in palace plans show the institutionalization of the role of the emperor and empress, who came from a semidivine hereditary line. Although the administrative center of the Yamato state at Asuka occupied a surprisingly small area (similar to that of other early secondary states in eastern Asia, such as the Silla capital of Kyŏngju), a constant supply of goods and services flowed to it from outlying regions, as documented in the *mokkan*. These wooden slips, together with precious writing utensils, provide archaeological evidence of a formalized, hierarchical pattern of authority, requiring documents of all kinds, including identification badges and passes.

Outlying garrisons and county seats were also linked to the center. Foreign elite were assimilated and gained positions of power in the rapidly advancing society. Specialization of craft production, land reform, and changes in agricultural techniques are borne out by excavation of production sites and farming villages.

Notes

1. This poem, which is here reprinted by permission of the publishers, concerns Fujiwara Palace, the seat of power from A.D. 694 to 710.

2. The *Kojiki* was based on materials recited to Ō no Yasumaro by Hieda no Are (born ca. A.D. 650), who had memorized the earlier written histories, the *Teiki* (Imperial Records) and *Kyūji* (Old Chronicles), which were burned at the time of the downfall of the Soga clan in A.D. 645.

3. It is likely that later historians condensed changes that had taken place over many years, attributing them all to the Taika Reform.

4. Kishi Toshio (Yamamoto Tadanao 1987, 192) has postulated an even larger area for Fujiwara. His estimate extends the city grid over irregular sloping land and places the palace in the southern portion of the capital. Since that configuration of the grid and placement of the palace are unknown in other capitals of this type, the larger estimate is not widely accepted.

5. The first two types are represented in the exhibition. These fragile documents must be conserved carefully, since the characters fade under excessive exposure to light. Unless humidity is controlled, they crumble to dust.

6. The vault ascended a twenty-nine-degree slope and was 45 feet (13.7 m) long, 5¼ feet (1.6 m) wide, and 5 feet (1.5 m) high inside.

7. Museums at Asuka, Dazaifu, and Kashihara help bring this period to life. In particular, the Nara Prefectural Kashihara Archaeological Research Institute presents a panorama of ancient cultures in the Nara Basin beginning from Paleolithic times.

THE MIZUOCHI WATER CLOCK

INOKUMA KANEKATSU

For the first time in Japanese history, in A.D. 660 (during the reign of Empress Saimei), a bell was used to signal time. A brand-new two-story clock tower had been completed in the southwestern corner of the temple grounds of Asukadera in Nara Prefecture.

In 1972 a mound and its surrounding stone-paved ditch were unearthed from a small rice paddy in the area called Mizuochi. The discovery occurred in the same year the painted murals of nearby Takamatsuzuka Kofun were opened to the public (see fig. 45). Archaeologists working at Takamatsuzuka found traces of postholes arranged in five lines and five rows, like the checkered board used in the game go. Although only a partial survey was possible that year, the site was determined immediately to be extremely important.

The Mizuochi area is assumed to have been the site of Kiyomigahara Palace, belonging to Emperor Temmu. The archaeological remains may represent the palace pavilion. On its east side was a water fountain with granite rock carvings representing Mount Sumeru and human figures (*sekijinzō*). A historical record states that the emperor entertained Indian and Persian guests at the site of these stones; some archaeologists have therefore regarded Mizuochi as the location of a reception hall. The key features unearthed at the structure—such as a bronze pipe, wooden conduit, and lacquer-painted box—underlined the special nature of the site as the location of a water clock.[1]

Ten years after its discovery the Mizuochi site was carefully examined (fig. 46). A full survey of the mound revealed a large hole at the center, like the foundation stone of the central pillar of a pagoda.[2] Passing over a footbridge to enter the structure, one encountered five lines of posts.[3] Placed at intervals of 9¼ feet (2.8 m), they created a grid of twenty-five posts. The foundation supporting the posts revealed traces of small socketed depressions under the posts. Rows of smaller stones were wedged between the foundation stones for the posts to prevent the tilting or sinking of the posts. The number of posts and nature of the foundation stones suggested that the original structure was quite elaborate. It probably had two stories, with the clock on the first floor and a bell and drum on the second (fig. 47). Other features of the site might have included a water-operated astrolabe.

Bronze pipes and clay vessels dating to about the mid-seventh century were also unearthed from the hole. Further below, a slight square depression on top of the granite-cut stone indicated traces of a lacquered box. Four boxes were painted with black lacquer and placed at the center of the structure to form a four-step stair, ascending from north to south (fig. 48). From top to bottom the boxes were named Yaten-chi (Night

Figure 46
Excavation of the Mizuochi site
(note surrounding pavement stones
and grid arrangement of postholes).

Figure 47
Reconstruction of the Mizuochi
clock tower (note placement of suspended bell on second floor and
location of five poles on the sides of
the structure).

Heaven Pond), Nitten-chi (Day Heaven Pond), Hei-ko (Flat Jar), and
Manbun-fu (Ten-Thousand-Portion Jar) or Suikai (Water Sea). Water
passed slowly from the upper to the lower boxes through a slender bronze
pipe soldered with an alloy of silver, brass, and cadmium. A buried
wooden conduit, which brought water from the Yatsuri River, was also
found, along with a stopper. Inserted in the side of the lacquered box,
the stopper would have blocked the water and diverted it through a
bronze pipe into an aboveground cistern.

The time is indicated on a graduated wooden rod attached to a float
in the shape of an arrow, which rises according to the water level in the
lowest box, the Suikai. The graduation is based on twelve divisions based
on the zodiac, each divided into four, indicating a lapse of thirty minutes.
A doll (holding an arrow in his left hand) stands and with his right hand
points to the mark that signifies the present time. By analogy with
the workings of a modern clock, the clock hands are fixed while the

Figure 48
Reconstruction of the Mizuochi
water clock in Nara Prefecture.

clockface moves. The discovery of the clock at Mizuochi indicates that
knowledge of the most recently invented water clock—by Lucai of Tang
dynasty China—had been quickly introduced to the Asuka capital.

According to the *Engishiki* (a detailed legal book compiled in the
early tenth century), sophisticated technology developed during the
seventh century enabled a bell and drum to be sounded every thirty
minutes throughout the palace and official residential areas of Asuka.
An alternate measuring stick was prepared for slight seasonal changes in
water temperature, which would affect water flow. Charcoal heating
was supplied in winter to prevent the water from freezing.

Asuka people, who had heretofore only determined time by the
movement of the sun, would have been amazed by the machine, which
worked day and night, rain or shine. Like modern salaried workers
who glance at their wristwatches as they hurry to their offices in the
morning, Asuka government officials were required to follow the time
indicated by the clock that had been built by order of a prince. The
governmental office assigned to look after the water clock was staffed
with twice the average number of workers, all of whom were low-level
laborers on duty twenty-four hours at a time.

The power to control time has always been a tool for rulers to demonstrate authority. The Mizuochi water clock points to the authority of the emperor or empress at the apex of the pyramid of state organization in ancient Japan. Excavations in Asuka have hitherto been focused mainly on the palace, temples, and tomb mounds. Future excavations will undoubtedly disclose the many features that were necessary to sustain the daily life of the ancient capital.

Notes

1. To understand the mechanism before proceeding with the excavation, investigators studied Joseph Needham's *Science and Civilization in China* (Cambridge: Cambridge University, 1954–). This unique, multivolume publication is regarded as the authoritative source for information regarding ancient Chinese science and technology.

2. A ditch 3¼ feet (1 m) deep and 5⅞ feet (1.8 m) wide surrounds a square building 36 feet (11 m) to a side.

3. Each post is 15¾ inches (40 cm) in diameter.

Asuka-Nara period,
7th–8th century
Excavated at Ōkita 24 Cliffside
Tomb, Shizuoka Prefecture
Stone
Height 14¾ in. (37.4 cm)
Izunagaoka Township Education
Commission, Shizuoka Prefecture

Forty-six grave chambers were found in a cluster of cliffside tombs at Ōkita, Shizuoka Prefecture. Excavations in 1978 unearthed about twenty graves with skeletons, twenty containers of cremated bones, and four container covers. In this type of square stone container were stored the cremated remains of the deceased.

On one side of the container are three characters representing the words *waka toneri*. The *toneri* were servants of aristocrats. It is assumed that Ō-toneri was an imperial servant, and Waka-toneri a servant for a prince. The inscription suggests that the particular family that held this hereditary occupation used the term as their family name. This container illustrates how firmly the structure of the ruling system of the ancient state, centered on the emperor and empress, had infiltrated local areas such as Shizuoka Prefecture.

According to historical documents, the custom of cremation entered Japan around A.D. 700, after the adoption of Buddhism as the state religion, and greatly changed traditional burial methods. Recent excavations such as that at Ōkita have made it clear, however, that cremation was already practiced in Japan by the beginning of the seventh century.

The writing of names on containers for cinerary urns suggests that the use of characters was well established, even though the ability to write was limited to an elite group of government officials and monks.

TANABE IKUO

China; Tang dynasty, 1st half
7th century
Excavated at Gobōyama 3 Kofun,
Nara Prefecture
Three-color glazed ware
Height 2 in. (5.2 cm); mouth
diameter 2⅝ in. (6.8 cm)
Nara Prefectural Kashihara Archae-
ological Research Institute, Nara
Important Cultural Property

The flat, slightly higher area of the ink stone, called *oka* ("the land"), provides the surface for rubbing an ink stick over the wet stone. The slightly lower, concave area in which the ink and water collect is called *umi* ("the sea"). A pale green glass cylinder more than five inches (12.7 cm) long, discovered in the same location, is assumed to be the stem of a brush belonging to this set of writing materials.

Ink stones first appeared in China during the Warring States period, and ceramic or earthenware ink-grinding slabs were known during the Western Han dynasty. Ink stones with supports, such as this example, date to the Eastern Han or later. Chinese ink stones most similar to

this one, glazed green with scattered brown dots, were made in the early Tang. This ink stone, excavated at Gobōyama 3 Kofun, was probably brought into Japan from China or a region under its influence.

Such glazed ink stones are rare. The few that are known were unearthed from Fujiwara Palace, built in A.D. 694, and Hōryūji, a seventh-century temple. The mounded tomb from which this ink stone was discovered is located about one-half mile (0.8 km) southwest of Hōryūji. This ink stone could well have belonged to a literary person closely linked to Prince Shōtoku, founder of Hōryūji.

MORIMITSU TOSHIHIKO

Nara period, 8th century
Excavated at Heijō Palace, Nara Prefecture
Agency for Cultural Affairs, Government of Japan, Tokyo; on deposit at Nara National Cultural Properties Research Institute

Note:
Objects from the Nara period, including those from the Heijō Palace and other sites, are discussed in the catalogue entries.

212
Ink stone
Stoneware
Height 2½ in. (6.5 cm);
diameter 6⅝ in. (17.0 cm)

213
Water dropper
Stoneware
2⅛ × 4¾ in. (5.5 × 12.2 cm)

214
Ink stone in form of a bird
Stoneware
3⅛ × 11⅜ in. (8.0 × 29.0 cm)

215
Ink stick
Ink
4¼ × 1 in. (10.7 × 2.6 cm)

216
Writing brush
Bamboo and animal hair
Length 5¾ in. (14.5 cm);
diameter ½ in. (1.4 cm)

217
Knife
Iron and wood
Length 6½ in. (16.7 cm);
diameter ½ in. (1.4 cm)

During the eighth century in Japan it was imperative for government officials to attain proficiency in calligraphy. A set of writing materials unearthed from Heijō Palace in Nara includes a writing brush [216] and its holder, made of slim bamboo, and a second brush. The brush in this set is the first writing brush to be excavated in Japan; writing brushes of badger or rabbit fur and with attached bamboo holders decorated with gold or ivory are preserved in the mid eighth-century Shōsōin Repository in Nara.

The ink stick in the shape of a boat [215] is called *karasumi,* which refers to Chinese ink. A similar ink stick, probably imported from either Tang China or the Korean kingdom of Silla, also can be seen in the Shōsōin Repository.

An ink stick was rubbed with water on an ink stone [212, 214]. In this set one ink stone is in the shape of a waterfowl and its lid is in the form of feathers. Ink stones in the shape of a sheep or flower were also excavated from Heijō Palace. The water dropper [213] was used to drop water onto the ink stone; liquid ink is made by rubbing the solid ink on the wet stone. The knife [217] was used to scrape written characters from wood for correction. Since paper was precious in ancient times, letters, notes, tags, labels, and other forms of everyday communication were written on wooden tablets.

MORIMITSU TOSHIHIKO

Ink on wood
Nara National Cultural Properties
Research Institute

The discovery of wooden tablets
(*mokkan*) with writing has greatly
influenced the historical research of
ancient Japan. Even though writing
on wooden tablets was often practiced in later periods, it was most
significant in ancient times, when
paper was more highly valued than
wood. Excavated examples have
been recovered primarily from early
eighth-century capital sites such as
Fujiwara, Heijō, and Nagaoka as
well as from local government offices
linked to the palaces, located at Dazaifu, Shimotsuke, and Taga Castle.

These wooden tablets with ink
inscriptions are from various sites in
the Heijō capital but also include
examples from Fujiwara Palace. The
recent excavation of the residence of
Nagaya no Ō, a second-rank minis-
ter of the early Nara period, yielded
as many as one hundred thousand
wooden tablets with ink inscriptions.
Those examples, many included
here, provide important new data
for researchers.

TATENO KAZUMI

218
Tablet
Nara period (A.D. 710–94)
Excavated at Heijō Palace, Nara
Prefecture
7⅜ × ⅞ × 1/16 in.
(18.7 × 2.2 × 0.2 cm)

The document identifies the soldiers
who guarded the palace gates and is
a request for their food provisions.

219
Tablet
Nara period, A.D. 764
Excavated at Heijō Palace, Nara
Prefecture
9½ × 1¼ × ⅛ in.
(24.1 × 3.3 × 0.3 cm)

The document reports on night-duty
officials at the training institution
for central government officials.

Back   *Front*

220
Tablet
Nara period (A.D. 710–94)
Excavated at Heijō Palace, Nara
Prefecture
9¾ × ¾ × ⅛ in.
(24.7 × 1.9 × 0.4 cm)

This is a request for cooked rice
needed to starch cloth.

221
Tag
Nara period (A.D. 710–94)
Excavated at Heijō Palace, Nara
Prefecture
9½ × 1¼ × ³⁄₁₆ in.
(24.2 × 3.3 × 0.5 cm)

The tag identifies by collective
title a batch of documents to which
it was attached.

Back　　　*Front*

222
Tablet
Nara period, A.D. 711–16
Excavated at Heijō-kyō (ancient
Nara capital), Nara Prefecture
11¾ × 1¼ × ⅛ in.
(29.9 × 3.2 × 0.4 cm)

Belonging to the Nagaya no Ō
family, this is an order for the presentation of rice and seaweed.

223
Tablet
Nara period, A.D. 714
Excavated at Heijō-kyō (ancient
Nara capital), Nara Prefecture
10 × 1³⁄₁₆ × ⅛ in.
(25.5 × 3.0 × 0.4 cm)

The tablet was written on the
occasion of the presentation of
vegetables from the Yamashiro
garden owned by the Nagaya no
Ō family.

Back   *Front*   *Back*   *Front*

224
Tag
Nara period (A.D. 710–94)
Excavated at Heijō Palace, Nara
Prefecture
11¾ × 1 × 3⁄16 in.
(29.7 × 2.5 × 0.5 cm)

The tag was attached to a package
containing shark, an offering from
Mikawa Province, modern Aichi
Prefecture.

225
Tag
Nara period, A.D. 746
Excavated at Heijō Palace, Nara
Prefecture
10⅛ × 1 × 3⁄16 in.
(25.7 × 2.6 × 0.5 cm)

The tag was attached to a package
containing hoes, an offering from
Bingo Province, modern Hiroshima
Prefecture.

226
Tag
Nara period (A.D. 710–94)
Excavated at Heijō Palace, Nara
Prefecture
2⅛ × ⅜ × 1⁄16 in.
(5.5 × 0.9 × 0.2 cm)

The tag was attached to a package
containing a milk product, an offering from Ōmi Province, modern
Shiga Prefecture.

227
Tag
Asuka period, before A.D. 701
Excavated at Fujiwara Palace, Nara
Prefecture
6¾ × 1¼ × ⅛ in.
(17.2 × 3 × 0.4 cm)

The tag was attached to a package
containing salt, an offering from
Wakasa Province, modern Fukui
Prefecture.

228
Tablet
Nara period (A.D. 710–94)
Excavated at Heijō Palace, Nara
Prefecture
7½ × 1¼ × ⅛ in.
(9.1 × 3.1 × 0.4 cm)

The document identifies the soldiers
who guarded the palace gates and
is a request for their food provisions.

Back　　　　　　*Front*

229
Tablet
Nara period (A.D. 710–94)
Excavated at Heijō Palace, Nara
Prefecture
5⅞ × 1½ × ⅛ in.
(15.0 × 3.8 × 0.3 cm)

This is an order by the head of the
official winery to his subordinate,
asking him to appear in his office.

230
Tablet
Nara period (A.D. 710–94)
Excavated at Heijō Palace, Nara
Prefecture
7⅜ × 1¼ × ⅛ in.
(18.9 × 3.2 × 0.4 cm)

This is a request for cooked rice
needed to starch cloth.

Back *Front*

Back *Front*

231
Tag
Nara period (A.D. 710–94)
Excavated at Heijō Palace, Nara
Prefecture
3½ × ⅞ × ¼ in.
(9.0 × 2.4 × 0.6 cm)

The tag identifies by collective title
a batch of documents to which it
was attached.

232
Tablet
Nara period, A.D. 711–16
Excavated at Heijō-kyō (ancient
Nara capital), Nara Prefecture
14½ × 1¼ × ⅛ in.
(36.9 × 2.9 × 0.4 cm)

Belonging to the Nagaya no Ō
family, this wooden tablet is a
request to present a recommen-
dation for employment.

Back   *Front*

Back   *Front*

233
Tablet
Nara period, A.D. 711–16
Excavated at Heijō-kyō (ancient
Nara capital), Nara Prefecture
11¾ × 1½ × 3/16 in.
(29.9 × 3.8 × 0.5 cm)

The tablet was written on the
occasion of the presentation of
vegetables from the Yaguchi garden,
owned by the Nagaya no Ō family.

234
Tag
Nara period (A.D. 710–94)
Excavated at Heijō Palace, Nara
Prefecture
10⅛ × 1³/16 × ¼ in.
(25.8 × 3.0 × 0.7 cm)

The tag was attached to a package
containing shark, an offering from
Mikawa Province, modern Aichi
Prefecture.

Back   *Front*

Back   *Front*

235
Tag
Nara period, A.D. 745
Excavated at Heijō Palace, Nara
Prefecture
14⅜ × ⅞ × ⅛ in.
(36.4 × 2.4 × 0.4 cm)

The tag was attached to a pack of
pit vipers, an offering from Kazusa
Province, modern Chiba Prefecture.

236
Tag
Nara period, A.D. 746
Excavated at Heijō Palace, Nara
Prefecture
11¾ × 1⅜ × ¼ in.
(29.8 × 3.5 × 0.6 cm)

The tag was attached to a pack of
seaweed, an offering from Mikawa
Province, modern Aichi Prefecture.

237
Tag
Asuka period, before A.D. 701
Excavated at Fujiwara Palace, Nara
Prefecture
6¾ × 1⅛ × ⅛ in.
(17.2 × 2.9 × 0.3 cm)

The tag was attached to a pack of
salt, an offering from Wakasa Province, modern Fukui Prefecture.

Back   *Front*

238
Tablet
Nara period (A.D. 710–94)
Excavated at Heijō Palace, Nara
Prefecture
9¾ × 1¼ × ⅛ in.
(25.0 × 3.1 × 0.4 cm)

The document identifies the soldiers
who guarded the palace gates and
is a request for their food provisions.

239
Tablet
Nara period (A.D. 710–94)
Excavated at Heijō Palace, Nara
Prefecture
7 × 1¼ × ¼ in.
(17.9 × 3.2 × 0.6 cm)

This is an order by a superior to his
subordinate, asking him to appear
in his office.

Back   *Front*

Back   *Front*

240
Tablet
Nara period (A.D. 710–94)
Excavated at Heijō Palace, Nara Prefecture
10³/₁₆ × ¾ × ⅛ in.
(25.9 × 1.9 × 0.4 cm)

This is a request for food by Hokkeji, a Buddhist temple.

241
Tablet
Nara period (A.D. 710–94)
Excavated at Heijō Palace, Nara Prefecture
25¾ × 1⅜ × ⅜ in.
(65.6 × 3.6 × 1.0 cm)

The tablet certifies that certain persons were permitted to pass a checkpoint.

Back   *Front*   *Back*   *Front*

242
Tablet
Nara period, A.D. 711–16
Excavated at Heijō-kyō (ancient
Nara capital), Nara Prefecture
8⅝ × 1½ × ⅛ in.
(22.0 × 3.7 × 0.3 cm)

This is an official letter from the
Court Music Office to the Nagaya
no Ō family.

243
Tablet
Nara period, A.D. 711–16
Excavated at Heijō-kyō (ancient
Nara capital), Nara Prefecture
9 × 1 × 1/16 in.
(23.0 × 2.5 × 0.2 cm)

This is a report of the offering of
vegetables from the Kataoka vegetable garden, owned by the Nagaya
no Ō family.

Back   *Front*   *Back*   *Front*

244
Tag
Nara period (A.D. 710–94)
Excavated at Heijō Palace, Nara
Prefecture
10½ × 1 × ⅛ in.
(26.7 × 2.6 × 0.4 cm)

The tag was attached to a package
containing shark, an offering from
Mikawa Province, modern Aichi
Prefecture.

245
Tag
Nara period (A.D. 710–94)
Excavated at Heijō Palace, Nara
Prefecture
5⅝ × 1⅛ × ⅛ in.
(14.4 × 2.9 × 0.4 cm)

The tag was attached to a pack of
salt, an offering from Wakasa Province, modern Aichi Prefecture.

246
Tag
Nara period (A.D. 710–94)
Excavated at Heijō Palace, Nara
Prefecture
7⅜ × ¾ × ⅛ in.
(18.8 × 2.1 × 0.4 cm)

The tag was attached to a pack of
soybean, an offering from Echizen
Province, modern Fukui Prefecture.

247
Tag
Asuka period, A.D. 691
Excavated at Fujiwara Palace, Nara
Prefecture
8⅜ × 1⅜ × ⅛ in.
(21.4 × 3.7 × 0.5 cm)

The tag was attached to a pack of
materials sent as tax payment from
Owari Province, modern Aichi
Prefecture.

 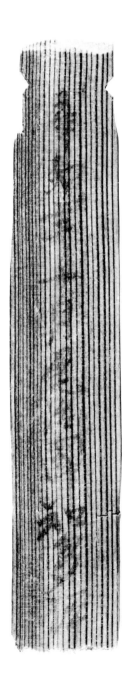

Back   *Front*

Asuka period, 2d half 7th century
Excavated at Matsuokayama,
Kashiwara City, Osaka Prefecture
Bronze
11¾ × 2⅝ in. (29.5 × 6.8 cm)
Mitsui Library Foundation, Tokyo
National Treasure

Usually inscribed with text about the deceased, tomb epitaphs may identify the individual by name, status, and date of death. The inscription on this bronze plaque refers to the career of Funa no Ōgo, who served two emperors, and gives A.D. 641 as the year of his death. In recognition of his service and ability, he was awarded a high rank. The year of his memorial service, A.D. 668 (in the reign of Emperor Tenji [r. A.D. 661–72]), dates this as the oldest among the nineteen ancient epitaphs recovered in Japan.

The epitaph was discovered in the eighteenth century, probably after a landslide, but there is no concrete information about the location or structure of the deceased's grave. It is assumed that the grave was small and consisted of a direct inhumation, a rarity, since most later epitaphs were found in graves with cremations.

The custom of writing an epitaph began in China in the Han dynasty. Many were incised in stone, and the contents were detailed and lengthy. Japanese epitaphs, in contrast, were simply written on thin, narrow, bronze plaques similar to this example.

The construction of planned capital cities, the acceptance of Buddhist thought, and the *ritsuryō,* a legal-code system influenced by judicial practices of the Sui and Tang dynasties in China, were introduced during the Asuka period. Accordingly, the concept of an afterworld drastically changed as did burial rituals. The custom of burying an epitaph, which praised the lifetime achievements of the deceased, was part of that changing world.

TANABE IKUO

Back

Front

惟船氏故
王後首者是
船氏中祖
王智仁首児
那沛故
首之子也
生於乎娑陁宮治天下
天皇之世
奉仕於等
與羅宮
治天下
天皇之朝至於阿須迦宮治天下
天皇之
朝
天皇照見其才異
仕有功
勲
勅賜官位大仁品為苐

二頃三年四頃並
天皇之末歳次辛丑十二月三日庚寅故
戊辰年十二月殯葬於松岳山上共婦
女理故
刀自
同墓其大兄
刀羅古首之墓並作墓也
即為安保万代
之靈基牢固永劫之寶地也

Late Kofun period, late 6th century
Excavated at Asukadera, Nara
Prefecture
Earthenware
Nara National Cultural Properties
Research Institute

249
Diameter 6⅛ in. (15.7 cm)

250
Diameter 6⅝ in. (16.2 cm);
length 17⅜ in. (44.0 cm)

These are examples of the round tiles used on the eaves of Asukadera, the oldest full-scale Buddhist temple in Japan. A design of eleven flower petals, each imperfectly rounded and decorated with a raised dot, is on one tile {249}. A lotus flower in which ten petals are attached to a central circle with six small holes is represented on the other tile {250}. The tip of each petal resembles that of a cherry blossom.

The oldest round eave tiles were made in Japan under the influence of the Korean kingdom of Paekche, although many ways of applying the tiles and finishing the roof seem to have been employed. At this time flat eave tiles were not decorated.

Asukadera, a Buddhist temple, was planned in A.D. 585 by Soga no Umako, a powerful political leader, and completed in A.D. 606. It was the first temple in Japan to be equipped with a complete cloister. The record shows that the Kondō (Great Hall) of the temple was erected with the guidance of technicians from Paekche. Located at the center of the temple enclosure, the Kondō was oriented to the north, east, and west. The plan of Asukadera is thought to have been influenced by the arrangement of Korean temples in the state of Koguryŏ.

KAWAGOE SHUN'ICHI

[250]

Detail [250]

Asuka period, 2d half 7th century
Excavated at Kawaradera, Nara
Prefecture
Earthenware
Nara National Cultural Properties
Research Institute

251
Diameter 7⅜ in. (18.6 cm);
length 1½ in. (3.8 cm)

252
Width 11 in. (28.0 cm);
length 1 in. (3.0 cm)

The round eave tiles used for roofing the Kawaradera were decorated with representations of the lotus, a flower sacred to Buddhists. The center is enlarged and exaggerated, and inside the flower are small, doubled circles. The eight double-lobed petals are thick and full, with sharply defined tips. A sawtooth design, reflecting the influence of early Tang dynasty China, edges the tile.

The flat eave tile, used in combination with the round tile, is simply made with a design of concentric arcs. This so-called Kawaradera-type tile combination was adopted during the latter half of the seventh century in the construction of temples in a wide area including not only the Kinai region but also the region from Chiba to Gumma prefectures in the east and from Fukuoka to Ōita prefectures in the west.

The Kawaradera, also called Gufukuji, was erected by Emperor Tenji for his mother, the deceased Empress Saimei, on behalf of the repose of her soul at the site of her residence. Even though opinions differ concerning the date of construction, it is generally assumed that the building of Kawaradera was begun in A.D. 663 and completed around A.D. 685. Excavations carried out from 1957 to 1959 revealed the plan of the temple enclosure in which a pagoda and the West Kondō were placed in contraposition to the central great hall. The layout of the temple enclosure was thereafter called the Kawaradera-type arrangement.

KAWAGOE SHUN'ICHI

Nara period, 1st half
8th century
Excavated at Heijō Palace,
Nara Prefecture
Earthenware
Nara National Cultural Properties
Research Institute

253
Diameter 6 in. (15.5 cm);
length 1⅞ in. (5.0 cm)

254
Width 10¼ in. (26.0 cm);
length 2¼ in. (5.7 cm)

These eave tiles represent those that were used for the roofs of Heijō Palace and government buildings. The round eave tile is decorated with eight radially arranged flower petals, each split in half, with two outer rings filled with small sawtooth-pattern circles [253]. An intertwining floral pattern, surrounded by papillae, decorates the flat eave tile [254]. Excavation of about 30 percent of Heijō Palace has yielded some four hundred kinds of roof tiles and sixty thousand specimens. It appears that on each occasion of reconstruction, not only of the central palace buildings but also of some government offices, the tiles were replaced.

Palaces in the Asuka period were roofed with cypress bark, similar to the roof material used on shrines today. The tradition was retained only for the imperial residences during the subsequent Nara and Heian periods. By the mid-seventh century the centralized power had implemented the *ritsuryō* administrative reforms following Chinese examples and, as a result, palaces and government offices were renovated. In A.D. 655 a vain attempt was made to tile the roof of Owarida Palace in Asuka following Chinese style. It was not until the building of Fujiwara Palace in A.D. 694 that tiled roofs were actually constructed. The roof tiles from ancient Japan reflect the maturation of political systems and concomitant advancements in architecture.

MORIMITSU TOSHIHIKO

Asuka period, late 7th century
Excavated at Kawaradera, Nara
Prefecture
Earthenware
10½ × 7¼ in. (26.7 × 18.6 cm)
Asuka Village Education Commission, Nara Prefecture; on deposit
at Asuka Historical Museum

This is the oldest relief tile in Japan to depict the image of the Buddha. Made in clay molds, then dried and fired, such tiles range in length from one to twenty-four inches (2.5–61.0 cm). Some were colored with pigment or decorated with gold or silver leaf.

In this example two bodhisattvas flank the Buddha, who rests his feet on a lotus-shaped base. Two celestial maidens scatter flowers on either side of the canopy (Sanskrit: *chatra*) above the head of the Buddha. Behind him

is a pipal tree, the large, long-lived tree indigenous to India.

Some Buddha-image relief tiles were kept in miniature shrines for daily worship, but most were set in the walls of temples or pagodas. Some were bronze reliefs, made by hammering a thin bronze sheet over a mold. Other Buddha images were embroidered on pieces of cloth, also for wall hangings.

MORIMITSU TOSHIHIKO

Asuka period, mid-7th century
Excavated at Nachi Mountain,
Wakayama Prefecture
Bronze
Max. height 12¼ in. (31.3 cm)
Tokyo National Museum

This small image is considered to
represent the bodhisattva known in
Japanese as Miroku (Sanskrit: Mai-
treya), the Buddha of the future.
The seated posture with the figure's
right foot on top of the knee of the
dangling left leg and the right hand
on the cheek as if in meditation was
particularly revered in China during
the Northern Wei dynasty (A.D.
386–535). This pose was used in
representations of Prince Siddhārtha
or of bodhisattvas, individuals who
had not yet attained enlightenment.

Several outstanding Buddhist
images from the Asuka and Nara
periods have survived in Japan. The
most famous is a wooden image of
the bodhisattva Miroku in the
Chūgūji, a temple adjacent to the
temple Hōryūji in Nara. The Tokyo
National Museum image of Miroku
seems to have imitated the bodhisattva of Chūgūji in the double
topknot hairstyle, gentle facial
expression, and slim body.
Relatively less attenuated than
Asuka period figures, this figure
would belong stylistically to a
slightly later period, perhaps to the
mid-seventh century.

The statue was found in 1918
from a sutra mound on Nachi
Mountain in Wakayama Prefecture,
which is famous for a Shinto shrine
and an adjoining Buddhist temple.
According to Buddhist belief,
mappō, the end of the world or "end
of the Law," was predicted to occur
at a future date that came to correspond to approximately the end of
the Heian period. People believed
that the power of Miroku would save
them, and in praying for his coming
they buried images of him.

TANABE IKUO

Asuka period,
late 7th–early 8th century
Bronze
15 ¼ in. (38.8 cm)
Agency for Cultural Affairs,
Government of Japan, Tokyo

The figure of the bodhisattva known
in Japanese as Kannon (Sanskrit:
Avalokiteśvara) stands on a lotus
platform and holds a bead necklace
in his right hand. On his head is a
miniature statue of the Buddha,
who sits cross-legged on a five-petal
lotus seat. Below the miniature is
a crown with large decorations.
Three layers of lotus petals form the
pedestal. The body and pedestal were
cast together; the pedestal is hollow,
whereas the body is solid.

The garments and detailed ornaments are extremely similar to those
of gilt-bronze images dedicated to
Hōryūji, a temple. Closer scrutiny
reveals, however, that Kannon's
youthful demeanor suggests that the
figure was made between the end of
the seventh and beginning of the
eighth century. The statue is generally well preserved, even though it
has survived a fire, from which remain scorch marks.

TANABE IKUO

Nara period, early 8th century
Bronze
Max. height 11⅜ in. (29.0 cm)
Nara National Museum

This standing figure wears a three-sided head decoration, celestial garment, and bead necklaces and holds a vase in the left palm. The figure and the pedestal were cast as one piece; only the bead necklaces were cast separately and later attached to the body. The lotus petals in reverse below the pedestal, also cast separately, are missing.

The figure has a round, youthful face. The shoulders are sloped, the celestial garment falls in soft folds like fish fins, and the pendant cords from the crown droop gracefully—all features effectively accentuating the slender image.

There are some very similar sculptures in the Hōryūji from the late seventh century, but these express a greater tranquility than this sculpture, which should be regarded as made after the beginning of the eighth century.

TANABE IKUO

GLOSSARY

Alloy. A mixture of two or more metals, intimately fused.

Archaeological Periods. Arbitrary units of time based on cultural similarities, such as comparable types of pottery, tools, or burial styles.

Archaeological Record. A general term for artifacts, features (pits, postholes, foundations, etc.), structures, and refuse; the remains of all types of human activities found by archaeologists.

Assemblage. All the artifacts found at a site or group of sites.

Bifacial Tool. A stone tool with flakes removed from both sides to form a cutting edge of symmetrical cross section, such as a chopper, ax, or projectile point.

Blade Flake. A long parallel-sided flake.

Block. An area of scattered stone tools thought to be left in one brief period of habitation.

Boreal Forest. Forest of northern regions, adapted to cool or cold climate, usually containing deciduous or coniferous trees. These forests provide evidence of cool climatic conditions in the past.

Burial Goods; Burial Offerings. Objects placed with the dead at the time of burial.

Burial Pavements. In the Jōmon period, the surface of the ground in which burials occurred, often covered with a pavement of stones up to twelve inches (30.0 cm) in diameter.

Clusters. Groupings of artifacts or features such as pits.

Comparative Sequence. A master archaeological sequence compiled from local sequences of adjacent areas, showing changes in the times of appearance of certain artifacts or cultures. In the Kantō Sequence, cruder stone tools are followed by knives, microblades, and stone points (see fig. 2).

Coniferous Forest. Forest composed of needle-leaved trees such as pine or cedar.

Controlled Excavation. Excavation in which records are kept of the exact locations of the objects and patterns in which they are found.

Core. Lump of stone from which human-struck flakes have been removed.

Cross Dating. Method by which objects found in dated sites can sometimes be used to date other sites. For example, a mirror or horse fitting found in a Chinese tomb with a written date could be used to date a Japanese tomb if the same type of material were found there.

Cultivation. The growing and tending of plants for human use.

Cultural Layer. A layer in an archaeological site that bears evidence of human activity, such as tools, debris, or structures, as opposed to a natural layer that contains no artifacts or debris but might be of silt or volcanic ash.

Deciduous Forests. Forests composed of trees that drop their leaves in winter, as in parts of the eastern United States.

Ecotone. A transition area between two adjacent ecological communities (as forest and grassland).

Exchange Network. The relationships created by exchanging goods and services between individuals and communities.

Fire Pit. The remains of a hearth, created by building a fire in a depression in the earth, sometimes lined with stones.

Firing Temperature. The maximum temperature to which fired clay objects are heated. Different firing temperatures affect the hardness, color, and porosity of clay objects.

Flake Tools. Stone tools fashioned from flakes struck or removed by pressure from stone cores. The flakes may be retouched by further removal of small flakes to thin the tools, by alteration of the edges, or by carving notches for hafting.

Horticulture. Small-scale cultivation of plants in plots or gardens.

Marine Deposit. Layers created by sea action, such as those formed on the ocean bottom.

Microblade. A tiny blade one inch or less in length, set in handles or hafts of bone or wood and used for cutting and engraving.

Microscopic Studies. Examination of objects under the microscope. Archaeological examination of edges of stone tools under a binocular microscope may reveal patterns of wear related to particular patterns of motion or of the material being cut or scraped.

Neolithic Cultures. The cultures of people who produced a significant portion of their food by growing crops and raising animals.

Phytoliths. Tiny silica particles, sometimes called plant opals, contained in plants, particularly in the stems. These survive after other parts of the plants decay. Their form is distinctive in different types of plants and different parts of the same plant.

Polity. A general term for a distinct political unit, useful when the exact nature of the political system is not clear, as in the investigation of chiefdoms and states. Anthropologists may be reluctant to use such specific interpretive words when the evidence is incomplete.

Post-Pleistocene Climatic Optimum. A period, from roughly 5000 to roughly 2000 B.C., when the climate was slightly warmer than today's climate.

Pumice. Porous lava rock produced in volcanic eruptions.

Radiocarbon Dating. A technique of dating organic materials by direct or indirect measurement of the amount of radioactivity of carbon from a sample. This radiocarbon disintegrates to stable nitrogen at a rate expressed as a half-life of 5,730 years.

Rice-Paddy Cultivation. The growing of rice in irrigated fields that are flooded while the rice is growing and are then drained for harvesting. The rice fields are bounded by earth walls, and the floor of the paddy is often stamped so it will retain water.
  Rice was cultivated in the Late Jōmon by 1000 B.C. on dry hill slopes, with no weeding or fertilizer. This method is termed "non-intensive." Around 500–400 B.C. wet rice cultivation began. It is called "intensive" because of the amount of labor required to maintain the irrigated fields.

Semisubterranean Pit Dwelling. A house in which the lower portion is dug into the ground. Posts set into the dug-out area support the roof.

Shell Mound. A human-made deposit of shells discarded after the meat contained within them was eaten. Since it is often located near a living area, it may contain tools, remains of houses, and burials.

Side-Blow Flakes. Stone flakes struck from oblong stone cores rather than circular or prismatic cores; these are typical of the Late Paleolithic of the Inland Sea region.

Social Ranking. Societies in which individuals have unequal inherited statuses.

Stratification. The formation of social classes, such as rulers, aristocrats, and commoners.

Subsistence; Subsistence Economy. The activity of food getting and the economy surrounding the provision of people with food. In some societies most of the daily work is devoted to the subsistence economy. In others, strongly developed craft or luxury production may be important.

Volcanic Glass. Natural glass produced in volcanic eruptions; also called obsidian.

Waterlogged Deposits. Sites, burials, or buried objects lying below the water table and usually well preserved because of the lack of oxygen and bacteria, which depend on oxygen.

X-ray Examination. Examination of objects by X-ray to penetrate thick encrustations of rust and other types of weathering; used for severely rusted iron swords or corroded bronze objects.

REFERENCES

Aikens, C. Melvin, and Don Dumond. 1986. "Convergence and Common Heritage: Some Parallels in the Archaeology of Japan and Western North America." In Pearson 1986, 163–80.

Aikens, C. Melvin, and Higuchi Takayasu. 1982. *Prehistory of Japan*. New York: Academic Press.

Akazawa Takeru. 1980. "Fishing Adaptation of Prehistoric Hunter Gatherers at the Nittano Site, Japan." *Journal of Archaeological Science* 7: 325–44.

———. 1982. "Cultural Change in Prehistoric Japan: Receptivity to Rice Agriculture in the Japanese Archipelago." In *Advances in World Archaeology,* ed. by Fred Wendorf and Pamela Close, 151–211. New York: Academic Press.

———. 1986. "Hunter-Gatherer Adaptations and the Transition to Food Production in Japan." In *Hunters in Transition,* ed. Mark Zvelebil, 155–66. New York: Cambridge University Press.

Akazawa Takeru and Maeyama Kiyoaki. 1986. "Discriminant Function Analysis of Later Jōmon Settlements." In Pearson 1986, 279–92.

Akazawa Takeru, Oda Shizuo, and Yamanaka Ichirō. 1980. *The Japanese Paleolithic: A Techno-Typological Study.* Tokyo: Rippū Shobō.

Anazawa Wakou and Manome Jun'ichi. 1986. "Two Inscribed Swords from Japanese Tumuli: Discoveries and Research on Finds from the Sakitama-Inariyama and Eta-Funayama Tumuli." In Pearson 1986, 375–96.

Aston, William G. 1956. *Nihongi: Chronicles of Japan from Earliest Times to A.D. 697.* London: Allen & Unwin.

Asuka Historical Museum. 1978. *Guide to the Asuka Historical Museum,* trans. William Carter. Nara: Nara National Cultural Properties Research Institute.

Asuka Shiryōkan. 1984. "Fujiwara-kyū: Han seiki ni okeru chōsa no kenkyū" (Fujiwara palace: Study of a half-century of investigation). In *Zuroku* (Illustrated publication) 13: 53–61. Nara: Asuka Shiryōkan.

Barnes, Gina Lee. 1983. "Protohistory." In *Kodansha* 1983, 3: 160.

———. 1987. "The Role of the *Be* in the Formation of the Yamato State" In *Specialization, Exchange, and Complex Societies,* ed. Elizabeth Brumfiel and Timothy Earle, 86–101. New York: Cambridge University Press.

———. 1988. *Protohistoric Yamato: Archaeology of the First Japanese State.* Michigan Papers in Japanese Studies No. 77; Anthropological Papers, Museum of Anthropology, University of Michigan No. 78. Ann Arbor: University of Michigan Center for Japanese Studies and the Museum of Anthropology, University of Michigan.

———. 1990a. "Ceramics of the Yayoi Agriculturalists." In *Rise of a Great Tradition* 1990, 28–39.

———, ed. 1990b. *Hoabinhian, Jōmon, Yayoi, Early Korean States.* Bibliographic Reviews of Far Eastern Archaeology. Oxford: Oxbow Books.

Carter, W. 1983a. "Aya Family." In *Kodansha* 1983, 1: 125.

———. 1983b. "Hata Family." In *Kodansha* 1983, 3: 111.

Center for Archaeological Operations News. 1983. *Asuka Hakuhō jiin kankei bunken mokuroku* (Bibliography of Asuka Hakuhō period temple sites). Vol. 40. Nara: Nara Kokuritsu Bunkazai Kenkyūjo.

Childe, Vere Gordon. 1942. *What Happened in History*. Harmondsworth: Penguin.

Crawford, Gary. 1987. "The Origins of Plant Husbandry in East Asia: The Japanese Perspective." Typescript. Department of Anthropology, University of Toronto, Canada.

Crawford, Gary, and Hiroto Takamiya. 1990. "The Origins and Implications of Late Prehistoric Plant Husbandry in Northern Japan." *Antiquity* 64: 889–911.

Esaka Teruya. 1983. *Jōmon doki to kaizuka* (Jōmon pottery and shell mounds). Vol. 2 of *Kodaishi hakkutsu* (Excavations of ancient history). Tokyo: Kodansha.

Farris, William Wayne. 1985. *Population, Disease, and Land in Early Japan*. Cambridge, Mass.: Council on East Asian Studies, Harvard Yenching Institute, Harvard University.

Fladmark, Knut. 1982. "An Introduction to the Prehistory of British Columbia." *Canadian Journal of Archaeology* 6: 95–154.

Frankenstein, Susan, and Michael Rowlands. 1978. "The Internal Structure and Regional Context of Early Iron Age Society in Southwestern Germany." *Bulletin of the Institute of Archaeology* (University of London) 15: 73–112.

Fried, Morton. 1967. *Evolution of Political Society*. New York: Random House.

Fujimoto Tsuyoshi. 1983. "Bosei seiritsu no haikei" (Background to the development of burial customs). In *Jōmonjin no seishin bunka* 1983, 12–31.

———. 1988. *Mō futatsu no Nihon bunka* (Two more Japanese cultures). Tokyo: University of Tokyo Press.

Fukunaga Shinya. 1989. "Kyōdō bochi" (Communal cemeteries). In *Kodaishi fukugen* 1989, 120–33.

Gekkan Bunkazai Hakkutsu Shutsudo Jōhō. 1990a. "Jōmon jidai no wankyū shutsudo" (Excavating a Jōmon [double-] curved bow). In *Gekkan Bunkazai Hakkatsu Shutsudo Jōhō*, 12: 34. Tokyo: Japan Tsūshinsha.

———. 1990b. "Kita Chōsen de aitsugi hatsumei" (Recent discoveries in North Korea). In *Gekkan Bunkazai Hakkutsu Shutsudo Jōhō*, 5: 177. Tokyo: Japan Tsūshinsha.

———. 1990c. "Kyokusen no ishigumi suidō" (Curved stone-lined water course). In *Gekkan Bunkazai Hakkutsu Shutsudo Jōhō*, 5: 8. Tokyo: Japan Tsūshinsha.

———. 1990d. "Saiko no haniwa mura" (Oldest *haniwa* village). In *Gekkan Bunkazai Hakkutsu Shutsudo Jōhō*, 2: 88. Tokyo: Japan Tsūshinsha.

Gumma Ken Kyōiku Iinkai. 1980. *Tsukamawari kofungun* (Tsukamawari *kofun* group). Maebashi: Gumma Ken Kyōiku Iinkai.

Habu, Junko. 1988. "Number of Pit Dwellings in Early Jōmon Moroiso Stage Sites." *Journal of the Anthropological Society of Nippon* 96, no. 2: 147–65.

Hanihara Kazurō. 1986. "The Origin of the Japanese in Relation to Other Ethnic Groups in East Asia." In Pearson 1986, 75–83.

Harunari Hideji. 1986. "Rules of Residence in the Jōmon Period Based on the Analysis of Tooth Extraction." In Pearson 1986, 293–312.

Helms, Mary W. 1979. *Ancient Panama: Chiefs in Search of Power*. Austin: University of Texas Press.

Hirose Kazuo. 1987; 1988. "Dai ō bo no keifu to sono tokushitsu" (Lineage and characteristics of the imperial tombs). *Kōkogaku kenkyū* (Archaeological research) 34, no. 3: 23–46; 34, no. 4: 68–78.

Howells, William W. 1986. "Physical Anthropology of the Prehistoric Japanese." In Pearson 1986, 85–99.

Hudson, Mark. 1990. "From Toro to Yoshinogari: Changing Perspectives on Yayoi Period Archaeology." In Barnes 1990b, 63–111.

Hudson, Mark, and Gina Lee Barnes. 1991. "Yoshinogari: A Yayoi Settlement in Northern Kyūshū." *Monumenta Nipponica* 46, no. 2: 211–35.

Ichihara Shi Kyōiku Iinkai. 1988. *Ō shi mei tekken gaihō: Chiba Ken Ichihara Shi Inaridai Ichigō fun shutsudo* (Brief report on the excavation of the iron sword with the inscription *ō shi* from the Inaridai 1 tumulus in Ichihara, Chiba Prefecture). Tokyo: Yoshikawa Kōbunkan.

Ikawa-Smith, Fumiko. 1978. "The History of Early Paleolithic Research in Japan." In *Early Paleolithic in South and East Asia*, ed. Fumiko Ikawa-Smith, 247–86. Hague: Mouton.

———. 1986. "Late Pleistocene and Early Holocene Technologies." In Pearson 1986, 199–216.

———. 1989. "Kanjōdori: Communal Cemeteries of the Late Jōmon in Hokkaidō." Paper prepared for the Circum Pacific Prehistory Conference, Seattle.

Inada Takashi. 1988a. "Kazanbai to hennen" (Volcanic ash and chronology). In Inada 1988c, 37.

———. 1988b. "Kyūsekki jidai no kōdō kiseki" (Traces of the shifting dwelling sites of the Paleolithic groups). In Inada 1988c, 105–24.

———, ed. 1988c. "Kyūsekki jin no seikatsu to shūdan" (Social groups and living patterns of the Paleolithic people). In *Kodaishi fukugen* 1988. Vol. 1.

Inano Yūsuke. 1983. "Gangū" (Stone figures). In *Jōmonjin no seishin bunka* 1983, 86–94.

Inokuma Kanekatsu. 1979. *Haniwa*. In *Nihon no genshi bijutsu* 1979. Vol. 6.

Inokuma Kanekatsu and Watanabe Akiyoshi. 1984. "Takamatsuzuka Kofun." *Nihon no bijutsu* (Japanese art) 217: 1–98.

Iwanaga Shōzō. 1989. "Seidōki no genryō o sagaru" (Search for the source of raw materials used in bronze artifacts). In Kuraku 1989b, 42–44.

Iwasaki Takuya. 1984. *Kofun jidai no chishiki* (Knowledge of the Kofun period). Tokyo: Niū Saiensu Sha.

Iwate Ken Maibun Sentā Bunkazai Chōsa Hōkokusho. 1982. *Gosho Damu kensetsu kanren iseki hakkutsu hōkokusho: Morioka Shi Shidanai iseki 1* (Report of site excavation relating to the construction of the Gosho Dam 1, Morioka, Shidanai 1 site). No. 32. Shimoiioka: Iwate Ken Maizō Bunkazai Sentā.

Jōmonjin no seishin bunka (Spiritual culture of the Jōmon people). 1983. Vol. 9 of *Jōmon bunka no kenkyū* (Study of Jōmon culture), ed. Katō Shinpei, Kobayashi Tatsuo, and Fujimoto Tsuyoshi. Tokyo: Yūzankaku.

Kamata Motokazu. 1987. "Naniwa Sento no keii" (Particular details on the moving of the capital from Asuka to Naniwa). *Rekishi tokuhon* (History reader) 32, no. 12: 171–79.

Kaneko Takuo. 1983. "Sankakukei doban, sankakukei gamban" (Triangular clay and stone plaques). In *Jōmonjin no seishin bunka* 1983, 114–27.

Kano Hisashi and Kinoshita Masashi. 1985. *Asuka Fujiwara no miyako* (Fujiwara capital in Asuka). Vol. 1 of *Kodai Nihon o hakkutsu suru* (Excavating ancient Japan). Tokyo: Iwanami Shoten.

Kashima Masaru. 1991. "Shutsudo no shō kondōbutsu" (Small gilt-bronze Buddha images). *Kikan kōkogaku* (Archaeology quarterly) 34: 60–65.

Keally, Charles T. 1990. "Environment and Distribution of Sites in the Japanese Paleolithic: Environmental Zones and Cultural Areas." Paper Presented at the Fourteenth Congress of the Indo-Pacific Prehistory Association, Yogyakarta, Indonesia.

Kidder, J. Edward. 1972a. *Early Buddhist Japan*. London: Thames & Hudson.

———. 1972b. "The Newly Discovered Takamatsu Tomb." *Monumenta Nipponica* 27, no. 3: 245–51.

———. 1985. "Archaeology of the Early Horse Riders in Japan." *Transactions of the Asiatic Society of Japan*, 3d ser. 20: 89–123.

———. 1990a. "Ceramics of the Burial Mounds (*Kofun*) (A.D. 258–646)," 40–52. In *Rise of a Great Tradition* 1990.

———. 1990b. "Saddle Bows and Rump Plumes: More on the Fujinoki Tomb." *Monumenta Nipponica* 45, no. 1: 75–85.

Kiley, Cornelius J. 1973. "State and Dynasty in Archaic Yamato." *Journal of Asian Studies* 33, no. 1: 25–49.

———. 1977. "Uji and Kabane in Ancient Japan." *Monumenta Nipponica* 32, no. 3: 365–76.

———. 1983. "Uji-Kabane System." In *Kodansha* 1983, 8: 131–37.

Kobayashi Tatsuo. 1979. *Jōmon doki 1* (Jōmon pottery 1). In *Nihon no genshi bijutsu* 1979. Vol. 1.

———. 1988a. "Jōmon bunka no kigen" (Origins of Jōmon culture). *Museum* 45: 4–10.

———, ed. 1988b. *Jōmonjin no dōgu* (Tools of Jōmon people). In *Kodaishi fukugen* 1988. Vol. 3.

———. 1989. *Jōmon no waza to dōgu* (Jōmon industry and implements). Vol. 2 of *Nihon no akebono* (Dawn of Japan). Tokyo: Mainichi Shimbunsha.

Kobayashi Tatsuo and Ogawa Tadahiro. 1988. *Jōmon doki taikan* (Overview of Jōmon pottery). 4 vols. Tokyo: Shōgakkan.

Kobayashi Yukio. 1961. *Kofun jidai no kenkyū* (Studies on the Kofun period). Kyoto: Aoki Shoten.

Kodaishi fukugen (Reconstruction of ancient history). 1988–90. 10 vols. Tokyo: Kodansha.

Kodansha Encyclopedia of Japan. 1983. 9 vols. Tokyo: Kodansha.

Kojima Toshiaki. 1983. "Sankaku tō-kei doseihin" (Triangular-shaped clay cylinders). In *Jōmonjin no seishin bunka* 1983, 128–40.

Kokuritsu Kagaku Hakubutsukan. 1988. *Nihonjin no kigenten: Nihonjin wa doko kara kita ka?* (Exhibition on the origins of the Japanese: Where did the Japanese come from?). Tokyo: Yomiuri Shimbun.

Kōmoto Masayuki. 1989. "Shoki Nihon shakai no futatsu no katachi" (Two forms of early agricultural society). In *Yayoi bunka no seiritsu to Higashi Ajia* (Formation of Yayoi culture and East Asia), 14–17. Fukuoka: Fukuoka Ken Kyōiku Iinkai.

Kondō Yoshirō. 1986. "The Keyhole Tumulus and Its Relationship to Early Forms of Burial." In Pearson 1986, 335–48.

Kuraku Yoshiyuki. 1979. *Yayoi doki* (Yayoi pottery). In *Nihon no genshi bijutsu* 1979. Vol. 3.

———. 1989a. "Shinshu to dentō: Kōgei gijutsu no tanjō" (Innovation and tradition: The birth of the techniques of ancient crafts). In Kuraku 1989b, 17–27.

———, ed. 1989b. *Yayoijin no zōkei* (Formation of the Yayoi people). In *Kodaishi fukugen* 1989. Vol. 5.

Kurosaki Tadashi. 1989. "Nōgu no kakushin" (Innovation in agricultural tools). In *Kodaishi fukugen* 1989, 61–65.

Kyoto Furitsu Yamashiro Kyōdo Shiryōkan. 1987. *Kagami to kofun* (Mirrors and *kofun*). Kyoto: Kyoto Furitsu Yamashiro Kyōdo Shiryōkan.

Kyūshū Rekishi Shiryōkan: Sōgō annai (Comprehensive guide to the Kyūshū History Museum). 1986. Dazaifu: Kyūshū Rekishi Shiryōkan.

Ledyard, Gari. 1983a. "Horse-rider Theory." In *Kodansha* 1983, 3: 229–31.

———. 1983b. "Yamatai." In *Kodansha* 1983, 8: 305–7.

Levy, Ian Hideo, trans. 1981. *The Ten Thousand Leaves: A Translation of the Man'yōshū, Japan's Premier Anthology of Classical Poetry*. Princeton, N.J.: Princeton University Press.

Mabuchi Hisaō, Hirao Yoshimitsu, and Masaki Nishida. 1985. "Lead Isotope Approach to the Understanding of Early Japanese Bronze Culture." *Archaeometry* 27, no. 2: 131–59.

Machida Akira, ed. 1989. *Kodai no kyūden to jiin* (Palaces and temples of ancient times). In *Kodaishi fukugen* 1989. Vol. 8.

Mellott, Richard. 1990. "Ceramics of the Asuka, Nara, and Heian Periods (A.D. 552–1185)." In *Rise of a Great Tradition* 1990, 56–67.

Miwa Karoku. 1990. "Sue Ware." In *Rise of a Great Tradition* 1990.

Miyagi Eishō and Takamiya Hiroe, eds. 1983. *Okinawa rekishi chizu* (Historical atlas of Okinawa). Tokyo: Kashiwa Shobō.

Miyamoto Nagajirō. 1988. "Samazama na ie" (Various houses). In *Kodaishi fukugen* 1988, 2: 85–103.

Miyazaki Ichisada. 1988. *Kodai Yamato chōtei* (Ancient Yamato imperial court). Tokyo: Chikuma Shobō.

Mori Kōichi. 1989a. *Ki to tsuchi to ishi no bunka* (Culture of wood, earth, and stone). Vol. 1 of *Zusetsu Nihon no kodai* (Illustrated ancient Japan). Tokyo: Chūōkōronsha.

———. 1989b. *Kome to kinzoku no jidai: Jōmon jidai banki-Yayoi jidai* (Period of rice and metal tools: Final Jōmon and the Yayoi period). Vol. 3 of *Zusetsu Nihon no kodai* (Illustrated ancient Japan). Tokyo: Chūōkōronsha.

———. 1989c. *Umi o watatta hitobito* (People who crossed the sea). Vol. 1 of *Zusetsu Nihon no kodai* (Illustrated ancient Japan). Tokyo: Chūōkōronsha.

Nagata Shin'ichi. 1987. "Torai shizoku to zōto" (Foreign clans and the building of the capitals). *Rekishi tokuhon* (History reader) 32, no. 12: 134–41.

Nakajima Eiichi. 1983. "Sekkan, dokan" (Stone and ceramic crowns). In *Jōmonjin no seishin bunka* 1983, 9: 149–69.

Nakamura Tomohiro. 1989. "Bui ni tsuite" (Concerning military power and prestige). In Kuraku 1989b, 36–41.

Nara Kenritsu Kashihara Kōkogaku Kenkyūjo. 1977. *Niizawa 126 go Kofun* (Niizawa 126 kofun). Nara: Nara Ken Kyōiku Iinkai.

———. 1986a. *Ikaruga Fujinoki Kofun*. Ikaruga-chō: Ikaruga-chō Kyōiku Iinkai.

———. 1986b. *Yamato no kōkogaku* (Archaeology of Yamato). Nara: Nara Kenritsu Kashihara Kōkogaku Kenkyūjo.

———. 1989. *Yayoi: Dōran no jidai* (Yayoi: A period of upheaval). Nara: Nara Kenritsu Kashihara Kōkogaku Kenkyūjo.

———. 1990. *Fujinoki Kofun gaihō Dai ichi chōsa—Dai sanji chōsa* (Fujinoki Kofun: Summary of first to third investigations). Tokyo: Yoshikawa Kōbunkan.

Nara Kenritsu Kashihara Kōkogaku Kenkyūjo Fūzoku Hakubutsukan. 1990. *Haniwa no dōbutsuen* (A zoo of animal *haniwa*). Kashihara: Nara Kenritsu Kashihara Kōkogaku Kenkyūjo Fūzoku Hakubutsukan.

Nara Kenritsu Kashihara Kōkogaku Kenkyūjo Fūzoku Hakubutsukan: Sōgō annai (Comprehensive guide to Museum of the Nara Prefectural Kashihara Archaeological Research Institute). 1988. Nara: Nara Kenritsu Kashihara Kōkogaku Kenkyūjo Fūzoku Hakubutsukan.

Nara Kokuritsu Bunkazai Kenkyūjo Asuka Shiryōkan. 1988. *Asuka jidai no kofun* (Kofun of the Asuka period). Kyoto: Dōhōsha Shuppan.

Nihon no genshi bijutsu (Primitive art of Japan). 1979. 10 vols. Tokyo: Kodansha.

Niiro Izumi. 1989. "Ō to ō no kōshō" (Connections between the kings). In *Kodaishi fukugen* 1989, 6: 145–61.

Nishida Masaki. 1989. *Jōmon no seitaishi kan* (Historical view of Jōmon ecology). Tokyo: Tokyo Daigaku Shuppankai.

Nomura Takeshi. 1983. "Sekken, sekito" (Stone swords, stone knives), 181–96. In *Jōmonjin no seishin bunka* 1983.

Ōbayashi Taryō. 1987. *Uji to ie* (Lineage and family). Vol. 11 of *Nihon no kodai* (Ancient Japan). Tokyo: Chūōkōronsha.

Oda Shizuo and Charles T. Keally. 1986. "A Critical Look at the Paleolithic and Lower Paleolithic Research in Miyagi Prefecture, Japan." *Zinruigaku zasshi* (Journal of the Anthropological Society of Nippon) 94, no. 3: 325–61.

Ogasawara Yoshihiko. 1985. "Iegata haniwa no haichi to kofun jidai gōzoku no kyokan" (Large residences of powerful families in the Kofun period as seen from the arrangement of *haniwa* houses). *Kōkogaku kenkyū* (Archaeological research) 31, no. 4: 13–38.

———. 1989. "Gōzoku no kyokan to kōzō" (Large residences of the powerful families and their organization). In *Kodaishi fukugen* 1989, 6: 79–89.

Ogawa Masumi. 1990. "Nihon to Chōsen hantō no tetsu seisan" (Iron production in Japan and the Korean peninsula). *Kikan kōkogaku* (Archaeology quarterly) 33: 72–75.

Okamura Michio. 1988. "Kyūsekki jidai jin torai no nami" (Waves of migrants of Paleolithic people). In Inada 1988, 149–56.

Okauchi Mitsuzane. 1986. "Mounded Tombs in East Asia from the Third to the Seventh Centuries A.D." In Pearson 1986, 127–48.

Okinawa Kōkogaku Kyōkai. 1978. *Sekki jidai no Okinawa* (Okinawa in the stone age). Naha, Okinawa: Nakahodo Masayoshi.

Ōtani Toshizō. 1983. "Kanjō dori" (Ring-shaped earth mounds). In *Jōmonjin no seishin bunka* 1983, 46–56.

Ōtsuka Kazuyoshi. 1988. "Jōmon no matsuri" (Jōmon religious ceremonies), 113–48. In *Kodaishi fukugen* 1988, 2: 113–48.

Ōzeki Kyōko. 1989. "Jōmon jidai no angin, orimono o jikken fukugen suru" (Experiment of restoration of knitted or woven cloth of the Jōmon period). In *Ki to tsuchi to ishi no bunka* (Culture of wood, earth, and stone), ed. Mori Kōichi, 99–104. Vol. 1 of *Zusetsu Nihon no kodai* (Illustrated ancient Japan). Tokyo: Chūōkōronsha.

Pearson, Richard. 1976. "The Contribution of Archaeology to Japanese Studies." *Journal of Japanese Studies* 2: 305–34.

———. 1982. "The Archaeological Background to Korean Prehistoric Art." *Korean Culture* 3, no. 4: 18–29.

———, ed. 1986. *Windows on the Japanese Past: Studies in Archaeology and Prehistory.* Ann Arbor: University of Michigan, Center for Japanese Studies.

———. 1990a. "Chiefly Exchange between Kyūshū and Okinawa, Japan, in the Yayoi Period." *Antiquity* 64, no. 245: 912–22.

———. 1990b. "Jōmon Ceramics: The Creative Expression of Affluent Foragers (10,500–300 B.C.)." In *Rise of a Great Tradition* 1990, 15–27.

———. N.d. "Trade and the Rise of the Okinawan State." *Bulletin of the Indo Pacific Prehistory Association* 12. In press.

Piggott, Joan R. 1989. "Sacral Kingship and Confederacy in Early Izumo." *Monumenta Nipponica* 44, no. 1: 45–74.

Price, T. Douglas. 1981. "Complexity in 'Non-complex' Societies," 55–97. In *Archaeological Approaches to the Study of Complexity,* ed. S. E. Van der Leeuw. Cingula VI. Amsterdam: University of Amsterdam.

The Rise of a Great Tradition: Japanese Archaeological Ceramics from the Jōmon through Heian Periods (10,500 B.C.–A.D. 1185). 1990. New York: Japan Society.

Rosenfield, John M. 1983. "Buddhist Art." In *Kodansha* 1983, 1: 184–94.

Rouse, Irving. 1986. *Migrations in Prehistory.* New Haven, Conn.: Yale University Press.

Ryūkyū Archaeological Research Team. 1981. *Subsistence and Settlement in Okinawan Prehistory—Kume and Iriomote.* Vancouver: Laboratory of Archaeology, University of British Columbia.

Sahara Makoto. 1979. *Jōmon doki 2* (Jōmon pottery 2). In *Nihon no genshi bijutsu* 1979. Vol. 2.

———. 1987a. *Nihonjin no tanjō* (Birth of the Japanese people). Vol. 1 of *Nihon no rekishi* (History of Japan). Tokyo: Shōgakkan.

———. 1987b. "The Yayoi Culture." In *Recent Archaeological Discoveries in Japan,* ed. Tsuboi Kiyotari, 37–54. Tokyo: Unesco and Centre for East Asian Studies.

———. 1989. "Sekai no naka no Yayoi bunka" (Yayoi culture in world perspective). In *Yayoi bunka no seiritsu to Higashi Ajia* (Formation of Yayoi culture and East Asia), 18–23. Fukuoka: Fukuoka Ken Kyōiku Iinkai.

Sahara Makoto, Takashima Chūhei, and Nishitani Tadashi, eds. 1989. *Yoshinogari iseki ten* (Exhibition of the Yoshinogari site). Fukuoka: Asahi Shimbunsha.

Sahlins, Marshall. 1968. *Tribesmen.* Englewood Cliffs, N.J.: Prentice Hall.

Saitō Tadashi. 1983. "Yayoi Culture." In *Kodansha* 1983, 8: 321, 322.

Sakaguchi Yutaka. 1983. "Warm and Cold Stages in the Past Seventy-six Hundred Years in Japan and Their Global Correlation." *Bulletin of the Department of Geography, University of Tokyo* 15: 1–31.

Sakamoto Yoshio. 1985. *Bagu* (Horse gear). Tokyo: Niū Saiensu Sha.

Sasaki Kenichi. 1990. "Development of Social Complexity in Prehistoric Japan." Typescript. Department of Anthropology, Harvard University, Cambridge, Mass.

Sasaki Kōmei. 1986. *Jōmon bunka to Nihonjin: Nihon kiso bunka no keisei* (Jōmon culture and the Japanese: The formation of Japan's basic culture). Tokyo: Shōgakkan.

Seki Toshihiko. 1985. *Yayoi doki no chishiki* (Knowledge of Yayoi pottery). Tokyo: Tokyo Bijutsu.

Service, Elman. 1971. *Primitive Social Organization: The Evolutionary Perspective.* New York: Random House.

Shiraishi Taiichirō. 1986. "Kofun jidai" (Kofun period). In *Kantō, Kōshinetsu Hen* (Kantō, Kōshinetsu regions), 157–95. Vol. 2 of *Zusetsu hakkutsu ga kataru Nihon Shi* (Illustrated Japanese history as told through excavation), ed. Tsuboi Kiyotari. Tokyo: Shin Jimbutsu Ōraisha.

———, ed. 1990. "Haniwa no sekai" (World of *haniwa*). In *Kofun jidai no kōgei* (Crafts of the Kofun period), 34–40. Vol. 7 of *Kodaishi fukugen* 1990.

Smith, Robert J. 1983. *Japanese Society: Tradition, Self, and the Social Order.* New York: Cambridge University Press.

Stark, Kenneth. 1989. "Wealth and Power in Yayoi Period North Kyūshū." Master's thesis. University of British Columbia.

Suenaga Masao and Inoue Mitsusada, eds. 1974. *Takamatsuzuka Kofun to Asuka* (Takamatsu *Kofun* and Asuka). Tokyo: Chūōkōronsha.

Sugibayashi Noboru, ed. 1989. *Yoshinogari, Fujinoki, Yamataikoku: Mietekita kodaishi no nazo* (Yoshinogari, Fujinoki, Yamataikoku: Seeing the riddles of ancient history). Yomiuri Special 31. Tokyo: Yomiuri Shimbun.

Suzuki Kimio, ed. 1988. *Jōmonjin no seikatsu to bunka* (Culture and daily life of the Jōmon people). In *Kodaishi fukugen* 1988. Vol. 2.

Suzuki Michinosuke. 1981. *Zuroku sekki no kiso chishiki* (Illustrated basic information on stone tools). Vol. 3 of *Jōmon.* Tokyo: Kashiwa Shobō.

Takakura Hiroshi and Yokota Kenjirō. 1986. "Asuka, Nara Jidai" (Asuka and Nara periods). In *Kyūshū, Okinawa Hen* (Kyūshū, Okinawa regions), 208–55. Vol. 6 of *Zusetsu hakkutsu ga kataru Nihon Shi* (Illustrated Japanese history as told through excavation), ed. Tsuboi Kiyotari. Tokyo: Shin Jimbutsu Ōraisha.

Takayama Jun. 1965. "Jōmon jidai ni okeru jisen no kigen ni kansuru ichi shiron" (Hypothesis concerning the origins of ear ornaments in the Jōmon period). *Zinruigaku zasshi* (Journal of the Anthropological Society of Nippon) 73: 23–44.

Tanaka Migaku. 1987. "The Early Historical Periods." In *Recent Archaeological Discoveries in Japan,* ed. Tsuboi Kiyotari, 72–91. Paris: Unesco and Centre for East Asian Studies.

Teramura Mitsuharu. 1980. *Kodai tamazukuri keiseishi no kenkyū* (Research on the history of the beadmaking industry). Tokyo: Yoshikawa Kōbunkan.

Terasawa Kaoru. 1989. "Seidōki mainō no igi" (Meaning of caches of bronze objects). *Kikan kōkogaku* (Archaeology quarterly) 27: 66–74.

Trewartha, George T. 1965. *Japan: A Geography.* Madison: University of Wisconsin Press.

Tsude Hiroshi. 1988. "Land Exploitation and the Stratification of Society: A Case Study in Ancient Japan." In *Studies in Japanese Language and Culture,* 107–30. Joint Research Report No. 4. Osaka: Faculty of Letters, Osaka University.

———. 1989a. "Daikaitaku to kaikyūsa no zōdai" (Widespread land clearance and increase in differences between social classes). In *Kodaishi fukugen* 1989, 6: 42–47.

———. 1989b. "Kofun bunmei to shoki kokka" (*Kofun* civilization and the early state). In *Kodaishi fukugen* 1989, 6: 48–52.

———. 1989c. "Kofun no tanjō to shūen" (Birth and death of the *kofun*). In *Kodaishi fukugen* 1989, 6: 27–40.

———. 1990. "Chiefly Lineages in Kofun Period Japan: Political Relations between Center and Region." *Antiquity* 64: 923–31.

Tsukada Matsuo. 1986. "Vegetation in Prehistoric Japan: The Last Twenty Thousand Years." In Pearson 1986, 11–56.

Tsunoda Ryōsaku and L. Carrington Goodrich. 1951. *Japan in the Chinese Dynastic Histories: Later Han through Ming Dynasties.* South Pasadena, Calif.: P. D. and Ione Perkins.

Ueno Yoshiya. 1987. "Senshijin no kokoro o motomete" (Search for the spirit of prehistoric people). In *Kokoro no naka no uchū* (Universe of the spirit), 33–72. Vol. 13 of *Nihon no kodai* (Ancient period of Japan), ed. Ōbayashi Taryō. Tokyo: Chūōkōronsha.

Uno Takao. 1988. "Nendai" (Chronology). In *Yayoijin to sono kankyō* (Yayoi people and their environment), 11–22. Vol. 1 of *Yayoi bunka no kenkyū* (Study of Yayoi culture), ed. Nagai Masabumi et al. Tokyo: Yūzankaku.

Wada Seigo. 1986. "Political Interpretations of Stone Coffin Production in Protohistoric Japan." In Pearson 1986, 349–74.

———. 1989. "Fukusō no hensen" (Changes in grave goods). In *Kodaishi fukugen* 1989, 105–19.

Waida Manabu. 1976. "Sacred Kingship in Early Japan: A Historical Introduction." *History of Religions* 15, no. 4: 319–42.

Wang Zhongshu. 1981. "Guanyu Riben sanjiaoyuan shengshoujing de wenti" (Problems concerned with the triangular-rim beast and deity mirrors in Japan). *Kaogu* (Archaeology), no. 4 (1981): 346–413.

Watanabe Hitoshi. 1986. "Community Habitation and Food Gathering in Prehistoric Japan: An Ethnographic Interpretation of the Archaeological Evidence." In Pearson 1986, 229–54.

———. 1990. *Jōmon shiki kaisōka shakai* (Jōmon stratified society). Tokyo: Rokkō Shuppan.

Watanabe Makoto. 1975. *Jōmon jidai no shokubutsu shoku* (Plant food in the Jōmon period). Tokyo: Yūzankaku.

———. 1984. "Jōmon jidai no sake" (Wine in the Jōmon period), 35. In *Jōmon jidai no sake zōgu* (Jōmon-period wine-making utensils). Yamanashi: Yamanashi Kenritsu Kōko Hakubutsukan.

Yamamoto Tadanao. 1987. "Temmu, Jitō tei no atarashii kyō" (New capital of Emperor Temmu and Empress Jitō). *Rekishi tokuhon* (History reader) 32, no. 12: 188–93.

Yamamoto Tadanao and Akira Matsui. 1988. *Japanese-English Dictionary of Japanese Archaeology.* Nara: Nara Kokuritsu Bunkazai Kenkyūjo.

Yamamoto Teruhisa. 1983. "Sekibō" (Stone rods). In *Jōmonjin no seishin bunka* 1983, 170–80.

Yamanashi Ken Kyōiku Iinkai, Nihon Dōro Kōdan. 1986, 1987. *Shakadō.* 3 vols. Yamanashi: Yamanashi Ken Maizō Bunkazai Sentā.

Yang Hong. 1984. "Wu, Dongjin, Nanchao de wenhua ji qi dui haidong de yingxiang" (On the cultures of the Wei, Eastern Jin, and Southern Dynasties and their influence on Korea and Japan). *Kaogu* (Archaeology), no. 6 (1984): 564–74.

———. 1985. "Riben gufen shidai jiazhou ji qi he Zhongguo jiazhou de guanxi" (On the relationship between Japanese armor and helmets in the Kofun period and their Chinese counterparts). *Kaogu* (Archaeology), no. 1 (1985): 61–77.

Yasuda Yoshinori. 1984. "Oscillations of Climatic and Oceanographic Conditions since the Last Glacial Age in Japan." In *Geology and Paleoclimatology Studies,* 397–413. Vol. 1 of *The Evolution of the East Asian Environment,* ed. Robert Orr Whyte. Hong Kong: University of Hong Kong, Center for Asian Studies.

INDEX

ILLUSTRATION CREDITS

Except as noted below, photographs are by Hashimoto Hirotsugu and Ushijima Shigeru, with the assistance of Kusumoto Makiko, courtesy the Agency for Cultural Affairs.

The following institutions kindly provided photographic material: Chitose City Education Commission, Fukuoka Municipal Museum, Gumma Historical Museum, Habikino City Education Commission, Ibaraki City Education Commission, Iwate Prefectural Museum, Kamiina Education Commission, Maebaru Township Education Commission, Minato Ward Education Commission, Prefectural Amagi Museum, Shimane Prefectural Education Commission, Tokyo Metropolitan Archaeological Center, Yamagata Prefectural Museum, Yasu Township Education Commission.

Line drawings have been adapted by Patricia Condit from several publications (references are cited in full beginning on p. 312).

Figs. 2, 4
Inada 1988c, 28, 29, 132 (courtesy Kodansha).

Fig. 3
Courtesy Imagane Township Education Commission.

Fig. 7
Kokuritsu Kagaku Hakubutsukan 1988, 95.

Fig. 8
Kobayashi Tatsuo 1989, 37, 41, 45, 49, 53, 57 (courtesy Mainichi Shimbunsha).

Fig. 9
Kobayashi Tatsuo 1988b, 76, 77 (courtesy Kodansha).

Fig. 10
Sahara 1979, 54 (courtesy Kodansha).

Figs. 11, 13
Suzuki Kimio 1988, 90–99, 123 (courtesy Kodansha).

Fig. 12
Iwate Ken Maibun Sentā Bunkazai Chōsa Hōkokusho 1982, 503 (courtesy Iwate Ken Maizō Bunkazai Sentā).

Fig. 15
Sugibayashi 1989, 45 (courtesy Yomiuri Shimbun).

Fig. 16
Kuraku Yoshiyuki 1979, 75 (courtesy Kodansha).

Fig. 17
Courtesy Shimane Prefectural Education Commission.

Figs. 18, 19
Courtesy Saga Prefectural Education Commission.

Fig. 22
Tsude 1989a, 43 (courtesy Kodansha).

Fig. 23
Machida 1989, 39 (courtesy Kodansha).

Fig. 24
Photograph courtesy Nara Prefectural Kashihara Archaeological Research Institute; drawing adapted from Nara Kenritsu Kashihara Kōkogaku Kenkyūjo 1990, 22.

Fig. 25
Courtesy Nara Prefectural Kashihara Research Institute.

Fig. 26
Niiro 1989b, 160 (courtesy Kodansha).

Fig. 27
Inokuma 1979, 74, 75 (courtesy Kodansha).

Fig. 28
Courtesy Gumma Prefectural Education Commission.

Figs. 29–31
Courtesy Archaeology Department, Kyoto University.

Fig. 38
Nara Kenritsu Kashihara Kōkogaku Kenkyūjo 1986a.

Fig. 39
Gumma Ken Kyōiku Iinkai 1980, 300.

Fig. 42
Courtesy Nara National Cultural Properties Research Institute.

Fig. 43
Courtesy Nara Kenritsu Kashihara Kōkogaku Kenkyūjo 1986b, 92.

Fig. 45
Courtesy Agency for Cultural Affairs.

Fig. 47
Machida 1989, 30 (Kiyomizu Shin'ichi, artist; courtesy Kodansha).